APR 1 8 2013

EAST MEADOW PUBLIC LIBRARY

3 1299 00883 9277

D1411273

HTML:
A Beginner's Guide

Fifth Edition

Wendy Willard

East Meadow Public Library
1886 Front Street, East Meadow, NY 11554
(516) 794-2570
www.eastmeadow.info

Mc
Graw
Hill
Education

New York   Chicago   San Francisco
Lisbon   London   Madrid   Mexico City
Milan   New Delhi   San Juan
Seoul   Singapore   Sydney   Toronto

Cataloging-in-Publication Data is on file with the Library of Congress

McGraw-Hill books are available at special quantity discounts to use as premiums and sales promotions, or for use in corporate training programs. To contact a representative, please e-mail us at bulksales@mcgraw-hill.com.

HTML: A Beginner's Guide, Fifth Edition

Copyright © 2013 by The McGraw-Hill Companies. All rights reserved. Printed in the United States of America. Except as permitted under the Copyright Act of 1976, no part of this publication may be reproduced or distributed in any form or by any means, or stored in a database or retrieval system, without the prior written permission of publisher, with the exception that the program listings may be entered, stored, and executed in a computer system, but they may not be reproduced for publication.

All trademarks or copyrights mentioned herein are the possession of their respective owners and McGraw-Hill makes no claim of ownership by the mention of products that contain these marks.

1234567890   DOC DOC   109876543

ISBN   978-0-07-180927-6
MHID   0-07-180927-9

Sponsoring Editor Brandi Shailer		**Proofreader** Claire Splan	
Editorial Supervisor Patty Mon		**Indexer** Karin Arrigoni	
Project Manager Sheena Uprety, Cenveo® Publisher Services		**Production Supervisor** Jean Bodeaux	
		Composition Cenveo Publisher Services	
Acquisitions Coordinator Amanda Russell		**Illustration** Cenveo Publisher Services	
Technical Editor Christie Sorenson		**Art Director, Cover** Jeff Weeks	
Copy Editor Lisa McCoy		**Cover Designer** Jeff Weeks	

Information has been obtained by McGraw-Hill from sources believed to be reliable. However, because of the possibility of human or mechanical error by our sources, McGraw-Hill, or others, McGraw-Hill does not guarantee the accuracy, adequacy, or completeness of any information and is not responsible for any errors or omissions or the results obtained from the use of such information.

To Corinna and Caeli—that you might remember your mom once knew some "cool stuff," even when HTML becomes for you what eight-track tapes are to me. "Heaven and earth will pass away, but my words will never pass away."

—Luke 21:33

About the Author

Wendy Willard is a designer, consultant, writer, and educator who has been involved in web design and development for more than 17 years. She has published on HTML, CSS, web design, and Photoshop. She's previously held the titles of Art Director, Creative Director, and Marketing Manager at firms in the Northeast, and now freelances for companies worldwide. Wendy has a degree in Illustration from Art Center College of Design in Pasadena, California, and splits her time between Maine, Maryland, and Nicaragua, with her husband and two daughters.

About the Technical Editor

Christie Sorenson is a senior software engineer at ZingChart. She has worked on JavaScript-based systems in analytics, content management, and business applications since 1997 and has been fascinated with the evolution of the language and its users. She has collaborated on several books, including *Ajax: The Complete Reference* and *HTML & CSS: The Complete Reference* and was also the tech editor on *JavaScript: The Complete Reference* and *JavaScript: A Beginner's Guide*. She has a B.S. in Computer Science from UC San Diego and now lives in San Francisco with her husband Luke and daughters Ali and Keira.

Contents at a Glance

PART I   Laying the Foundation

1	Getting Started	3
2	Document Setup	23
3	Style Sheet Setup	41
4	Working with Text	57
5	Page Structure	79
6	Positioning Page Elements	105

PART II   Adding the Content

7	Working with Links	133
8	Working with Images	159
9	Working with Multimedia	197
10	Creating Lists	217
11	Using Tables	235

12 Creating Forms **267**

13 Formatting and Styling Forms **297**

14 Beyond Static HTML **321**

PART III   Going Live

15 Publishing Pages **349**

16 HTML for Email **373**

PART IV   Appendixes

A Answers to Self Tests **405**

B HTML/CSS Reference Table **429**

C Troubleshooting (FAQs) **455**

D Special Characters **465**

E File Types **471**

Index **475**

Contents

ACKNOWLEDGMENTS xvii
INTRODUCTION xix

PART I Laying the Foundation

1 Getting Started **3**
Understand the Internet as a Medium for Disseminating Information 4
    The Anatomy of a Web Site 4
    Web Browsers 7
    Internet Service Providers 8
Be Aware of the Current Version of HTML 9
Plan for the Audience, Goals, Structure, Content, and Navigation of Your Site 10
    Identify the Target Audience 10
    Set Goals 11
    Create the Structure 12
    Organize Content 12
    Develop Navigation 13
Identify the Best HTML Editor for You 14
    Which Is Best? 16
Learn from the Pros Using the View Source Command of Popular Web Browsers 17

2 Document Setup **23**

Create an HTML File 24

Naming Conventions 24

Preview an HTML File in a Browser 25

Describe and Apply the Basic HTML Document Format 27

Types of Elements 28

Types of Tags 30

Attributes 30

Required Tags 31

Capitalization 33

Quotation Marks 34

Nesting 34

Spacing and Breaks Within the Code 34

Spacing and Breaks Between Tags 35

Spacing Between Lines of Text 35

Use Character Entities to Display Special Characters 36

Add Comments to an HTML File 38

3 Style Sheet Setup **41**

Set Up Style Sheets in an HTML File 42

Define the Style 42

Define the Values 43

Create the Structure 44

Understand the Cascade 47

Identify the Ways in Which Color Is Referenced in Web Development 48

Hexadecimal Color 48

RGB Values and Percentages 50

Color Names 51

So Which Should I Use? 52

New and Notable Color Options 52

RGBA 52

Opacity 52

Specify Document Colors 52

4 Working with Text **57**

Ensure Onscreen Readability of Text 58

Markup Text 60

Style Text 61

Font Faces 63

Font Sizes 66

Font Colors 70

Other Font Style Properties 70

Offer Printer-Friendly Versions of Text Content 72
    PDFs 72
    Printer-Specific Style Sheets 73
    Final Tips for Printer-Friendly Pages 75

5 Page Structure **79**
Organize Sections of Content 80
    Identifying Natural Divisions 80
    Set the Outline 87
    Get Inspired 89
Organize Text 89
    Paragraphs 89
    Line Breaks 93
    Quotation Blocks 95
    Box Properties 96
    Alignment 100

6 Positioning Page Elements **105**
Understand the Concept and Uses of Style Sheets for Page Layout 106
Create a Single-Column, Centered, Fluid Page Layout 107
    Break Down the Code 109
    Pull It All Together 110
    Browser Support 111
Create a Multicolumn Fluid Page Layout 111
    Break Down the Code 113
    Pull It Back Together 120
    Browser Support 120
Other CSS Page Layouts 121
Layer Content Within a Layout 122
    Realistic Uses of Layers in Web Pages 125
Use External Style Sheets 126
    Link to an External Style Sheet 126
    Import an External Style Sheet 127

PART II Adding the Content

7 Working with Links **133**
Add Links to Other Web Pages 134
    Absolute Links 135
    Relative Links 135
Add Links to Sections Within the Same Web Page 138
    Create an Anchor 139
    Link to an Anchor 140

Add Links to Email Addresses and Downloadable Files 143
    Email Addresses 143
    FTP and Downloadable Files 146
Recognize Effective Links 146
    Extra Credit 149
Style Links 149
    Default Link Colors 150
    Beyond Colors 151
Customize Links by Setting the Tab Order, Keyboard Shortcut, and Target Window ... 152
    Title 152
    Tab Order 153
    Keyboard Shortcuts 153
    Target Windows 154

8 Working with Images **159**
Locating Web Image Sources 160
    Use Stock Images 160
    Creating Your Own Graphics 161
Become Familiar with Graphics Software 162
    Adobe Photoshop and Illustrator 162
    Other Options 163
Recognize Appropriate Web Image File Formats 164
    Terminology 164
    GIF 166
    JPEG 167
    PNG 169
    Choose the Best File Format for the Job 170
Use Images as Elements in the Foreground of a Web Page 172
Specify the Height and Width of Images 173
Provide Alternative Text and Titles for Images 175
Link Images to Other Content on a Web Site 177
    Link the Entire Image 178
    Link Sections of an Image 178
Add Figure Captions 181
Style Foreground Images 182
    Borders 182
    Floats 185
    Padding and Margins 187
    Centering 188
    Pulling It All Together 189
Use Images as Elements in the Background of a Web Page 192
    Extra Credit 195

9 Working with Multimedia **197**
Understand How Plug-ins Are Used with Web Browsers 198
    Identify the Installed Components 199
    Recognize File Types, Extensions, and Appropriate Plug-ins 199
Link to Different Types of Media from a Web Page 200
Embed Different Types of Media onto a Web Page 202
    Start with the audio and video Elements 203
    Customize with Attributes 203
    Specify Sources 203
    Provide Fallback Options 207
    Add Text Tracks 209
    Use embed for Non-native Multimedia Content 211
Style Multimedia Content 212

10 Creating Lists **217**
Use Ordered Lists in a Web Page 218
Use Unordered Lists in a Web Page 221
Use Definition Lists in a Web Page 222
Combine and Nest Two or More Types of Lists in a Web Page 223
Style Lists 226
    Customize the Bullets 226
    Customize the Spacing 227
    Customize the Entire Layout 228

11 Using Tables **235**
Understand the Concept and Uses of Tables in Web Pages 236
Create a Basic Table Structure 237
    Table Structure 238
    Cell Content 239
Format Tables Within Web Pages 242
    Borders and Margins 242
    Width and Height 244
    Basic Alignment 246
    Colors 248
    Background Images 249
    Captions 250
Format Content Within Table Cells 252
    Alignment 252
    Width and Height 253
    Cell Padding 255
    Colors 256
    Prohibit Line Breaks 257
    Spanning Columns 257
    Span Rows 258

Additional Formatting Techniques for Tables 259
    Group Rows 259
    Group Columns 261

12 Creating Forms **267**
  Understand the Concept and Uses of Forms in Web Pages 268
  Create a Basic Form 268
    Text Input 270
    Radio Buttons 275
    Check Boxes 277
    Date and Time Inputs 278
    Other Number Inputs 279
    Contact Methods 281
    Color Selectors 283
    Select Menus 284
    Disable Form Elements 286
    Hidden Fields 286
    File Uploads 286
    Buttons 287
  Validate the Form Content 290
    Using Patterns 291
  Provide a Way for Your Form to Be Processed 292
    The action Attribute 292
    The method and enctype Attributes 295

13 Formatting and Styling Forms **297**
  Apply Tables to Forms 298
  Make Forms More User-Friendly 299
    Set Tab Order and Keyboard Shortcuts 300
    Include Labels 301
    Group-Related Controls 302
    Add Data Lists 304
    Show Progress 304
    Assist Your Users 307
  Style Forms 308
    Use Styles and Fieldsets to Eliminate the Table Layout 311
    Use Styles for Client-Side Validation 315

14 Beyond Static HTML **321**
  Understand the Concept and Uses of JavaScript and HTML5 APIs in Web Pages 322
    Troubleshoot JavaScript 323
    Terminology 324
    JavaScript Logic 329

New and Notable 330
   Multitasking 330
   Storage 330
   Offline 331
   Geolocation 332
   Canvas 333
Sample Scripts 336
   Add the Current Date and Time 336
   Format a New Window 336
   Create a Dynamic Navigation Bar 337
   Display a User's Location on a Map 340
Learn More 345
   Online References and Scripts 345

PART III Going Live

15 Publishing Pages **349**
Select Possible Domain Names for Your Site 350
Determine the Most Appropriate Type of Hosting for Your Site 351
   Personal Site Hosting 351
   Business Site Hosting 353
Prepare Your Site for Its Public Debut 354
   Update Meta Content 355
   Troubleshoot the Code 356
   Validate the Code 359
   Preview on Mobile Devices 360
   Preview in Other Browsers 362
Upload Your Site to a Host Computer 363
   Desktop FTP Programs 364
   Web-Based FTP 367
Test Your Published Site 368
Publicize Your Web Site 368
   Marketing Tips 370
Make the Site Live! 371

16 HTML for Email **373**
Email Standards Project 374
Determine Whether HTML Email Is Appropriate for Your Needs 375
   The Purpose of Email Is to Communicate 375
   The End-User Display Is Unknown 375
   Plain-Text Email Is Safer and Smaller 376
   But ... HTML Email Marketing Works 376

Don't Send Spam 377
    Email the Right People 377
    Always Provide a Way to Opt Out 378
    Adhere to Other FTC Rules 378
Identify the Necessary Tools for the Task 378
    Send Live Web Pages with a Personal Email Account 378
    Using an Email Service Provider 379
Code for Email Readers, Not Web Browsers 380
    Absolute Paths 382
    Images 382
    Tables for Layout 384
    Inline CSS 386
Reference Guide to CSS Support in Email Clients 389
Interactivity and Multimedia in HTML Email 389
    Video in Email 389
    Flash 393
    Forms 393
Test, Test, Test 395
    Spam Test 397

PART IV Appendixes

A Answers to Self Tests **405**
  Chapter 1: Getting Started 406
  Chapter 2: Page Setup 407
  Chapter 3: Style Sheet Setup 408
  Chapter 4: Working with Text 409
  Chapter 5: Page Structure 410
  Chapter 6: Positioning Page Elements 411
  Chapter 7: Working with Links 413
  Chapter 8: Working with Images 414
  Chapter 9: Working with Multimedia 416
  Chapter 10: Creating Lists 418
  Chapter 11: Using Tables 420
  Chapter 12: Creating Forms 422
  Chapter 13: Formatting and Styling Forms 423
  Chapter 14: Beyond Static HTML 424
  Chapter 15: Making Pages Available to Others 426
  Chapter 16: HTML for Email 426

B HTML/CSS Reference Table **429**
  Generic Attributes 430
    Group Type: Core 430
    Group Type: Events 431
    Group Type: Intl 434

HTML Tags 434
CSS Properties 447

C Troubleshooting (FAQs) **455**
My Page Is Blank in the Browser! 456
All I See Is Code in the Browser! 457
My Images Don't Appear! 457
I Tried to Change the Font, But Nothing Happened! 457
When I Use a Special Character, It Doesn't Appear! 457
My Links Don't Work! 458
My Page Looks Great in One Browser, But Terrible in Another! 458
When I Link My Images, They Have Little Colored Dashes Next to Them! 459
I Saved My Image as a JPEG, But the Browser Says It's Not a Valid File Format! 459
Strange Characters Are at the Top of My Page! 459
I Added Internal Links to Sections of a Web Page, But When I Click Them,
  the Browser Launches a Brand New Window! 460
I Specified One Color, But Got a Totally Different One! 460
I Need to Protect Some of My Pages from Unwanted Visitors! 460
I Need to Prevent People from Stealing My Images! 461
I Tried to Send My Web Page in an Email, But the Page Looked Terrible! ... 461
I Updated My Web Page, But I Don't See the Changes in the Browser! 461
My Whole Page Is _____! (Fill in the Blank) 462
My Page Has a White Background in One Browser, But Not in Others! 462
I Shrank My Images, But They Still Take Forever to Download! 462
I Embedded a Flash File That Works Fine on My Computer, But Doesn't Work
  Properly on Other Computers! 463
My Tables Look Fine in One Browser, But Terrible in Another! 463
I Still Have Questions! 464

D Special Characters **465**
Standard HTML Entities 466

E File Types **471**

  Index **475**

Acknowledgments

As always, I'm so grateful to everyone at McGraw-Hill Education for making it easy to write and update this book. This edition underwent a pretty significant overhaul, which meant it needed a careful and dedicated technical editor. Thankfully, Christie fulfilled that role beautifully.

Because I wrote this revision during the first three months after my family and I moved to Nicaragua for a year, I cannot forget to acknowledge the various friends and family who helped make it happen. The support, prayers, and encouragement we received were instrumental in getting our family's grand adventure off to a successful start.

And finally, Wyeth, Corinna, and Caeli—you are my inspiration and my reward. I am humbled and honored to be able to share this adventure with you.

Introduction

When I was first approached about writing this book—over 13 years ago now—I must admit that my thought was, "Another HTML book—how many do we need?" I learned HTML by experience when there was only one version of Netscape, and it had been a long time since I'd even looked at an HTML book. But after I researched the other HTML books on the market, I felt compelled to write a book that gives readers a realistic, easy-to-understand approach to learning HTML while at the same time offering real-world practice activities and advice on related issues.

HTML: A Beginner's Guide is that book, offering you practical tools and knowledge that can easily be applied to a variety of development situations, without the boring rhetoric or lengthy technical fluff. This book tells you what you need to know, when you need to know it. In revising this book for the fifth edition, I again reviewed competing books to determine what readers wanted and needed in a "new" HTML book. Again and again, I saw that you wanted a book that combined an explanation of HTML5 and the latest aspects of CSS in a way that was easy to understand and use. Furthermore, readers clamored for a beginning-level HTML book that covered the standards-compliant way to code usable web pages. This is that book.

Who Should Read This Book

Since this book is geared toward anyone with little or no prior HTML knowledge, it's perfect for anyone wishing to learn HTML. If you are a stay-at-home mom who wants to create a web site for your family without relying on half-baked tools or cookie-cutter templates, you've come to the right place. If you are a business professional seeking to acquire web development skills, this is the book for you. If you are interested in learning HTML to further your programming skills, this book is for you.

You don't need to know anything about computer programming or web development in order to learn HTML, and you certainly don't need to know either of those things to get a lot from this book.

What This Book Covers

The book is divided into four parts: Laying the Foundation, Adding the Content, Going Live, and Appendixes.

Part I, "Laying the Foundation," covers all you need to know in order to start coding effective and efficient web pages with HTML. Part I consists of six chapters in which information is broken up into manageable chunks. Each chapter contains one or more step-by-step, real-world suggestions for practicing what you've learned.

Chapter 1, "Getting Started," helps you understand the Web by answering common questions, such as "Who created HTML?" and "Who maintains HTML?" and also by tackling the anatomy of a web site, web browsers, and HTML. Issues surrounding how to plan your web site, using HTML editors, and learning from the pros are also discussed.

Chapter 2, "Document Setup," explains beginning terminology, such as tags, attributes, and nesting, while also describing naming conventions and proper page structure.

Chapter 3, "Style Sheet Setup," gives you details on how to set up style sheets in an HTML file, as well as ways to work with and reference color in your web pages.

Chapter 4, "Working with Text," teaches you how to format text within your web pages, whether that means changing the font style or color, or adding line breaks and emphasis. In addition, this chapter provides essential dos and don'ts for working with web content.

Chapter 5, "Page Structure," expands on the content covered in Chapter 4 to help you organize and structure various sections of content, as well as to format paragraphs and other page elements. All of this is setting the stage for Chapter 6, in which you'll learn how to position those page elements.

Chapter 6, "Positioning Page Elements," is the capstone chapter in this first section. It is here that we pull all you've learned thus far together to enable you to create single- and multicolumn page layouts with HTML and CSS.

Part II, "Adding the Content," helps you add all the page details necessary for the bulk of your site's text, image, and multimedia content. In this section, we'll cover not only how to add images to your sites, but also using lists, tables, and forms—all of which are key components of usable and effective web pages.

Chapter 7, "Working with Links," discusses the core of HTML: hypertext links. This chapter gives details on how to add and customize links in your web pages, whether you're linking to another web page, a section on a web page, or an email address.

Chapter 8, "Working with Images," helps you use images in your web pages by describing different image types, how to add them to a page, and how to link to and from them. A review of popular web graphics software, as well as guidelines you can use when creating images for the Web, are also provided.

Chapter 9, "Working with Multimedia," explains different types of multimedia you can add to your pages and tells how to do so in ways that work in multiple browsers.

Chapter 10, "Creating Lists," teaches you how to create and format the three different types of lists available in HTML, as well as how to style them with CSS.

Chapter 11, "Using Tables," tackles the somewhat tricky but very useful topic of HTML tables. In step-by-step fashion, this chapter takes you through creating a very basic table structure and then formatting it with CSS.

Chapter 12, "Creating Forms," introduces a key ingredient for most web sites—forms providing communication methods for customers. Various types of input controls are taught, including text fields, check boxes, file uploads, select menus, and buttons, as well as information about providing a way for your form to be processed.

Chapter 13, "Formatting and Styling Forms," builds upon the skills you learned in Chapter 12 to make forms more user-friendly and efficient. Layout techniques specific to web forms are discussed, as well as client-side form validation.

Chapter 14, "Beyond Static HTML," offers you an introduction to JavaScript, a technology used to add dynamic aspects to otherwise static HTML pages. Sample scripts allow you to add the current date and time to a web page, create a dynamic navigation bar, and display a user's location on a map.

Part III, "Going Live," includes two chapters that cover ways to publish the pages you've created, as well as tips for translating them to be accessed via email readers.

Chapter 15, "Publishing Pages," teaches you to prepare your pages for online distribution before guiding you on important decisions, such as where to host your site, what domain name to use, and how to upload the site. Testing, submission to search engines and directories, and general marketing tips are also discussed.

Chapter 16, "HTML for Email," is a brand-new chapter in this edition of the book, added to help web editors translate web page development skills to the world of HTML email (specifically for business marketing purposes).

Part IV, "Appendixes," provides additional information in quick-reference formats and puts commonly used details at the fingertips of both beginning and advanced HTML coders.

Appendix A, "Answers to Self Tests," contains the answers to the questions asked at the end of each chapter.

Appendix B, "HTML/CSS Reference Table," outlines all of the HTML tags and CSS properties taught in the book in an easy-to-read alphabetical reference format.

Appendix C, "Troubleshooting (FAQs)," provides answers to commonly asked questions from beginning and advanced HTML coders.

Appendix D, "Special Characters," lists the character entities used to embed special characters, such as the copyright symbol and an ampersand, into a web page.

Appendix E, "File Types," includes a list of the file types you are most likely to encounter while creating web pages, as well as a brief description and MIME type for each.

How to Read This Book

The content is structured so that you can read a single chapter as needed or the entire book from cover to cover. While beginners should read through the book, chapter by chapter, in order to efficiently grasp the concepts taught, intermediate and advanced users can use certain chapters as reference materials.

The projects at the end of each chapter are intended to build upon each other as you create your own web site, but you could certainly adapt a specific project to your own needs if you read them out of order.

Special Features

Each chapter includes Tips and Notes to provide additional reference information wherever needed. Detailed code listings are included, many times with certain tags or features highlighted with further explanation.

Many chapters contain Ask the Expert question-and-answer sections to address potentially confusing issues. Each chapter contains Try This exercises and step-by-step projects to give you a chance to practice the concepts taught thus far. The intention is that you use these projects to build a web site from scratch for yourself or the business or organization of your choosing.

Self Tests are included at the end of each chapter to give you another chance to review the concepts taught in the chapter. The answers to the Self Tests are in Appendix A.

Throughout the development of this book, our objective has always been to provide you with a cohesive, easy-to-understand guide for coding HTML to help you get up and running in no time. As you'll hear me say countless times, HTML is not that difficult and is definitely within your reach. I applaud your decision to learn HTML and encourage you to use the Internet to its fullest potential, both during the learning process and in your ensuing web development aspirations. As Chapter 1 discusses, visit the web sites you love and love to hate to determine how they accomplished various features. Follow the links identified in the book for additional information, and don't forget to perform your own web searches for related content. Have fun and good luck!

Part I

Laying the Foundation

Chapter 1

Getting Started

Key Skills & Concepts

- Understand the Internet as a Medium for Disseminating Information

- Be Aware of the Current Version of HTML

- Plan for the Audience, Goals, Structure, Content, and Navigation of Your Site

- Identify the Best HTML Editor for You

- Learn from the Pros Using the View Source Command of Popular Web Browsers

For as long as I've been involved in making web pages, people have asked me to teach them the process. At the start, many are intimidated by the thought of learning HTML. But fear not! After all, one of the reasons I decided to attend art school was to avoid all the math and science classes. So, as I tell my students ... if I could learn HTML, so can you.

HTML is not rocket science. Quite simply, it is a means of telling a web browser how to display a page. That's why it's called *HTML,* which is the acronym for *Hypertext Markup Language.* Like any new skill, HTML takes practice to comprehend what you are doing.

Before we dive into the actual creation of web pages, you must first understand a few things about the Internet. I could probably fill an entire book with the material in this initial chapter, but the following should provide you with a firm foundation.

Understand the Internet as a Medium for Disseminating Information

When you're asked to write a term paper in school, you don't sit down and just start writing. First, you have to do research and learn how to format the paper. The process for writing and designing a web page is similar.

The Anatomy of a Web Site

Undoubtedly, you've seen more than a few web sites by now. Perhaps you know someone who's a skilled web navigator, and you've watched him surf through a web site by chopping off pieces of the web address. Have you ever wondered what he's doing? It's not too difficult. He just knows a little about the anatomy of a web site and how the underlying structure is laid out.

URLs

The fancy word for "web address" is *uniform resource locator,* also referenced by its acronym URL (pronounced either by the letters U-R-L or as a single word, url, which rhymes with "girl"). Even if you've never heard a web address referred to as a URL, you've probably seen one—URLs start with http://, and they usually end with .com, .org, .edu, or .net. (Other possibilities include .tv, .biz, and .info. For more information, see **www.networksolutions.com**.)

Every web site has a URL—for instance, Google's is **www.google.com**. The following illustration shows another example of a URL as it appears in a common web browser (Firefox) on the Mac.

The first part of the URL is commonly referred to as a *protocol* or *scheme*. In the previous illustration, HTTP was the scheme used. HTTP stands for Hypertext Transfer Protocol, and tells the browser how to access the rest of the URL. In this case, HTTP specifies the browser should display the file using hypertext.

HTTPS is another common scheme, and indicates the browser should connect securely to the server before displaying the content.

The next significant part of a URL is the *domain,* which helps identify and locate computers on the Internet. To avoid confusion, each domain name is unique. You can think of the domain name as a label or shortcut. Behind that shortcut is a series of numbers, called an *IP address,* that gives the specific address of where the site you're looking for is located on the Internet. To draw an analogy, if the domain name is the word "Emergency" written next to the first-aid symbol on your speed dial, the IP address is 9-1-1.

NOTE

Although many URLs begin with "www," this is not a necessity (depending on how the server is set up). Originally used to denote "World Wide Web" in the URL, using www caught on as common practice. The characters before the first period in the URL are not part of the registered domain and can be almost anything. In fact, many businesses use this part of the URL to differentiate between various departments within the company. For example, the GO Network includes ABC, ESPN, and Disney, to name a few. Each of these is a department of go.com: abc.go.com, espn.go.com, and disney.go.com. Type **www.abc.com** in the address bar of your favorite web browser, and you'll notice the URL changes to abc.go.com. That's because www.abc.com is an alias—or a shortcut—for abc.go.com.

Businesses typically register domain names ending in a .com (which signifies a commercial venture) that are similar to their business or product name. Domain registration is like renting office space on the Internet. Once you register a domain name, you have the right to publish a web site under that name on the Internet for as long as you pay the rental fees.

TIP

Wondering whether *yourname.com* is already being used? You can check to see which domain names are still available for registration by visiting a registration service like **www.godaddy.com** or **www.networksolutions.com**.

The rest of the address contains the exact path to the specific file on the server being displayed. For example, when I visit **http://www.fox.com/glee/recaps**, I am viewing the content from Fox housed in the "recaps" folder, which is then housed in the "glee" folder on the web server. Here, the slashes separate the domain from each folder name.

Web Servers

Every web site and web page also needs a web server. Quite simply, a *web server* is a computer, running special software, that is always connected to the Internet.

NOTE

Some people talk about the computer as the server, as in "We need to buy a new server." Others call the software the server, saying "We need to install a new web server." Both uses of the word essentially refer to the same thing—web servers make information available to those requesting it.

When you type a URL into your web browser or click a link in a web page, you send a request to the server housing that information. It's similar to the process that occurs when you dial a phone number with your telephone. Your request "calls" the computer that contains all the files necessary to show you the web page you requested. The computer then "serves" and displays all the pages to you, usually in your web browser.

Ask the Expert

Q: I've heard the phrase "the World Wide Web" used so many times, but I'm a little confused about what it actually means and how it relates to the Internet.

A: The *World Wide Web* (*WWW* or the *Web*) is often confused with the *Internet*. The actual term "Internet" was first used in the early 1970s, when academic research institutions developed a way to connect computers to create better communication and to share resources. Later, universities and research facilities throughout the world began using the Internet. In the early 1990s, Tim Berners-Lee created a set of technologies that allowed information on the Internet to be connected through the use of *links* in documents. The language component of these technologies is Hypertext Markup Language (HTML). If you want to find out more, a good resource on the history of the Internet is available at **http://www.internetsociety.org//internet/internet-51/history-internet**.

The Web was mostly text-based until a division at the National Center for Supercomputing Applications (NCSA) created the first graphical web browser in 1993. Called Mosaic, this paved the way for the use of video, sound, and photos, and many other aspects of the modern web browser. As a large group of interconnected computers all over the world, the Internet comprises not only the Web, but also things like *newsgroups* (online bulletin boards) and e-mail. Many people think of the Web as the graphical or illustrated part of the Internet.

Sites

A URL is commonly associated with a web site. You've doubtless seen plenty of examples of such addresses on billboards and in television advertising. For instance, **www.amazon.com** is the URL for Amazon's web site, while **www.cbs.com** is the URL for CBS.

Most commonly, these sites are located in directories or folders on the *server,* just as you might have your C: drive on your personal computer. Then, within this main site, there may be several folders that house other sections of the web site.

For example, Chop Point is a summer camp and K–12 school in Maine. If you look at the URL for Chop Point Camp's "about us" section, you can see the name of the folder after the site name:

www.choppointcamp.com/about

If you access the main page for the enrollment section, the URL changes to:

www.choppointcamp.com/enroll

Pages

When you visit a web site, you look at pages on the site that contain all its text, graphics, sound, and video content. Even though a web page is not the same size or format as a printed page, the word "page" is used to help us differentiate among pages, folders, and sites. The same way that many pages and chapters can be contained within a single book, many pages and folders (or sections) can also be kept within a web site.

Most web servers are set up to look automatically for a page called "index" as the main page in any folder. So if you were to type in the URL used in the previous example, the server would look for the index page in the "about" folder, which might look like the following:

www.choppointcamp.com/about/index.html

If you want to look for a different page in the about folder, you could type the name of that page after the site and folder names, keeping in mind that HTML pages usually end with .html or .htm, such as in:

www.choppointcamp.com/about/donate.html

NOTE

Sites built on content management systems like Wordpress typically use a different type of file naming convention than the traditional structure I've outlined here. The latest version of Chop Point Camp's site uses Wordpress, and therefore doesn't default to index.html pages like those mentioned here. We'll talk about Wordpress later, but at this point just keep in mind there are a variety of file naming conventions currently in use.

Web Browsers

A *web browser* is a piece of software that runs on your personal computer and enables you to view web pages. Web browsers, often simply called "browsers," interpret the HTML code and provide a visual layout displayed on the screen. Browsers typically can also be used to check web-based e-mail and access newsgroups.

The most popular browsers are Microsoft Internet Explorer (also called IE), Google Chrome, and Firefox. In previous years, IE garnered as much as 65 percent of the market share. But as of this writing, the three browsers I mentioned each enjoy roughly 25 percent of the market. The remaining quarter is divided among Safari (Apple's default browser), Opera, Android, and other miscellaneous browsers.

TIP

To keep current on statistics about browser use, visit **http://en.wikipedia.org/wiki/Usage_share_of_web_browsers**.

Browsers are updated regularly, changing to address new aspects of HTML or emerging technologies. Some people continue to use older versions of their browsers, however. This means that at any given time there may be two or three active versions of one browser and several different versions of other browsers being employed by the general public.

What if there were several versions of televisions that all displayed TV programs differently? If this were true, then your favorite television show might look different every time you watched it on someone else's television. This would not only be frustrating to you as a viewer, it would also be frustrating for the show's creator.

Web developers must deal with this frustration every day. Because of the differences among various browsers and the large number of computer types, the look and feel of a web page can vary greatly. This means web developers must keep up-to-date on the latest features of the new browser versions, but we must also know how to create web pages that are backward-compatible for the older browsers many people may still be using.

TIP

Most browsers can be easily customized, meaning you can change the text sizes, styles, and colors, as well as the first page that appears when you start your browser. This is usually called your "home" page or your "start" page, and it's the page displayed when you click the "home" button in your browser. For easier access, many people change their home page to a search engine or a news site customized according to their needs. These personalized sites are often called portals and also offer free e-mail to users. A few examples are Yahoo!, Google, and MSN.

Internet Service Providers

You use an *Internet service provider (ISP)* to gain access to the Internet. Traditionally, this connection is made through your wired phone line with a company like Verizon or AT&T, or you can connect through a cable line with a company like Comcast or Time Warner.

With the rise of high-speed wireless options, many users access the Internet via wireless broadband connections, either on their phone or through a small device that plugs into a Universal Serial Bus (USB) port, called a dongle. Verizon, Clearwire, Xanadoo, and CLEAR are just a few of the many companies offering high-speed wireless service in the United States.

Regardless of which connection method you choose, the company providing that service is called your ISP. Many ISPs offer you a choice of browsers, and may even provide a particular web browser customized with quick links for things like checking your e-mail and reading local news.

Be Aware of the Current Version of HTML

In its earliest years, HTML quickly went through much iteration, which led to a lack of standardization across the Internet. The *World Wide Web Consortium* (W3C—**www.w3.org**) stepped in and began publishing a list of recommendations, called standards, for HTML and other web languages. The last *official* standard for HTML was HTML 4.01 in 1999.

In an attempt to move the standards away from the old-style HTML and closer to a more flexible language, *Extensible Markup Language (XML),* the W3C rewrote the standard in 2000. The resulting set of standards, called *Extensible Hypertext Markup Language (XHTML),* provided a way for HTML to handle alternative devices, such as cell phones and handheld computers.

XHTML 1.0 offered many new features to make the lives of web developers easier, but it was poorly supported by web browsers at its launch in 2001. It was much stricter and had little tolerance for sloppy HTML. In the years immediately following, the W3C updated its recommendation to XHTML 2.0. However, the world didn't adopt XML as quickly or as warmly as the W3C had anticipated, and the organization ended up switching gears.

In 2008, the W3C released a working draft of the future of hypertext markup: HTML5. Since then, even though HTML5 has been a consistent "work in progress," the modern browser creators have worked to incorporate as many features as possible. (You can check the status of HTML5 on the W3C's web site: **www.w3c.org/TR/html5**.)

Unlike XHTML, HTML5 is intended to allow the best of HTML and XML simultaneously. The development team has been studying the modern use of HTML and its content in an effort to create code standards that will carry us easily into the next generation of the Web.

Previously we needed plug-ins like Flash and QuickTime—which essentially are stop-gaps—to do the things HTML wasn't able to accomplish. Now the combination of HTML, cascading style sheets (CSS), and JavaScript, working together as HTML5, is capable of just about anything web designers and developers need.

Although the standard is technically still in development (as of this writing), plenty of the new features are now supported by the major browsers. I will call attention to those as needed throughout the course of this book, but here are a few highlights:

- **More intuitive structure** The latest revision offers new HTML elements that make it easier to group related content and structure pages, among other things.

- **Better portability** It is easier to port your pages from one device to another, whether the content consists of text, images, animation, and interactivity, or a combination of each.

- **Next-generation forms** HTML5 enables us to create much more interactive and user-friendly forms, both in desktop browsers as well as mobile versions.

- **Rich media** Speaking of animation and interactivity, HTML removes the need for plug-ins to handle dynamic images. (And yes, this means HTML5 is now a *competitor* of Flash.)

- **Audio and video** Embedding audio and video in HTML pages used to be quite a chore. Thankfully the new spec adds elements to easily embed—and style!—both.

You can read more about the specific differences at **www.w3.org/TR/2008/WD-html5-diff-20080610**.

Plan for the Audience, Goals, Structure, Content, and Navigation of Your Site

In addition to learning about the medium, you need to do the following:

- Identify your target audience.

- Set goals for your site.

- Create your web site's structure.

- Organize your web site's content.

- Develop your web site's navigation.

Identify the Target Audience

If you are creating a web site for a business, a group, or an organization, you are most likely targeting people who might buy or use the company's products or services. Even if your site is set up purely for the purpose of disseminating information, you must target a certain audience. Consider whether you have existing research regarding your client or user base. This might include demographics, statistics, or other marketing information, such as age, gender, and web experience.

TIP

If your site represents a new company or one that doesn't already have information about its clients' demographics, you might check out the competition. Chances are good that if your competition has a successful web site, you can learn from them about your target audience.

Knowing your target audience will influence how you design and develop your web site. For example, if you are developing a site for beginners to learn about the Internet, you want to create a site that is extremely easy to use and does not stray from standard computer conventions. If your site targets teens and young adults, you can expect lots of visits from mobile phone and tablet devices.

Once you identify your target audience, you need to think about what functions each part of that audience can perform at your site. Try drawing up a chart like Table 1-1 to make your plans. The example in the table is designed for a bank, but you can use it as a starting point for any site you create.

You can use this information to determine the appropriate direction for the site. For new sites, consider taking it a step further to identify a few sample customers in each category. To do so, give your pretend customer a name, age, job, and location, and then specify his or her brand preferences, Internet usage, and what influences and inhibits him.

You might also specify whether he is an "accidental tourist" or a "navy seal" type of visitor. Most sites have a little of both. Have you ever surfed a certain site and then wondered

User Group	Functions Performed	Ages	Gender	Web Habits
Current customers	Bank online contact Customer service Research additional services/ products	16+	Male/female	Daily use for business interaction, email, and social networking
Potential customers	Research services/products Contact sales	16+	Male/female	Daily use for business interaction, email, and social networking
Potential employees	Search job openings Research company Contact HR	18–60	Male/female	Daily use for job search, email, social networking
Financial consultants	Research services/products View company financials Contact sales	30–60	Male/female 60/40	Daily use for both business and personal reasons

Table 1-1   Functions Performed by a Target Audience

how you got there from here? This is the "accidental tourist," aka the serendipitous visitor. At the other end of the spectrum is the student on a mission—looking for a specific piece of information for a homework assignment. I call these the "navy seals."

TIP

Does your site target mostly "navy seal" visitors? These individuals prefer search engines, especially when trying to locate information quickly. Providing a good search engine or site map on your site can greatly increase your repeat visitors.

This type of detailed user information can give extremely beneficial insights to any developer working on the project.

Set Goals

Since the Web's inception, millions of new web sites have been created. To compete in such a large market, you need to set clear goals for the site that meet the needs of the target audience. For instance, the site might

- Sell products/services
- Recruit potential employees
- Entertain
- Educate
- Communicate with customers

Always remember the goals when developing the site to avoid unnecessary content. If a page or section of content on your site doesn't meet one of the goals, it may confuse or turn away visitors.

Create the Structure

Once you align your site's goals with the functions performed by the target audience, you will see a structure forming. Consider a site whose primary goal is to sell office supplies to businesses and whose secondary goal is to recruit potential employees. This site would most likely contain two main topic areas: shop for office supplies and browse available jobs.

Many people use tree diagrams, such as the one shown in Figure 1-1, to help define the structure of the site. Others use flow charts, wire frames, or simple outlines.

Organize Content

All the content for the site should fit under each of the topic areas in the site structure, and you might have several subcategories in each topic area. So, the "Enrichment" section from the preceding example might be broken down into several subcategories, according to the different types of programs available. Table 1-2 shows how the category names might relate to the folder names.

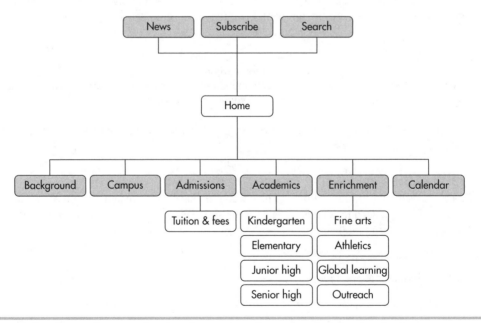

Figure 1-1 A tree diagram showing the structure for a sample school web site

Category Name	Folder Name
Fine arts	enrichment/finearts/
Athletics	enrichment/athletics/
Global learning	enrichment/globallearning/
Outreach	enrichment/outreach/

Table 1-2   Content Organization

Develop Navigation

After the site structure has been defined and the content has been placed into the structure accordingly, you will want to plan out how a visitor to this site navigates between each of the pages and sections. A good practice is to include a standard navigation bar on all pages for consistency and ease of use. This navigation bar probably should include links to your home page and any major topic areas. It should probably also contain the name of your business or a logo so that a simple visual clue lets the user know she has not moved beyond your site by accident.

Many sites also offer an additional level of navigation, usually to content related to the currently active section. Highlighting the current section on the navigation bar is important so visitors can more easily distinguish where they are in your site's structure. This means if your site has two sections—jobs and résumés—the jobs button would look different when you were inside that section and, in some way, should identify it as the current section.

In addition, consider giving your visitors as many visual clues as possible to aid in the navigation of your site (see Figure 1-2). This might be accomplished by repeating the page name in:

- The page's title (the text that appears at the top of the browser window, as well as in search engines)

- The page's filename

- A headline

- Buttons and links to the page (highlighted if you are viewing that page)

The URL clues the visitor to the name and location of the section being viewed.

This button has a different color scheme to show the visitor which section is currently being viewed.

This page title lists the name of the site as well as the page and section names.

This text is darker to show the visitor which aspect of the iPod section is currently being viewed.

Figure 1-2 Apple's site gives the user plenty of visual clues to aid in navigation.

Identify the Best HTML Editor for You

At some point, you may wonder: "Why go to the trouble of learning HTML if I can use a program that does it for me?" With so many new software packages available to help you develop HTML, that's a valid question. We'll discuss the pros and cons of each type after reviewing the features of some of the most common editors in Table 1-3. This is by no means an exhaustive list of valid HTML editors. It is merely meant to help get you started by pointing out the key benefits of each.

After reviewing Table 1-3, you likely noticed that most tools fall into one of two categories. First, text-based editors require you to know some HTML to use them. They can be customized to help speed your coding process, and often have sophisticated checks and balances in place to check for errors in coding. Hundreds, if not thousands, of editors exist. I've listed a few of the most popular text-based HTML editors here, and I encourage you to try out a few before settling on one.

Tool	Average Price (U.S.)	Key Features
Amaya www.w3.org/Amaya/	Free	Open-source software project hosted by W3C Windows/Mac/Linux WYSIWYG visual editor (but no browser preview) Spell-checking Internationalized
BBEdit http://barebones.com/ products/bbedit/	$49.99	Also offers a free, scaled-down version called TextWrangler Mac only Browser preview FTP upload Multiuser editing Text-based editor capable of handling many popular programming languages, including C, C++, CSS, Java, JavaScript, JSP, Perl, PHP, Ruby, HTML, SQL, and XML
CoffeeCup Pro/Free www.coffeecup.com	$69/free	Windows and Mac options available WYSIWYG visual editor FTP upload Spell-checking Templates Shopping cart creator Form builder
Dreamweaver www.adobe.com/ products/dreamweaver	$399 (or $19.99/month)	Windows/Mac WYSIWYG visual editor with browser preview FTP upload Spell-checking Templates Server-side scripting Multiuser editing E-commerce building tools Mobile app/site development
Expression Studio 4 Web Professional www.microsoft.com/ expression **Note:** *Expression Web replaced Microsoft's Front Page.*	$149	Windows only WYSIWYG visual editor with browser preview FTP upload Spell-checking Templates Server-side scripting Multiuser editing Web graphics editor Additional editing tools available
TextWrangler http://barebones.com/ products/textwrangler/	Free	Mac only Text-based editor perfect for beginners Also has server administration tools

Table 1-3   Common Tools Used to Edit HTML (*continued*)

Tool	Average Price (U.S.)	Key Features
Visual Web Developer www.microsoft.com/ express/download	Free	Windows only WYSIWYG visual editor with browser preview FTP upload Spell-checking Templates Server-side scripting Multiuser editing
NoteTab www.notetab.com	Free/$39.95	Free and pro versions available Windows only (but Mac and Linux users can install via Wine or another emulator) Text-based HTML editor The Pro version is highly customizable and includes features such as a spell-checker and templates

Table 1-3 Common Tools Used to Edit HTML

Second, WYSIWYG editors don't require knowledge of HTML. Instead of looking only at the HTML code of your pages, you have the option to view a "preview" of how the page will look in a browser. This way, you can simply drag and drop pieces of your layout as you see fit. These types of programs can have some drawbacks, but they can also be quite useful for the purposes of learning different aspects of HTML or for quickly publishing a basic web page.

Which Is Best?

Some web developers prefer to use the text-based HTML editors rather than have a WYSIWYG editor do it for them, for the following reasons:

- **Better control** WYSIWYG editors may write HTML in a variety of ways—although not all of them will have the same outcome. This means your pages can look different in each browser. Unfortunately, this has caused some older WYSIWYG programs to be labeled "WYSINWYG" or What-You-See-Is-*Not*-What-You-Get.

- **Faster pages** WYSIWYG editors sometimes overcompensate for the amount of code needed to render a page properly, and so they end up repeating code more times than necessary. This leads to large file sizes and longer downloads.

- **Speedier editing** The large-scale WYSIWYG editors can take a lot of memory and system resources, slowing both the computer and the development process.

- **More flexibility** Some older WYSIWYG editors are programmed to "fix" code they think is faulty. This may make you unable to insert code or edit the existing code as you wish.

That said, modern WYSIWYG editors have come a long way in terms of control and flexibility. Those developers who sing their praises typically make the following comments:

- **Preview**   WYSIWYG editors allow you to preview your pages within the HTML editor, which means you get an idea of how the page is shaping up even before switching to the browser view.

- **Drag-and-drop editing**   Because WYSIWYG editors have previewing tools, you can actually edit your HTML by dragging and dropping elements throughout the page.

- **Advanced inline edition**   Tools like Dreamweaver offer the capability to code extras beyond static HTML, like CSS, Dynamic HTML (DHTML), and JavaScript, all within the same visual editor used to code basic HTML.

- **Best of both worlds**   With the ability to dig right into the code and still see a visual representation of the output, it's no surprise that editors like Dreamweaver have become so popular.

Quick confession time: If I sound a bit biased toward Dreamweaver, that's because I am. I find it does everything I need an HTML editor to do, while still giving me ultimate control over my code. In addition, its companion tool—Contribute—allows me to give access to certain aspects of the web pages to clients, so they can maintain their own pages without altering the underlying structure or format of the site.

In the end, both text-based HTML editors and WYSIWYG editors have their benefits. My recommendation is to download free trials of the various programs and decide for yourself which one works best for your needs.

To achieve the goals of this book, you are free to use any editor or software package you like, provided it gives you access to the source code. To begin, I recommend you use the basic text editor that came with your computer system, such as SimpleText or TextEdit (Mac) or Notepad (Windows). Once you have the basics of HTML down, you can move on and experiment with other available programs.

Learn from the Pros Using the View Source Command of Popular Web Browsers

One of the best ways to learn HTML is to surf the Web and look at the HTML for sites you like (as well as those you don't like). Most web browsers enable you to view the HTML source code of web pages (as shown in Figure 1-3), using the following commands:

- In your favorite web browser, bring up the page whose source you would like to view.

- In Chrome, choose View | Developer | View Source. In Firefox or Mozilla, right-click and select View Page Source. In IE, choose View | Source or Page | Source.

- In Safari, you must first choose Safari | Preferences | Advanced and check the option to Show Develop menu in menu bar. Then, choose Develop | Show Page Source.

Figure 1-3 Viewing the source of a web page allows you to see the HTML code used to create it.

You'll notice there are often additional types of code visible. For example, aside from standard HTML code, you might also find references to other files on the server, or even other types of scripts or code altogether. Furthermore, what you're seeing in the View Source display is only what has been sent by the server for the browser to display. This means there may have been other code used to actually tell the server where to get this code, when to send it, or even how to send it.

If you'd like, you can print or save these pages to review at a later time or to keep in a reference library. Because the Web is *open source,* meaning your code is free for anyone to see, copying other developers' code is tempting. But remember, you should give credit where credit is due and never copy anything protected by a copyright, such as graphics and text content.

NOTE

A few browsers don't let you use View Source. If you find you cannot view the HTML source of a web page, try saving the page to your local hard drive, and then opening it in a text editor instead.

Try This 1-1 Develop a Web Site

The best way to practice HTML is to develop web sites. While developing a personal site might be fun, I think you can sometimes learn more about the whole development process by working on a site for a business or organization. In fact, volunteering your time to develop a web site for a nonprofit organization or a start-up business is a wonderful way to start.

Throughout the course of this book, I'll give you projects that relate to the development of such a web site. If you already have an organization or business in mind for which you want to develop a site, then use that one. If not, you can follow along while I start a site for a friend's online tutoring business, and customize it as you see fit.

This specific project takes you through the planning phase of the web development project. Goals for this project include

- Identifying your target audience

- Setting goals for your site

- Creating your web site's structure

- Organizing your web site's content

- Developing your web site's navigation

1. Spend some time researching your organization. Try to learn as much about its business as possible. If you know people within the company, do some interviews to help you identify your target audience, as well as the site goals. If you can't speak with them, visit other similar sites to determine what type of people the competition is targeting. Some questions to ask and things to consider include

   - What business issues or problem(s) will the web site address? What do you want to accomplish? What are your goals for the web site?

   - Who are the targeted users/visitors of the site? Do you have any existing research regarding your client or user base, such as demographics, statistics, or other marketing information?

   - To determine the appropriate direction for the site, you must match the targeted users and the functions they will perform when visiting the site. For example, will the targeted users be "accidental tourists" directed to the site by an advertisement, or potential investors looking for the financials? How do the audience demographics affect this? (You can use a table like the following to help you plan the targeted users and the functions they might perform at the site.)

(continued)

User Group	Functions Performed at Site	Ages	Web Habits
1. Parents of students needing tutoring	Check services and prices Schedule a session Contact the tutor	35–60	Daily email use, uses online searches to research services and opportunities for family
2.			
3.			

2. Pull out one or two key user groups and create a sample user scenario for fictional members of each group. Use the following table to get started.

Name and Quick Bio	Online Habits and Preferences	Influencers	Inhibitors
Nancy is a stay-at-home mom to two teenage daughters who lives in Ohio.	Engages daily with family and friends through Facebook and Pinterest. Is comfortable using text and video chat for online services. For online customer service, prefers knowing she is talking with an actual person, rather than a computer.	Strongly influenced by likes and dislikes of friends and family via social media. Primary motivator is whatever helps her kids and family.	Money is tight since she doesn't work outside the home. Shops based on price first.

3. After you decide on the target audience and goals for the site, it's time to evaluate your content. This is best accomplished through conversations with the people you're developing the site for. If this isn't possible, be creative and come up with a list of content you think could be appropriate.

4. Use the answers to the following questions as a springboard for building the structure of your site. Then develop a tree diagram, similar to the one shown in Figure 1-1, to identify all the pieces of your site and where they fit within the overall structure.

   - Does an official logo have to be used on the web site?

   - Is all the content written and available in digital format?

   - What are the main sections of the site? Does all the content fit within those sections?

   - List all the content for the site. Assign each piece of content to a section (as necessary) and define the filenames.

✓ Chapter 1 Self Test

1. What is a web browser?

2. What does HTML stand for?

3. Identify the various parts of the following URL:
   http://www.mcgrawhill.com/books/webdesign/favorites.html
   _____://_____/_____/_____/_____

4. What is WYSIWYG?

5. Fill in the blank: The latest version of HTML currently under development is
   _____.

6. What is the Adobe Dreamweaver program used for?

7. What is one of the three most popular web browsers?

8. Fill in the blank: When you type a URL into your web browser, you send a request to the
   _____ that houses that information.

9. What does the acronym "URL" stand for?

10. What organization maintains the standards for HTML?

11. How can you give your site's visitors visual clues as to where they are in your site's
    structure?

12. Fill in the blank: A good practice is to include a standard _____ on all pages
    for consistency and ease of use.

13. Fill in the blank: Selling products and recruiting potential employees are examples of web
    site _____.

14. Fill in the blank: Before you can begin developing your web site, you must know a little
    about the site's target _____.

15. If your site represents a new company or one that doesn't already have information about its
    client demographics, where might you look for information?

Chapter 2

Document Setup

Key Skills & Concepts

- Create an HTML File

- Preview an HTML File in a Browser

- Describe and Apply the Basic HTML Document Format

- Use Character Entities to Display Special Characters

- Add Comments to an HTML File

N ow that you know a little about the Web and what to think about before creating a web page, let's talk about the basic setup of an HTML page.

Create an HTML File

At their very core, HTML files are simply text files with two additional features:

- *HTML files have an .html or .htm file extension.* A *file extension* is an abbreviation that associates the file with the appropriate program or tool needed to access it. In most cases, this abbreviation follows a period and is three or four letters long.

- *HTML files have tags.* Tags are commands or code used to tell the computer how to display the page content.

NOTE
You might also see other types of pages on the Internet, such as files ending with .php, .asp, or .xml. For the most part, these are beyond the scope of the traditional HTML page, and therefore not covered in this book.

Naming Conventions
Remember the following few points when naming your HTML files:

- Although in most cases it doesn't matter whether you use .html or .htm, you should be consistent to avoid confusing yourself, the browser, and your users.

NOTE
Wondering why some people use .html and some use .htm? Older systems such as Windows 3.1 and DOS could not understand four-letter file extensions, so anyone creating web pages on those systems used .htm as the extension. In any case, because the first three letters of .html and .htm are the same, those systems simply ignored the "l" and recognized the file type without any problems.

- Some web servers are case-sensitive, so remember this when naming and referencing filenames and try to be consistent. If you name your file MyPage.html, and then reference it later using mypage.html, you may end up with a broken link. One good technique is to use only uppercase or lowercase to name your files. This way, if you see a file with a letter in it that doesn't match, you know instantly that file is probably the problem. Even the pros run into case-sensitivity problems on an almost daily basis.

- Use simple filenames with only letters and numbers. Don't use spaces, punctuation, or special characters other than hyphens (-) and underscores (_). Good examples might be home.html, my-story.html, and contactme.html.

TIP

While it's perfectly acceptable to use an underscore (_) in a file or folder name, I suggest using a hyphen instead. Underscores can easily become confused with an underline, especially when displayed as a link on a web page (because links are usually underlined).

These same recommendations hold true for any folder names you use. If you were creating a web site that had your favorite links, family photos, and résumé, you might find it useful to put each of those things in a separate folder.

TIP

If you decide to use Microsoft Word or WordPad to type your HTML, you need to choose the file type "Text Document" or "Text Only" and give the file an .html extension the first time you save it. This is because both of those programs default to saving "Word for Windows" or "Microsoft Word" documents with a .doc or .docx extension.

Preview an HTML File in a Browser

You can view HTML files located on your personal computer within your own web browser. It isn't necessary for your files to be stored on a web server until you are ready to make them visible on the Internet.

When you want to preview a page, open your web browser and choose File | Open File (or Open Page or simply Open, depending on your browser), and then browse through your hard drive until you locate the HTML file you want to open. (Note: If you don't see any File menus in IE, try pressing the ALT key to reveal those menus. Also, Windows users can right-click the file and choose Open With and then choose the browser name.)

If you're going to make frequent changes to the HTML file in an editor without a preview tool and then switch back to a web browser to preview the page, keeping both programs (a text editor and a web browser) open at the same time makes sense. When using a basic text editor, the steps to edit and preview HTML files are as follows:

1. Open/return to your HTML file in an editor.

2. Edit your HTML file in an editor.

3. Save your HTML file in an editor.

4. Open/return to your HTML file in a web browser.

5. Click the Refresh or Reload button in your web browser to update the HTML page to reflect the changes you just made to it.

By keeping your HTML file open in both an editor and a browser, you can easily make and preview changes. I'll have you give this a try shortly.

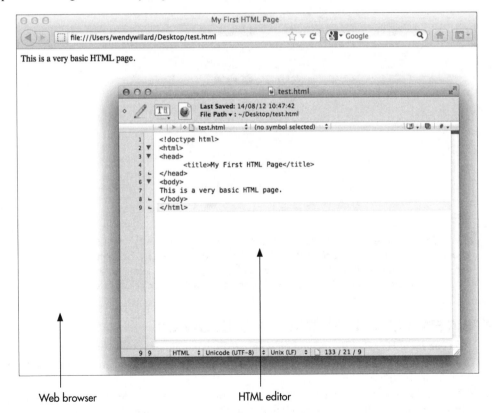

Web browser   HTML editor

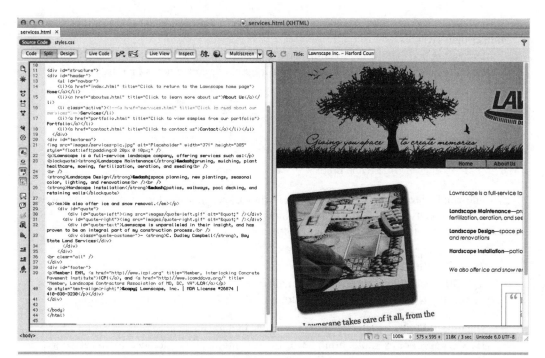

Figure 2-1   Accessing both the code and browser preview at once with Adobe Dreamweaver

If you're using a graphical or WYSIWYG editor, the ideal steps are slightly different because these types of programs include a browser preview option. For example, Adobe Dreamweaver offers three ways to work with an HTML file. One option is to view only the code, as you would in a basic text editor. Another option is to work in the preview mode, moving page elements around on the page by clicking and dragging. Finally, you can use a combination, where the code is visible on part of the screen and the browser preview is visible on the rest (as shown in Figure 2-1).

Describe and Apply the Basic HTML Document Format

An *HTML element* is used to tell the browser how to display content on a page. HTML elements have opening and closing *tags* to tell the browser when to start and stop applying commands. These commands are similar to what happens behind the scenes when you highlight some text in a word processor and click the Italic button to make the text italicized.

With HTML, instead of clicking a button to make text italicized, you can type a tag before and after the text you want to emphasize, as in the following:

```
<em>Reminder:</em> There will be no band practice today.
```

You can easily recognize tags because they are placed within *brackets* (< >), or less-than and greater-than symbols.

Did you notice that the tag to emphasize text and make it italic is em? Given that piece of information, can you guess the tags to add a paragraph or create items in a list?

Purpose	Tag
Create paragraphs	<p>
Create list items	<li>
Add a line break	

Now do you believe me when I say HTML is not rocket science? Don't worry—most of the elements are pretty intuitive and easy to remember. We will work through each of these tags, and plenty more, throughout the course of the book.

Types of Elements

Most HTML tags fall into one of several main categories. While the actual category names vary according to who you ask, for the purposes of this book I group them like this:

- **Document Setup** Elements in this category include those necessary to set up a basic HTML page. For example, html, head, and title might all be included in this category. We'll talk about these types of elements in this chapter.

- **Text-Level Semantics** These elements help the browser understand the meaning behind bits of text content. We'll cover this category in Chapters 4 and 6.

- **Sectioning** Elements used to section large chunks of content and divide up the page belong in this category. Examples include section, div, and header, all of which are covered in Chapter 5.

- **Grouping** Elements used to section smaller chunks of content, like lists and paragraphs, fall into this category. Lists are explained in Chapter 10, while paragraphs are covered in Chapter 3.

- **Embedding** Often times, we need to embed content from other sources into a web page. Examples include images (discussed in Chapter 8), audio and video (explained in Chapter 9), and other interactive elements (some of which are discussed in Chapter 14).

- **Tables** Those elements useful for managing tabular data can easily be grouped together. We'll go over those in Chapter 11.

- **Forms** Any element used in the development of a web form falls into this category. I'll discuss these in Chapters 12 and 13.

Josh Duck has a great interactive example on his web site that can really help us visualize the various types of elements and how they work together to create web pages. Figure 2-2 shows a screen shot, but be sure to visit **www.joshduck.com/periodic-table.html** to see it live.

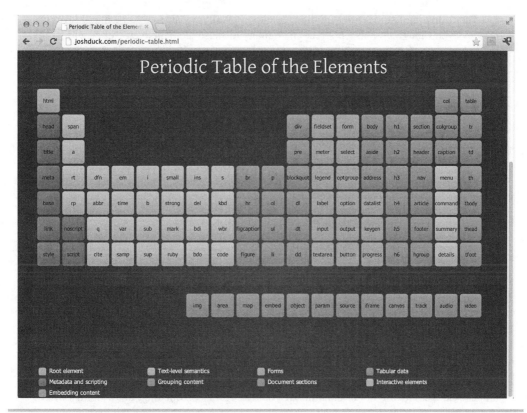

Figure 2-2   This interactive "Periodic Table of Elements" helps us visualize all the HTML5 elements together.

Block-Level vs. Inline

Beyond those basic categories, there are two other types of elements I want to touch on before we go any further. Of those HTML elements that are added to the body of a web page, most can be classified as either a *block-level* or *inline,* or text-level, element by default.

Generally speaking, block-level elements have the following key differences from inline elements:

- They can contain other block-level elements, as well as inline elements.

- They are formatted to start on blank lines by default.

- They are styled as "boxes" on the page.

By contrast, inline elements cannot contain other block-level elements and do not begin on new lines. In addition, inline elements cannot be fully styled the same way block-level elements are formatted. We'll discuss more about those differences when we get to some of the affected elements.

The following list identifies all the elements typically considered to be block-level in nature. Even though you may not recognize many of these elements yet, I'm providing this list as a reference to help you style the elements appropriately when you get to that point.

<address>	<hr>
<article>	<li>
<aside>	<noscript>
<audio>	<ol>
<blockquote>	<output>
<canvas>	<p>
<dd>	<pre>
<div>	<section>
<dl>	<table>
<fieldset>	<tbody>
<figcaption>	<td>
<figure>	<tfoot>
<footer>	<th>
<form>	<thead>
<h1> (and the other heading elements)	<tr>
	<ul>
<header>	<video>
<hgroup>	

Types of Tags

In HTML, many elements actually have two types of tags: one used for *opening* an element and another for *closing* it. For example, if you use <p> as an opening tag to signify where to start a new paragraph, you have to use a closing tag to signify where that paragraph ends (unless you want your entire page to be contained within one paragraph). To do so, add a forward slash before the element name: </p>.

```
<p>This paragraph has both opening and closing tags surrounding it.</p>
```

Having said that, HTML5 does not require all elements to have both opening and closing options. This means some elements have only one type of tag. Such elements are referred to as being *empty* because they stand alone and do not contain any other content.

```
The line break tag is an example of a tag that is empty. It looks like this: <br>.
```

Attributes

Many tags have additional aspects that you can customize. These options are called *attributes* and are placed after the element name, but before the final bracket. Specific attributes for each element are discussed as we move through the book. But to give you an idea of how attributes work, let's look at an example using the img element:

```
<img src="mypicture.jpg" width="100" height="100" alt="A photo of me">
```

In this example, the base element is img, which tells the browser I want to insert an image at this spot. The attributes are src, width, height, and alt. Each attribute has a *value,*

Opening Tag	Closing Tag	Description
!doctype	n/a	Tells the browser which set of standards your page adheres to.
<html>	</html>	Frames the entire HTML page.
<head>	</head>	Frames the identification information for the page, such as the title, that is transferred to the browser and search engines.
<body>	</body>	Frames the content of the page to be displayed in the browser window.
<title>	</title>	Gives the name of the page that will appear at the top of the browser window and be listed in search engines. Is contained within <head> and </head>.

Table 2-1   Required HTML Page Elements

which comes after an equal sign (=) and is placed within quotation marks. The whole thing—from the left angle bracket to the right angle bracket—is referred to as the *tag*.

There's no need to repeat the img tag, because multiple attributes can be included in a single tag. When you add attributes to a tag, you only put them in the opening tag. Then, you only need to close the tag (not the attributes), if necessary. (Note that this tag is one that doesn't have a separate closing tag in HTML5.)

Required Tags

All HTML pages need to have the html, head, title, and body tags, along with the doctype identifier. This means, at the very least, your pages should include the following (which are also outlined in Table 2-1):

```
<!doctype html>
<html>
<head>
     <title>My First HTML Page</title>
</head>
<body>
This is a very basic HTML page.
</body>
</html>
```

Here is the result of this page when displayed in a browser.

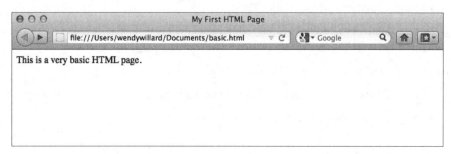

To test this basic HTML page for yourself, try the following:

1. Open a basic HTML editor, such as the free versions of TextWrangler (Mac) or CoffeeCup (PC).

2. Copy the preceding code into a new document.

3. Save it and name it **test.html**.

4. Launch your browser and choose File | Open File or File | Open.

5. Browse your hard drive to locate the test.html file, and you're off and running!

NOTE

If you're using IE7+ and don't see the File menus, press ALT to reveal those menus.

Doctype

The `doctype` element is used to tell the browser which type of coding or scripting language is used in the document. In versions prior to HTML5, this element specified which variation of HTML/XHTML should be used by the browser to interpret the page.

Thankfully the W3C greatly simplified this element in HTML5, which also makes it somewhat obsolete. At this point, all you need to do is to include the following brief tag at the top of each page to prevent the browser from using an older interpretation method:

```
<!doctype html>
```

HTML

The `html` element contains all of the remaining HTML elements. That means all the HTML of your page—except for the `html` and `doctype` elements—should be placed in between the opening and closing `html` tags.

```
<html>
...other HTML elements go here...
</html>
```

Head

The `head` element is used to tell the browser *about* the page, as opposed to including the content that will display *on* the page. There are a few other elements that belong in between the opening and closing `head` tags to help tell about the page. Those elements include

- `title`   Specifies the page title.

- `meta`   Specifies additional information about the page, such as which character set is used in the page.

- `style`   Defines internal style information.

- `link`   Defines a link to an external file needed to process the content of this page.

- `script`   Specifies non-HTML script content.

Note that of those five elements, only the `title` element is required. We'll discuss these elements further in later sections.

Body

The `body` element contains all of the HTML elements that define the content displayed on the page, including the tags necessary to format text, links, images, and so on. The bulk of the next few sections and chapters will outline exactly what to do in the body section of your pages.

Capitalization

Original versions of HTML were case-insensitive and, in fact, very forgiving. This means all of the following examples would be considered the same by the browser:

- `<html>`

- `<HTML>`

- `<HTml>`

But then HTML4 and XHTML came along, with all its restrictions, requiring all tags to be lowercase. This means of the three preceding examples, the browser might properly interpret only the first.

Thankfully, HTML5 returns to being case-insensitive, where pretty much anything goes in terms of capitalization. But given the differences between the various versions of HTML currently in use, I still recommend using all-lowercase tags.

Ask the Expert

Q: I typed the preceding HTML into a text file, but when I tried to preview the page in my browser, nothing happened. Why?

A: There are several possible reasons why your page might appear blank. First, review the code in the preceding example and compare it line by line with the code you typed. Forgetting a closing tag or maybe just a forward slash (/) is easy. Sometimes it's helpful to take a quick break before returning to scrutinize your page. If you do make a change, be sure to save the file in your text editor before clicking Refresh or Reload in your web browser.

If you're certain the code in your page matches the example, try resaving your file under a new name. Close your browser, and then relaunch your web browser and open the page in the browser again.

Additional troubleshooting techniques are located in Appendix C.

Quotation Marks

Earlier versions of HTML also required all values to be placed within straight quotation marks, as in the following example:

The value of the attribute

```
<p style="font-family: verdana;">
```

I suggest continuing this practice, for continuity and usability reasons.

Nesting

The term *nesting* appears many times throughout the course of this book and refers to the process of containing one HTML tag inside another:

The em tag is nested within the strong tag.

```
<strong>This text is bold and <em>italic</em></strong>
```

You have a proper way and an improper way to nest tags. All tags should begin and end starting in the middle and moving out. Another way of thinking about it involves the "circle rule." You should always be able to draw semicircles that connect the opening and closing versions of each tag. If any of your semicircles intersect, your tags are not nested properly.

Using the following example, the first one is proper because the strong tags are both on the outside and the em tags are both on the inside:

```
<strong><em>These tags are nested properly.</em></strong>
<strong><em>These tags are not nested properly.</strong></em>
```

Even though both may work in some browsers, you need to nest tags the proper way to ensure that your pages display the same across all browsers.

Spacing and Breaks Within the Code

Let's look closely at some example HTML to identify where proper spacing should occur. (Note that the a tag and href attribute are used to link something—in this case, text.)

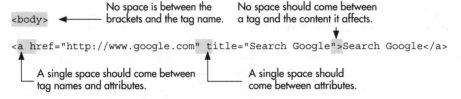

Two places exist within an HTML file where you might like to add breaks:

- In between tags, to help you differentiate between sections of the page

- In between lines of text within the body of the page

Spacing and Breaks Between Tags

The first place you might like to add breaks is in between tags, as in the following example:

```
<html>
<head>
    <title>My First Web Page</title>
</head>
```

Although this is not required, most people use the ENTER or RETURN key to separate tags with line breaks. Others also indent tags that are contained within other tags, as in the preceding example: The `title` element is indented to show it is contained or nested within the `head` element. This may help you to identify the tags more quickly when viewing the page in a text editor.

Spacing Between Lines of Text

The second place you add breaks is between the lines of text in the body of the page. If you use the RETURN or ENTER key on your keyboard to add a line break in between two lines of text on your page, that line break will not appear when the browser displays the page.

```
<!doctype html>
<html>
<head>
    <title>My first HTML page</title>
</head>
<body>
Welcome.

Thank you for visiting my first web page. I have several other pages
that you might be interested in.
</body>
</html>
```

In this code, I pressed the RETURN key twice after the word "Welcome." In this example, you can see that the browser ignored my returns and ran both lines of text together.

To make those line breaks appear, I'd have to use an HTML element to tell the browser to insert a line break. Two tags are used for breaks in content:

```
<br>
<p></p>
```

The br element inserts a simple line break. It tells the browser to drop down to the next line before continuing. If you insert multiple br tags, the browser will drop down several lines before continuing.

The p element signifies a paragraph break. The difference between the two is that paragraph breaks cause the browser to skip a line, while line breaks do not. Also, the p element is considered a *container* element because its opening and closing tags should be used to *contain* paragraphs of content. The br and p tags are discussed in more detail in Chapter 5.

NOTE

Because the br element doesn't contain any text, as the p element does, it doesn't have opening and closing versions. In previous versions of HTML, you were required to place a slash before the closing bracket to "terminate" the tag, as in: <br />. HTML5 does not require us to close empty tags like this.

If I enclose each of these paragraphs in p tags, like the following:

```
<p>Welcome.</p>
<p>Thank you for visiting my first web page. I have several other
pages that you might be interested in.</p>
```

the browser will know to separate them with a blank line. The following illustration shows how the browser displays the text now that I have contained each of the paragraphs in p tags.

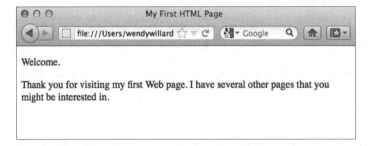

In addition, HTML neither recognizes more than a single space at a time nor interprets a tab space as a way to indent. This means that in order to indent a paragraph or leave more than one space between words, you must use style sheets (see Chapter 5) or special characters.

Use Character Entities to Display Special Characters

As crazy as this sounds, you technically shouldn't include any characters in your HTML files that you can't type with only one finger. This means if you have to hold down the SHIFT key to type an exclamation mark or a dollar sign, you are supposed to use a *character entity* to include that special character in your HTML file.

Even though you might be able to type a certain character on your computer system without any problems, some characters may not translate properly when visitors to your web site view your page. So, I recommend you use character entities to maintain consistency across computer systems.

Character entities can be typed as either a *numbered* entity or a *named* entity. All character entities begin with an ampersand (&) and end with a semicolon (;). Although every character entity has a numbered version, not every one has a named version. While a full list of special characters is included in Appendix D, a few are listed in the following table to give you an idea of what they look like.

NOTE

A few characters are reserved and given special meaning in HTML. For example, the brackets (< and >) are used to signify HTML tags, while the ampersand (&) is used to begin these entities. If you need to use a bracket within the content of your HTML page, such as when a greater-than symbol is needed, in the case of 3 > 2, you should use the corresponding character entity (>) to do so.

Character	Numbered Entity	Named Entity
"	&#34;	&quot;
&	&#38;	&amp;
(nonbreaking space)		
©	&#169;	&copy;
®	&#174;	&reg;
é	&#233;	&eacute;
<	&#60;	&lt;
>	&#62;	&gt;

Having now made the case for using character entities, let me just say here that it's been my experience that certain characters *can* actually be used in a web page without causing any problems. These include straight—not curly—quotation marks ("), exclamation marks (!), question marks (?), colons (;), and parentheses (). While I haven't noticed any of these to cause problems in the majority of browsers, you should still test your pages thoroughly when using any special characters.

Here's an example of how the most commonly used character entity—the non-breaking space—might be used in a code snippet:

```
<p>Welcome! I just used a non-breaking space between the first
two words to ensure they stay on the same line, no matter how wide or
narrow this text box is displayed.</p>
```

Add Comments to an HTML File

Sometimes you might not want your web site visitors to see personal comments or notes you've added to your web pages. These notes might be directions to another person or reminders to yourself.

```
<!-- Remember to update this page after the new product becomes
available -->
```

After the opening bracket, an exclamation mark and two hyphens signify the beginning of a comment. A space should appear after the opening comment code, as well as before the closing comment code.

Comments are not restricted in size but can cover many lines at a time. The end comment code (-->) doesn't need to be on the same line as the beginning comment code. If you forget to close your comment tag, the rest of the page will not appear in your browser. If this happens, don't be alarmed. Simply go back to the code and close that comment. The rest of the page will become visible when you save the file and reload it in the browser.

NOTE

Comments can be seen by anyone who views the source code of your page, so it is wise to avoid placing any personal or secure information in that space.

Try This 2-1 ## Create the First Page of Your Site

To continue with the site you began planning for in the first chapter, we now begin the first page in your site. These are the main goals for this project:

- Use all the necessary elements to create a basic web page.

- Use a character entity to add a copyright symbol to the page.

- Save the page as an HTML file that can be read by a web browser.

- Preview the page in a web browser.

1. Open an HTML editor on your computer. Copy the following code to begin your web page. Feel free to make edits wherever necessary to personalize your site for your organization.

```
<!doctype html>
<html>
<head>
<title>Izzo Teaches Math | Online Math Tutor</title>
</head>
<body>
<p>Izzo Teaches Math</p>
<p>Erinn Izzo provides online math tutoring for students in North America.</p>
</body>
</html>
```

2. After the end of the second paragraph, use the code you learned in this chapter to add two breaks and a copyright symbol (©), followed by the name of the organization. (Example: © Erinn Izzo.)

3. Create a new folder on your hard drive, called **mathtutor** (or the name of your organization or web site). Save this file as **index.html** in the folder you just created.

4. Open your web browser and choose File I Open (or Open File, depending on the browser you're using). Locate the file index.html you just saved.

5. Preview the page. If you need to make changes, return to your HTML editor to do so. Once you have made those changes, save the file and switch back to your web browser. Click the Reload or Refresh button in your browser to update your page according to the changes you just made. The complete code for your page might look like this.

```
<!doctype html>
<html>
<head>
<title>Izzo Teaches Math | Online Math Tutor</title>
</head>
<body>
<p>Izzo Teaches Math</p>
<p>Erinn Izzo provides online math tutoring for students in North America.</p>
<br>
<br>
&copy; Erinn Izzo
</body>
</html>
```

TIP

Does your browser window appear blank when you try to preview your page? If so, return to your HTML editor and make sure you have included all the necessary closing tags (such as `</body>` and `</html>`). In addition, if you are using a basic text editor (as opposed to an HTML editor), don't forget to save the file as "text only" within an .html file extension. For more tips, see Appendix C.

Chapter 2 Self Test

1. What file extensions do HTML files use?

2. The following line of HTML code contains errors. What is the correct way to write this line?

```
<p This is a paragraph of text p>
```

3. At the very least, which tags should be included in a basic HTML page?

4. Identify the tag name, attribute, and value in the following line of HTML code:

```
<a href="page.html">
```

5. Fill in the blank: HTML5 is case-_____.

6. Which option is *not* acceptable for an HTML filename?

   A. myfile.html

   B. my-file.html

   C. my file.html

   D. my1file.html

7. What is the named character entity used to add a copyright symbol to a web page?

8. You just created a web page, and you're previewing it in a web browser when you notice an error. After fixing the error and saving the web page, which button should you click in the browser to view the changes made?

9. The tags in the following line of code aren't nested properly. Rewrite the code so that the tags are nested properly.

```
<p><strong><em>Hello World!</p></em></strong>
```

10. How can you rewrite the following text so that it doesn't display when the page is viewed in a browser?

```
Hide Me!
```

11. Which two options will the browser ignore when they are coded in a web page?

   A. `<p>`

   B. A tab

   C. `<br>`

   D. `<br><br>`

   E. Single space with the SPACEBAR

   F. Double space with the SPACEBAR

12. Fill in the blank: The p tag is an example of a _____ tag because it contains sections of text.

13. The following line of HTML code contains errors. What is the correct way to write the code?

```
< img src = "photo.jpg" >
```

14. What symbols must start and end all HTML tags?

Chapter 3

Style Sheet Setup

Key Skills & Concepts

- Set Up Style Sheets in an HTML File
- Identify the Ways in Which Color Is Referenced in Web Development
- Specify Document Colors

Before we go any further with document setup, we need to cover a very important aspect of web page development with HTML5: the use of style sheets.

Set Up Style Sheets in an HTML File

I've already mentioned the phrase "style sheets" a few times, but haven't really given them a full explanation yet. Part of the reason is that style sheets weren't really a part of HTML until it was rewritten a few times. The purpose of *cascading style sheets* (abbreviated CSS) is to separate the *style* of a web page from its *content.*

The current HTML "rules" dictate that we only use HTML to identify the content of the page, and then use a style sheet to specify the presentation of that content. This not only makes web pages more accessible and usable to all users (regardless of their browsers, platforms, operating systems, physical limitations, and so forth), but also to search engines and other types of software.

TIP

If you've ever used the Style drop-down menu in Microsoft Word, you've already used a style sheet of sorts. The most basic style sheet might include a style called "Body Text" that specifies how the body text of the web page should look—which font and color to use, how much space to leave around it, and so on.

Define the Style

To define a basic formatting style, you first must identify which HTML element you want to affect. This tag is then called a *selector* in CSS. So, if you wanted to specify the style of all the level-2 headlines (which is accomplished with the <h2> tag) on a page, for example, you would use h2 as your selector.

```
h2
```

In fact, the selector is essentially the tag without the brackets. With that in mind, can you guess what the selector for <p> would be?

```
p
```

Once you have a selector, you can define its properties. Similar to how attributes work in HTML, CSS *properties* alter specific attributes of a selector. Returning to the preceding example, if you want to change the style of the level-2 headlines on your page to a 14-point Verdana font, italic, and blue, you can use the following properties:

```
font-family
font-style
font-size
color
```

When you specify values for properties, you are creating a *declaration* for that selector. The declaration and selector together are then referred to as a set of *rules,* or a *ruleset.* In the typical ruleset, the declaration is enclosed in curly brackets after the selector.

So here are the first few pieces of our ruleset:

```
h2  ◄── Selector
font-family  ◄── Property
verdana  ◄── Value
{font-family: verdana;}  ◄── Declaration
```

And here is how they all fit together to tell the browser to display all level-2 headlines in the Verdana font:

```
h2 {font-family: verdana;}
```

To specify the font size, color, and style (italic), we simply add on a few more of those properties:

```
h2 {font-family: verdana;
     font-size: 14pt;
     color: blue;
     font-style: italic;}
```

At this point, you can probably start to see the pattern—a CSS property is followed by a colon, and then its value, which in turn is followed by a semicolon.

TIP

Appendix B includes a list of popular CSS properties.

Define the Values

As with attributes in HTML, properties have values. However, contrary to HTML values, CSS values are not placed in between quotation marks.

Most values can be specified in terms of color, keyword, length, percentage, or URL, as listed in Table 3-1. Length and percentage units can also be made positive or negative by adding a plus (+) or minus (−) sign in front of the value.

Type of Value	Description
Color	When specifying color in a value, you can do so in one of three ways (see the end of this chapter for more information on color): <ul><li>Hexadecimal code, such as #000000</li><li>RGB values, such as rgb (0,0,0) or rgb (0%, 0%, 0%)</li><li>One of the predefined keywords</li></ul>
Keyword	A keyword is a word defined in CSS that's translated into a numerical value by the browser. For this reason, keywords are often considered *relative* because, ultimately, it's up to the browser to decide how to render the content. An example of a keyword is small.
Length	In HTML, most units are defined in pixels. When styling content with CSS, however, you have the option of using many other types of units. For example, when specifying text sizes with the font-size property, you can use any of the following (abbreviations are shown in parentheses): <ul><li>points (pt) —72 points in an inch</li><li>picas (pc) —12 points in a pica</li><li>pixels (px) — dots on the screen</li><li>ems (em) — refers to the height of the font in general</li><li>exs (ex) — refers to the height of an *x* in a particular font</li><li>inches (in)</li><li>millimeters (mm)</li><li>centimeters (cm)</li></ul>
Percentage	Relative percentages can be useful in CSS when used to position elements on a page. This is because percentages allow elements to move around, depending on how large the screen and window sizes are. When used in CSS, a percentage sign (%) following a numerical value, such as 100%, indicates a relationship between the surrounding elements.
URL	When you reference an absolute URL in CSS, use the following form: url (http://www.mhprofessional.com) Similarly, relative URLs (typically those found within the current web site) are referenced in the following manner: url (home.html).

Table 3-1   Types of CSS Values

Create the Structure

After you know a little about the individual parts of CSS, you can put them together to create a few styles. The organization of these pieces depends a bit on which type of style sheet you are creating. There are three key places where we can style web pages:

- **Inline**   Styles are embedded right within the HTML code they affect.

- **Internal**   Styles are placed within the header information of the web page, and then affect all corresponding tags *on a single page*.

- **External**   Styles are coded in a separate document, which is then referenced from within the header of the actual web page. This means a single external style sheet can be used to affect the presentation on a whole group of web pages.

You can use any or all of these types of style sheets in a single document. However, if you do include more than one type, the rules of *cascading order* take over: These rules state that inline rules take precedence over internal styles, which take precedence over external styles.

In a nutshell, CSS styles apply from general to specific. This means a ruleset in the head element of a document overrides a linked style sheet, while a ruleset in the body of a document overrides one in the head element. In addition, more local (or *inline*) styles only override the parent attributes where overlap occurs.

Inline

Inline styles are created right within the HTML of the page, hence the name. In the previous examples, a declaration was surrounded by curly quotes, but inline declarations are enclosed in straight quotes using the style attribute of whichever tag you want to affect:

```
<h2 style="font-family: verdana;">
```

You can separate multiple rules by semicolons, but the entire declaration should be included within quotes:

```
<h2 style="font-family: verdana; color: #003366;">
```

Inline styles are best for making quick changes to a page, but they aren't suited for changes to an entire document or web site. The reason for this is that when styles are added to a tag, they occur only for that individual tag and not for all similar elements on the page.

TIP
Inline styles overrule internal and external styles when multiple types of style sheets are found on the same page.

Internal

When you want to change the style of all the h2 elements on a single page, you can use an *internal,* or *embedded,* style sheet. Instead of adding the style attribute to a tag, use the style element itself to contain all the instructions for the page. The style element is placed in the header of the page, in between the opening and closing head tags. Here's an example of what an internal style sheet might look like:

```
<head>
<title>CSS Example</title>
<style type="text/css">
h2 {font-family: verdana; color: blue;}
h3 {font-family: verdana; color: red;}
</style>
</head>
```

As this example shows, the selector is placed before the declaration, which is enclosed in curly brackets. This entire ruleset can be contained on a single line or broken up into multiple lines, as in the following example:

```
h2
{font-family: verdana;
color: blue;}
```

You can write styles in several ways. The following example is just as valid as the preceding one and is preferred by some people because it is easier to read:

```
h2 {font-family: verdana;
    color: blue;}
```

In addition, you can use certain shorthand properties to reduce the amount of coding necessary. For example, instead of specifying both *font family* (Verdana) and *font size* (12 point), you could type the following because both properties begin with *font*:

```
h2 {font: verdana 12pt;}
```

TIP

Chapter 4 discusses how to style text in much more detail.

External

An *external* style sheet holds essentially the same information as an internal one, except an external style sheet is contained in its own text file and then referenced from within the web page. Using external style sheets is a way to apply the same styles to multiple pages, thereby allowing an entire web site to share the same look and feel.

Thus, an external style sheet might look like this:

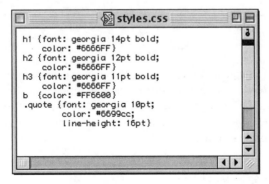

Notice that external style sheets don't use the `style` element or attribute, but simply include a list of rulesets as instructions for the browser. Once you create your external style sheet, save it as a text file, with the .css file extension. Then, return to your HTML file and add the `link` element to the page header to reference the external style sheet, as in the following example:

```
<head>
<title>Using an External Style Sheet</title>
<link rel="stylesheet" href="styles.css">
</head>
```

This is where the name of
your style sheet is placed.

In this case, I only needed to write styles.css because the style sheet is in the same folder as my HTML page. However, if your style sheet is in a different folder than your HTML page, be sure to reference that path appropriately.

NOTE

External style sheets can be overruled by internal and inline style sheets.

Understand the Cascade

The C in CSS means *cascade,* but rarely is this term discussed with beginning web developers. While this is understandable, given the ability for this discussion to become very complex, we can't avoid the topic altogether. So, let's dive right in…

Officially, you know the C stands for cascade, but what exactly does that word mean? You might swap out *cascade* for *combine* to help clarify. When the browser comes across multiple style declarations for a single page or bit of content, it essentially *combines* them together into a single style sheet and assigns levels of importance to each declaration to determine how to process.

The most basic order of importance is one I just mentioned: External style sheets are overruled by internal and inline style sheets. This means if an external style sheet specifies all text should be black, but an internal style sheets says it should be blue, it will ultimately be blue. Table 3-2 helps further explain how the browser determines importance.

While Table 3-2 doesn't delve into the more complex aspects of cascading rules, it gives you a basic understanding of what sort of styles can override others. To reiterate, using this table, can you determine which of these styles would actually display in the browser?

1. p {color: black;} in an external style sheet

2. p {color: blue;} in an internal style sheet

	Least Important	←-------------------→	Most Important
Styles generated by:	Browser default	Custom user style sheet	Page developer style sheet
Styles specified by:	External style sheet	Internal style sheet	Inline style sheet
Styles assigned by:	Element selector	Class selector	ID selector

Table 3-2 Style Importance

You might have guessed that the internal style sheet (#2) takes precedence. This is a pretty clear-cut example, but what happens when things aren't so cut and dry? The W3C has actually set up some pretty sophisticated rules to help with complex situations. These rules dictate a point scale, where more points are assigned, depending on how the style was generated, specified, and assigned. The higher the points received, the more important a particular style is considered. In situations where styles conflict, the most important are used. Take a look at **www.w3.org/TR/CSS2/cascade.html** to learn more about cascading rules.

NOTE
It's common for new web developers to become frustrated when the browser seems to flat out ignore certain style declarations. Nine times out of ten, this is caused by conflicting declarations. If this happens to you, take a break and then use your browser's troubleshooting tools to help identify the conflict. (Refer to Chapter 14 for more on testing and troubleshooting tools.)

Declaring Importance
I can't leave a discussion on cascading without mentioning the !important rule. CSS allows for an override, so to speak, to be used when conflicting levels of importance might prevent a particularly desirable style from being used. To declare a style more important, you can add the important keyword, like this:

```
p { color: blue; !important }
```

As you can see, the keyword must be prefaced by an exclamation mark in order to be properly interpreted by the browser. An !important declaration ultimately takes precedence over a normal style sheet declaration.

Identify the Ways in Which Color Is Referenced in Web Development

At the beginning of time—Web time—the only way to reference color in an HTML page was to use its hexadecimal color value. When CSS became the preferred method of referencing color in web pages, we were permitted to use a variety of other units to measure color, including RGB (which stands for Red Green Blue) values, RGB percentages, hexadecimal shorthand, and color names.

Hexadecimal Color

The "normal" number system in the United States is *decimal*—based on the number 10. This means we have 10 units (0–9) to use before we have to repeat a unit (as with the number 10, which uses the 0 and the 1).

The *hexadecimal* system (hex) uses the same concepts as the decimal system, except it's based on 16 units (see Table 3-3). Because standard HTML cannot handle decimal color values, the hexadecimal system is used to specify color values on web pages. Instead of

Decimal	0	1	2	3	4	5	6	7	8	9	10	11	12	13	14	15
Hex	0	1	2	3	4	5	6	7	8	9	A	B	C	D	E	F

Table 3-3   Decimal and Hexadecimal Units

making up new characters to represent the remaining units after 9, the hexadecimal system uses the first six letters of the English alphabet (A–F).

Computer monitors display color in *RGB* mode, where R = Red, G = Green, and B = Blue. Each letter (R, G, and B) is represented by a value between 0 and 255, with 0 being the darkest and 255 representing the lightest in the spectrum. In RGB, white and black have the following values:

	Red Value	Green Value	Blue Value
White	255	255	255
Black	0	0	0

This is how one graphics program—Adobe Photoshop—displays the RGB values for blue (R:00 G:00 B:255). Most other graphics programs have similar ways of helping you determine the RGB values of your colors.

In Photoshop, one way to find out what the hexadecimal values are for that shade of blue is to click the triangle in the upper-right corner of that color window and choose Web Color Sliders from the menu.

The resulting window shows the corresponding hex values for that same blue are R:00 G:00 B:FF.

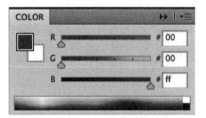

When using hexadecimal color values in an HTML page, you translate the color from decimal (RGB) to hex. Each red, green, and blue value translates into a two-digit hex value. You then combine all three of those two-digit hex values into a single string, preceded by a hash mark. The following is an example where a hexadecimal color is used to change the text in one paragraph to blue:

```
<p style="color: #0000FF;">
```

TIP
While you previously needed a scientific calculator to convert between decimal and hexadecimal values, many charts, software programs, converters, and even web pages are now available to do this for you. Check out **www.psyclops.com/tools/rgb/** to see an example.

Hexadecimal Shorthand
When referencing a color that has value pairs, you can use a bit of shorthand to reduce the amount of typing necessary. For example, a color with a hexadecimal code of 003366 can be shortened to 036. This is because each of the two red values is the same, as are each of the blue and green values. That wouldn't work for a hexadecimal code of 003466, because the green values—34—aren't the same.

The following shows how the same blue used in the preceding code example could be referenced using hex shorthand:

```
<p style="color: #00F;">
```

RGB Values and Percentages
If hexadecimal color values already have your head spinning, I have good news! If a color's RGB values are handy, use those in your style sheet in place of the hexadecimal code, like in the following:

```
<p style="color: rgb(0,0,255);">
```

If you don't have the RGB values handy, as when working in some page layout or design programs other than Photoshop, you can also use the RGB percentages, like that shown in the following example:

```
<p style="color: rgb(0%,0%,100%);">
```

Notice that a comma separates each RGB value, and the entire set of values is placed inside parentheses. A lowercase rgb precedes those parentheses, as in the case of the previous code example, R = 0, G = 0, and B = 255. As was the case with hexadecimal shorthand, RGB values and percentages are only used to describe color in style sheets, not the older HTML color tags.

Color Names

With each successive version of HTML, we have gained additional color names that have standard values. Table 3-4 lists the 17 color names that are almost uniformly supported by browsers. Over 100 more exist, so check out **http://www.w3schools.com/html/html_colornames.asp** to see visual examples of each.

```
<p style="color: blue;">
```

Color Name	Hex Value	RGB Value
black	#000000	0,0,0
white	#ffffff	255,255,255
silver	#c0c0c0	192,192,192
gray	#808080	128,128,128
lime	#00ff00	0,255,0
olive	#808000	128,128,0
green	#008000	0,128,0
yellow	#ffff00	255,255,0
maroon	#800000	128,0,0
navy	#000080	0,0,128
red	#ff0000	255,0,0
blue	#0000ff	0,0,255
purple	#800080	128,0,128
teal	#008080	0,128,128
fuchsia	#ff00ff	255,0,255
aqua	#00ffff	0,255,255
orange	#ffa500	255,165,0

Table 3-4 Popular Standard Color Names

So Which Should I Use?

The wonderful thing about using style sheets to define color in web pages is that we are free to use any of the previously mentioned methods. This means you can tailor your color presentation method to your particular needs and use whichever makes the most sense to you.

New and Notable Color Options

One of my favorite aspects of the latest HTML5/CSS3 updates is transparency. The W3C has defined two new ways to create transparency in web pages.

RGBA

With RGBA, you can specify the "alpha value," or the transparency of a color. The transparency is defined by a number between 0.0 (completely transparent) and 1.0 (fully opaque). For example, you might use the following code to tell the browser to display a headline at 50 percent of the defined color:

```
h1 {color: rgba(255,68,253,0.5);}
```

The latest versions of Safari, Firefox, and Google Chrome have all supported RGBA color specification for awhile. Unfortunately, Internet Explorer only started supporting it with version 9. So if your target audience includes many users with older versions of IE, I don't recommend using this.

TIP

The closer to 0.0, the more the background will show through.

Opacity

Another new addition to the CSS3 specification is the opacity property. Similar to the RGBA values just described, opacity values are defined between 0.0 (completely transparent) and 1.0 (fully opaque).

```
div.transparentbox {
   background-color:#036;
   opacity: 0.7;
}
```

Specify Document Colors

Now that you know a little about how colors are handled in web development, let's talk about the way in which we go about actually specifying them. Changing document colors, such as the background and the text, is accomplished via your style sheet.

As with any style declaration, you can specify the background, text, and link colors in an inline, internal, or external style sheet. The actual properties used to do so are the same, however, regardless of which type of style sheet you use. Look at the following example of an internal style sheet used to change the main background color as well as the link colors of a page:

```
<style type="text/css">
body {background-color: white;
      color: gray;}
a:link {color: blue;}
a:visited {color: purple;}
a:active {color: orange;}
</style>
```

NOTE
Remember, internal style sheets are those placed in between the opening and closing head tags in the HTML code of your web page.

The color property specifies the color of the foreground, whereas the background-color property identifies the background color. So when both of those properties are specified, the foreground color becomes the color of the text content.

The trick here is to consider which *element* actually creates the content whose color you want to change, and use *that* as your CSS selector. So, in the preceding internal style sheet example, I first tell the browser to change the background color of the entire page to white (the body element determines the underlying features of a page, such as background color and default text color). Adding the color property to the body selector also specifies that all text on the page should be gray in this case.

Next, I'm telling the browser to select all content affected by a tags (a:link) and make them blue. When those links have been visited, I want the browser to render them purple, as indicated by the line a:visited {color: purple;}. And, finally, the color of active links—that is, the color visible when the user is clicking a link—is orange, as defined by the line beginning with a:active.

TIP
Although we used the same property—color—to change the default text color and the various link colors, remember that it is the *selector* (in this case, body and a) that tells the browser exactly which content's color to alter.

Try This 3-1 Add a Style Sheet
and Change the Colors of Your Page

Let's take the index.html page from the last Try This, and change the background and text colors of that page. Goals for this project include

● Add an internal style sheet

● Choose coordinating colors

● Specify the background and text colors of the web page

● Reference the colors with the appropriate color codes

1. Open your text editor and load the index.html page saved earlier in this book.

2. Use the style element to create space for an internal style sheet in the header of the document.

3. Add the background-color and color properties to your internal style sheet as the following shows. (Feel free to replace these color values with any you deem appropriate.) Save the file.

```
<style type="text/css">
body {background-color: #ffe188;
      color: #602b00;}
</style>
```

You can find a color in several different ways:

● Go to **www.colorblender.com** and use the sliders to select your favorite colors. As a bonus, this online tool will then suggest matching colors to create a harmonious color palette.

● Use a color from Table 3-4.

● Choose one from the color-picker in your favorite graphics program (such as Adobe Photoshop).

4. Open your web browser and choose File | Open Page (or Open File or Open, depending on the browser you're using). Locate the file index.html.

5. Preview the page to determine if you approve of your color choices. If you don't, return to your HTML editor to make changes. After making any changes, save the file and switch back to the browser. Choose Refresh or Reload to preview the changes you just made.

Because style sheets are so integral to web development, it's wise to review this chapter again after you learn some more about HTML page structure in the next few chapters.

Chapter 3 Self Test

1. What file extension is used for external CSS files?

2. The following line of HTML code contains errors. What is the correct way to write this line?

```
h2 (font-family="verdana")
```

3. *font-family*, *font-size*, and *color* are all examples of what in CSS?

4. Update the following code to reference the URL of the background image *images/background.jpg*:

```
body {background-image:                    ;}
```

5. Fill in the blank: CSS _____ alter(s) specific attributes of a selector.

6. The second two numbers in a six-digit hexadecimal code refer to which color?

7. Which element is used as a CSS selector when you want to change the color of a page's links?

8. Which element is used as a CSS selector when you want to change the background color of a page?

9. Which takes precedence when there are conflicting style declarations?

    A. A style applied to all p tags

    B. A style applied with an ID selector

    C. A style applied to the body element

    D. A style applied with a class selector

10. Which takes precedence when there are conflicting style declarations?

    A. An inline style

    B. An internal style sheet

    C. An external style sheet

    D. A browser default style sheet

Chapter 4

Working with Text

Key Skills & Concepts

- Ensure Onscreen Readability of Text
- Add Logical Emphasis to Sections of Text
- Style Sections of Text by Changing Font Characteristics
- Offer Printer-Friendly Versions of Text Content

Before we dive into the nitty-gritty of structuring and laying out web pages, let's go over one of the most important aspects of page development: working with text.

First, we'll cover ways to optimize text content for web readability. Then, we'll identify plenty of style sheet properties to help customize your text content. Finally, we'll take a look at ways to offer printer-friendly versions of the text content to ensure your pages are readable both online and off.

Ensure Onscreen Readability of Text

Reading extensive amounts of text on a screen is not only difficult on the eyes, it's also tiresome and inconvenient. Even so, many people use the same text content written for the printed page on their web sites. This repurposing of content detracts from a company's overall identity and can make reading the web site content quite difficult.

TIP

In the "Writing for the Web" section of his web site, usability expert Jakob Nielsen instructs, "Write no more than 50 percent of the text you would have used in a hardcopy publication" (**www.useit.com/papers/webwriting/**). Even though some of the articles found here were written several years ago, the content is still relevant.

To make things easier on web readers, try following these guidelines:

- **Keep it short and concise** Chances are good that most web readers won't last through more than a few screens of text on a web page. If you have a long article that needs to be made available to web surfers, try breaking it into several pages to avoid the super-long page-scroll. Remember, you only have a few seconds to grab a user's attention, and long-winded "speeches" (even if they are on the Web) rarely work.

- **Separate paragraphs with blank lines** On the printed page, paragraphs are designated by an indent of the first sentence in each paragraph. On the screen, such paragraphs seem to run together. For easier onscreen reading, surround paragraphs with paragraph elements (<p>) to leave a blank line between them.

- **Limit column widths**   Ever wonder why newspaper columns are so short? One reason is it eases and speeds reading for the viewer. The same is true online, so be wary of 500-pixel-wide columns. I like to stay between 200 and 400 pixels.

- **Avoid underlining**   On the Web, underlined text signifies a link. When you give nonlinked text an underline, it's confusing to users.

- **When centering text, use moderation**   Avoid centering a whole section or paragraph of text, because more than a line or two of centered text is difficult to follow.

- **Do place emphasis on important text, but don't overemphasize**   While bold and italics draw attention to important text, you can easily overdo it by bolding too much.

- **Avoid using all capital letters**   Consider which is used more on street and highway signs: all caps or a mix of lowercase and capital letters. You rarely see all caps used on street signs, because it's much easier to read words with a mix of uppercase and lowercase letters. In addition, the use of all capital letters is considered "screaming" in online communication.

- **Use lists and group related information**   Lists improve the "scannability" of your page, making them easier to scan quickly in search of particular information. Headlines can also help differentiate between sections and offer users quick insight on the section's content.

- **Place the most important information at the top of the page**   If users have to scroll for it, you may lose them. Avoid pages that are too busy by limiting paragraphs to one main idea and pages to no more than seven main options or thoughts.

- **Use descriptive headlines and subheads**   Eyetracking software in conjunction with usability tests has shown just how little web users actually read web pages and e-mail newsletters (see **www.useit.com/alertbox/newsletters.html**). This is why it's important to break up large sections of text with informative headlines to help your readers decide where to pause—and hopefully read—on the page.

- **Make information easy to find**   Most studies show users don't click more than three times on a web site to try to find the information they want. Avoid burying content more than three levels deep if you expect anyone to find it. And, if you have a search engine on your site (which you should if your site contains more than a few dozen pages), take care to ensure the titles of each page are descriptive.

Overall, remember most people *scan* web pages, as opposed to reading them. When you create a web page, put it away for a day or two and then look at it from a user's standpoint. If you had no idea what the purpose of the page was because you just stumbled on it, would you be able to pick out the main point(s) within five seconds? If not, you might want to rework the content.

Or, ask a friend to look at the page and identify the first, second, and third things that pop out. If those three things aren't the most important things on the page, perhaps you need to reevaluate the page.

Markup Text

Now that we've covered some key points for optimizing web text content, let's talk about the different ways we can mark up that content. HTML includes different types of formatting elements to identify the purpose of certain bits of text.

Text-level semantics define how the affected text is to be used on the page, not how it will be displayed. This means the browser ultimately decides how to display the text (see Table 4-1). For example, if you were writing the HTML for the first sentence in this paragraph, you could use the dfn element to tell the browser the phrase "text-level semantics" should be highlighted as a defined term.

```
<dfn>Text-level semantics</dfn> define how the affected text will be
used on the page, not how it will be displayed.
```

Table 4-1 lists the most common elements used for differentiating bits of text from surrounding content. While previous versions of HTML actually dictated how text marked up with these elements should be displayed, HTML5 merely advises us to use them to help describe meaning to the browser.

Element	Description	Default Graphical Browser Display
abbr	Indicates an abbreviation	No change in graphical browsers (each letter is spoken in audio browsers)
acronym	Indicates an acronym	No change in graphical browsers (each letter is spoken in audio browsers)
b	Specifies the text should be emphasized	Bold
cite	Marks a reference to another source or a short quotation	Italic
code	Displays a code example	Monospace font (such as Courier)
del	Text marked for deletion	Strikethrough
dfn	Highlights a definition or defined term	Italic
em	Provides general emphasis	Italic
i	Identifies text that should be read in an alternate voice or mood	Italic
ins	Text marked for insertion	Underlined
kbd	Identifies text a user will enter (kbd is short for keyboard)	Monospace font (such as Courier)
mark	Highlights text for referencing elsewhere	Yellow highlight
q	Identifies quoted text	Surrounds text with quotation marks

Table 4-1 Text-Level Semantics in HTML (*continued*)

Element	Description	Default Graphical Browser Display
s	Text that is no longer accurate or necessary	Strikethrough
samp	Describes sample text or code, typically output from a program	Monospace font (such as Courier)
small	Classifies the fine print	Lowers the font size
span	Enables text to be styled in whatever manner necessary	No change until you use it to apply CSS styles
strong	Provides a stronger general emphasis than with <em>	Bold
sub	Subscripts text	Moves the text below the baseline
sup	Superscripts text	Moves the text above the baseline
var	Suggests a word or phrase that is variable and should be replaced with a specific value	Italic
wbr	Provides the opportunity for a line break (used when a group of words is written as one long word, but must be broken across multiple lines for readability)	Allows line breaks to occur

Table 4-1   Text-Level Semantics in HTML

So in the previous example, the dfn tag would tell the browser to differentiate between the phrase "text-level semantics" and the rest of the sentence. Exactly how it does so depends on the different browsers, but many browsers display it as italicized text. It is then up to you to customize the display of the marked-up text in your style sheet.

All of these elements must be opened and closed when they are used in an HTML document. Figure 4-1 shows how these tags are typically displayed before any CSS styles are applied.

Style Text

There are style properties to affect just about any aspect of text necessary. Some, like those that alter font faces and sizes, enjoy wide support among browsers and operating systems. Others, like those that allow us to load our own fonts into the browser, are newer and perhaps not quite ready for widespread use.

By far, the most commonly changed text characteristics all have something to do with the fonts used to display the text. For that reason, we'll look at which style sheet properties affect font display first.

But before you begin changing the font characteristics of a web page, you should note that visitors to your web site have the ultimate control over these font characteristics. The following screen shows how the user can customize the way text displays in Firefox. Users can even

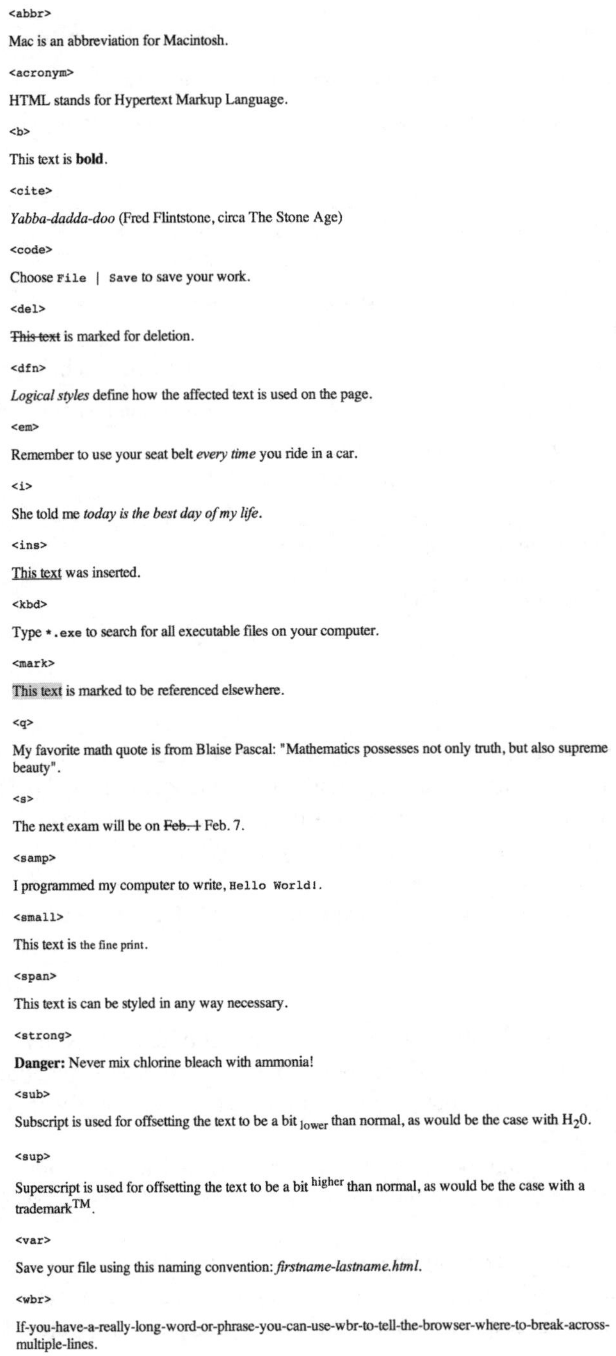

`<abbr>`

Mac is an abbreviation for Macintosh.

`<acronym>`

HTML stands for Hypertext Markup Language.

`<b>`

This text is **bold**.

`<cite>`

Yabba-dadda-doo (Fred Flintstone, circa The Stone Age)

`<code>`

Choose `File` | `Save` to save your work.

`<del>`

~~This text~~ is marked for deletion.

`<dfn>`

Logical styles define how the affected text is used on the page.

`<em>`

Remember to use your seat belt *every time* you ride in a car.

`<i>`

She told me *today is the best day of my life.*

`<ins>`

<u>This text</u> was inserted.

`<kbd>`

Type `*.exe` to search for all executable files on your computer.

`<mark>`

This text is marked to be referenced elsewhere.

`<q>`

My favorite math quote is from Blaise Pascal: "Mathematics possesses not only truth, but also supreme beauty".

`<s>`

The next exam will be on ~~Feb. 1~~ Feb. 7.

`<samp>`

I programmed my computer to write, `Hello World!`.

`<small>`

This text is the fine print.

`<span>`

This text is can be styled in any way necessary.

`<strong>`

Danger: Never mix chlorine bleach with ammonia!

`<sub>`

Subscript is used for offsetting the text to be a bit $_{lower}$ than normal, as would be the case with H_2O.

`<sup>`

Superscript is used for offsetting the text to be a bit ^{higher} than normal, as would be the case with a trademark^{TM}.

`<var>`

Save your file using this naming convention: *firstname-lastname.html*.

`<wbr>`

If-you-have-a-really-long-word-or-phrase-you-can-use-wbr-to-tell-the-browser-where-to-break-across-multiple-lines.

Figure 4-1 Here's how a Mozilla browser (in this case, Firefox) displays text-level semantics.

choose to use their fonts, overriding page-specified fonts, so you should consider these tags as recommendations for the browser, but never rely on them for your page display. In other words, there is little you can do to absolutely guarantee your pages will look the way you want them to every single time. Rather than become frustrated by this fact, I encourage you to embrace it. Being flexible is an important characteristic of a web designer, just as the flexibility of the Web is one of its greatest assets.

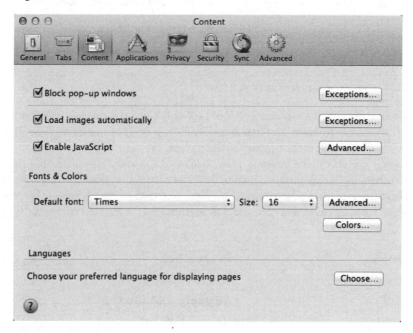

Font Faces

When used in conjunction with the term *font, face* refers to the name of the font you'd like to use on your page. In style sheets, we specify the font face with the font-family property.

You can use the font-family property to specify virtually any font name you can think of, but the person viewing your web page will be unable to see your page in that font face unless he already has it loaded on his computer, or you provide access to that font. So, if you specify your page should be displayed in the Gill Sans font, but the person viewing your page doesn't have access to Gill Sans, he will see your page in his browser's default font face (usually Times New Roman).

```
<p style="font-family:'gill sans';">This text will be displayed in
Gill Sans.</p>
```

When a style sheet value includes a space, as this one does, use single quotes to contain the value.

To compensate for the possibility that not all visitors will have the font you specify, you can specify backup fonts in the value of the font-family property. If the browser cannot find the first font face listed on the viewer's computer, it then looks for the second font face, and the third, and so forth until it comes up with a match. Once again, if the browser doesn't find a font face listed in your HTML file that is actually installed on the viewer's system, it displays the page in the default font.

NOTE

This process of providing a backup font name is also referred to as *cascading*.

In this example, the browser would first look for Gill Sans.

```
<p style="font-family:'gill sans', verdana, arial, helvetica;">Here I
have given the browser four choices, in hopes that it will find one of
them on the viewer's system.</p>
```

In the previous code, the browser first looks for Gill Sans. If it doesn't find that font face, it looks for Verdana, followed by Arial and Helvetica. If none of those font faces is available, it would display the text in the browser's default font.

Several font faces have become quite popular on the Web. This is because these faces offer the best chance of being installed on a majority of viewers' systems. In addition, most of these fonts have been found to be more readable on the Web than others. Table 4-2 shows many readable font faces for your pages that enjoy default support from at least 80 percent of typical users.

Font Name	Example Text
Arial	ABCdefg 123456 !?@
Arial Black	**ABCdefg 123456 !?@**
Arial Narrow	ABCdefg 123456 !?@
Century Gothic	ABCdefg 123456 !?@
Comic Sans MS	ABCdefg 123456 !?@
Courier	ABCdefg 123456 !?@
Courier New	ABCdefg 123456 !?@
Georgia	ABCdefg 123456 !?@
Helvetica	ABCdefg 123456 !?@
Impact	ABCdefg 123456 !?@
Tahoma	ABCdefg 123456 !?@
Times	ABCdefg 123456 !?@
Times New Roman	ABCdefg 123456 !?@
Trebuchet MS	ABCdefg 123456 !?@
Verdana	ABCdefg 123456 !?@

Table 4-2   Popular and Widely Supported Web Fonts

The more products a font ships with, the more likely it is that viewers of your web site will have the font installed. The information on the availability of fonts was drawn from Microsoft's discussion on web typography and Visibone's font survey. To learn more, visit **www.microsoft.com/typography/** and **www.visibone.com/font/FontResults.html**.

TIP

Font names may be a bit different across computer systems. Therefore, I recommend using lowercase names and sometimes even including two possible names for the same font. For example, the font Comic Sans can sometimes be installed as Comic Sans or Comic Sans MS. You can code your page to allow for both instances by using: `'comic sans, comic sans ms'`.

Google Web Fonts

What if you want to use a font not listed in Table 4-2? Say, for example, you're working on a web site for someone whose logo contains a fairly unique font not normally found on most users' systems. You should definitely include the logo as an image to ensure it displays consistently across the widest possible audience. But you would never want to include all, or even a majority, of the text on a site in images because that text wouldn't be searchable or accessible by nonimage-based browsers (such as those used by vision-impaired readers or some mobile phone browsers).

Thankfully, there are a few ways around being limited to the fonts listed in Table 4-2. The first I want to discuss is Google Web Fonts (**www.google.com/webfonts**). Google maintains a database of open-source fonts that can easily be made accessible to web users. Simply browse through hundreds of font families and choose those you want to use on your pages. Then, copy the code necessary to make the selected font(s) accessible to your users.

Here's an example. Suppose I wanted to use a font called Skranji for the navigation on my page. First, I need to make the font available to my users in one of three ways:

- HTML link element: `<link href='http://fonts.googleapis.com/ css?family=Skranji" rel="stylesheet" type="text/css">`

- CSS @import rule: `@import url(http://fonts.googleapis.com/ css?family=Skranji);`

- Javascript (using the following code snippet)

```
<script type="text/javascript">
  WebFontConfig = {
    google: { families: [ 'Skranji::latin' ] }
  };
  (function() {
    var wf = document.createElement('script');
    wf.src = ('https:' == document.location.protocol ? 'https' : 'http') +
      '://ajax.googleapis.com/ajax/libs/webfont/1/webfont.js';
    wf.type = 'text/javascript';
    wf.async = 'true';
    var s = document.getElementsByTagName('script')[0];
    s.parentNode.insertBefore(wf, s);
  })(); </script>
```

After you make the font available to users, you can simply reference it from within your style sheet, like this:

```
#nav { font-family: Skranji; }
```

Pretty cool, huh? Google Web Fonts puts hundreds of open-source fonts right at our fingertips. The only drawback—if there is one—is that fonts must be open source in order to be included in the Google database. This means most of our favorite commercial fonts are not available this way.

Other Ways to Access Fonts

Still wondering how to use your favorite commercial font in your web pages? There are a few other options, but nothing that has a huge amount of browser support as of this writing. HTML5/CSS3 does bring us a new font tool in the @font-face rule. With this new style sheet feature, we can actually load a copy of a font onto the web server and make it accessible to our site visitors. Here's an example of how it's coded:

```
@font-face { font-family: FontName; src: url('FontName.ttf'); }
```

Then, you could use that font for your header section, for instance:

```
header { font-family: FontName; }
```

Looks pretty straightforward, right? It is, for the most part. The trick is that not all the browsers support the different font formats uniformly. For example, TTF (short for TrueType Format) fonts are supported this way on iOS devices. SVG (short for Scalable Vector Graphic) fonts are supported on iOS devices, but not in IE or on Android devices.

TIP

Want to learn more about the different font formats, like TTF? Check out **http://computer.howstuffworks.com/question460.htm**.

And to make matters worse, most commercial font companies do not allow you to load their fonts on your web server without purchasing an additional license. One notable exception is Fontspring (**www.fontspring.com**), which sells its professional fonts with licenses for both online and offline use.

My advice is this: Stick to fonts that are either already loaded on most users' machines or those that can be freely loaded (without breaking any licensing rules).

Font Sizes

You can also use style sheets to change the size of the text. This is accomplished with the font-size property and any of the following possible values, as in: `font-size: 12pt`.

- **Keyword**   xx-small, x-small, small, medium, large, x-large, or xx-large
- **Relative size**   Smaller or larger
- **Measured size**   Number followed by the unit, as in 12pt (for 12 point) or 8px (for 8 pixels)

CSS Absolute-Size Values	Approximate Point Size
xx-small	8
x-small	9
small	10
medium	12
large	14
x-large	16
xx-large	18

Table 4-3   Font Sizes

Keywords

A keyword doesn't identify an exact size measurement, but instead suggests a basic guideline for the browser to follow. Table 4-3 *attempts* to explain how the font-size keywords correlate to other default sizing measurements. I use the word "attempts" because default text sizes can vary given the operating system and browser used to display text. So, based on Table 4-3, you can see that font-size: x-small roughly translates into text that is approximately 9pt. Likewise, font-size: x-large would produce text approximately 16pt.

NOTE

Although these sizes loosely correspond to the point sizes you use in a word processor, most text in a web page tends to look a tad bit smaller on a Mac than it does on a PC because the two systems render type differently.

Figure 4-2 shows how these keywords translate into the four most popular browsers on the Mac OS (Opera, Safari, Chrome, and Firefox, from left to right). Thankfully, the sizes are fairly consistent when viewed in different browsers on the same platform. To be sure the results end up as expected, always test your pages on a variety of different systems, including mobile devices.

Relative Sizes

Relative sizes can work together with keywords to provide additional customization of font sizes. For example, if you specify one section of your page should use "medium" text, then want to style a small bit of content inside of that section just a bit smaller than medium, you could use "smaller." Note the *er* at the end of the keyword. That is what differentiates it from the small and x-small keywords previously mentioned. Adding the *er* to small or large basically gives you the ability to refine font sizes.

Wondering why you wouldn't just use "small" for the text inside the "medium" section? Suppose you later decided to change the font size of that section from "medium" to "large." If you had used "small" for that bit of text you wanted to make just a tad bit smaller than the rest, you would have to go edit that style as well. But, if you had used "small*er*" instead, the browser would automatically understand your intent—that the text should be one step smaller

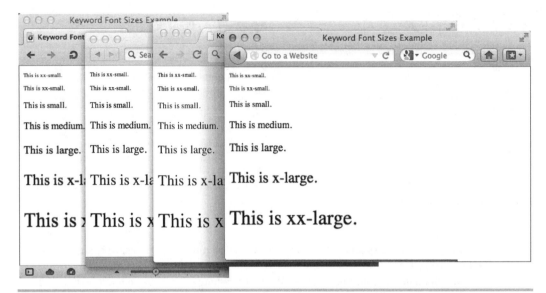

Figure 4-2 Here's how font-size keywords are displayed in four browsers on the Mac OS.

than the rest—and adjust the size accordingly. So, in essence, the relative keywords small*er* and larg*er* help you get your point across to the browser while still remaining flexible and easily updatable.

Measured Sizes

With measured font sizes, you are telling the browser—using a length measurement—what size you want the text to be. (It should be noted, however, that ultimately the size of the text will also be impacted by the screen resolution.) The four most popular categories of measured sizes are pixels (px), percentages (%), ems (em), and points (pt).

Pixel measurements are the most common in web design, because they are the most specific to pages being displayed on the screen. When you specify a font should be rendered at 12px, the browser knows to only allot 12 pixels of vertical space for each letter.

Percentages are pretty straightforward, in that they are just percentages of the page's default font size. For example, if the default font size of the browser were 16px (which is true for a lot of browsers), then text set to display at 50% would show up as 8pt type.

Ems also relate to the default font size. In fact, 1em equals whatever the default font size is. If you haven't specified otherwise, this would mean 1em was 16px (or whatever the user's default browser font size is set to). Using 1.5em would get you a font size of 24px.

As you can see, percentages and ems are ultimately less *absolute* in nature, because they are affected by the user's default font size. This means the trick to using percentages and ems successfully is to set your preferred default font size at the start of your style sheet:

```
<style>
body {font-size: 12px;}
</style>
```

Then, if you want to specify a section of text should be larger or smaller, you can use something like 50% or .8em.

TIP

When you start mixing pixels, ems, and other font measurements, things can get pretty confusing quite quickly. The best summary I've read regarding how to wade through all the details is here: **www.css-tricks.com/css-font-size**.

Point sizes are specific to the printed page, and should therefore be reserved for use in printer-friendly style sheets (which are discussed at the end of this chapter).

Ask the Expert

Q: If I can reliably use an absolute font size, such as 18pt, with the font-size property, why would I ever use a keyword or relative font size?

A: The answer lies in the Web's adaptability to different user scenarios. Older versions of some browsers (namely IE6 and earlier) got a bit funky when handling absolute font sizes. In particular, older browsers rendered absolute font sizes unadjustable in the browser. This means a user with limited eyesight could not increase the font size in her browser if the text was displayed in pixel measurements. That translated into a pretty significant failure for the Web in general, which prides itself on being easily adaptable to a wide audience.

So, many web designers got comfortable using keywords and relative font sizes, which are always adjustable by the user. Thankfully, the modern browsers allow just about all text (except those embedded in images or multimedia files) to be adjusted in size by the user. But you can still use nonabsolute font sizes as needed. In fact, many designers prefer to set the default font size for the page using the body element as a selector, and then use relative keywords to change the size throughout the design. Here's an example of that type of styling in action:

```
body {font-size: 12px;}
h1 {font-size: larger;}
.byline {font-size: smaller;}
```

In this case, text is set to 12 pixels for the whole page. Then, text enclosed in level-1 headings will be "larger" than 12px, while text with the .byline class attached will be "smaller."

Font Colors

As discussed in Chapter 3, the CSS color property is used to change the color of any item in the foreground of a web page, including text. Alternatively, the background-color property is used to change the color of anything in the background of a web page. This means you can attach two color characteristics to a single paragraph, for instance. The following code shows how this might be done to add a yellow highlight behind some purple text with an inline style sheet.

```
<p style="color: purple; background-color: yellow;">Remember to bring
your notebooks back to class tomorrow, because we will be starting a
new unit in English Literature.</p>
```

Other Font Style Properties

We just covered how to change basic font characteristics, like the font face, size, and color, but what about other aspects of text like the space between the letters, as well as the space between words, the thickness of the font, underlines, and so on. Thankfully, there are style sheet properties available for just about any type of formatting you want to apply to text. For your convenience, the most commonly used properties—including those just covered—are outlined in Table 4-4.

Sample Property and Value	Description	Possible Values	Notes
font-family: verdana	Changes the font face.	Can use font names. Multiple values are separated by commas.	Fonts identified in this manner must be loaded on the user's system in order to be displayed.
font-size: 14pt	Changes the size of the text.	Can use absolute or relative sizes. Absolute sizes can be specified with a numeric value and a unit (such as 12pt) or a keyword (xx-small, x-small, small, medium, large, x-large, xx-large). Relative keywords are larger and smaller.	The default is usually medium, but the size ultimately depends on the user's browser and platform.
font-style: italic	Changes the style of the text, causing it to appear vertical or slightly slanted.	Can be normal, italic, or oblique.	Italic and oblique appear the same in most cases.
font-variant: small-caps	Lets you specify text as small capitals.	Can use normal or small caps.	n/a

Table 4-4 Common CSS Properties for Styling Text (*continued*)

Sample Property and Value	Description	Possible Values	Notes
font-weight: bold	Changes how heavy or thick the font appears.	Can use keywords (normal, bold, bolder, lighter) or numbers (100, 200, 300…900). Normal is 400, bold is 700; bolder and lighter cause the weight to be one step lighter or darker than the rest of the text.	Some browsers only understand normal and bold.
letter-spacing: 10em	Changes the spacing between the letters. Similar to kerning in other programs and print methods.	Can be specified by a length value (such as 5em) or the keyword normal.	Negative values provide for a tighter, more condensed display, where letters run together.
line-height: 2	Changes the spacing between lines. Similar to leading in other programs and print methods.	Can be specified as a percentage of the font size (such as 200% to achieve a "double-spaced" look), multiples of the font size (1.5 or 2), lengths (72px), or with the keyword normal.	n/a
text-decoration: overline	Lets you alter the appearance of the text in a variety of ways.	Can use none, underline, overline, line-through, or blink.	Nonlinked text defaults to none, while linked text defaults to underline.
text-transform: uppercase	Changes the case of the text.	Can use none, capitalize (capitalizes all words), uppercase (makes all letters uppercase), or lowercase (makes all letters lowercase).	n/a
word-spacing: 20em	Changes the spacing between words. Similar to tracking in other programs or print methods.	Can be specified by a length value (such as 20em) or the keyword normal.	Negative values provide for a tighter, more condensed display where words run together.
font-stretch: wider	Lets you expand and condense characters in fonts.	Can be absolute keywords (ultra-condensed, extra-condensed, condensed, semi-condensed, normal, semi-expanded, expanded, extra-expanded, ultra-expanded) or relative keywords (wider and narrower).	Browser support varies.

Table 4-4 Common CSS Properties for Styling Text (*continued*)

Sample Property and Value	Description	Possible Values	Notes
text-shadow: 10px, 20px, 5px, blue	Allows for text to have a shadow effect.	Can specify a length value for both the top and left side of the shadow, as well as a color and optional color blur radius. The order described here matches the example shown. (Commas separate these values.)	Browser support varies.
color: black	Changes the text color.	Can use hexadecimal code: #000000, RGB values: rgb (0,0,0), or color names: black.	n/a
background-color: #336699	Changes the background color of a page or element.	Can use hexadecimal code: #000000, RGB values: rgb (0, 0, 0), or color names: black.	Can be used with many types of elements (not just text).

Table 4-4   Common CSS Properties for Styling Text

NOTE

There are many other new CSS3 properties for styling text. To learn more about these advanced options, visit **www.w3.org/TR/2012/WD-css3-fonts-20120823**.

Offer Printer-Friendly Versions of Text Content

Even though many people use electronic documents to avoid having reams of paper on their desks, plenty of us still print lots of pages from the Web. The fact of the matter is we are more likely to read long articles of text when they're printed. The problem with this is that most web pages were not created to be printed and, as such, don't print well.

PDFs

One solution to this problem is to enable users to download PostScript versions of the documents. A *PostScript* file, in contrast to an HTML file, was created with a printer in mind and contains specific instructions on how the file should be printed. Different types of PostScript files can be created from all kinds of software titles, regardless of the computer platform.

For example, Adobe's *Portable Document Format (PDF)* enables you to take any file from another program (such as Microsoft Publisher or Adobe InDesign) and save it in a universally recognizable file format, characterized by the .pdf file extension. Adobe PDF has become a standard in electronic document delivery because of its ease of use, reliability, and stability.

Unlike HTML pages, which look different depending on the browser and computer system, PDF files look the same across different platforms, even when printed. This makes it easy to distribute documents, such as your company's annual report or newsletter.

TIP

Some programs, such as Adobe Photoshop, Adobe InDesign, and Microsoft Office 2010, automatically allow you to save files as PDFs. Check with your page layout or publishing program's manual before purchasing Adobe Acrobat. Also, Mac users can save as PDF from most applications by default. Microsoft Office 2007 users can download a plug-in from Microsoft that allows you to save as PDF right from within tools like Word and Excel (see **http://www.microsoft.com/en-us/download/details.aspx?id=7**).

To save text files in the PDF format, you typically must have the Adobe Acrobat software loaded on your system. Once you do, it's only a matter of selecting a few menu items before the file is converted to the PDF format.

To view PDF files, you typically must have the Adobe Acrobat Reader installed on your system. This free utility is available from Adobe's web site. Even if you've never downloaded the Reader, you may already have it because it's included with many other software titles and computer systems. If you do include a link to a PDF file on your web page, remember also to tell users what is needed to view the file and where to download the Reader.

NOTE

Visit **www.adobe.com/products/acrobat/readermain.html** to download the free Acrobat Reader.

Because users must have the Reader to view a PDF, avoid using PDFs as the *only* means for electronically delivering important information. Whenever possible, it's good to have both an HTML version—for online viewing—and a PDF version—for printing—of important documents. (Visit **http://access.adobe.com** for tips on creating accessible PDFs, as well as tools for converting PDFs to HTML documents and vice-versa.)

Printer-Specific Style Sheets

Ever visited a web page and seen a button labeled "click for printer version" or something similar? While that link may have led to a PDF version of the page, it more likely led to another HTML version of the page—this one using a printer-specific style sheet.

When using external style sheets it's possible to add the `media` attribute to your `link` tag to tell the browser when to use a particular style sheet. For example, the following shows some code that loads two different style sheets: one if the page is printed, and one if the page is displayed on the screen:

```
<link type="text/css" media="print" href="print.css">
<link type="text/css" media="screen" href="screen.css">
```

Once you've linked to your printer-specific style sheet, you just need to edit that style sheet to make the page display appropriately when printed. I recommend starting with a copy of your normal style sheet, and then editing as necessary. So what should you change? The text that follows presents a few things to look out for.

Backgrounds

Always set your background color to white and remove any background images you might have already assigned to the page. This will ensure the user doesn't waste precious ink printing a black background with white text for no real reason. What may have looked attractive on screen might only be a big bleed of ink on the printed page.

```
body {background: white;}
```

NOTE

Some of these concepts—like links and margins—will be covered in later chapters, but I mention them here just to give you an idea as to what needs to be customized for printer-specific style sheets.

Links

If you turned your link underlines off, be sure to turn them back on. Likewise, consider making them bold or otherwise emphasized so they'll stand out even when printed in black and white. You can even specify that links should display the actual URL after the link. This would be quite useful if someone prints your page and then wants to access its links at a later date, because the link addresses would be printed on the page.

The following code specifies that the URL should be printed after both visited and unvisited links. (While the code that follows doesn't look like the rest of the code you've learned thus far in this book, it is correct. The spaces, in particular, are important to the code, so be sure to type this CSS exactly as you see it.)

```
a:link:after, a:visited:after {
   content: " (" attr(href) ") ";
   }
```

If you have a lot of internal links on your pages, you may need to add your domain name to this code. Without it, users might see only a portion of the URLs printed: index.html or aboutus/address.html. The following shows how the code should look in order to make those links display completely:

```
a:link:after, a:visited:after {
   content: " (http://www.mywebsite.com " attr(href) ") ";
   }
```

Finally, consider turning off any graphical navigation bars, advertisements, or buttons when styling a printed version of the page. Not only do web navigation bars typically print poorly, but they are frequently of no use to the reader of a printed page.

Fonts

The standard font measurement for printed pages is points. Therefore, if you used another measurement for your screen pages, such as pixels, be sure to change that for your printer-specific style sheet.

```
body { background: white;
       font-size: 12pt;
       }
```

Margins and Padding

If you've removed all margins and padding on your page to make things snug against the edges, you should remove those style declarations in your printer version. I like to leave the margins and padding at their default values so as not to have content cut off when printed. However, many designers prefer to add a 5- or 10-percent margin to either side so the content has a good amount of buffer space when printed.

Ultimately, the choice is yours. As with all web pages, it's important to test your printer-specific pages by printing them on at least two different printers from two different browsers until you are happy with the results.

NOTE

If you styled any aspects of your page to be absolutely positioned, consider removing that declaration and allowing the content to flow freely on the printed page.

Final Tips for Printer-Friendly Pages

Whenever you create pages that will be printed, whether PDF files or printer-specific style sheets, remember the following things:

- **Page Size**   Whereas web pages are designed for screen format, printed pages should be designed for the paper on which they will be printed. Most users in the United States will probably print in portrait format on standard letter-size paper (8.5" by 11"). Be sure to leave at least a 1/2" margin on all sides.

- **Color**   Avoid dark background colors on printed pages. Many browsers don't print background colors anyway, so someone might end up with light-colored text on white paper and have trouble reading anything. Remember, many people have black and white printers as opposed to color, so printed documents should be readable in both formats.

- **Reference**   Always include the web page address (URL) on a printed page, so users can return to the page for more information as needed.

- **Image Resolution**   Images created for the Web are low in screen resolution (72 dpi) because that makes them quicker to download. It does not, however, make them pretty when printed. In fact, printed web graphics often look quite bad. Therefore, when creating alternate versions of web pages that will be printed, avoid graphics whenever possible.

Try This 4-1 Style Text in Your Web Page

Returning to the index.html page, let's vary the font characteristics of the text on that page and add some style. Goals for this project include

- Adding emphasis to the page where necessary

- Changing the face, size, and color of the text on a page

1. Open your text/HTML editor and load the index.html page saved previously.

2. Add a level-1 heading.

3. Add a level-2 heading in between the first and second paragraphs. Align this heading to the center of the page.

4. Add emphasis to the name of the business or organization wherever it displays in the body copy.

5. Change the font face of the body copy to one listed in Table 4-2.

6. Change the size of the level-1 headings to be approximately 16pt.

7. Change the size of the level-2 headings to be approximately 14pt.

8. Change the color of the footer text to a lighter color than the rest of the text on the page.

9. Change the font size of the footer section to be approximately 10pt.

10. Open your web browser and choose File | Open Page (or Open File or Open, depending on the browser you are using). Locate the file index.html you just saved.

11. Preview the page to check your work. If you need to make changes, return to your text editor to do so. After making any changes, save the file and switch back to the browser. Choose Refresh or Reload to preview the changes you just made.

TIP

Do any of your changes continue past where you want them to stop? Make sure to use the appropriate closing tag to tell the browser where to stop. For more tips, see Appendix C.

Chapter 4 Self Test

1. Which file format has become a standard in electronic document delivery because of its ease of use, reliability, and stability?

2. Why should you avoid underlining text on a web page?

3. What is a reasonable range for column widths on web pages?

4. What are three key things to consider when designing a printable version of a web page?

5. Name four possible values of the `font-size` CSS property.

6. What is the default characteristic of text marked with the `del` element?

7. What is the default characteristic of text marked with the `mark` element?

8. Fill in the blank: You use the _____ property in CSS when specifying the font name in which the text should be rendered.

9. When you specify a font size in ems, that size is relative to what?

10. Fill in the blank: The process of providing a backup font name in the `font-family` property is also referred to as _____.

Chapter 5

Page Structure

Key Skills & Concepts

- Organize Sections of Content
- Format Paragraphs and Page Elements

Now that you've learned the basics of planning for, opening, editing, and saving a web page, and know a little about working with text, you're ready to learn about structuring the content.

Organize Sections of Content

As we've discussed, planning is an important aspect of developing a web page—especially when it comes to organizing sections of content on that page. A great strength of style sheets is the ability to easily apply groups of formatting characteristics to whole sections of text. For example, suppose you have three paragraphs and a list making up the main body copy of a page, and you want to see how the text in that section looks with a different font face and size. As long as you've organized your content appropriately, the code changes will be minimal.

The key to all this is the use of some appropriately placed container elements. Prior to HTML5, the primary container element was the `div` element, but we now have several others to use as well.

So at this point in the process, here's an important concept to understand: When structuring web pages, we first group content into sections with HTML; then we apply style and formatting with CSS later. Let's take a closer look at the HTML used to create those content sections.

Identifying Natural Divisions

When developing HTML5, the authors took a look at how web designers were using div containers. Over and over again they saw the same types of sections being contained within div tags: headers, footers, navigation bars, and so on. The code used to separate each section might look similar to the following:

```
<body>
<div>
Header content goes here.
</div>
<div>
Body copy goes here.
</div>
<div>
Footer content goes here.
</div>
</body>
```

To help speed up the development process, and to make it all more user-friendly, HTML5 added six new container elements. The original div element and the six new container elements are briefly described in Table 5-1.

Once you've set up basic divisions like this—leaving the styling and formatting to CSS— the possibilities are endless. Need to move the navigation from the top of your page to the bottom ... on ten different pages? If you put all of it into its own content areas ... piece of cake! Not only is it easy to move that entire navigation bar, you only have to edit the style sheet— and not the individual HTML pages—to do so.

To help you understand how these natural divisions work, let's look at the sample web page shown in Figure 5-1.

Then, let's take that page and reverse-engineer it, so to speak, to try and identify the natural content divisions. Figure 5-2 shows one *possible* way this page might be coded using the new container elements. In this instance, I choose to put the logo, navigation, and search fields into a header section, and then nest the nav section inside of it. Next, I used the section elements to contain the main body content, plus an aside element for the related content in the sidebar. Finally, I finished the structure with the footer.

Because the specific use of these elements is flexible, there are plenty of additional ways this page could be coded too. Keep that in mind as you begin to structure your page content. As long as you follow the general W3C guidelines for container elements, you have some leeway in regard to which elements are used where.

On their own, the container elements will not change the way the page displays. It is through the combination of this structure, and the style information added later, that the page display is created. You might think of it this way: Before you can paint a wall, it has to be built with construction materials first. At this point in the process, we are using container elements in HTML to "build" the wall, which will then be "painted" with a style sheet.

Now let's take a closer look at those six new container elements.

Opening Tag	Closing Tag	Description
<section>	</section>	Used to group thematically related content, such as chapters in a book, that will usually become part of a database.
<header>	</header>	Used to hold the header aspects of a section or document, such as the title, subtitle, tagline, and navigation.
<footer>	</footer>	Used to hold the footer aspects of a section or document, such as contact information and copyright data.
<aside>	</aside>	Used to group tangentially related content, such as pull-quotes, biographical information, and related links.
<nav>	</nav>	Used to hold the important navigational elements of a section or document.
<article>	</article>	Used to hold content available for syndication.
<div>	</div>	Used to hold generic sections of content, primarily for the purpose of applying styles.

Table 5-1 HTML Container Elements

Figure 5-1 Sample web page for a school

Figure 5-2   Sample web page for a school with content divisions identified

The Header and Footer Elements

The header and footer elements can be used to contain the primary header and footer areas of a page, as well as other minor header and footer sections. This means you can actually have multiple headers and footers on a single page. Here's an example of how the header tags are used:

```
<header>
Header content goes here
</header>
<footer>
Footer content goes here
</footer>
```

Both opening and closing tags are required for these elements; the content to be displayed inside the header or footer goes in between the opening and closing tags.

NOTE

Even though the names are similar, the header element has nothing to do with the head element. Headers go *inside* the body content, while the head element is placed *outside* the body of the web page.

The Nav Element

The nav element can be placed inside of another section or can stand on its own. However, it is not necessary to enclose every single link on your page inside of a nav container. On the contrary, only the most important navigation block(s) should go inside nav tags.

```
<nav>
Nav content goes here
</nav>
Both opening and closing tags are required.
```

The Aside Element

An aside in HTML is a chunk of content related to the main article or section, but not part of the main flow of the page. Most commonly, that results in the aside element being used for pull quotes, biographical information, and related advertising or links.

```
<aside>
Aside content goes here
</aside>
```

Both the opening and closing tags are required for the aside element.

The Section and Article Elements

I left these two last because they are most easily confused with each other. Both primarily contain the same type of content, but only one—the article element—is ear-marked for *syndicated content.* Some examples of syndicated content include blog posts and newspaper or magazine articles.

TIP

On the Web, syndication refers to content made available to other web sites for reproduction. Oftentimes a site makes it known that its content is available for syndication by displaying a small orange icon like this:

By contrast, the section element works better for chapters in a story, general sections of a web site (such as About Us, Contact Information, and Company History), and other nonsyndicated page content.

```
<section>
Section content goes here
</section>
<article>
Article content goes here
</article>
```

Both opening and closing tags are required for these elements. You can have multiple sections and articles on a single web page. Also, each of these elements can be nested inside one another, depending on the use case.

For instance, suppose you were creating an online book. You might place each chapter in the book inside section elements, and then put the entire book in an article element for syndication. Here's a very rudimentary example of how the structure of such a book might be created:

```
<article>
    <header>My Book</header>
    <section>Chapter 1 goes here</section>
    <section>Chapter 2 goes here</section>
    <section>Chapter 3 goes here</section>
</article>
```

NOTE

According to the W3C, the section element was specifically created for chunks of content *to be stored in a database.* This means it should not be used as a generic container for content; if you're just looking for a generic container element to house content for styling purposes, use a div element instead.

Element + ID

If it doesn't make sense to use any of those six container elements, you'll want to use the div element, which essentially is the most generic container element. It's important to note that you needn't try to force your content areas into one of the new elements. It is perfectly acceptable, and even sometimes preferable, to use the generic div element for most or even all of your page's content areas.

But whenever you use any of these container elements *multiple times* on a page, you'll likely want to add an `id` attribute to give each content area a name.

```
<section id="introduction">
Section content goes here
</section>
<section id="summary">
Section content goes here
</section>
```

In the same way that a unique Social Security number is assigned as identification—ID—for each person living in the United States, so, too, should a name be given to each content area you intend to style uniquely. Once you've named your divisions, these content areas can then easily be formatted in the site's style sheet, which might look something like the following:

```
#introduction {border: 1px;}
#summary {font-family: Verdana; font-size: 12pt;}
```

TIP

Avoid spaces in ID names. Instead, I typically use capital letters to help make the name more readable if it contains several words.

In the style sheet, the # before each content area name is necessary because this isn't a normal tag selector. Instead of using an HTML tag as my selector, like p, I've essentially made up my own selectors and given them names like introduction and summary. And because I used the `id` attribute to do so, I prefaced my selector name with a hash mark (#).

Element + Class

Wait—what about instances where you want to style multiple sections the same, or with only minor adjustments? In these cases, you can apply a *class*—instead of or in addition to an ID, depending on the situation—to the opening tag. In the following example, I set up two different classes for the chapters in a series of books. First, the class titled "introChapter" will be styled one way; then the rest of the chapters—"normalChapter"—will follow a different style.

```
<article id="scienceBook">
    <header>Science</header>
    <section class="introChapter">Chapter 1 goes here</section>
    <section class="normalChapter">Chapter 2 goes here</section>
    <section class="normalChapter">Chapter 3 goes here</section>
</article>
```

The corresponding style sheet might then start off with something like this:

```
#scienceBook {font-family: Verdana; font-size: 12pt; color: green;)
.introChapter {border: double medium;}
.normalChapter {margin: 2em;}
```

(We'll cover these and a lot of other styling options throughout the course of the book, but for now I just want you to understand styles as they relate to the structure of the web page.)

You'll notice I added a hash mark (#) before "scienceBook" and a period before the two chapter styles. The difference is simple: "scienceBook" was created with an id attribute, whereas the other two were created with class attributes. Even though I named them all, they need to be prefaced by specific characters to let the browser know where to find them in the rest of the code (in other words, whether they should follow id or class attributes). So, when you use the class attribute, you always preface the class name with a period in your style sheet. Likewise, you use a hash mark or pound sign before your id names.

We've just added two types of selectors to those mentioned in previous chapters. So to help solidify your knowledge, refer to Table 5-2 for an overview of the most commonly used CSS selectors. There are tons of other types of selectors too. Check out **www.w3schools.com/cssref/css_selectors.asp** for a great online CSS selector reference.

TIP

While there are many people in a *class,* your personal identification (ID) is unique to you. This holds true in CSS—id selectors can only be used once on a page, whereas classes can be repeated as many times, and in as many tags, as necessary.

Set the Outline

One of the intentions of HTML5 is to make our web pages more structurally sound and easily interpreted by nonvisual users. This is achieved largely through the new sectioning elements we just discussed, but also through well-placed headings.

Selector Type	CSS Example	HTML Example	Description
Tag selectors	header {color: white;}	<header>	Uses an HTML tag—as is—to apply styles to a section of content
ID selectors	#intro {color:white;}	<header id="intro">	Applies the style only to the element whose id attribute matches
Class selectors	.intro {color:white;}	<header class="intro">	Applies the style to all the elements with matching class attributes
Descendent selectors	header p {color:white;}	<header><p>	Applies a style only to certain elements contained within another element, such as only the paragraphs within the header section
Multiple selectors	header, footer {color: white;}	<header></header> <footer></footer>	Applies a style to a variety of elements at once

Table 5-2 Commonly Used CSS Selectors

Heading tags are similar to the headings you might use in a word processor such as Microsoft Word. And just like outlines in Microsoft Word, HTML headings are intended to be used only in the proper order, from h1 down to h6.

```
<h1>This is an example of a level 1 heading.</h1>
<h2>This is an example of a level 2 heading.</h2>
<h3>This is an example of a level 3 heading.</h3>
<h4>This is an example of a level 4 heading.</h4>
<h5>This is an example of a level 5 heading.</h5>
<h6>This is an example of a level 6 heading.</h6>
```

For example, you wouldn't create an outline that began with a small letter *a* and was followed by the Roman numeral *I*. Instead, you would begin with the Roman numeral *I*, follow that with a capital *A*, and, most likely, follow it with a number *1*. In like manner, an <h1> should be followed by an <h2>, as opposed to an <h3>.

NOTE

Using a heading tag automatically adds breaks before and after the heading because these tags are block-level container tags. You can refine the spacing around a heading in your style sheet.

You can add headings to each of your content areas, as dictated by the content. Here's a quick example to show you how this might work in combination with the section containers:

```
<article id="scienceBook">
    <header>Science</header>
    <section class="introChapter">
        <h1>Chapter 1 Heading</h1>
        First part of chapter 1 goes here
        <h2>Chapter 1 Sub Heading</h2>
        Second part of chapter 1 goes here
    </section>
    <section class="normalChapter">
        <h1>Chapter 2 Heading</h1>
        First part of chapter 2 goes here
        <h2>Chapter 2 Sub Heading</h2>
        Second part of chapter 2 goes here
    </section>
</article>
```

Styling Headings

You use the heading tags to tell the browser which pieces of text function as headings, and then specify how to style them with CSS. So, you could quickly adjust the alignment of your headings with an inline style by using <h3 style="text-align: right;">. Likewise, you could use h3 as a selector in an internal style sheet (placed in between the opening and closing head tags on your page) to specify the formatting options of all level-3 headings on the page.

```
<style type="text/css">
h3 {text-align: right;}
</style>
```

Get Inspired

Now that we've covered the basics about the structural elements, let's pause to remind ourselves why it is important to structure well. One of my favorite sources of inspiration on this topic is the CSS Zen Garden (**www.csszengarden.com**). This web site shows how one web page can be drastically altered simply by changing the style sheet attached to the page. Each content area of this page is clearly and structurally defined in the HTML code.

NOTE

This site was created before the development of HTML5, and therefore uses only div tags for structuring the page. Even so, the site is a wonderful example of how structural markup and styles work together to display pages.

After dividing his page into sections, the author then attached a style sheet with directions for how to display each of those content areas. Style sheets are so powerful that a few simple changes to them can cause the page to appear completely different, as you can see in Figures 5-3 and 5-4.

Organize Text

After you've structured your page into the key content areas and added headings, you can further organize the text in those content areas. As discussed briefly in Chapter 2, HTML is different from traditional word processors because you cannot simply press the RETURN or ENTER key to end a paragraph, and then the TAB key to indent a new one. Instead, you have to use tags to tell the browser where to start and end paragraphs, as well as any other types of breaks.

Paragraphs

The p element functions specifically as a container *for paragraphs*. This means you use an opening p tag at the beginning of your paragraph and a closing p tag at the end. If each line in this nursery rhyme were a paragraph, it might look like this:

```
<div class="nurseryRhyme">
<p>Jack and Jill went up a hill</p>
<p>To fetch a pail of water</p>
<p>Jack fell down and broke his crown</p>
<p>And Jill came tumbling after</p>
</div>
```

Zen Garden

The Beauty of CSS Design

The Road to Enlightenment

A demonstration of what can be accomplished visually through CSS-based design. Select any style sheet from the list to load it into this page.

Download the sample html file and css file.

Littering a dark and dreary road lay the past relics of browser-specific tags, incompatible DOMs, and broken CSS support.

Today, we must clear the mind of past practices. Web enlightenment has been achieved thanks to the tireless efforts of folk like the W3C, WaSP and the major browser creators.

The css Zen Garden invites you to relax and meditate on the important lessons of the masters. Begin to see with clarity. Learn to use the (yet to be) time-honored techniques in new and invigorating fashion. Become one with the web.

So What is This About?

There is clearly a need for CSS to be taken seriously by graphic artists. The Zen Garden aims to excite, inspire, and encourage participation. To begin, view some of the existing designs in the list. Clicking on any one will load the style sheet into this very page. The code remains the same, the only thing that has changed is the external .css file. Yes, really.

CSS allows complete and total control over the style of a hypertext document. The only way this can be illustrated in a way that gets people excited is by demonstrating what it can truly be, once the reins are placed in the hands of those able to create beauty from structure. To date, most examples of neat tricks and hacks have been demonstrated by structurists and coders. Designers have yet to make their mark. This needs to change.

Participation

Graphic artists only please. You are modifying this page, so strong CSS skills are necessary, but the example files are commented well enough that even CSS novices can use them as starting points. Please see the CSS Resource Guide for advanced tutorials and tips on working with CSS.

You may modify the style sheet in any way you wish, but not the HTML. This may seem daunting at first if you've never worked this way before, but follow the listed links to learn more, and use the sample files as a guide.

Download the sample html file and css file to work on a copy locally. Once you have completed your masterpiece (and please, don't submit half-finished work) upload your .css file to a web server under your control. Send us a link to the file and if we choose to use it, we will spider the associated images. Final submissions will be placed on our server.

Benefits

Why participate? For recognition, inspiration, and a resource we can all refer to when making the case for CSS-based design. This is sorely needed, even today. More and more major sites are taking the leap, but not enough have. One day this gallery will be a historical curiosity; that day is not today.

Requirements

We would like to see as much CSS1 as possible. CSS2 should be limited to widely-supported elements only. The css Zen Garden is about functional, practical CSS and not the latest bleeding-edge tricks viewable by 2% of the browsing public. The only real requirement we have is that your CSS validates.

Unfortunately, designing this way highlights the flaws in the various implementations of CSS. Different browsers display differently, even completely valid CSS at times, and this becomes maddening when a fix for one leads to breakage in another. View the Resources page for information on some of the fixes available. Full browser compliance is still sometimes a pipe dream, and we do not expect you to come up with pixel-perfect code across every platform. But do test in as many as you can. If your design doesn't work in at least IE5+/Win and Mozilla (run by over 90% of the population), chances are we won't accept it.

We ask that you submit original artwork. Please respect copyright laws. Please keep objectionable material to a minimum; tasteful nudity is acceptable, outright pornography will be rejected.

This is a learning exercise as well as a demonstration. You retain full copyright on your graphics (with limited exceptions, see submission guidelines), but we ask you release your CSS under a Creative Commons license identical to the one on this site so that others may learn from your work.

Bandwidth graciously donated by mediatemple. Now available: Zen Garden, the book.

xhtml   css   cc   508   aaa

select a design:

Under the Sea! by Eric Stoltz

Make 'em Proud by Michael McAghon and Scotty Reifsnyder

Orchid Beauty by Kevin Addison

Oceanscape by Justin Gray

CSS Co., Ltd. by Benjamin Klemm

Sakura by Tatsuya Uchida

Kyoto Forest by John Politowski

A Walk in the Garden by Simon Van Hauwermeiren

archives:

next designs »

View All Designs

resources:

View This Design's CSS

CSS Resources

FAQ

Submit a Design

Translations

Figure 5-3 Creator Dave Shea's original design for the CSS Zen Garden

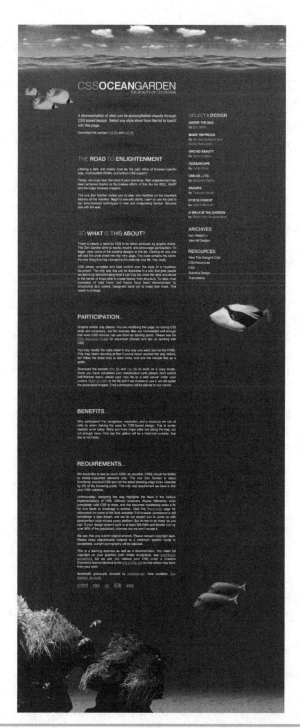

Figure 5-4 One of the additional designs, achieved simply by altering the style sheet (and not the HTML code)

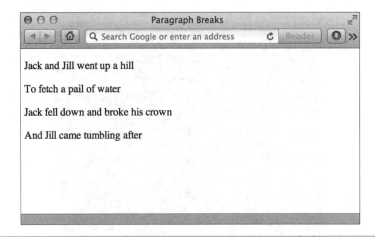

Figure 5-5 The paragraph element defines sections of text.

Figure 5-5 shows how the browser would render this code. Notice how the p tag forces a blank line between each of the paragraphs or sections by default.

Even though the p tag is most often used to contain paragraphs of text, it doesn't automatically indent them. There's no regular HTML tag to indent and, as discussed in Chapter 2, the browser ignores any tabs and multiple spaces you enter using the keyboard.

Indenting

To indent the first line of a paragraph, you can use the text-indent property in your style sheet. In the following example, I specify that the first line should be indented 25 pixels from the left edge of the paragraph:

```
<p style="text-indent: 25px">This is the first sentence in my
paragraph...
```

While the preceding example uses an *inline* style to affect this paragraph only, you could add the same declaration to an internal or external style sheet to achieve this effect on all the paragraphs in a page or a whole site. For example, if I wanted all of the paragraphs in the *normalChapter* sections of my page to be indented 25 pixels, I might add the following declaration to my style sheet:

By placing the p tag selector after my *normalChapter* selector, I'm telling the browser to indent only those paragraphs that fall within the *normalChapter* section of my page.

```
.normalChapter p {text-indent: 25px;}
```

Here's how the HTML for the related paragraph might look:

```
<section class="normalChapter">
<p>This paragraph's first line will be indented.</p>
</section
```

NOTE

On the printed page, such as in books and newspapers, paragraphs are indented to ease readability. But on the Web, the p tag automatically adds blank lines between paragraphs to ease readability, thus removing the need for additional indentations.

Line Breaks

You can also use the br tag to add a line break in your HTML page. Typing the br tag in HTML is the same as clicking the RETURN or ENTER key on your keyboard in a word processor. It causes the browser to stop printing text on that line and drop down to the next line on the page. The following code uses the same nursery rhyme with line breaks instead of paragraph breaks between each line. Figure 5-6 shows how the browser would display this code.

```
<p>
Jack and Jill went up a hill <br>
To catch a pail of water <br>
Jack fell down and broke his crown <br>
And Jill came tumbling after <br>
</p>
```

In most cases, it doesn't matter if you click the RETURN or ENTER key after typing <br> to begin again on the next line (as shown in the preceding code). In fact, that code would have the same output if you let all the text run together, as in the following example:

```
<p>
Jack and Jill went up a hill<br>To catch a pail of water<br>Jack fell
down and broke his crown<br>And Jill came tumbling after<br>
</p>
```

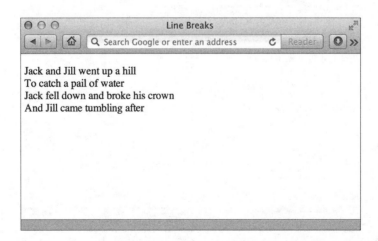

Figure 5-6   The browser understands the br tag as a signal to stop and begin again on the next line.

Unlike when using the p tag, which cannot be repeated to add multiple paragraph breaks in a row, you can use the br tag to add several line breaks. To do so, simply repeat the tag in your HTML file. Figure 5-7 shows how the browser renders this code.

```
<p>
Jack and Jill went up a hill <br><br><br><br> To fetch a pail of water
</p>
```

Preformat

The only time pressing the RETURN or ENTER key in your page creates line breaks in the browser view is when the pre tag is used. Short for preformat, the pre tag renders text in the browser exactly as you type it. Why, then, wouldn't I just use the pre tag for everything, since it sounds so much easier? Two reasons:

- The pre tag usually displays text in a monospaced font, such as Courier, that looks similar to what a typewriter prints. While this may be appropriate for examples of programming code, it probably isn't the look you want for your entire web site.

- The output isn't guaranteed to remain as you envisioned it. Even though you're able to use the TAB key to format text in the pre tag, browsers may interpret a tab as a greater or lesser number of spaces than your text editor did. This could cause any tables you lay out to render incorrectly.

With that said, the pre tag can be quite useful for displaying code examples or even creative illustrations.

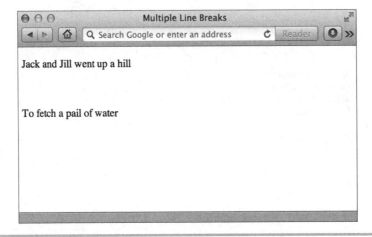

Figure 5-7   You can use multiple br tags to add as many breaks as you want to your page.

```
<pre>
This text will display exactly as I type it. Watch this:
     x  |  o  |  o
     ---------------
     x  |  x  |
     ---------------
     o  |     |  x
</pre>
```

Here's how one browser displays the preceding code:

```
This text will display exactly as I type it. Watch this:
     x  |  o  |  o
     ---------------
     x  |  x  |
     ---------------
     o  |     |  x
```

Quotation Blocks

The blockquote element is used to set apart content quoted from another source. By default, this element indents the entire selection on both the right and the left, and also adds a blank line above and below. The browser determines the exact amount of the indentation, so it may vary from browser to browser. The result of the following code is shown in Figure 5-8.

```
<p>Consider this thought from Dinah Maria Mulock Craik:
<blockquote>"Oh, the comfort - the inexpressible comfort of feeling
safe with a person - having neither to weigh thoughts nor measure
words, but pouring them all right out, just as they are, chaff and
grain together; certain that a faithful hand will take and sift them,
keep what is worth keeping, and then with the breath of kindness blow
the rest away."</blockquote>
</p>
```

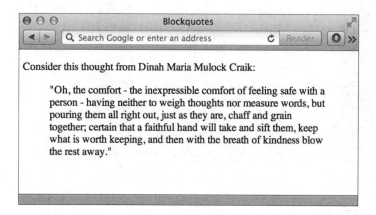

Figure 5-8   Notice how the blockquote element causes the text to be indented on both sides.

TIP

You can include br or p elements within the content of your blockquote. In addition, you can nest blockquote elements as needed.

To achieve a specific amount of indentation, as well as control the blank space above and below, you can use CSS's margin and padding properties in your style sheet. But wait, you say, we haven't even learned those yet! Here we go…

Box Properties

Every element on a web page is contained within a box of sorts, or at least it's considered a box in coding standards. This means you can format content on the page by adjusting its box dimensions, for example, or by indicating how far away from the browser edges it lies.

Unfortunately, this has been known to get pretty tricky because some of the browsers have interpreted the box properties a bit differently. Thankfully, HTML5/CSS3 now gives us the ability to even out the playing field, so to speak, by first using the box-sizing property to specify exactly which interpretation method should be used.

- **box-sizing: border-box;** Tells the browser the borders and padding values are included inside the height and width values (see Figure 5-9)

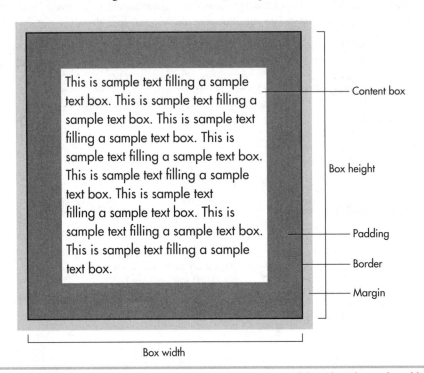

Box width

Figure 5-9 The border and padding are *included* in the overall box height and width when the box-sizing property is set to border-box.

- **`box-sizing: content-box;`** Tells the browser the borders and padding values are not included inside the height and width values (see Figure 5-10)

In Figure 5-9, notice how the padding is contained *within* the borders of the box. By contrast, it is not included in the overall content box height and width in Figure 5-10. It doesn't matter which of these methods you use, as long as you first tell the browser how to interpret your measurements and plan accordingly. However, if you want to use content-box as your sizing method, you're in luck because that is now the default option. To clarify, you only need to specify the box-sizing property in your style sheet if you intend to change it from the default (content-box) to border-box.

Height and Width

After you specify which type of box properties you're using, you may want to also identify the box's intended height and width. Note it is not required to do so, if all you're doing is adding a border or adjusting the buffer space around the content. (If you're trying to position a section of content on the page, the height and width values become more critical. We'll cover that in the following chapter.)

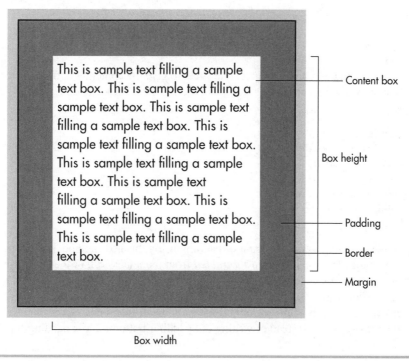

Figure 5-10 The border and padding are *not included* in the overall box height and width when the box-sizing property is set to content-box.

Height and width properties are referenced with a unit of measurement:

- px (pixels)
- cm (centimeters)
- % (percentage of the containing box)

TIP

The most common unit of measurement is pixels, particularly for sections of content that need to always be displayed in a certain size "box." However, a growing number of designers are sticking to percentage widths because they allow the content to grow and shrink according to the available space in the browser window.

So, if I wanted to specify that my nav box should run the entire width of the page, but only 20 percent of the page height, here's how that code might look:

```
nav {
    box-sizing: content-box;
    width: 100%;
    height: 20%;
}
```

Padding

You can use the padding property in a style sheet to give the content a buffer zone of white space on one, two, three, or all four sides, as I did for the `blockquote` tag in the following example:

```
blockquote {
    box-sizing: border-box;
    padding-bottom: 20px;
    padding-top: 25px;
    padding-right: 15px;
    padding-left: 35px;
    }
```

If you do specify a certain amount of padding using this box method, such as padding-right: 15px, those 15 pixels are then *subtracted* from the total width of the content box. So if your box is 200 pixels wide by 200 pixels tall, and you code a 25-pixel padding on all four sides, you are left with 150 pixels across and 150 pixels down for the actual content.

Speaking of using the same padding dimension on all four sides … we can use *shorthand* to speed up that process. Instead of writing out padding-bottom: 25px; padding-top:25px; and so on, we can simply use:

```
p {padding: 25px;}
```

TIP

A faster way to code padding that is different for each side is this: blockquote {padding: 25px 15px 20px 35px;}, where the sides are specified in the following order: top, right, bottom, left (clockwise, starting with top).

Margins

The margin property affects the buffer space *outside* the box boundaries, so it won't subtract space from the overall size of the content box. As with the padding property, you can define the margins for one, two, three, or all four sides of the box, such as in the following:

```
p {
    box-sizing: border-box;
    margin-bottom: 25px;
    margin-top: 25px;
    margin-right: 15px;
    margin-left: 15px;
    }
```

TIP

You might think of margins and padding in terms of a framed painting. The padding affects how far the paint is from the edge of the canvas, while the margin corresponds to how wide the matte and/or frame is.

TIP

A faster way to code margins that want to specify one value for the horizontal margin and another for the vertical margin is this: p {margin: 25px 15px;}, where the sides are specified in the following order: top/bottom, left/right.

Borders

Boxes can have both horizontal and vertical borders. You can easily alter the size and style of borders, which can be placed around all sorts of page elements—from images to paragraphs of text. Table 5-3 identifies the properties used to control borders and rules for web pages.

The following bit of code shows an inline example of using the border property to add a single-pixel black line below a paragraph:

```
<p style="border-bottom-width:1px;border-color:#000;border-style:solid;">
```

Sample Properties and Values	Description	Possible Values
border-bottom-width: thick border-left-width: 4px border-right-width: 6px border-top-width: thin border-width: medium	Controls sizes of an element's borders, individually (any of the first four shown) or as a whole (border-width).	Can use length units or keywords (thin, medium, or thick).

Table 5-3 Style Sheet Properties Used to Control Borders and Rules (*continued*)

Sample Properties and Values	Description	Possible Values
border-color: #ffffff, #cccccc, #999999, #666666	Specifies the border's color.	Can use between one and four color values.
border-style: double	Specifies the border's style.	Can use none, dotted, dashed, solid, double, groove, ridge, inset, or outset.
border-bottom-left-radius: 10px border-radius: 25px	Controls the shape of the border's corners, individually or as a whole, to make them rounded or square (default).	Can use length units or percentages.

Table 5-3   Style Sheet Properties Used to Control Borders and Rules

NOTE

Did you see all those border style declarations and wonder if there was a simpler way to write them? There is. Using shorthand, you could also write the following code to specify a single-pixel black border below a paragraph. While older web browsers had trouble with shorthand, all modern browsers understand such code without any trouble:

```
<p style="border: 1px solid #000;">
```

Alignment

The normal text alignment depends on how text is read across the page in the browser's default language. If text is read from left to right, the normal alignment is left. If text is read from right to left, however, the normal alignment is right. In either case, when text is aligned to one side or the other, the opposite side is *ragged,* in that it doesn't continue all the way to the margin. When text does continue to both margins, it is called *justified.*

The text-align style sheet property allows you to realign text on your page in any of the following ways:

- left
- right
- center
- justify

Styles also enable you to align text vertically with the vertical-align property, as listed in Table 5-4.

Sample Property and Value	Description	Possible Values
text-align: left	Changes the alignment of the text.	Can be left, right, center, or justify.
vertical-align: text-bottom	Allows text to be aligned vertically, without the use of tables.	Can be specified by relative keywords (baseline, middle, sub, super, text-top, text-bottom, top, bottom) or percentages. (Note: negative percentages result in text below the baseline.)

Table 5-4   Style Sheet Text Alignment Properties

The following code provides an example of how embedded style sheets can change the text alignment of three different paragraphs. Figure 5-11 shows how the browser interprets this code.

```
<p style="text-align: center;">My family moved to Nicaragua to
volunteer and do mission work. As a way to support ourselves, I
started an online tutoring business. I have taught math at the middle
school, high school, and college levels for over 12 years.</p>
<p style="text-align: right;">I believe everyone has the potential to
learn math. All that is needed is the right motivation, focus, and
someone who can explain the material in a way that makes sense to the
learner.</p>
<p style="text-align: justify;">I pride myself on being able to
explain difficult material in different ways so that the student can
```

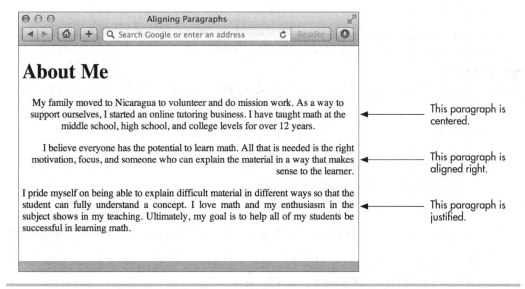

Figure 5-11   The example code is illustrated here, showing different alignment possibilities for the text-align property.

```
fully understand a concept. I love math and my enthusiasm in the
subject shows in my teaching. Ultimately, my goal is to help all of my
students be successful in learning math.</p>
```

But what if you wanted to justify all three of those paragraphs—would you have to add the same style sheet information to each p tag? Definitely not! For one thing, if you planned your page appropriately and separated the content areas with the appropriate container tags, you could take advantage of that planning by adding the text-align property to the appropriate selector in your style sheet, instead of any individual tags within each content area. For example, the following code shows how I named one division with the three paragraphs:

```
<section id="aboutMe">
<p>Paragraph 1</p>
<p>Paragraph 2</p>
<p>Paragraph 3</p>
</section>
```

Then, in my site's main style sheet, I use that name—*aboutMe*—when assigning the formatting of that section. Remember, the # before *aboutMe* is necessary because this isn't a normal style sheet selector. Instead of using a *tag* as my selector, like <p>, I've made up my own selector and given it the name of *aboutMe*. And because I used the id attribute to do so (instead of the class attribute), I prefaced my selector name with a hash mark or pound sign.

```
#aboutMe {text-align: justify;}
```

NOTE

Beyond this most basic style of alignment, style sheets also offer advanced alignment and positioning options. Refer to Chapter 6 for more details.

Try This 5-1 Format Paragraphs and Page Elements

This project gives you practice in structuring content and then applying basic page formatting. Goals for this project include

- Using logical container elements to structure a page

- Adding a header, footer, and navigation

- Adding at least one other natural division to house the main page content

- Formatting one of the content areas with some of the style properties discussed in this chapter

1. Open your HTML editor and load the index.html page saved from the previous activity. Make the following changes and save the file.

2. Create content areas for the header, footer, and navigation sections.

3. Create another content area for the main body copy.

4. Add at least one more paragraph of text in between the existing paragraph(s) and the copyright information. Use a logical container tag (such as article, section, or div) and id attribute to contain all these paragraphs in a section called *homeIntro* (or something appropriate to your particular page content). *If you are using my sample business, you can use the text shown after this numbered list.*

5. Add a quote and format it as an aside. *If you are using my sample business, you can use the text shown after this numbered list.*

6. Add at least one style declaration to the internal style sheet. You might try adding a top border above the footer or justifying the paragraphs.

7. Open your web browser and choose File | Open Page (or Open File or Open, depending on the browser you are using). Locate the file index.html you just saved.

8. Preview the page to check your work. If you need to make changes, return to your HTML editor to do so. After making any changes, save the file and switch back to the browser. Choose Refresh or Reload to preview the changes you just made.

Added Paragraphs

The following paragraphs were mentioned previously in Step 4 and can be added to your web page if you're using my sample company.

My family moved to Nicaragua to volunteer and do mission work. As a way to support ourselves, I started an online tutoring business. I have taught math at the middle school, high school, and college levels for over 12 years.

I believe everyone has the potential to learn math. All that is needed is the right motivation, focus, and someone who can explain the material in a way that makes sense to the learner.

I pride myself on being able to explain difficult material in different ways so that the student can fully understand a concept. I love math and my enthusiasm in the subject shows in my teaching. Ultimately, my goal is to help all of my students be successful in learning math.

Quotation

The following quote is the new text (as mentioned previously in Step 4) and can be added to your web page.

"No human investigation can be called real science if it cannot be demonstrated mathematically."—Leonardo da Vinci

Chapter 5 Self Test

1. What is the purpose of the br element?

2. What happens when you code three p elements in a row?

3. List two style sheet properties used for text alignment.

4. How is the div element different from the article element?

5. Which element—head or header—goes inside the body of an HTML document?

6. True/False: The blockquote element indents text on both the left and right sides by default.

7. True/False: You can only use one header element in each page.

8. Using #introduction indicates the style named *introduction* was applied to an element using which HTML attribute?
   <section _____ = "introduction">

9. What is the primary difference between the article and section elements?

10. Which CSS property is used to specify the buffer space around a content box, inside of the box's border?

11. Which CSS property is used to specify the buffer space around a content box, outside of the box's border?

Chapter 6

Positioning Page Elements

Key Skills & Concepts

- Understand the Concept and Uses of Style Sheets for Page Layout

- Create a Single-Column, Centered, Fluid Page Layout

- Create a Multicolumn Fluid Page Layout

- Layer Content Within a Layout

- Use External Style Sheets

So far, we've talked about how to set up a web page and which elements create the page structure. You learned the importance of organizing content according to natural divisions, and using the appropriate elements to do so. But at this point you may wonder how to actually get those sections to display where you want them to on the screen. This chapter seeks to answer that question.

Understand the Concept and Uses of Style Sheets for Page Layout

To summarize my earlier discussions on CSS, style sheets were created to provide a way to separate the content of a web site from the formatting, or style. The theory is that content is king (which it should be, in most cases), and so anything else is simply icing on the proverbial cake. So we keep the content in the main HTML body and pull the design aspects into the style sheet.

The most striking benefit to this arrangement is in maintenance of the web site. In the past, if you wanted to change the color of the links on all the pages of your site, for example, you had to edit the body element on every page. But now, if that information is contained in a single style sheet, which is then linked from each page on the site, you need only make a single change to alter the link colors for the entire web site.

This also holds true for the overall page layout. It used to be an expensive and exhaustive process for businesses to redesign their web sites every few years. If the content is separated from the formatting with style sheets, the site can be redesigned much more quickly, at a mere fraction of the cost. The reason is simple—instead of recoding every page on the site, the developer only has to recode the site style sheet.

TIP

Remember the CSS Zen Garden mentioned in a previous chapter? That web site is a
perfect example of this concept. Refer to **www.csszengarden.com** to see how the entire
look and feel of the site is completely altered after changing only a single style sheet.

Create a Single-Column, Centered, Fluid Page Layout

So now that you understand the key reasons for using style sheets to lay out your web pages,
let's get to it! Before the modern page layout options became available, a centered "box" was
the standard design. Because screen sizes varied from very small (640 × 480) to much larger
(1024 × 768), that box was often a fixed width so as not to hide any of the content from those
using small monitors.

Thankfully, times have changed and there is no longer a need to design for 640 × 480
monitors. In fact, the typical screen size for over 85 percent of users, as of this writing, is
greater than 1024 × 768, with more and more people getting larger monitors. I still advocate
limiting the horizontal size of graphics, however, so you don't end up forcing the user to
scroll horizontally just to see the rest of the content. But with that said, I see no reason the
text content of your page can't be fluid so as to grow and shrink according to the size of the
browser window.

TIP

Refer to **www.w3schools.com/browsers** to see up-to-date statistics on average screen
resolution.

Many other designers agree, and the centered, fluid page layout is quite popular, whether
used with one or more columns of content. For our first page layout with style sheets, I decided
to keep it simple and create a single-column, centered, fluid page design. Compare Figures 6-1
and 6-2 to see how this layout grows according to the size of the browser window.

The style sheet for this layout is quite simple. In fact, the layout portion includes only the
following declarations to style the body element and the content division labeled *content*:

```
body {
    margin: 0px;
    padding: 0px;
}
#content {
    margin: 50px;
    padding: 20px;
    color: black;
    background-color: #ccc;
    border:1px dashed black;
}
```

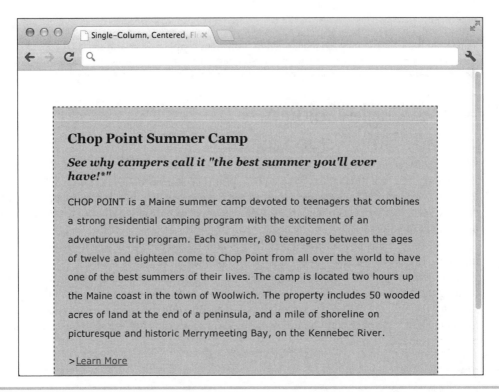

Figure 6-1 The centered, fluid layout is shown in a relatively narrow browser window.

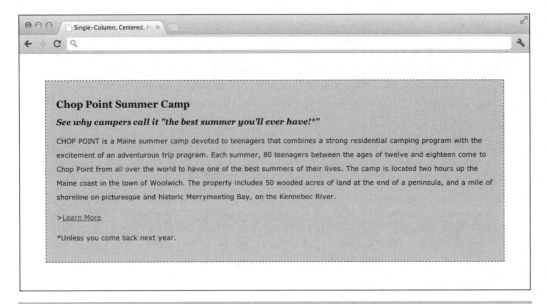

Figure 6-2 The centered, fluid layout is shown in a wider browser window.

Break Down the Code

Even though the styles used for positioning this layout are relatively simple, it helps to break each section down to really understand how each style sheet property works. So let's look at the properties applied to the body element:

```
body {
    margin: 0px;
    padding: 0px;
}
```

Whenever you set out to use style sheets to position elements on the page, it's best to get off to a good start. That usually means letting all the browsers know exactly where to begin displaying your content, because some browsers have different default "starting points" than others. If you remember to think of the available space within the browser window as a big box, the "starting point" identifies any margins outside that box and the padding inside of it.

For the purposes of this layout, we're essentially turning off all margins and padding. This means we can place content all the way up to the edge of the browser window if we choose, and it gives us the flexibility to design accordingly.

#content

The main content area (outlined with a dotted line in Figures 6-1 and 6-2) is contained within a division called *content* using code like this:

```
<div id="content">Content goes here</div>
```

All the formatting of that content is achieved by adding properties to the style sheet declaration for that section:

```
#content {
    margin: 50px;
    padding: 20px;
    color: black;
    background-color: #ccc;
    border: 1px dashed black;
}
```

The margin property adds a 50-pixel margin around all sides of the content box. Because div tags are block-level elements in HTML, the content box fills the remaining available space. And, because there is an equal amount of space around all four sides, the content box becomes centered in the browser window. Voilà!

To create some empty space between the edge of the box and the content inside, the padding property is added. This makes a 20-pixel buffer zone along all internal edges of the box. The background-color, color, and border properties aren't used for positioning but to add character to the box itself.

Pull It All Together

The complete code used to create this layout, as shown previously in Figures 6-1 and 6-2, is as follows:

```
<!doctype html>
<html>
<head>
<title> Single-Column, Centered, Fluid Layout </title>
<style type="text/css">
body {
    margin: 0px;
    padding: 0px;
}
#content {
    margin: 50px;
    padding: 20px;
    color: black;
    background-color: #ccc;
    border:1px dashed black;
}
p {
    font-size: 10pt;
    line-height: 20pt;
    font-family: verdana, arial, helvetica, sans-serif;
    margin: 0px 0px 12px 0px;
}
h1 {
    font-size: 14pt;
    font-family: georgia;
}
h2 {
    font-size: 12pt;
    font-family: georgia;
    font-style: italic;
}
</style>
</head>
<body>
<div id="content">
<h1>Chop Point Summer Camp</h1>
<h2>See why campers call it "the best summer you'll ever have!* "</h2>
<p>CHOP POINT is a Maine summer camp devoted
to teenagers that combines a strong residential camping program with
the excitement of an adventurous trip program. Each summer,
80 teenagers between the ages of twelve and eighteen come to Chop
Point from all over the world to have one of the best summers of their
lives. The camp is located two hours up the Maine coast in the town
of Woolwich. The property includes 50 wooded acres of land at the end
of a peninsula, and a mile of shoreline on picturesque and historic
```

```
Merrymeeting Bay, on the Kennebec River.</p>
<p>&gt;<a href="">Learn More</a></p>
<p>*Unless you come back next year.</p></div>
</body>
</html>
```

TIP

I always show internal style sheets in my examples, because it's easier when teaching. However, if you're adding these layouts to multiple pages, it makes much more sense to save the style sheet as an external style sheet, and simply reference it from each page. The final section in this chapter discusses several ways to accomplish this task.

Browser Support

This style sheet layout actually enjoys wide support among the popular browsers. It is simple enough in concept that there really aren't any offending properties or values used. But with any CSS page layout, it's important to test your page in as many browsers as possible. This becomes even more important if you customize this layout to add columns.

Create a Multicolumn Fluid Page Layout

Probably the most widely used web page layout is one with three columns, one or more of which grows according to the size of the browser window. Typically, the site's navigation is placed in the left column, while ads or other supplemental information is added to the far-right column.

This leaves the center column for the real meat of the site—its text content. In situations like this, the left and right columns remain static in size, while the center column grows or shrinks according to the width of the browser window. There may also be a header and a footer area to complete the layout, as shown in the following example.

NOTE

The code provided is meant as a starting point to help you build the basic page structure. You will likely need to alter your style sheet, depending on the length of content used in each of the content areas.

Continuing with our three-column, fluid page layout, the following shows what the style sheet might look like:

```css
body {
    margin: 10px 10px 0px 10px;
    padding: 0px;
}
header {
    height: 50px;
    background-color: #ccc;
    padding: 5px;
}
nav {
    position: absolute;
    left: 10px;
    top: 70px;
    width: 150px;
    border: 1px solid #000;
    padding: 5px;
}
#extras {
    position: absolute;
    right: 10px;
    top: 70px;
    width: 150px;
    border: 1px solid #000;
    padding: 5px;
}
section {
    margin-left: 162px;
    margin-right: 162px;
    padding: 5px;
}
footer {
    border-top: 2px solid #000;
    padding: 5px;
}
```

And the corresponding HTML is quite simple in this case:

```html
<header>Header</header>
<section>Content</section>
<nav>Navigation</nav>
<div id="extras">Extras</div>
<footer">Footer</footer>
```

TIP

Notice how the content section is placed before the navigation section in the HTML code, but appears to the right of it in the browser view? That's intentional, and very important. Search engines and other tools that "read" the code need to "see" the real meat of the site as soon as possible. CSS enables us to place that content before other, less important aspects, such as the navigation, because the actual placement of the content is done in the style sheet instead of the HTML code. This means Braille readers, for example, can access the content quicker. In fact, many search engines give extra weight to keywords found in the first part of the code.

Break Down the Code

To really understand what's happening in this style sheet in order to position the elements appropriately on the page, let's break it down a bit. First, take a look at the style sheet declaration for the body element:

```
body {
    margin: 10px 10px 0px 10px;
    padding: 0px;
}
```

When you use CSS shorthand for properties with four edges, you always specify values in the following order: top, right, bottom, left.

This particular layout allows for a 10-pixel margin around the top, right, and left edges, but no margin along the bottom edge. Internally, the style sheet turns off padding on all four sides. The following is a graphical representation of what we've created thus far:

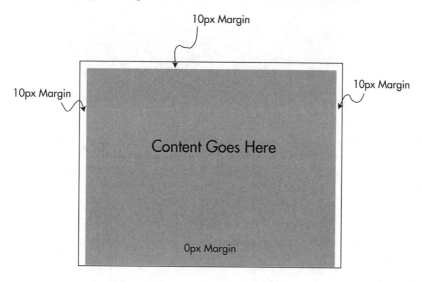

#header

Next, consider the division called *header* by looking at its portion of the style sheet:

```
header {
    height: 50px;
    background-color: #ccc;
    padding: 5px;
}
```

This element's style declaration is very basic, specifying only its height, background color, and padding size. Even so, there are a couple of important aspects to this element. First, even though the header's height is 50 pixels, it will actually cover 60 pixels from the top edge of the available window space, as shown graphically in the following illustration.

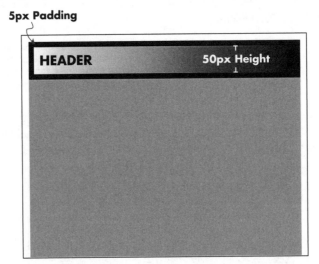

Why? Because we must remember that according to the W3C specifications for the default box-sizing method, padding is *added to* the width or height. This means our header takes up 50 pixels in content height, plus 5 pixels of padding along the top edge and 5 pixels of padding along the bottom edge, for a total of 60 pixels in height. Keep that in mind as we move on to the navigation box.

NOTE

Wondering how the browser knew to draw the header box all the way across the width of the screen even though we didn't specify a width? The answer lies in the fact that the header is contained within a block-level element. By default, the browser normally displays block-level items one after the other, from top to bottom on the page, and fills the available space horizontally. Thus, our header will automatically span across the entire width of the browser window.

#navigation

Now that we have our header positioned, let's consider the first column in our multicolumn layout—the navigation:

```
nav {
    position: absolute;
    left: 10px;
    top: 70px;
    width: 150px;
    border: 1px solid #000;
    padding: 5px;
}
```

Right off the bat we have a new style sheet property to consider: `position`. Possible values for the `position` property include

- **static**   This is the default normal flow of a document that results with standard HTML. In many ways, you might consider this to be no positioning at all, because a declaration of `position: static` ultimately leaves the browser to determine where an element is placed.

- **relative**   This is actually a way to adjust an element's position on the page, relative to itself. So, for example, to move an image 50 pixels up from where it normally sits on the page, you'd use `position: relative` and `bottom: 50px` (thus adding 50 pixels to the bottom edge of the image, pushing it up that much).

- **absolute**   Absolute positioning is used to precisely place elements on the page, thereby taking them out of the normal flow. This means an absolute positioning element could, in fact, be placed on top of another element. One additional note about absolute positioning is this: Items are positioned absolutely in relation to their *parent* element, or rather the object in which they are contained.

So in the case of our navigation column, we're absolutely positioning it in a specific spot on the page. Because it is not contained within any other HTML element, the browser window is the parent object relative to which our first column is being positioned. Let's look at the code again to see exactly where it's being positioned:

```
nav {
    position: absolute;
    left: 10px;
    top: 70px;
    width: 150px;
    border: 1px solid #000;
    padding: 5px;
}
```

The `left` property specifies where the left edge of the column will be placed in relation to the browser window. What can be confusing is even though we specified that the column

Ask the Expert

Q: Wait, I'm confused. You said absolute positioning places items precisely on the page, but then you said those items are placed in relation to something else? How is that *absolute*?

A: To absolutely position an element, you specify its exact location with the `top`, `bottom`, `left`, and `right` properties. The potentially tricky part is this: The element is then placed *relative* to its container block. So, yes, even though you're specifying an item's location, you must do so in relation to the positioned block that contains the object. In many cases, where there isn't any such positioned "ancestor," this ends up being the actual body of your page, so the element is positioned in relation to the *browser window*.

However, suppose you want to absolutely position an image contained within a news story on your page. Here's where the mix of relative and absolute positioning comes into play. By placing the news story in an article element whose positioning is set to `relative` but not further altered, you've achieved your goal: You can absolutely position the image within the context of the news article, since the news article now functions as the image's positioned container.

should be 10 pixels from the edge of the browser window, we must also consider any style sheet properties already attached to the browser window. With that in mind, can you figure out where the left edge of the navigation column will actually be placed?

The left edge of the navigation column will begin 10 pixels from the edge of the browser window, so it sits just below the header area.

Here's another brainteaser for you: Can you determine how I even came up with the value of 70 for the `top` property? To answer this question, you might need to refer back to the `header` code:

```
header {
    height: 50px;
    background-color: #ccc;
    padding: 5px;
}
```

The navigation column needed to be positioned below the header. We already determined that the header takes up 60 pixels of vertical space (50px + 5px padding on top + 5px padding on bottom). So, to place our navigation column right below the header, I added 60 to the 10-pixel top margin and used a value of 70 for the `top` property.

The remaining pieces of the style sheet declaration for the navigation column determine the column's width (150px), border style, and padding (5px around all internal sides). The following graphic helps visualize what we've achieved thus far.

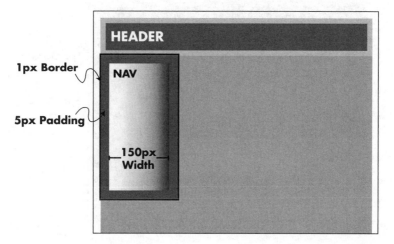

TIP

Want to see an example of someone experimenting with this type of page layout? Style sheet guru Eric Meyer has created CSS/edge for that very purpose. Check it out at **www.meyerweb.com/eric/css/edge**.

#extras

The column to the far right in the layout is very similar to the navigation column. I've used a generic div container and labeled this column *extras* because it is typically used to house bonus elements not integral to the content of the page. For example, you might include advertisements or links to related information in that area.

A review of the style declaration for the extras column shows just how similar it is to the navigation column. In fact, the only difference is this column is placed 10 pixels from the *right* edge of the browser, while the navigation column was placed 10 pixels from the *left* edge:

```
#extras {
    position: absolute;
    right: 10px;
    top: 70px;
    width: 150px;
    border: 1px solid #000;
    padding: 5px;
}
```

This means our graphical representation now includes two of the three columns we're trying to create, and I've updated the graphical representation accordingly.

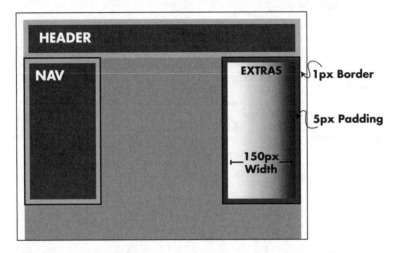

section

While the navigation and extras sections were absolutely positioned, the middle content column is designed to fit within the normal (static) flow of the document. However, that doesn't mean we can't specify where the element should sit on the page. Refer to the style declaration to see what I mean.

```
section {
    border: 1px solid #000;
    margin-left: 162px;
    margin-right: 162px;
    padding: 5px;
}
```

First, we don't need to specify how far down on the page the column will display, because it will sit below the header by default. (If we wanted to allow for space between the header and this section, we would have to use the `margin-top` property to push the element down a bit.) But if we leave all four edges of the center column to chance, it will end up overlapping the navigation column. By adding margins to either side of the column, I am essentially telling the browser how much space to leave on those two sides, which means the element will fill the space left over in the middle of the two absolutely positioned columns.

The trick is figuring out just how much space to allow on either side of the element so that it sits perfectly in the middle. In this particular example, I first needed to consider the total horizontal space covered by the navigation column, because it lies to the left of the main content area I'm currently positioning. The result was 162 pixels (150px width + 5px left padding + 5px right padding + 1px left border + 1px right border).

TIP

Specifying a left margin of 162 pixels places the center content exactly next to the navigation column. If you want to leave some blank space between the two, simply increase the size of the left margin. The right margin needs to be the same size as the horizontal space used by the extras column. Just like the navigation column, the result is 162 pixels (150px width + 5px left padding + 5px right padding + 1px left border + 1px right border).

Finally, a five-pixel padding ensures the text in this column doesn't smash right up against the borders of the other columns. The following shows how the center column fits in our graphical representation:

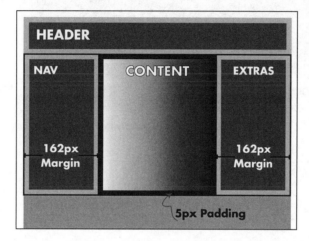

footer

The final piece in our multicolumn fluid layout is the bottom footer. This could hold something as simple as a copyright notice, or additional content such as text links and supplemental graphics. The style sheet declaration reflects the simplicity of this content area.

```
footer {
    border-top: 2px solid #000;
    padding: 5px;
}
```

As with the header, this section will automatically fill the horizontal space in the browser window. Unless we specify otherwise, the height will be determined by the amount of content placed within the footer. In fact, in my style sheet, I only added a five-pixel border to allow some buffer space around the content, and a two-pixel border along the top edge to help separate the footer from the content above. The following illustration finalizes our graphical representation of this layout.

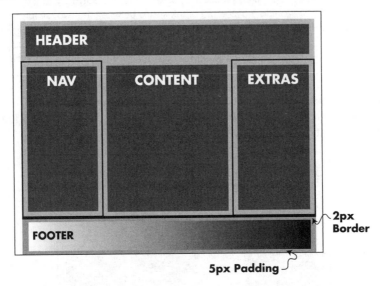

Pull It Back Together

Viewing this very layout in a browser gives us a real glimpse as to just how fluid and flexible it is. Check out Figure 6-3 to see the layout with some generic content.

NOTE

Sometimes, with layouts like this, there is an unequal amount of content in the various columns, causing the borders to be different heights. One way around this, if it bothers you, is to only add the borders on the tallest column. In other words, instead of adding a full border around both the left and right columns, you could add left and right borders just to the center column to serve as dividers.

Browser Support

What would a layout example be without a few caveats? Anytime style sheets are involved, there are questions about compatibility (whether the style sheet properties are supported the same in the popular browsers) and degradation (what happens to the elements when certain properties are not supported). So on that note, I have good news and bad.

The good news is that style sheet support among browsers has come a long way over the past few years, and layouts like this are widely supported.

The only real bad news has more to do with platforms than the browsers. Why? Well, this layout "breaks" if you shrink the browser window below about 400 pixels in width. This is

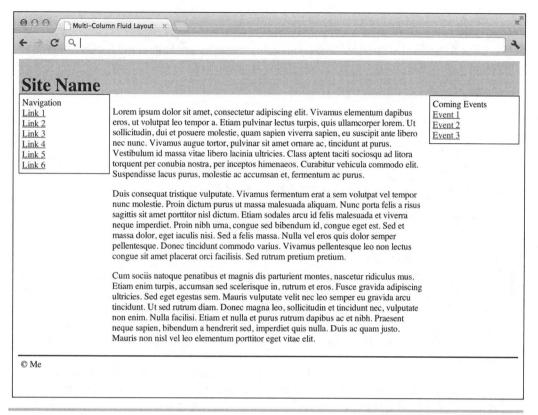

Figure 6-3   The multicolumn fluid layout is shown using some sample content.

important because it means you should offer a different style sheet for users of handheld, web-enabled devices, if those types of users are a large part of your target audience.

The moral of this story is to test, test, and test some more, until you're satisfied with the results in the browsers and platforms used by your target audience.

Other CSS Page Layouts

The preceding two sections listed two sample CSS page layouts: a very basic one and another one that's a bit more complex. These are really just the tip of the iceberg when it comes to CSS page layout, and are meant to simply show you examples of what's possible.

One of the wonderful aspects of the Web itself is its open-source nature. If you see a page layout that inspires you, choose View | Source (or something similar depending on your browser) to *learn* from the site's author. (Of course, I'm not advocating plagiarizing at all—please contact the author to request permission if you want to copy the code explicitly.)

The following list provides additional online resources and inspiration for CSS page layout:

- www.meyerweb.com/eric/css/edge

- www.alistapart.com

- www.mezzoblue.com

- www.onextrapixel.com/2012/01/05/23-interesting-html5-and-css3-websites/

- http://tympanus.net/Development/FlipboardPageLayout/

- www.cssportal.com

Layer Content Within a Layout

If you've ever played with a graphics program like Adobe Photoshop, you know the power of layers. I like to explain layers like this: Imagine if you had two transparencies (you know, like the ones your teachers used with overhead projectors in school), each of which had different pictures on them. If you put one transparency behind the other, the front image would block portions of the back image. If you reversed them, the back image would now block part of the front image.

Using layers on a web page is quite similar. In the last section, I discussed how the center content area of the layout would overlap the navigation if the correct left margin weren't specified. That is true, but what I haven't yet mentioned is that you can actually control which content area is "on top" whenever multiple sections do overlap. In fact, you can control the entire stacking order with the z-index property.

NOTE

The z-index property only works on elements that are positioned (in other words, those that have the position property set to either relative or absolute).

To help explain this concept, let's compare apples to oranges. The following code creates two boxes on the screen. The first one, labeled "Apples," is absolutely positioned 20 pixels from the top and left edges of the browser window. The second box, labeled "Oranges," is relatively positioned. This means it is allowed to flow relative to any other elements on the page. However, because absolutely positioned elements are *removed* from the normal page flow, there are no other elements for the Oranges box to flow around! So the Oranges box is simply placed in the upper-left corner of the screen, as shown in Figure 6-4.

```
<html>
<head>
<title> Layers </title>
<style type="text/css">
```

```
body {
    font-family: verdana;
}
#apples {
    position: absolute;
    top: 20px;
    left: 20px;
    width: 200px;
    padding: 10px;
    text-align: center;
    background-color: #ccc;
    border: 1px dashed black;
}
#oranges {
    position: relative;
    width: 200px;
    padding: 10px;
    text-align: center;
    background-color: #333;
    color: #fff;
    border: 3px solid #999;
}
</style>
</head>
<body>
<div id="apples">APPLES</div>
<div id="oranges">ORANGES</div>
</body>
</html>
```

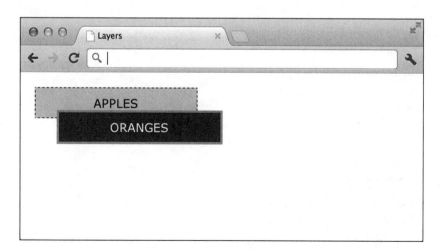

Figure 6-4   By default, the relatively positioned element (Oranges) is placed above the absolutely positioned element (Apples) in this layout.

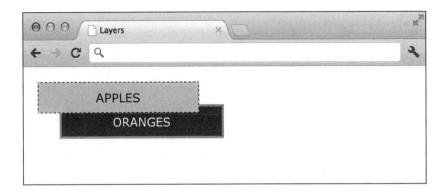

Figure 6-5 After the Apples layer is given a z-index higher than the Oranges layer, it becomes visible.

What if you didn't mind the fact that these were overlapping, but just wanted the Apples layer to be in front of the Oranges layer? One way to accomplish this is to use the z-index property. Compare Figures 6-4 and 6-5 to see the effects. In Figure 6-5, the content area labeled "Apples" is given a z-index property of 2, while "Oranges" has a z-index property of 1. With this property, the element with the highest z-index value is the one "on top." The code used to create Figure 6-5 is shown next.

TIP
You can also use negative z-index values to force a layer to drop *behind* others.

```
<html>
<head>
<title> Layers </title>
<style type="text/css">
body {
      font-family: verdana;
      }
#apples {
      position: absolute;
      top: 20px;
      left: 20px;
      width: 200px;
      padding: 10px;
      text-align: center;
      background-color: #ccc;
      border:1px dashed black;
      z-index: 2;
}
```

```
#oranges {
      position: relative;
      width: 200px;
      padding: 10px;
      text-align: center;
      background-color: #333;
      color: #fff;
      border: 3px solid #999;
      z-index: 1;
      }
</style>
</head>
<body>
<div id="apples">APPLES</div>
<div id="oranges">ORANGES</div>
</body>
</html>
```

Realistic Uses of Layers in Web Pages

While the apples and oranges comparison may not have been the most realistic web page layout scenario, it did help explain the concept of layers in web pages. So what are some more realistic uses for this powerful tool? The following are just a few:

- **Advertising**   Ever clicked a link in a banner ad, only to have that ad appear to grow larger without the actual web page changing? Very likely, the larger version of the ad was a *hidden* layer set to appear when you clicked that link.

- **Games**   While many online games use Flash for interactivity, some use a combination of HTML, JavaScript, and CSS. These games often place different elements on layers so that they can be easily moved around on the page, independent of the other page content.

- **Navigation**   You've likely visited a web site and used navigation that had submenus or drop-down menus. These types of navigation systems can be accomplished by placing the drop-down menu content into a layer that is "brought forward" or "made visible" with the click of a particular link.

TIP

The `display` and `visibility` properties are used to determine whether an element is visible. We'll cover those more in Chapter 14, but in the meantime, check out **www.w3schools.com/css/css_display_visibility.asp** for an online reference.

You probably noticed that most realistic examples of layers within web pages involved some sort of interaction on the user's part, whether that's to make a layer visible or move a player in a game. Unfortunately, this interaction is not achieved through HTML or CSS alone, but involves the use of some sort of scripting, like JavaScript. While this is technically beyond the scope of this book, I wanted to give you an idea as to what was possible. Refer to Chapter 13 for a bit more information, as well as links to online references and other ways to learn more.

Use External Style Sheets

The vast majority of style sheet examples in this book have been shown as internal or embedded styles, meaning they were placed within the actual web page they affected. But when you use style sheets for layout purposes, you're typically planning to use the same (or very similar) layout with other pages on your site. In such cases, using an internal style sheet would almost defeat the purpose of using style sheets altogether, because you'd have to edit each and every page to make a change to the layout.

A better solution is to create an external style sheet with the page layout information, and then reference that style sheet from each page it should affect. There are essentially two ways to reference an external style sheet—linking or importing.

TIP

When developing my site's style sheet, I usually create it as an internal style sheet within my test page. Then, after I'm satisfied with the results, I copy and paste it into an external style sheet and add a reference to it from all of the pages it should affect.

Link to an External Style Sheet

The concept of linking to an external style sheet was introduced in an earlier chapter, but I want to reiterate it here where it's most appropriate. It's accomplished by using the `link` element, as shown next:

```
<link rel="stylesheet" href="styles.css">
```

This code simply tells the browser to use the content of `styles.css` when displaying the current page.

To take it one step further, you can add the `media` attribute to your `link` tag to specify to which medium the style sheet applies. This means you could link to multiple style sheets for multiple media. The following shows an example that specifies one style sheet to use when the page is displayed on the screen, and another when the page is sent to a printer:

```
<link rel="stylesheet" href="screen.css" media="screen">
<link rel="stylesheet" href="print.css" media="print">
```

Other possible values for the `media` attribute are as follows:

- `projection` (for projected presentations)
- `aural` (for speech synthesizers)
- `braille` (for presentation on Braille tactile feedback devices)

- `tty` (for display using a fixed-pitch font)
- `tv` (for televisions)
- `all`

TIP
If a particular linked style sheet applies to multiple media, separate them with a comma, as in `media="screen,projection"`.

Import an External Style Sheet

Another way to reference an external style sheet is to import its styles into the current document. Instead of a separate HTML tag, this is accomplished with the `@import` statement between the opening and closing `style` tags:

```
<style type="text/css" media="screen">
    @import "/layouts/screen.css";
</style>
```

Because the `@import` statement is placed between the opening and closing `style` tags, you can actually mix internal and external style sheets with this method. This can be particularly useful if, perhaps, you want to use the same general layout on all the pages of your site (with an imported style sheet), but also want to include a few custom internal styles on certain pages.

Another important aspect of this method is the ability to import multiple style sheets. Say, for example, you had one style sheet for the layout of your pages, and another one for different design aspects (colors, fonts, and so on). This might be accomplished with code like the following:

```
<style type="text/css" media="screen">
    @import "/styles/layout.css";
    @import "/styles/design.css";
</style>
```

NOTE
Whenever you combine different style sheets, it's good to remember the rules of precedence discussed in Chapter 3. These state that styles are applied with the following order of importance: Embedded styles take precedence over internal styles, which take precedence over external styles.

Try This 6-1 Use CSS for Page Layout

In this project, select a file you already created and apply a CSS page layout. The goals for this project include

- Using CSS for page layout

- Creating a style sheet that works in most modern browsers

- Using an external style sheet

1. Open your HTML editor and load the index page, or any other pages you've developed thus far.

2. Determine the type of layout that will work best on the page you selected. To get started, consider the following questions: *Will the page have content that easily fits into two or more columns? Or is it a page whose content flows best as a single column with perhaps a top header and a bottom footer for navigation, and so on?*

3. After selecting your layout, return to your code and add the necessary container elements to divide the content into manageable sections.

TIP

Remember to use ID names that describe the content itself, as opposed to how you plan to style it. For example, if you plan to put a calendar of events in column three, and also want to give that column a yellow background, naming your ID "events" would be much better than "column3" or "yellowcolumn." Why? At some point, you may move the events to another column, or you may change the background color, but they will always be events.

4. Work with your internal style sheet to add the appropriate CSS properties to lay out the page. Refer to the samples provided in this chapter, as well as the online resources I suggested.

5. Save the file and test it often in your favorite browser, as well as any others you can get your hands on.

TIP

Some web sites offer the ability to display your site on multiple web browsers so you can see how it looks without having to actually install those browsers on your machine. Adobe's BrowserLab (**browserlab.adobe.com**) offers a free online tool to preview your page in a variety of viewing conditions (i.e., different browsers and operating systems).

6. When you're satisfied with the layout, copy and paste your internal style sheet (without the `style` tags) into a blank text document. Then save it as **style.css**.

7. Return to your HTML file and use the `link` element or the `@import` statement to reference the external style sheet you just created. Save the file and switch back to the browser. Choose Refresh or Reload to preview the changes you just made and make sure your external style sheet works.

TIP

If your style sheet no longer works after you switched from internal to external, check the location of the external style sheet. Is it in the same folder as your HTML file? If not, be sure to add the folder path to your `link` element or `@import` reference. For more tips, see Appendix C.

Cascading style sheets have come a long way, and now provide excellent page layout options for web designers. This project gave you practice developing your own layout using style sheets.

For added practice, perform this project again on other pages you developed while working through this book.

Chapter 6 Self Test

1. Fill in the blank: _____ positioning takes an element out of the normal page flow and positions it in a particular place on the page.

2. Which property determines whether a layer is hidden or visible?

3. Which two properties are set in the `body` element to ensure all browsers use the same "starting point" for page layout?

4. According to the W3C default specifications, if you had a box that was 150 pixels wide, with 10 pixels of padding on all four sides, and a 2-pixel border all the way around, what would be the total horizontal space used by the box?

5. Which HTML element is used to create generic sections of content to be formatted with style sheets?

6. Fill in the blank: The _____ attribute identifies the medium for which a particular external style sheet should be used.

7. Add the appropriate code so the content area has a 20-pixel margin around the top, right, and left sides, but a 5-pixel margin around the bottom.

```
#content {                                    }
```

8. Which HTML element can be used to reference an external style sheet?

9. Add the appropriate code to import a style sheet called design.css.

```
<style>

</style>
```

10. Fill in the blank: _____ positioning is the default type of positioning.

11. True/False: Relative positioning adjusts an element's location on the page relative to itself.

12. Add the appropriate code to place the content area 50 pixels from the left edge of the browser and 150 pixels from the top edge.

```
#content {                                }
```

13. Which property is used to specify an element's stacking order on the page?

14. True/False: When adjusting an element's stacking order on the page, lower values take precedence over higher values.

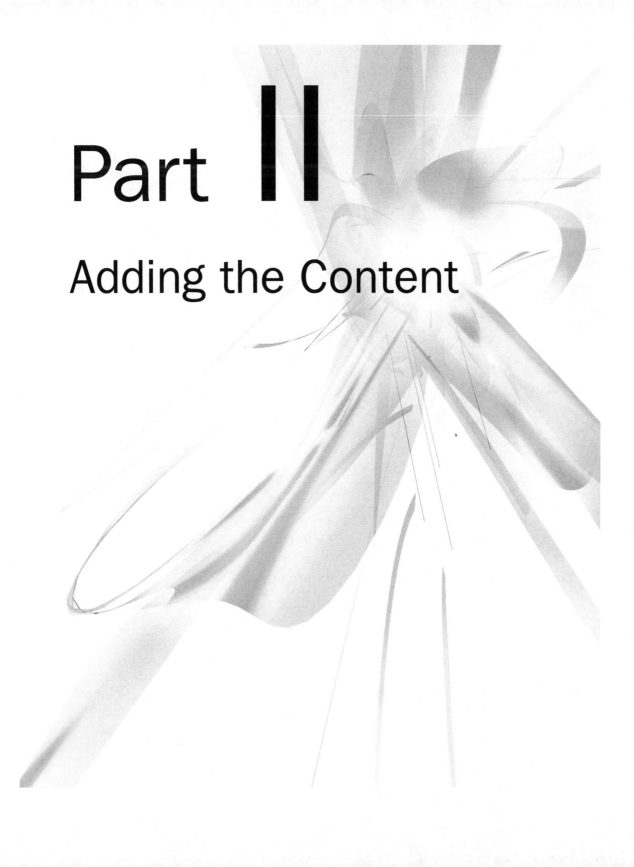

Part II

Adding the Content

Chapter 7
Working with Links

Key Skills & Concepts

- Add Links to Other Web Pages

- Add Links to Sections Within the Same Web Page

- Add Links to Email Addresses and Downloadable Files

- Recognize Effective Links

- Style Links

- Customize Links by Setting the Tab Order, Keyboard Shortcut, and Target Window

The crux of HTML is its capability to reference countless other pieces of information easily on the Internet. This is evident because the first two letters in the acronym HTML stand for *hypertext,* or text that is linked to other information.

HTML enables us to link to other web pages, as well as graphics, multimedia, email addresses, newsgroups, and downloadable files. Anything you can access through your browser can be linked to from within an HTML document. In fact, one of the easiest ways to identify the URL of a page you want to link to is to copy it from the location or address toolbar in your web browser. You can then paste it directly into your HTML file.

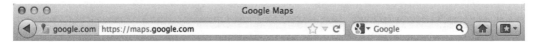

Add Links to Other Web Pages

You can add links to other web pages, whether they are part of your web site or someone else's. To do so requires using the a element:

```
<a href="http://maps.google.com">Use this link to find us on Google Maps.</a>
```

TIP

While adding a link to your favorite web site on your page is usually considered acceptable, it is never acceptable to copy someone else's content without their permission. If you have any doubts, check with the site's administrator whenever you're linking to a site that isn't your own.

This is the text in between the opening and closing a tags in the example code.

When a visitor to your web site moves the mouse over a link, it usually changes to a hand to show the text can be clicked.

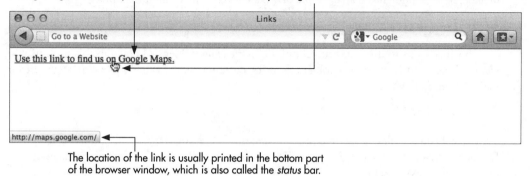

The location of the link is usually printed in the bottom part of the browser window, which is also called the *status* bar.

Figure 7-1 This screen shows the browser view of the previous example code.

The a element itself doesn't serve much purpose without its attributes. The most common attribute is href, which is short for *hypertext reference*: It tells the browser where to find the information to which you are linking. Other attributes are name, title, accesskey, tabindex, and target, all of which are discussed in this chapter.

The text included in between the opening and closing a tags is what the person viewing your web page can click. In most cases, this text is highlighted as a different color from the surrounding text and is underlined, as shown in Figure 7-1.

In deciding what to use as the value of your href attribute, consider what type of link you want to use. The following are the two basic types of links:

- Absolute
- Relative

Absolute Links

Absolute links are those that include the entire pathname. In most cases, you use absolute links when linking to pages or sites that are not part of your own web site. Absolute links must include the protocol (such as http://) at the beginning of the link. For example, if you are linking from your web site to Yahoo!, you type **http://www.yahoo.com** as your link.

```
<a href="http://www.yahoo.com">Visit Yahoo!</a>
```

Relative Links

Relative links are so called because you don't include the entire pathname of the page to which you are linking. Instead, the pathname you use is relative to the current page. This is similar to saying, "I live in Summershade Court, about three miles from here," which is relative to wherever "here" is. A more *absolute* way to say this might be "I live at 410 Summershade Court in Anytown, USA 55104."

Relative links are most commonly used when you want to link from one page in your site to another. The following is an example of what a relative link might look like:

```
<a href="contactme.html">Contact Me</a>
```

This link looks for the contactme.html file in the same folder that contains this page. If you were linking to a file in *another* folder *below* the current one, the value of your `href` might look like the following:

```
<a href="wendy/contactme.html">Contact Me</a>
```

If you need to link to a file in a folder above the folder your page is in, you can add "../" for each directory up the tree. So, if the file you are linking to is two folders higher than the one you are in, you might use

```
<a href="../../contactme.html">Contact Me</a>
```

Suppose you were building a web site for yourself and your family, using the following directory structure. You might remember something similar from Chapter 1, where we talked about file naming and the anatomy of a URL. Folders and files are indented to indicate that they are located on a different level.

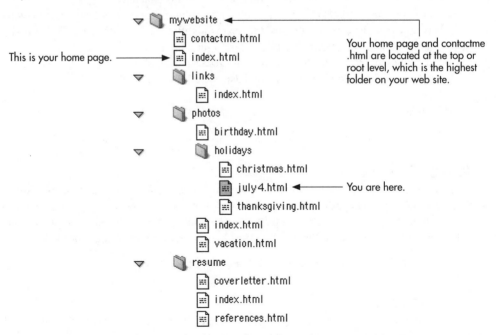

You are working on the highlighted file: july4.html. This file is located two folders below the home page (index.html) in a folder called *holidays*. If you want to link back to that home page from the july4.html page, you would include a relative link similar to this one:

This tells the browser   This tells the browser to look for the
to go up a level.   index.html file in the destination folder.

`<a href="../../index.html">Return Home</a>`

This tells the browser to
go up one more level.

Another way to tell the browser to return back to the root—or base—level is to simply use a single slash, like this:

`<a href="/index.html">Return Home</a>`

The vast majority of servers are set up to recognize a single slash as a shortcut, so to speak, back to the home directory. This makes it easy to assign a single link "home," for example, that works from any page on the web site.

NOTE

Remember that most servers consider index.html to be the index of a folder. This means a link to <a href="holidays/"> would be the same as <a href="holidays/index.html">. If you don't specify a filename, but only a folder name, the index page will be shown (provided it exists).

Now, suppose you are working on the birthday.html file and you want to link to the july4 .html page. Can you imagine how you would do that?

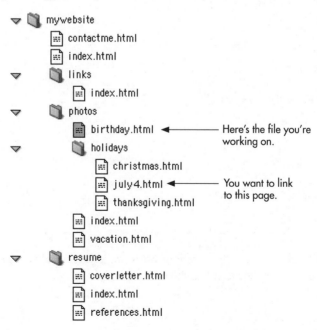

To link from birthday.html to july4.html, use the following code:

```
<a href="holidays/july4.html">Check out these photos from July 4.</a>
```

Because the july4.html file is one folder below the birthday.html file you are currently working on, you simply list the folder name followed by a forward slash and the filename (as shown in the preceding example).

Add Links to Sections Within the Same Web Page

When you link to a page, the browser knows what to look for because each page has a name. But sometimes you may want to link to a section of text *within* a page on your web site (see Figure 7-2 for an example). To link to a section of a web page, you must first give that section a name.

Figure 7-2 When you have multiple sections on a single page that you want to link to, you can use an anchor to name them.

Create an Anchor

An *anchor* is a place within a page that is given a special name, enabling you to link to it later. Without first naming a section, you cannot link to it. The following is an example of an anchor:

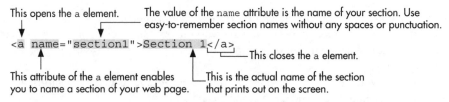

This opens the a element.

The value of the name attribute is the name of your section. Use easy-to-remember section names without any spaces or punctuation.

```
<a name="section1">Section 1</a>
```

This closes the a element.

This attribute of the a element enables you to name a section of your web page.

This is the actual name of the section that prints out on the screen.

In this example, the phrase in between the opening and closing a tags is displayed in the web page and labels the anchor as "Section 1." If you prefer not to include a label for your anchor, you can leave that space blank, as in the following example:

```
<a name="top"></a>
```

Here, you could use this invisible anchor at the top of your page, and then link to it from the bottom of your page. This would enable visitors to return to the top of a long page easily, with only one click and no scrolling (see Figure 7-3 for an example).

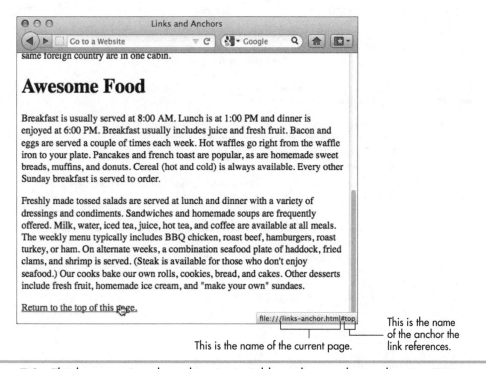

This is the name of the current page.

This is the name of the anchor the link references.

Figure 7-3   This browser view shows how an invisible anchor can be used to give visitors an easy link back to the top of the page.

Ask the Expert

Q: How do I know when to use relative or absolute pathnames?

A: Whenever you are linking to a page *that is not contained within your web site,* you will use an absolute pathname. For example, if you are working on a summer camp's web site and you want to link to a national summer camp association, you need to use the full (absolute) pathname to do so.

However, if you are linking to *a page on your own web site* that contains information about that association, you could use a relative pathname.

Remember, if you do decide to use *absolute* pathnames to link to a page located in the same folder on your web site, this may cause problems for maintenance in the long run. If, at a later date, you decide to change the name of the folder these files are located in, you need to go back and change all the absolute links. If you used a relative link, though, you wouldn't have to change anything.

Link to an Anchor

To create the link to an anchor, you also use the a element and the href attribute, as you would when creating any other type of link. To finish the link, you need to include a hash symbol (#) and the anchor name as the value of the href attribute.

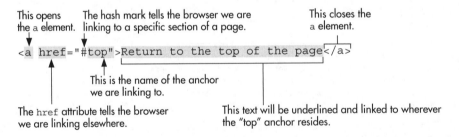

The following shows how it all might look when you code it in an HTML document:

```
<!doctype html>
<html>
<head>
<title>Links and Anchors</title>
</head>
<body>
<a name="top"></a>
<h1>Cabin Life</h1>
<p>Campers sleep in cabins with eight or nine other campers of similar
age and two counselors. The cabins are rustic but comfortable. The
```

girls' cabins all have a large closet and drawer space, two sinks, a toilet and a shower. Three of the boys' cabins share a latrine with plenty of sinks and toilets and two showers. They also have a number of other bathrooms available to them. The oldest boys' cabin has bathrooms with showers and sinks. All cabins are equipped with comfortable bunk beds.</p>
<p>Campers are responsible for keeping their own cabins clean, taking a turn at waiter duty, and sharing the upkeep of the common area. On a typical night, campers return to their cabins at 9pm to spend time with their cabin-mates before lights-out at 10pm. A weekly laundry service is provided. Friends of similar age who come to camp together may request to be placed in the same cabin. Due to space limitations however, we may not be able to accommodate all such requests.</p>
<p>Foreign camper enrollment is limited, so that no more than two campers from the same foreign country are in one cabin.</p>
<h1>Awesome Food</h1>
<p>Breakfast is usually served at 8:00 AM. Lunch is at 1:00 PM and dinner is enjoyed at 6:00 PM. Breakfast usually includes juice and fresh fruit. Bacon and eggs are served a couple of times each week. Hot waffles go right from the waffle iron to your plate. Pancakes and french toast are popular, as are homemade sweet breads, muffins, and donuts. Cereal (hot and cold) is always available. Every other Sunday breakfast is served to order.</p>
<p>Freshly made tossed salads are served at lunch and dinner with a variety of dressings and condiments. Sandwiches and homemade soups are frequently offered. Milk, water, iced tea, juice, hot tea, and coffee are available at all meals. The weekly menu typically includes BBQ chicken, roast beef, hamburgers, roast turkey, or ham. On alternate weeks, a combination seafood plate of haddock, fried clams, and shrimp is served. (Steak is available for those who don't enjoy seafood.) Our cooks bake our own rolls, cookies, bread, and cakes. Other desserts include fresh fruit, homemade ice cream, and "make your own" sundaes.</p>
<p><a href="#top">Return to the top of this page.</a></p>
</body>
</html>
    ⌐—This tag links to the predefined anchor "top."

As suggested, a good case for using anchors involves a long page with many small sections, such as the example shown in Figure 7-2. Whenever you do have long pages with an index and several sections, it's nice to offer your visitors a "Back to Top" link to bring them back to the index easily. The following shows the HTML code used to create this page:

```
<!doctype html>
<html>
<head>
<title> Using Anchors on Long Pages </title>
</head>
```

```
<body>
<nav>
<h1><a name="top">Title</a></h1>
<p><a href="#one">Jump to Section 1</a><br />
<a href="#two">Jump to Section 2</a><br />
<a href="#three">Jump to Section 3</a></p>
</nav>
<section id="NameOfSection1">
<h2><a name="one">Section 1</a></h2>
<p>Text for section 1 goes here.</p>
<p><a href="#top">Back to Top</a></p>
</section>
<section id="NameOfSection2">
<h2><a name="two">Section 2</a></h2>
<p>Text for section 2 goes here.</p>
<p><a href="#top">Back to Top</a></p>
</section>
<section id="NameOfSection3">
<h2><a name="three">Section 3</a></h2>
<p>Text for section 3 goes here.</p>
<p><a href="#top">Back to Top</a></p>
</section>
</body>
</html>
```

This links to the anchor lower on the page named "one."

This links to the anchor lower on the page named "two."

This links to the anchor lower on the page named "three."

The anchor names this "one."

The anchor names this "two."

The anchor names this "three."

NOTE

If the anchor you are linking to is already visible on the screen (such as how the first section is already visible in Figure 7-2), then the browser may not jump to that anchor. Similarly, if the anchor being linked to is at the very bottom of the visible screen (such as the second section is in Figure 7-2), then the browser also may not jump to that anchor, according to your screen size.

If you need to create a link to a specific section with another page (not the one you are currently working on), then you use that page's filename and the anchor name separated by a hash mark (#), as in the following example:

```
<a href="genealogy.html#intro">View names beginning with an "A" on our
genealogy page.</a>
```

In this case, the browser will first look for genealogy.html and then locate an anchor named "intro" on that page.

Add Links to Email Addresses and Downloadable Files

Although links to and within web pages are the most common types of links you'll create, you can also link to other types of content on the Internet.

Email Addresses

When you want to give someone easy access to your email address, you can include it on your page as a *mailto* link. This means instead of using `http://` in front of your link, you use the email protocol `mailto:` to preface your email address.

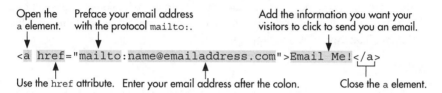

Open the a element.   Preface your email address with the protocol `mailto:`.   Add the information you want your visitors to click to send you an email.

`<a href="mailto:name@emailaddress.com">Email Me!</a>`

Use the `href` attribute.   Enter your email address after the colon.   Close the a element.

Clicking this link in a browser causes the visitor's email program to launch. Then it opens a new email message and places your email address in the To: box of that message.

NOTE

For a mailto link to work, visitors to your web site must have an email program (such as Outlook or Mac Mail) set up on their computers. Email links like these may not work if the visitor uses only a web-based email service such as Gmail or Hotmail.

Customize the Email Message

Some browsers will even let you add content to the subject and cc fields in the email by entering additional text into the `href` value. To do so, you add a question mark after the end of your email address, and type the word **Subject** followed by an equal sign (=), along with the word or phrase you'd like to use as your subject. This can be particularly useful in helping you distinguish mail sent through your web site from your other email.

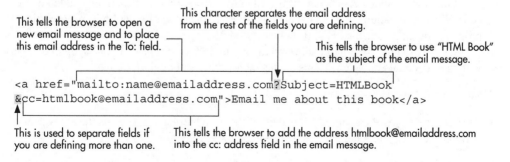

This tells the browser to open a new email message and to place this email address in the To: field.   This character separates the email address from the rest of the fields you are defining.

This tells the browser to use "HTML Book" as the subject of the email message.

`<a href="mailto:name@emailaddress.com?Subject=HTMLBook`
`&cc=htmlbook@emailaddress.com">Email me about this book</a>`

This is used to separate fields if you are defining more than one.   This tells the browser to add the address htmlbook@emailaddress.com into the cc: address field in the email message.

Remember, no spaces should be in the value of the `href` attribute, unless they are part of the subject line.

Spam-Proofing Your Email Links

Many people who send spam use programs called mail harvesters to search the Web looking for email addresses. This means any time your email address is listed, displayed, or otherwise included on a web page, you open yourself to potential spam.

What tips these harvesting programs off is the at symbol (@) in your email address, because we all know an email address can't exist without one of those symbols. So the key to spam-proofing your email address is not to display it with an @ symbol.

Using [at] Instead of the @ Symbol A quick, pure-text way to avoid displaying your complete email address on a web page is to replace the @ symbol with something like [at] so that savvy visitors can still get your email address, but the harvesting programs miss it. This might make your email address look something like this:

me[at]mail.com

This only works if you merely *display* the email address and don't *link* to it. For more on that, keep reading.

Using an Image to Replace the @ Symbol The second easiest way to spam-proof displayed email addresses is to replace the text @ symbol with a graphic @ symbol. This causes your site's visitors to see the email address in its entirety, but fools email harvesters because they don't read images.

However, this and the previous technique only work to hide email addresses that are merely *displayed* in the browser. If you're *linking* your email address so people can click it to send an email, you must also hide the version of the email address embedded in the a tag. To do so, try one of the following two tricks.

Using Code to Replace the @ Symbol The problem with the first two ways to spam-proof your email address is that they only work if the email address is *displayed* and not *linked*. For example, consider the following:

```
<a href="mailto:me@mail.com">Email Me</a>
```

While the email address is not displayed in the browser view, it's still embedded in the code. When you include your actual email address in the code of a mailto link, harvesting programs reading the actual HTML will still find it!

One way to hide the email address in the mailto link is to replace the @ symbol and period with their decimal equivalents. This means me@home.com might look like:

```
me&#64;home&#46;com
```

Here, `&#64;` is the decimal equivalent of the @ symbol and `&#46;` is the equivalent of a period. The complete a tag using this technique looks like this:

```
<a href="mailto:me&#64;home&#46;com">
```

The vast majority of email programs recognize these decimal characters and will replace them with the appropriate equivalents when preparing the actual email.

Using JavaScript to Hide the Email Address   Arguably the most effective way to avoid spammers and still include a mailto link is to hide the email address with some sort of scripting language or other type outside of HTML, such as JavaScript. The following sample script would be placed within your HTML code exactly where your `<a href="mailto:me@ home.com">` should have been:

```
<script language="JavaScript">
<!--
var name = "me";
var domain = "mail";
var ext = "com";
document.write('<a href="' + 'mail' + 'to:' + name + '@' + domain +
'.' + ext + '">Email Me</a>');
//-->
</script>
```

When displayed in a browser, this script prints "Email Me" and links it to me@mail.com, all the while never displaying the complete email address in a way spammers can interpret.

TIP

One of the best ways to avoid posting your email address for all to see (and harvest) is to create a web form for visitors to send you email. Refer to Chapters 12 and 13 for more information.

Ask the Expert

Q: What about linking to an RSS feed?

A: RSS—Really Simple Syndication—has grown so quickly in recent years that even though you might not have known what it meant, you've likely seen it referenced at one web site or another. Many news sites and web blogs include little orange or blue rectangular buttons near a story that is available for syndication by the general public. For example, visit **www .foxnews.com/rss** to see a list of the Fox News content available for syndication.

To "read" such syndicated content, you need to open the RSS feed in a news reader (also called an aggregator). Most email apps include news readers. Google *RSS news reader* if you'd like to find a stand-alone option.

Anyone can create his or her own RSS feeds. Refer to **www.mnot.net/rss/tutorial** for a great tutorial on doing just that. Once you've created your own syndicated content, you'll need to put a link on your page to advertise that content (similar to those little orange buttons you've probably seen at other sites). Links to RSS feeds look very similar to other HTML links, with a few minor variations: `<a type="application/rss+xml" href="feed.rss">RSS feed for this page</a>`.

FTP and Downloadable Files

The Internet provides many companies with an easy way to transmit files to customers. For example, suppose you purchased a piece of software to protect your computer against viruses. Eventually, your software must be updated so that it can recognize new viruses. The quickest and easiest way to obtain such an update is to download it from the company's web site.

When you download files from the Internet that cannot be displayed in your web browser (such as software applications and add-ons), you usually do so by accessing the company's FTP site.

FTP, which stands for *File Transfer Protocol*, is a way in which you send and receive files over the Internet. Many companies have both HTTP servers, which house their web site, and FTP servers, which house their downloadable files.

To reference a file on an FTP site, you use an `a` tag and `href` attribute with the FTP protocol, as in the following example:

```
<a href="ftp://sunsite.unc.edu/pub/">Visit the SunSite FTP</a>
```

Although some FTP sites are anonymous and don't require a password for access, most are private. Secure content is typically made available to a limited audience, which is given specific credentials for accessing the content. You won't be able to access a private FTP site without a qualified username and password. If you are linking to a private FTP site, you should also consider providing a way for visitors to register or sign up to receive a username and password.

Of course, in some cases, you could have downloadable files located right on your web server with your web page. These might be movies, sounds, programs, or other documents you want to make available to your visitors. Or, they might be located on a file server like Dropbox. In either case, you can link to these just as you would any other web page, keeping the proper file extension in mind.

```
<a href="http://www.wendywillard.com/downloads/baby.mov">View the baby
movie!</a>
```

Recognize Effective Links

The Web is all about links. If users cannot find the links on your page and successfully use them, that linked content might as well be deleted. One of the problems with so many web pages is what's commonly referred to as the "click here syndrome."

NOTE

Even more than a decade after the first edition of this book was published, I continue to see web designers fall victim to the "click here syndrome." For this reason, I feel compelled to add this note to further emphasize just how bad the phrase "click here" is! Please, please don't ever underline (link) the words "click here" in your web pages. Instead, link words that describe what the user will actually find when they click the link!

Discussed briefly earlier, this occurs when the phrase *click here* is used as a link's label text. Consider the following example:

Woolwich is a rural community on the eastern shore of the Kennebec River, opposite the historic city of Bath and approximately 12 miles from the Atlantic Ocean. First settled in the 1600s and incorporated in 1759, the town is named for Woolwich, England, which in like manner is situated on a large, navigable river. (Click here for information about Woolwich, England.)

The words *click here* that were underlined in the preceding example don't shed any light on exactly what you would find if you clicked that link. A better example might be the following:

Woolwich is a rural community on the east shore of the Kennebec River, opposite the historic city of Bath and approximately 12 miles from the Atlantic Ocean. First settled in the 1600s and incorporated in 1759, the town is named for Woolwich, England, which in like manner is situated on a large, navigable river.

Now, when you scan the paragraph, the words *Woolwich, England* jump out and you know more information about that place can be found by clicking the linked words.

Another common pitfall is using entire sentences as link labels. Compare the two links in the next paragraph. The shorter link at the end is easier to spot because you have to read the entire first sentence to understand the content of the link.

Woolwich is a rural community on the east shore of the Kennebec River, opposite the historic city of Bath and approximately 12 miles from the Atlantic Ocean. First settled in the 1600s and incorporated in 1759, the town is named for Woolwich, England, which in like manner is situated on a large, navigable river.

If you needed to place multiple links within a paragraph of text, it might be better to convert the paragraph into a list, where each link is at the beginning of the list item.

Woolwich is a rural Maine community on the east shore of the Kennebec River.

Historic Bath is located opposite Woolwich

Atlantic Ocean is approximately 12 miles down river

First settled in the 1600s

Incorporated in 1759

Woolwich, England, gives the town its name

To summarize, it's important to scan over your web pages from the user's perspective to determine if your links are easy to spot and use. Short, meaningful words and phrases work better than lengthy marketing jargon.

Try This 7-1 Add Links

Returning to the pages we've been completing for our practice site, let's add some links. You can tailor the project to your particular needs. Goals for this project include

- Adding links to web pages
- Adding links to sections within a web page
- Adding links to email addresses

1. Open your text/HTML editor and load one of the pages saved from a previous chapter.

2. Add a link to a page describing the company/person's services (services.html). Title the link something appropriate for the link's content.

3. Save the file.

4. Create a new file using the name you just linked to: **services.html**. Include the basic elements of all web pages, and add a few paragraphs of content.

5. Add the phrase "email us" to the page. Specify an email address to which the messages should be sent, and specify a subject of *Services*.

6. Save this file.

7. Open your web browser and choose File | Open Page (or Open File or Open, depending on the browser you're using). Locate the first file you just saved.

8. Click the link you added to ensure it works. The link should bring up the services.html page.

9. If you need to make changes, return to your text editor to do so. After making any changes, save the file and switch back to the browser. Choose Refresh or Reload to preview the changes you just made.

10. Return to the services.html file in your text editor.

11. Add sections for each of the services offered. Add anchors to each of the section headings, using the section name (without any spaces) as the anchor name.

12. Add links to each of the anchors you just created so that the category names near the top of the page become links to the actual category content below.

13. Add an anchor to the top of the page named **top**.

14. Add **Back to Top** links at the end of each section to enable a visitor to have easy access back to the category listing at the top of the page.

15. Save the file.

16. Return to your web browser and choose Refresh or Reload to confirm your changes.

TIP

Does your link work? If not, make sure the pathname is correct. Both the index.html and services.html pages should be located in the same folder. If they aren't, you need to change the pathname to reflect the proper folder name. In addition, be sure to check your capitalization (or lack thereof). Remember, links like this are case-sensitive, so if you named a section "Intro" with a capital *I,* but linked to "intro" with a lowercase *i,* then your link won't work. For more tips, see Appendix C.

The a element enables you to add links to many types of information on the Internet. This project gives you practice using that element to link to another web page, an email address, and sections within the same web page.

TIP

Do each of your target links work? If not, make sure the anchor name is correct. Remember, in most cases links are case-sensitive, so if you capitalized the anchor name, you need to capitalize it again when you link to it. In addition, check to see you have included a hash mark (#) before each anchor name when you link to it (that is, href="#a"). For more tips, see Appendix C.

Extra Credit

1. To prepare for the next project, switch from using an internal style sheet to an external style sheet. (Use the internal style sheet from index.html as the basis for your external style sheet.)

2. Name it **styles.css** and save it in the same folder as the other two files.

3. Add a link to your external style sheet from both index.html and services.html.

Style Links

We previously discussed changing the text and background colors for pages. As with other attributes that change color in HTML pages, you need to specify the color, whether by hexadecimal code, RGB values, or a predefined color name. (More information about how to find color values is listed in Chapter 3.)

You specify these colors with style sheets. As with any style declaration, you can specify the background, text, and link colors in an inline, internal, or external style sheet. The actual properties used to do so are the same, however, regardless of the type of style sheet you use.

You actually use the a element to change link colors with style sheets, as in the following example:

```
<style type="text/css">
body {background-color: white;}
a:link {color: blue;}
a:visited {color: purple;}
a:hover {color: orange;}
a:active {color: red;}
</style>
```

This allows you to specify the color of the links *before* they're clicked.

This allows you to specify the color of the links *after* they've been clicked and visited.

This allows you to specify the color of the links *while the cursor is positioned over them* (same as a "rollover").

This allows you to specify the color of the links *while they are being clicked.*

While this specific style declaration changes the links on the entire page, you could also use classes to adjust only certain link colors. This is particularly handy if, for example, most of the links on your page are the default blue but the background of your navigation bar is also a deep blue. One way to take care of this is to create a *class* with a different color link, as I did in the following style sheet:

The period tells the browser that a class name follows, which means this declaration only applies to a tags with that class name.

```
a.navlinks:link {color: white;}
a.navlinks:visited {color: gray;}
a.navlinks:hover {color: yellow;}
a.navlinks:active {color: orange;}
```

After you create these classes in your internal or external style sheet, you just need to apply it to the links you want affected. This is achieved by adding the class attribute to the appropriate a elements, as in:

```
<a href="link.html" class="navlinks">Home</a>
```

If you placed all of your navigation links inside of a nav element, then there's another way to easily change the colors of only those links. This is a perfect chance to use what is referred to as a *descendant selector.* In the following code example, we first tell the browser to look for the nav section, and then to adjust only the a elements that fall *inside* that section:

```
nav a:link {color: white;}
nav a:visited {color: gray;}
nav a:hover {color:yellow;}
nav a:active {color:orange;}
```

Default Link Colors

In most cases, the default link color for browsers is blue. The default visited link color is purple, and the active link color is red. Remember, as with many other features of web browsers, the user ultimately controls these default colors.

TIP

Although not required, and certainly not always possible, staying with a blue/purple/red color scheme for your link/visited link/active link colors is nice. Visitors to your site may adjust to the navigation more quickly if the color scheme is similar to that of other web sites.

I recommend using the same link colors on all the pages in your web site to give a consistent look and feel across the pages. In addition, it's wise to pick visited link colors that don't stand out as much as your unvisited links. Both of these recommendations enable visitors to scan your page easily and identify which pages they've been to and which ones they haven't visited.

Finally, remember to test your colors on a number of different computer systems to ensure they appear as you intend. I also recommend changing your monitor settings to black and white for a minute, just to make sure your links are visible in a grayscale environment.

Beyond Colors

If you ever changed link colors with older HTML tags, you know that there wasn't much else you could do to links beyond changing their colors. With CSS, you can style your links to really stand out from the rest of the text on your page. In fact, you can format links in much the same way you learned to style regular text content in the previous chapter. This means you can substitute link colors, make links bold or italic, or even change the perpetual underline that comes with text links by default. Table 7-1 contains code to give you a few ideas.

The only one of these properties we haven't covered thus far is text-decoration. This is the CSS property used to specify whether your link underlines are visible. By default, all linked text is underlined with a single line beneath it, the same color as the linked text. With this property, you can switch to an overline, a line-through, or no line at all (none).

Link State	Description	Code Used
Normal	Blue Bold	```a:link {color: blue;``` ``` font-weight: bold;}```
Visited	Purple	```a:visited {color: purple;}```

Rollover	Orange
	Bold
	No underline
	Yellow highlight
		```a:hover {color: orange;```
		``` font-weight: bold;```
		``` text-decoration: none;```
		``` background-color: yellow;}```

Active	Red Bold	```a:active {color: red;``` ``` font-weight: bold;}```

Table 7-1   Explanation on Sample Code Used to Style Links

The possibilities are endless, so I encourage you to experiment with ways to creatively style your links. Having said that, I do have a few words of caution:

- Avoid using different size fonts in each link state, unless the size change in no way affects the surrounding content. (It can be very annoying to move your mouse across a web page and then not be able to read the page content because the links become large enough to block the text around them.)

- Avoid making any changes that cause text to move or jump around on the page when a link is activated.

- Make sure to pick colors that complement the rest of the page. While you want your links to be visible, you don't want them to distract the reader.

Customize Links by Setting the Tab Order, Keyboard Shortcut, and Target Window

You can further customize the links on your page by setting the title, tab order, keyboard shortcuts, and target windows. Although many of these options have little effect on the outward display of the page, they provide added benefit to users, particularly those with disabilities (such as the hearing- or vision-impaired) and those viewing the site from web-enabled mobile devices.

Title

The `title` attribute is actually pretty easy to use and understand, and goes a long way toward helping users navigate a web site. When you add it to a link (or any other page element), you're giving the browser and user a little bit more detail regarding the content—in this case, of the linked file. What the browser does with the contents of your `title` attribute varies, but in most situations the text appears as a "tool tip" when the cursor is placed over the link.

For example, in the following code snippet and illustration, the `title` attribute serves to alert users to the fact that clicking the link will take them to another web site:

```
<a href="http://www.yahoo.com" title="Click this link to leave our
site and visit Yahoo!">Visit Yahoo!</a>
```

TIP

The W3C encourages you to add the `title` attribute to as many page elements as you can—everything from images and links to paragraphs and sections of text—because the `title` attribute can also aid in style sheet development and general page usability.

Tab Order

Frequent users of screen-based forms understand that pressing the TAB key advances your mouse pointer to the next available form field. Usually, the tab order of those fields is specified by the programmer who created the form.

In like manner, you can customize the tab order of links and form field elements on your web page by using the `tabindex` attribute:

This attribute defines the tab order.

```
<a href="page1.html" tabindex="1">Page 1</a><br>
<a href="page2.html" tabindex="2">Page 2</a><br>
```

The value of the `tabindex` attribute defines which link is to be highlighted first, second, and so forth when a visitor uses the TAB key to navigate a web page.

When a visitor uses the TAB key to navigate your web page, each link or clickable element on the page is, in turn, highlighted. If no order has been specified by the `tabindex` attribute, the browser will make its best effort to use a reasonable tab order, usually from top to bottom of the code.

After successfully using the TAB key to highlight the link the person wants to visit, he or she can press the RETURN or ENTER key to visit that link.

NOTE

You can use any number between 0 and 32,767 for the value of the `tabindex` attribute, or use a negative number to exclude an element entirely from the tab order.

Keyboard Shortcuts

Many computer users are familiar with some common keyboard shortcuts, such as copy (CTRL-C/Windows or COMMAND-C/Mac) and paste (CTRL-V/Windows or COMMAND-V/Mac). Similarly, you can assign keyboard shortcuts to links in your web page. To do so requires adding the `accesskey` attribute to the a element:

This attribute defines the keyboard shortcut.

```
Click the link or type the appropriate keyboard shortcut and press RETURN
to visit the page of your choice:<br>
<a href="page1.html" tabindex="1" accesskey="1">Page 1</a> (Alt-1)<br>
<a href="page2.html" tabindex="2" accesskey="2">Page 2</a> (Alt-2)<br>
```

The value of the `accesskey` attribute specifies which key the user must enter.

A good idea is to include the keyboard shortcut next to your link; otherwise, visitors to your web page wouldn't know it exists. Note that in some versions of IE on Windows, users must press ENTER after typing the `accesskey` to actually visit the web page.

TIP

Try to remember any universal keyboard shortcuts when you come up with your own. You wouldn't want to disable someone's ability to print, for example, in favor of a link in your web page.

Target Windows

Have you ever visited a web site and noticed that a second instance—either a new window or tab—of the web browser opened when you clicked a link? This happens when web developers use the `target` attribute to load links in a browser window other than the one you're currently using.

For example, you may want to offer visitors to your site a link to search Yahoo!, but you don't want to encourage them to leave your site. If you use `_blank` as the value of the `target` attribute in your link to Yahoo!, the browser will launch a new browser window or tab (depending on the browser settings) to load **http://www.yahoo.com**.

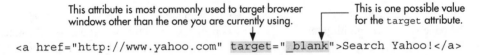

```
<a href="http://www.yahoo.com" target="_blank">Search Yahoo!</a>
```

Aside from targeting new windows, you can also target specific windows you have named. For instance, instead of using `_blank` to launch a new window, you might use "cars" to launch a window that is named "cars." Then, any time you have a link related to cars, you can add `target="cars"` to your link and all those links will load into the "cars" window. Table 7-2 lists three of the possible options for the `target` attribute.

Value of `target` Attribute	Description
_blank	Opens the link in a new unnamed browser window
_self	Opens the link in the same window currently being used
name (where *name* is any name you have given to a window)	Opens the link in the window of that name (if no window is currently open by that name, the browser launches a new window and gives it that name)

Table 7-2 Commonly Used Values for the `target` Attribute

Try This 7-2 Customize Links

This final project in Chapter 7 gives you practice customizing links by changing the default colors, tab order, keyboard shortcuts, and target windows. Goals for this project include

- Changing the link colors for a page

- Targeting a link to open in a new browser window

- Adding titles for all links on a page

1. Open your HTML editor and open both the index.html page and the services.html page saved from Try This 7-1.

2. Change the link colors on both pages to the color scheme of your choice. Save all files. (If you created styles.css in the Extra Credit for the previous project, you only need to change the link colors in that one file to alter them on both pages! Refer back to the end of Try This 7-1 if you missed it.)

3. Close index.html.

4. Switch to services.html and add a link to a related external web site somewhere on the page. Target a new browser window with this link.

5. Add titles to each link with the `title` attribute.

6. Save the file.

7. Open your web browser and choose File | Open Page (or Open File or Open, depending on the browser you're using). Locate the file services.html you just saved.

Preview the page to check your work. If you need to make changes, return to your text editor to do so. After making any changes, save the file and switch back to the browser. Choose Refresh or Reload to preview the changes you just made.

Although users and browsers ultimately control the link colors on your pages, you can make recommendations in your style sheets. This project gives you practice changing those colors, as well as customizing the target windows for your links.

Chapter 7 Self Test

1. What does the `href` attribute do?

2. Which of these can be classified as a relative link?

   A. `<a href="../email.html">`

   B. `<a href="http://www.yahoo.com/email.html">`

   C. `<a href="/email.html">`

   D. `<a href="http://email.yahoo.com">`

3. What must be installed and activated on a user's machine to take advantage of an email link in a web site?

4. How do you tell the browser to launch a link in a new window?

5. Which style sheet selector enables you to change the color of the links on your page after someone has clicked them?

6. In Windows, what must users type to highlight the following link?

   ```
   <a href="contact.html" tabindex="2" accesskey="t">Contact Me</a>
   ```

7. Fill in the blank: After successfully using the TAB key to highlight a link, you must press the _____ key to actually visit that link.

8. Fix the following code:

   ```
   < ahref="contact.html" >Contact Me</a>
   ```

9. Add the appropriate code so that this link enables users to email you at your personal email address.

   ```
   <           > Email Me </ >
   ```

10. Which tag links to a section within the current page?

    A. `<a href="page1">Page 1</a>`

    B. `<a href="#page1">Page 1</a>`

    C. `<a href="*page1">Page 1</a>`

    D. `<a href="page1.html">Page 1</a>`

11. Which common phrase should always be avoided when naming links?

12. Fill in the blank: By default, all linked text is _____.

13. True/False: A dot-dot-slash tells the browser to go up a level in the directory structure before looking for a file.

14. Which links to a section named *Intro* within the web page named genealogy.html?

    A. `<a href="genealogy.html">Intro</a>`

    B. `<a href="genealogy.html#intro">Intro</a>`

    C. `<a href="genealogy.html#Intro">Intro</a>`

    D. `<a href="genealogy.html=Intro">Intro</a>`

    E. `<a href="genealogy.html=intro">Intro</a>`

15. What does `_blank` do when used as the value of the `target` attribute?

Chapter 8

Working with Images

Key Skills & Concepts

- Become Familiar with Graphics Software

- Recognize Appropriate Web Image File Formats

- Use Images as Elements in the Foreground of a Web Page

- Specify the Height and Width of Images

- Provide Alternative Text and Titles for Images

- Link Images to Other Content on a Web Site

- Add Figure Captions

- Style Foreground Images

- Use Images as Elements in the Background of a Web Page

At its beginning, information pages on the Internet were text only and didn't contain any images. We've come a long way since then, with some web sites now consisting *solely* of images. While, in most cases, I wouldn't advocate using only images, I do advocate employing images to spice up your web pages wherever they make sense. The saying "a picture is worth a thousand words" definitely holds true for the Internet.

Locating Web Image Sources

Whenever you create a web site, you will undoubtedly want to include images. It isn't always necessary to create your own images. In fact, thousands of stock images are available, both online and off. Some require minimal fees, while others are free. Let's run through a few different types to help you decide what to use.

Use Stock Images

The use of high-quality photography and illustration can often add a sense of professionalism to a business web site, but many businesses don't have the budget to hire photographers to do private photo shoots for them. If you're in this predicament, have no fear. Plenty of stock imagery houses offer royalty-free photography and illustrations to be used for almost any purpose, except for resale.

You can purchase entire CDs of images with a particular theme at your local computer or office supply store. These CDs range in cost from $40 to $500, depending on the quality of the work and the type of license you're given.

You can also search online and purchase the right to use an individual photograph or graphic. The costs vary according to how you plan to use it. For example, if you want to purchase the right to use a photo only on your web site, you can expect to pay a minimal fee as low as a few dollars (especially on sites like **istockphoto.com**). If, however, you want to use the same image in all your printed publications, as well as in any digital presentations, the fees typically start around $100 and go up from there.

You might also check the software licenses that came with your favorite graphics or presentation program. For instance, registered owners of Microsoft Office have access to Microsoft's free image gallery at **http://office.microsoft.com/clipart**.

NOTE

Just because you find an image online doesn't mean it's available for you to use!
Always check the license—if available—and ask for permission before using personal
or business photos that belong to someone else.

When using any stock images, be sure to read the terms of use and license carefully. While you may find free stock images, they are often restricted only to noncommercial use. Here are a few other resources to consider:

- **www.sxc.hu**
- **www.stockvault.net**
- **www.kozzi.com**
- **www.morguefile.com**
- **www.public-domain-photos.com**
- **www.flickr.com/creativecommons**
- **www.highresolutiontextures.com**
- **www.istockphoto.com**
- **www.shutterstock.com**
- **www.gettyimages.com**

Creating Your Own Graphics

If you do not use existing graphics on your pages, you may need to create some of your own or hire a web designer to do so. The best web designers typically have a background in graphic design and know how to make fast-loading, good-looking graphics for the Web. You can locate web designers either by word of mouth or by searching an online directory such as The Firm List: **www.firmlist.com**.

The next few sections provide an overview of the process of creating and saving web graphics.

Become Familiar with Graphics Software

If you check out the software section (virtually or otherwise) of your favorite computer store, you might be surprised by the sheer volume of graphics-related software available. You can buy clip art and photography, fonts, scanning utilities, animation titles, photo editing programs, desktop publishing applications, drawing tools, and so forth.

NOTE

You'll hear the term *layers* used a lot when discussing graphics software. Using layers in a graphics program is similar to making a bed. You place sheets, blankets, and pillows over the mattress, but you can change any of those items freely if you decide you dislike one. The same is true with layers—you can paint on a layer, and then delete it later if you don't like it. Layers offer much flexibility in graphics programs. However, once you export a file for use in a web page, those layers are merged, or flattened, to save file size and make it easily portable. So if you want to make changes to that file, you'll need the original—layered—source file.

For the purposes of this chapter, I focus on those software titles that offer you the best tools for creating web graphics. Two main categories of graphics software titles exist: vector and bitmap.

Bitmap applications, also called *raster* applications, create graphics using tiny dots known as *bits*. These types of images are more difficult to resize because you must change each individual dot, but they have been around longer and enjoy more support from file formats. GIFs and JPEGs are bitmap images.

Vector applications, also called *object-oriented* applications, are based on mathematically calculated lines and curves that are easily changed and updated. Images created with vectors tend to be smaller in file size and, for that reason, are increasing in popularity on the Internet.

TIP

Can't decide which graphics program to purchase? Most options have trial or demo versions available for free. Visit each company's web site for details.

The programs discussed here are by no means the only products available for creating web graphics. Given the scope of this book, though, I thought it best to limit the discussion to the most popular programs. If none of these tools suits your needs, try searching in Yahoo! (**www.yahoo.com**) or CNET's download center (**www.downloads.com**) for "web graphics," and perhaps you'll find one more suitable for your purposes.

Adobe Photoshop and Illustrator

Adobe is the world leader in graphics and imaging software. It offers such renowned titles as Photoshop and Illustrator, which have been used in the printing and design industry for years.

TIP

Adobe's products are available for Windows and Macintosh systems. For more information, visit **www.adobe.com**.

Photoshop is a bitmap program, best known for image manipulation, using layers to allow for virtually limitless flexibility in design. In fact, if you've recently bought a new scanner or printer, you might have acquired a scaled-back version of Photoshop with it. Illustrator, on the other hand, is a vector tool, more suited for freehand drawing and illustration. However, both programs save and open multiple formats.

In many cases, Adobe's Photoshop is the product to use. For the typical home user, however, the cost of the full version is a bit steep (over $650). If you're familiar with Adobe's products and enjoy them, I recommend sticking with Photoshop. Likewise, if you're interested in creating web graphics as well as editing images for printed publications, Photoshop is your best bet. But if your particular interest is more in the graphical or illustrative realm, I suggest you download a trial of Illustrator to see if that better serves your needs.

If you don't fall into these use categories, you might be interested in Photoshop Elements (a scaled-back, but still fabulous, version), which costs around $100. While this version doesn't have all the high-powered image editing tools used by the professionals, it's more than capable of handling the needs of someone just starting, and it even has a few bells and whistles that the full version doesn't. Photoshop Elements, available for both the Mac and the Windows SDFX, is a great choice for the typical home user.

If you are a student or are employed by an academic institution, remember to check into academic pricing for software like this one. Adobe offers significant academic discounts that can make their creation options for their software quite affordable. For example, you might pay around $9.99/month if you pay for a year at a time.

Other Options

While the Adobe tools are by far the most popular web graphics applications, there are alternatives available that might be more appropriate for you. Corel fans particularly enjoy Draw and PaintShop Pro (www.corel.com), which are Corel's competitors to Illustrator and Photoshop. Features include animation, direct digital camera support, layers, filters, brushes, special effects, and advanced text tools, such as text typed along a curve or custom path.

Xara (www.xara.com) is another company that offers a few competing tools for cost-conscious web designers looking to ease into design. Photo & Graphic Designer FX is less than $100, and touts all of the basic features you'll likely need. But if you're looking for a full-blown suite of options, like Pantone color libraries or built-in PayPal integration, consider the Xara suite. (Note that Xara's software packages are Windows-only.)

Everyone likes free, so did you know you can get some software for free. Normally, I'd say, "no, really," but in this case there actually is an option for you: GIMP, which is an acronym for GNU Image Manipulation Program. GIMP is freely distributed from **www.gimp.org** for the Mac, Windows, and UNIX platforms. Its features include photo retouching, image composition, and so on. If you're just getting started with creating your own web graphics, you may not want to spend a lot of money until you know if this is something to pursue. A free program like GIMP might be the perfect way to start. And who knows, you may even decide you don't need anything else.

10/04/2018

Items checked out to:
p105703473

Title: 101 ready-to-use Excel formulas / by
Barcode: 31299009097222
Call #: 005.369 A
Due: 10-18-18

Title: Excel outside the box / by Bob Umlas.
Barcode: 31299008652472
Call #: 005.369 U
Due: 10-18-18

Title: Microsoft Excel 2013 / by Michael Miller.
Barcode: 31299009041568
Call #: 005.369 M
Due: 10-18-18

Title: HTML : a beginner's guide / Wendy
Barcode: 31299008839277
Call #: 005.72 W
Due: 10-18-18

Total items checked out: 4

You just saved an estimated $112 by
using the Library today.

Thank you for visiting!

East Meadow Public Library
1886 Front Street ∘ East Meadow, NY 11554
516.794.2570 ∘ 516.794.2949 (TTY)
www.eastmeadow.info

Recognize Appropriate Web Image File Formats

Now that you have some ideas about software to use, let's talk about the file formats necessary. If you try to load a TIFF or PICT into your web page, users will see a broken image symbol. This occurs because graphics in web pages must be in a format understood by the web browser. The most popular graphics file formats recognized by web browsers are GIF, JPEG, and PNG.

Terminology

Before you dive into the nuts and bolts about those file types, you need to learn a few terms that relate to web file formats.

Compression Methods

Web graphic file formats take your original image and compress it to make it smaller for web and email delivery. Two types of compression methods are used for web graphics:

- Lossy
- Lossless

Lossy compression requires data to be removed—permanently—from the image to compress the file and make it smaller. Typically, areas with small details are lost as the level of lossy compression is increased. *Lossless* compression is the opposite of lossy, in that no data is lost when the file is compressed. In these cases, the actual data looks the same whether it's compressed or uncompressed.

Resolution

You might have considered your monitor's resolution previously, but in this case I'm referring specifically to *file* resolution. Whenever you create or edit a file in a graphics editor, you need to specify a file resolution (see Figure 8-1). The standard file resolution for web graphics is 72 *pixels per inch (ppi)*.

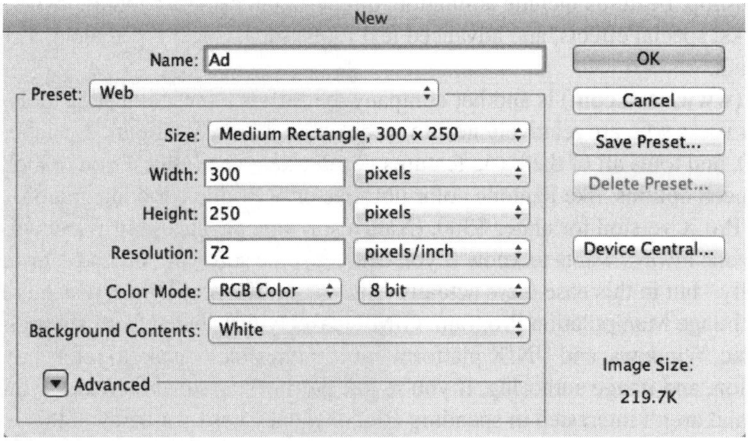

Figure 8-1 When working with web graphics, use a file resolution of 72 ppi.

Figure 8-2 When a file with transparency is displayed in a graphics program, you typically see a gray and white checkerboard in the transparent areas of the image.

NOTE
Don't be confused if you see dpi (dots per inch) used interchangeably with ppi. Technically speaking, dpi is more often linked to a printer's "dots per inch," while monitors are considered to have "pixels per inch."

Transparency
When you view an image and are able to *see through* parts of it, that image is said to have *transparency*. Some graphics editors show this transparency by displaying a gray and white checkerboard behind the image. Figure 8-2 shows an example of this in Photoshop.

When a web graphic contains transparency, the page's background color or background tile shows through in the transparent areas.

File types that support transparency fall into two categories: binary and variable. *Binary transparency* means any given pixel is either transparent or opaque. *Variable transparency*, also known as *alpha channel,* allows pixels to be partially transparent or partially opaque; therefore, it is capable of creating subtle gradations.

Certain file types don't support transparency. If the image shown in Figure 8-2 were to be saved in a file format not supporting transparency, the areas shown in a checkerboard would be filled in with a solid color.

Animation
Some web file formats support animation as well as still images. These animation files contain two or more individual files called *animation frames*. The following illustration shows three frames of an animation. Notice that the position of the rattle changes slightly from frame to frame.

When the file is played back through the browser, viewers watch the various frames of the animation appear, one after the other. The rate at which the frames change can vary between a speedy filmstrip and a slowly blinking button. In the preceding example, the rattle appears to shake.

The most common example of this type of animation—bitmap animation—is GIF animation. More robust animation tools are those that use vectors instead of bitmaps. This means the animation is sent as a series of instructions instead of actual pixel renderings. The result is much more fluid animation that downloads in a fraction of the time a similar bitmap animation would. Flash is the most common type of vector animation. In addition, HTML5 introduces animation right within the page, using the canvas element and JavaScript. I'll discuss that a bit more in Chapter 14.

GIF

GIF is the acronym for *graphic interchange format*. Originally designed for online use in the 1980s, GIF uses a compression method that is well suited to certain types of web graphics. This method, called *LZW compression*, is lossless and doesn't cause a loss of file data. However, several characteristics of GIFs restrict the type of files capable of being saved as GIFs. Table 8-1 lists these and other characteristics of the GIF file type.

NOTE

According to its creator, GIF is officially pronounced with a soft *g*. Because the word is an acronym, though, many people pronounce it with a hard *g*.

Because of these characteristics, the following types of images lend themselves to being saved as GIFs. Notice all of these are limited in colors.

- Text
- Line drawings
- Cartoons
- Flat-color graphics

Characteristic	Description
Color mode	Restricted to no more than 256 exact colors (8-bit)
Compression method	Lossless
Animation	Supported
Transparency	Supported (binary only)

Table 8-1 GIF File Format Characteristics

Ask the Expert

Q: I noticed photographs aren't on this list. I've seen plenty of photographs used on web pages—can't they be saved as GIFs?

A: Images with photographic content shouldn't usually be saved as GIFs, unless they're part of an animation or require transparency. Other file types are more capable of compressing photographs. In fact, the JPEG file format was created specifically for photographs and shouldn't be used for other types of images such as flat-color graphics and text.

Save a GIF

When you save a file as a GIF in a graphics program, you have the option of saving your image with or without *dithering*. GIF color palettes only have a limited number of colors, and the fewer colors present, the smaller the file size. When you want to reduce the number of colors in the palette, the program must know what to do with the areas in your image that contain the colors you're removing.

TIP

The *g* in GIF gives you a hint about what types of images are best saved as GIFs: graphics (as opposed to photographs).

If you tell the program to use dithering (you can specify any amount of dithering between 0 and 100 percent), it may use multiple colors in a checkerboard pattern in those areas to give the appearance of the color you removed. If no dithering is used, the removed colors are replaced with another solid color (see Figure 8-3). Dithering can be useful in giving the appearance of gradations or subtle color shifts, but be forewarned—it adds to the file size.

TIP

Few images actually need all 256 colors available in a GIF color palette. Try reducing the number of colors all the way down to 8 or 16, and work your way back up as high as you need to go to make the image look acceptable. This assures that you reach the minimum colors more easily than if you try to work from the most colors on down. Remember, the fewer colors in the palette, the smaller the file size.

JPEG

The *JPEG* file format (pronounced *jay-peg*) was created by the *Joint Photographic Experts Group*, who sought to create a format more suitable for compressing photographic imagery. After reading Table 8-2, review Table 8-1 to compare JPEG's characteristics with those of GIF.

Figure 8-3 In this example, the photograph on the bottom is dithered, while the photograph on the top is not.

One major difference between GIFs and JPEGs is that JPEGs don't contain an exact set of colors. When you save a photograph as a JPEG, you might consider all the colors in the file to be *recommended*, because the lossy compression might require some colors to be altered. In addition, all web JPEG files must be in the RGB (Red, Green, Blue) color mode, as opposed to the print standard—CMYK (Cyan, Magenta, Yellow, Black).

Characteristic	Description
Color mode	Displayed in 24-bit color, also called millions of colors. If the user's monitor isn't set to view 24-bit color, the file is displayed with as many colors as are available.
Compression method	Lossy
Animation	Not supported
Transparency	Not supported

Table 8-2 JPEG File Format Characteristics

Save a JPEG

When you save an image as a JPEG, you choose between several different quality levels. The highest-quality JPEG has the least amount of compression and, therefore, the least amount of data removed. The lowest-quality JPEG has the most amount of data removed and often looks blotchy, blurry, and rough. I usually save JPEG images with a medium quality. The decision is made based on how low in quality you can go without compromising the integrity of the file: The lower the quality level, the lower the file size.

PNG

PNG, which stands for *Portable Network Graphics* and is pronounced *ping*, is the newest and most flexible of these three graphics file formats. After looking at the list of characteristics for PNG in Table 8-3, you might think of PNG as being the best of both the GIF and JPEG formats.

TIP

The 32-bit color format is similar to 24-bit color because it also has millions of colors. However, 32-bit color also has a masking channel, which can be used for alpha transparency.

An additional benefit of PNG is its gamma correction. The PNG file format has the capability to correct for differences in how computers and monitors interpret color values.

Save a PNG

When saving a file as a PNG, you must first choose how many colors to include in its palette. Saving as PNG-8 uses an exact palette of 256 colors or less. Transparency and dithering are available in the PNG-8 setting. PNG-24 and PNG-32 offer 24-bit (millions) and 32-bit (millions, plus an alpha channel) color modes, respectively.

Characteristic	Description
Color mode	Can be stored as 8-bit, 24-bit, or 32-bit
Compression method	Lossless
Animation	Not supported
Transparency	Supported (variable/alpha)

Table 8-3   PNG File Format Characteristics

Choose the Best File Format for the Job

Now that you know a little about the different web graphics file formats, you're probably wondering how you might select the best format for the job. While I wish I could give you a foolproof method, the answer, ultimately, lies in your own testing.

Luckily, many of the popular graphics programs make this testing easy. For example, Photoshop enables you to compare how a single image might look when saved in any of these file formats.

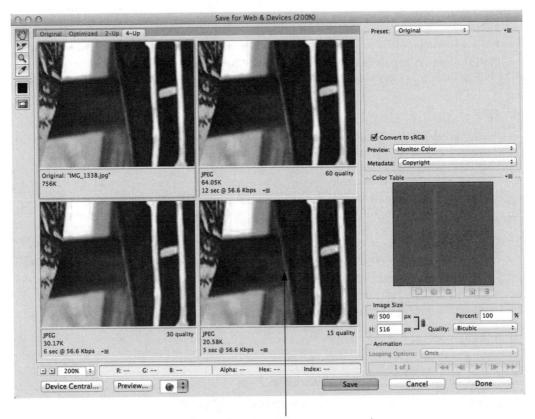

With magnification at 200 percent, you can better see how the lower quality affects the image.

TIP

If the graphics program you're using doesn't allow you to compare and preview file types, save several different versions of the same file and preview each one in a browser. Compare their file size (with regard to download speed) and appearance to determine which file type and settings are the best.

In the preceding example, I used Photoshop's Save For Web feature to compare three different quality levels for the JPEG file format. The settings and file sizes are printed below each example to help decide which would work the best.

Choosing the best file format is like shopping—you are looking for the file format that looks the best, but costs the least. In this case, the cost comes in download time for web page visitors.

Try This 8-1   Save Web Graphics

Designers often receive images for web pages on disc, via email, or even in printed format. On receipt of these files, you need to put them in a web-ready format by saving them as GIFs, JPEGs, or PNGs.

If you have a graphics program, this project gives you a chance to practice saving different types of images in the appropriate web file format. If you don't already have a graphics program, you might visit the web sites listed in the beginning of this chapter to download trial copies or demo versions. Goals for this project include the following:

- Saving a photograph in an appropriate web file format

- Saving an illustration in an appropriate web file format

NOTE

You will need a few image files to use for this project. Search your computer's hard drive and/or Google Images to find a few practice files. At this point, we are less concerned about the actual image content as much as the process by which web graphics are saved.

1. Open your graphics editor and load a logo file, an illustration, or another graphical image (something other than a photograph).

2. Adjust the dpi and pixel dimensions to be more suited toward placement of this image in a web page.

3. Determine which file format is the most appropriate for this image, using any of the following techniques. If necessary, keep track of your progress by entering each file's setting in the following table. The first two rows give examples of how the table might be used.

   - Review the guidelines in this chapter.

   - If available, use the program's preview and compare features.

   - Save multiple versions of the file, using different settings in each one, and view them in a web browser.

(continued)

4. Repeat this process for a photographic image.

5. Open your web browser and choose File | Open Page (or Open File or Open, depending on the browser you're using). Locate the graphics you just saved. Make sure the image appears as you intended.

6. If you need to make changes, return to your graphics editor to do so. After making any changes, save the file and switch back to the browser. Choose Refresh or Reload to preview the changes you just made.

TIP

Do you see broken image symbols instead of your images? Make sure the filenames end in a three-letter extension (such as .gif or .jpg). If they don't, go back to your graphics editor and resave or re-export the file as a GIF, JPEG, or PNG. For more tips, see Appendix C.

Creating your own web graphics can be a great way to add your own personal style to your web pages. This project gave you a chance to practice saving files in formats viewable on the Web.

Use Images as Elements in the Foreground of a Web Page

Now that you have a basic understanding of how to save web images, let's discuss how to insert them into your site. You can easily add images anywhere on your web page by using the img element, where img is short for *image*. Add the src attribute (short for source), supply the appropriate value, and you're off and running.

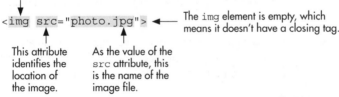

This opens the img element.

`<img src="photo.jpg">` ← The img element is empty, which means it doesn't have a closing tag.

This attribute identifies the location of the image.

As the value of the src attribute, this is the name of the image file.

When you use the `img` element, you're telling the browser to display the image right within the web page. In doing so, remember the following few things:

- Your image should be in a web-friendly file format, such as GIF, JPEG, or PNG.

- The value of your `src` attribute should include the correct pathname and location of your file. So, if the image you want to use is not located in the same folder as the HTML page you're working on, you need to tell the browser in which folder that image is located. For example, if you want to include an image located one directory higher than the current directory, you would use `src="../photo.jpg"`, where the `../` tells the browser to go up one directory before looking for the image file. If you want to reference an image from another web site, first you must obtain permission from the image's owner. Then, you could use `src="http://www.websitename.com/images/photo.jpg"`, where the URL is the full name of the image location on the other site.

- In general, each image should serve a unique purpose and add something to your web page. Because visitors have to wait while images download to their computers, it's wise not to bog down your page with gratuitous graphics that serve little or no purpose.

Specify the Height and Width of Images

After you start adding several images to your web pages, you may notice they sometimes cause the browser to wait a few seconds before displaying the page. Because they don't know the size of the image, some browsers actually wait until the images are all loaded before displaying the web page.

Therefore, you can help speed the display of your web pages by telling the browser the sizes of your images right within the `img` tag. You do so with the `height` and `width` attributes.

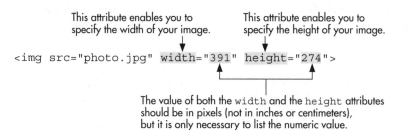

This attribute enables you to specify the width of your image.

This attribute enables you to specify the height of your image.

```
<img src="photo.jpg" width="391" height="274">
```

The value of both the `width` and the `height` attributes should be in pixels (not in inches or centimeters), but it is only necessary to list the numeric value.

If you don't know the size of your image, you can open it in a graphics editor to find out. Or you can use the browser to determine the size of your images.

- **In Firefox/Mozilla for the Mac and PC, as well as in Safari for the Mac**   First, load the image by itself into the browser window (choose File | Open or File | Open Page and locate the image file on your computer). Then, look at the top of the browser window where the title is usually displayed. When you view an image file, these browsers print the width and height of the image (in that order) in the title.

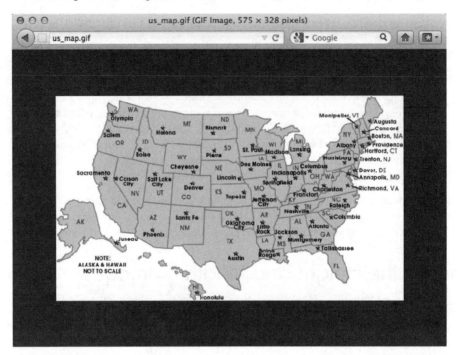

- **In Internet Explorer**   Load the image into the browser window (choose File | Open and locate the image file on your computer, or drag it from the desktop into an open browser window). Then, right-click the image and choose Properties. The size is displayed as *dimensions* (width × height).

TIP

If a magnifying glass is displayed when you hover over the image in the browser, you are not viewing the full-size image. Click the magnifying glass to enlarge the image to its full size, and then view the dimensions.

You can also use the `height` and `width` attributes to change the size of an image. For example, if you were given an image that was 50 pixels high by 60 pixels wide, you could change that size by specifying a different size in the HTML (such as 50 pixels wide by 50 pixels high). This causes the browser to attempt to redraw the image at the newly specified size. I don't recommend doing this—and neither does the W3C—because it may not only slow down the display of your pages, it may also cause the image to lose proper proportions. Creating the image at whatever size you need it to be within your page is best.

Provide Alternative Text and Titles for Images

Some people visiting your site won't be able to see the images on your pages. This might be the case for a variety of reasons, but here are a few of the most common ones:

- **They have turned images off in their browsers**   Most browsers have a setting in the preferences that enables you to disable images on pages. By turning off images, visitors are able to view web pages more quickly, and then choose which (if any) images they want to see.

- **They are using text-only browsers**   Although a small minority of people using desktop computers have text-only browsers, some of those with handheld devices do use text-only browsers on a daily basis. These handheld devices might include Internet-ready telephones, pagers, and palm-size computers. In addition, those who are vision-impaired often use text-only browsers with additional pieces of software that read the pages to them. In these cases, your alternate text may be the only way vision-impaired people can understand the purpose of your images.

- **The image doesn't appear**   Sometimes, even though you coded the page properly, the visitor to your site doesn't see every single image on the page. This could happen if too much traffic occurs, or when visitors click the Stop button in their browser before the page has fully loaded.

The good news is you can do something to help visitors to your site understand the content of your images, even if they can't see them. You can use the `alt` attribute in the `img` tag to provide alternative text for an image.

```
<img src="art-turtle.gif" width="600" height="412" alt="Drawing of a
Turtle">
```

The text value of the `alt` attribute displays in the box where the image should be located if the browser cannot find the image or if it isn't set to display images (see Figure 8-4).

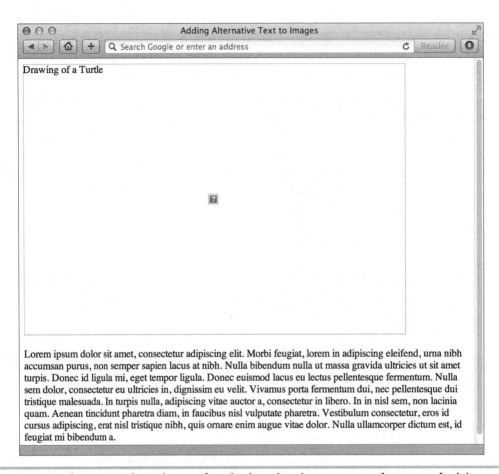

Figure 8-4 This screen shows how Safari displays the alternative text if it cannot find the image. Without that alternative text, viewers wouldn't have any idea what they were supposed to see.

In addition to the `alt` attribute, it's a good idea to add the `title` attribute to your `img` tag. While the `alt` attribute specifies alternative text for images in case the images don't load, the `title` attribute is displayed in a box near your pointer arrow when the arrow is positioned over the image. In addition, the `title` attribute can be added to images as well as links and other page elements. It serves as a quick tip for users to briefly explain the contents of the page element or, in this case, the image.

```
<img src="art-turtle.gif" width="600" height="412" alt="Drawing of a
Turtle" title="Drawing of a Turtle">
```

TIP

This process of showing informative text when the mouse moves over an image is also called a *tool tip* in other software programs.

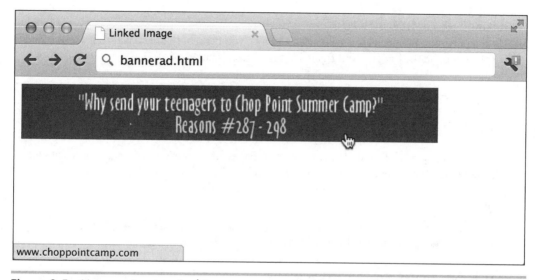

Figure 8-5   Here, an image—in this case, an animated banner ad—is used as a link to another web page.

Link Images to Other Content on a Web Site

In the preceding chapter, you learned how to create links to other pieces of information on the Internet. Text phrases were used to mark links and give visitors something to click. You could also use an image to label a link, with or without an additional text marker. Figure 8-5 shows an example of an image used as a link without an additional text label, while Figure 8-6's linked image does have a text label.

Figure 8-6   As an alternative, a text label has been added in this example to help users understand where the link will take them.

Link the Entire Image

To link an entire image, as in Figures 8-5 and 8-6, you need only to add an a tag and the href attribute around the image. Both figures show a linked banner ad. The associated code looks like this:

```
<a href="http://www.choppointcamp.com"><img src="choppoint_468x60.gif"
width="468" height="60" alt="LINK: Chop Point Summer Camp in Woolwich,
Maine"></a>
```

As with any other linked elements in a web page, the visitor's pointer turns to a hand when she moves her mouse over the linked image (refer to Figures 8-5 and 8-6 for examples).

TIP

When I link an image, I like to add "LINK:" to the beginning of my alternative text. This immediately lets users who can't see the image know it is also a link.

Link Sections of an Image

You can also link sections of an image, creating what are called *image maps*. When only sections of an image are linked (as opposed to the entire image), the visitor's pointer only changes to the hand when he moves his mouse over one of the predefined hot spots on the image. Each *hot spot* within an image map can link to its own web page, if wanted.

So, looking back at the drawing of a turtle, an image map could be used to link the eyes to one web page and the shell to a different one. Another example of an image map is a picture of the United States, where each state could be designated as a hot spot, with its own link.

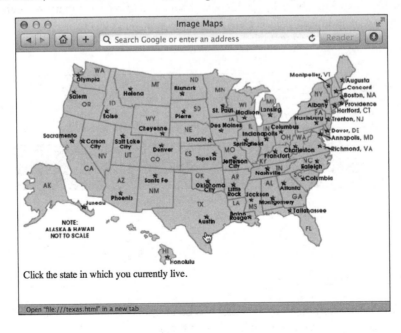

In this example, when you move your mouse over the state of Texas, for example, the pointer changes to a hand telling you Texas is a link. You can see in the status bar at the bottom that the Texas hot spot links to a page called texas.html. If you moved your mouse over another state, such as New Mexico, you would see it's linked to newmexico.html.

The technical term for the type of image map discussed here is "client-side image map." *Client-side image maps* are so called because all the work is done on the client's (or visitor's) computer. The "work" I refer to is the computation of where the hot spot is located and to which link it corresponds. All the information about which hot spot is where and what it links to is included within the original HTML file. This makes for easy access by your visitor's web browser because it doesn't have to look for the information elsewhere. The following example shows what that code looks like. First, we have to tell the browser this image will be used as an image map. Use the usemap attribute to do that and tell the browser where to look for the map file:

```
<img src="map.gif" width="575" height="328" alt="Click your state"
 usemap="#usa"><br>Click the state in which you currently live.
```

Then we name the map:

```
<map name="usa">
```

…and define each hot spot:

```
<area shape="poly" coords="193,174,247,178,244,236,187,243,192,175"
href="/newmexico.html" alt="New Mexico">
<area shape="poly" coords="215,243,304,309,335,260,326,214,275,210,275,
184,248,182,245,238,216,244" href="/texas.html" alt="Texas">
```

After defining all the hot spots in the image, don't forget to close the map tag:

```
</map>
```

You use the usemap attribute of the img tag to specify the image as a client-side image map. This attribute works similarly to something you learned in the preceding chapter: links within a page. The reason for this is that the map tag contains a name attribute that enables you to link to it.

When you use the usemap attribute, you reference whatever name you gave to your map in the map tag. So, in the previous example, the image references an image map called "usa" (usemap="#usa"), which is defined further down the page by <map name="usa">.

NOTE
Remember, whenever you reference a client-side image map, you need to use the hash mark (#) before the name of the map to tell the browser you're referencing something contained within a named section of the page.

Let's look at the code a little more closely.

```
<img src="map.gif" width="575" height="328" alt="Click your state"
usemap="#usa"><br>Click the state in which you currently live.
```

Here's your basic `img` tag, with the addition of the `usemap` attribute. The value of the `usemap` attribute (in this case, usa) should be enclosed in quotes and preceded by a hash mark (#).

```
<map name="#usa">
```

The `map` element surrounds all the other information defining hot spots in your image. The opening and closing tags are both required. The `map` element and its enclosed information can actually be located anywhere within your HTML page and needn't be immediately below the corresponding `img` tag. The `name` attribute is used with the `map` tag to enable you to reference it from anywhere else on the page (or any other page, for that matter).

```
<area shape="poly" coords="193,174,247,178,244,236,187,243,192,175"
href="/newmexico.html" alt="New Mexico">
<area shape="poly" coords="215,243,304,309,335,260,326,214,275,210,275,
184,248,182,245, 238,216,244" href="/texas.html" alt="Texas">
```

In between the opening and closing map tags are `area` tags for each hot spot. The `area` element has four basic attributes (see Table 8-4).

```
</map>
```

Finally, you end this section by closing the `map` tag.

Finding Hot-Spot Coordinates

If you need to, you can likely use your favorite graphics program or HTML editor to find the coordinates of your hot spots. Alternatively, there are plenty of online tools that can help you find the hot spots and code the image map for you. Check out **www.kolchose.org/simon/ajaximagemapcreator** to see one in action.

Attribute	Value	Description
shape	rect, poly, or circle	Defines the shape of your hot spot: rect for rectangles, poly for polygons, and circle for circles.
coords	rect: x1, y1, x2, y2 poly: x1, y1, x2, y2, x3, y3 circle: x, y, r	Defines the boundaries of your hot spot, where x and y are the horizontal and vertical coordinates, respectively, and r is the radius (for circles only): • Rectangles are defined by the upper-left and lower-right points. • Polygons are defined by each of their points, in x,y couples. • Circles are defined by the x,y coordinates of the center point and the radius.
href	filename.html	Defines the page to which you want this hot spot to link.
alt	text string	Defines the alternative text that appears for that hot spot.

Table 8-4 Attributes for the `area` Element

Add Figure Captions

Prior to HTML5, there was no easy way to semantically connect a figure caption to the actual image. Thankfully, we can use the `figure` and `figcaption` elements to do just that. The following code snippet and illustration show the code and resulting browser display for a single photo and caption:

```
<figure>
<img src="fabric-banner.jpg" alt="Fabric banner">
<figcaption>Fabric banner handmade by the women of Nueva Imagen
</figcaption>
</figure>
```

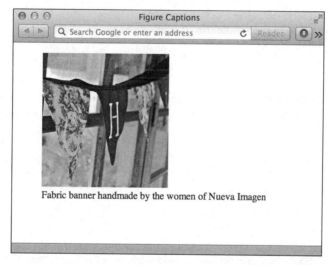

When you use the `figcaption` element, it must be placed inside the `figure` element, and must contain both opening and closing tags. You can then use the `figcaption` tag as a selector in your style sheet to format the caption to match your site's look and feel. (We'll look at an example of this shortly.)

NOTE

It's not necessary, or even recommended, to put *all* of your images inside `figure` elements. Logo and navigational items, for instance, are not part of the actual informational content of a document, and therefore should not be placed inside `figure` elements.

You can also use the `figure` and `figcaption` elements to connect more than just images with their captions. Suppose you created a table of reference information and wanted to place it within a large text block. You could place the table or other diagram within a figure element, and then add a caption to explain the purpose of the `figure`.

Style Foreground Images

While the basic `img` element provides an easy way to add images to your web pages, you likely want to do a whole lot more than just plop those images down on the page. Style sheets enable you to customize the borders, align images with text, and a whole lot more.

Borders

You might have noticed that many linked images have borders around them. This happens because all linked images automatically have borders, just as all linked text automatically has underlines. The earlier HTML specifications allowed for a `border` attribute, which was used to specify the size of an image's border, as in the following example:

```
<img src="map.gif" width="575" height="328" alt="Click your state"
usemap="#usa" border="0"><br>Click the state in which you currently
live.
```

NOTE

Some versions of Internet Explorer turn off borders for images by default. However, because this is not true for all browsers, you should turn it off yourself if you indeed want it to be off.

The value of the `border` attribute is expressed in pixels, where the default is 1 for linked images and 0 for nonlinked images. If you wanted to make it thicker, you would use a larger number, such as 4. In this example, the value is 0. This turns the border off completely, making it invisible.

NOTE

You could also use the `border` attribute to add a border to an image that is not linked by specifying the value as any number greater than 0.

With that said, the W3C retired the `border` attribute and now prefers that you adjust the display of borders with style sheets, just as you learned in a previous chapter. One reason for this is that style sheets offer significantly more control over your borders. For example, if you have multiple images on your page and wish to turn the borders off for all of them, instead of adding "border=0" to each of the `img` tags on the page, you can add the following code to the page's style sheet:

```
img {border-width: 0;}
```

Actually, you could use `border-style: none;` instead of `border-width: 0;` and it would also make the border invisible. Additional style sheet properties related to borders are as follows:

- **border-width**   Controls the size of the borders, individually (border-left-width, border-right-width, and so on) or as a whole (border-width). Values can be specified in length units (0 or 1, for example) or keywords (thin, thick, or medium).

- **border-color**   Controls the border's color by specifying between one and four values. When you specify one value, that color is set for all four border edges. When two values are specified, the top and bottom edges take on the color in the first value and the left and right edges take on the second. When three values are specified, the top is set to the first, the right and left are set to the second, and the bottom is set to the third. When four values are set, the top, right, bottom, and left edges are set, respectively, as in the following example: img `{border-color: #ccc #666 #333 #999;}`. To specify a value for only one side, add the side's name (top, bottom, right, or left) to the property, as in "border-top-color."

- **border-radius**   Allows you to round the corners of the border by specifying between one and four values (just like the border-color property). To round an image's border, use any pixel dimension greater than zero for the value, such as border-radius: 25px.

- **border-style**   Changes the style of the border. Options include

  - none

  - dotted

  - dashed

  - double

  - solid

  - groove

  - ridge

  - inset

  - outset

As you can see, another powerful aspect of the border properties is that they can be altered either as a whole (so that all four edges look the same) or individually. To alter the characteristics individually, you simply add the side specification (top, bottom, right, or left) to the border property, after `border` and before any final characteristic. To give you an idea how

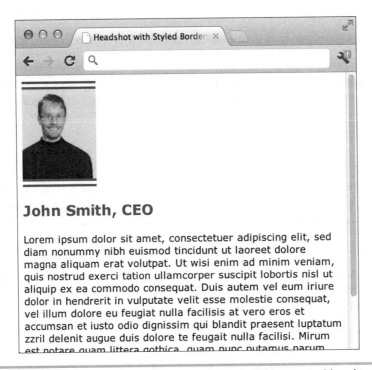

Figure 8-7 The *headshot* class tells the browser to add double, 10-pixel borders to the top and bottom edges of the photo, but leave the left and right edges blank.

this is done, consider the following example and Figure 8-7. Here, I've created a class called *headshot* and then set the border properties in my style sheet.

```
.headshot {border-style: double;
           border-left-style: none;
           border-right-style: none;
           border-width: 10px;
           border-left-width: 0px;
           border-right-width: 0px;
           border-color: #C00;}
```

After adding that style declaration to my style sheet, I can add the class reference to my `img` tag to complete the task:

```
<img src="jsmith.gif" alt="John Smith, CEO" class="headshot">
```

TIP
As discussed previously, with style sheets these types of borders can be added not just to images but to any other element on the page! This means you can quickly add border styles to things like table cells or pull-out quotes, or virtually any other piece of content.

Floats

Whenever images appear within a section of text, you may want to alter the alignment so that the image floats within the text flow instead of above or below it. (By default, the text starts wherever the image ends and flows below it, as shown previously in Figure 8-7.)

While the text-align property discussed previously works for basic alignment of text, it does not align images. Chapter 6 introduced the process of more complex alignment and positioning, but sometimes that is not necessary for quick image alignments. So, I want to mention a very quick and easy way to "float" an image on the page—the CSS float property and a value of either left or right.

Floating an Image Within Text

The float property essentially tells the browser to place the floated element nearest whichever browser edge is specified, and then flow the rest of the page's content around it. To say it another way, content automatically flows along the right side of a left-floated image, and to the left side of a right-floated image. For example, if you had a lengthy paragraph of text and wanted to place an image in the upper-right corner of that paragraph, like this:

you could use the float property on that image, and set the value to *right* to tell the browser to keep the image on the right side of the text. Possible values for the float property are left, right, or none.

```
<img src="jsmith.gif" alt="John Smith, CEO" width="100" height="116"
style="float: right;">
```

NOTE
When coding floats, your floated content must be placed *before* any other content to wrap around it.

Clearing Floats

From time to time you'll encounter an instance in which you actually need to stop or clear a float. One example might involve the same situation I just used—an image floated to the right of a long paragraph of text. Suppose you wanted to break the long paragraph up into two paragraphs, and then you only wanted the first paragraph to wrap around the image. The remaining paragraph would then take up the entire width of the page. To accomplish this, you have to "clear the float" by adding the clear property to the section in question, such as:

```
<p style="clear: right;">Remaining paragraph of text. . .</p>
```

This causes the paragraph to be "pushed down" until it is below the bottom edge of the floated image, like this:

NOTE

Possible values for the clear property are left, right, both, or none.

Floating Groups of Images

Suppose you had a page with lots of images, maybe one with several photos of products for sale. If all of the images were the same size, it would be very easy to use the float property and let the browser automatically place them in lines across the page. The following code shows one way to accomplish this task by placing each of the images (and their accompanying captions) into separate figure elements:

```
<figure>
  <img src="christmas.jpg" alt="Merry Christmas Banner">
  <figcaption>"Merry Christmas" Banner</figcaption>
</figure>
<figure>
  <img src="itsaboy.jpg" alt="It's a Boy Banner">
  <figcaption>"It's a Boy" Banner</figcaption>
</figure>
<figure>
  <img src="names.jpg" alt="Names Banner">
  <figcaption>Names Banner</figcaption>
</figure>
```

Then you would add the declaration for that element to your style sheet:

```
figure {float: left;}
```

The float: left code tells the browser to put the first image next to the left margin of the page. Then, each subsequent image with the float: left style follows suit and sits in a row next to the first image until it reaches the right edge of the browser. If the browser is open wide enough for all the floated images to fit in a single row, they will do so. If the user has the browser window open only enough for two images to fit in a row, then the remaining images will begin a new row beneath the first row (starting again near the left margin).

This is the true meaning of a "liquid layout" in web design, because the page is able to grow or shrink according to the browser window size. Figure 8-8 shows how the images line up next to each other when the browser window is open wide enough.

Padding and Margins

In Chapter 5, we discussed how to use the padding and margin properties to add blank space within and around an element's borders. Those same properties can also be applied to images to specify the space around an image on one, two, three, or all four sides.

For example, suppose you wanted to add a small block of space on the left side of an image, but you didn't want to add any space on the right side because that side fits perfectly with another image. If you added the margin-left property to your style sheet or within your img tag, you could add space only on the left side:

```
<img src="photo.jpg" width="200" height="200" style="margin-left:
25px;">
```

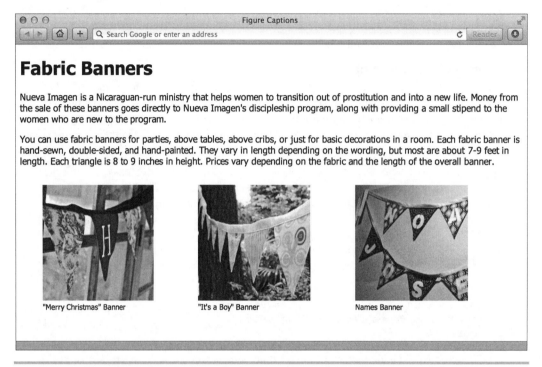

Figure 8-8 A very simple style sheet declaration allows these three photos to float next to each other on the page.

NOTE

The figure element has a default margin of 15 pixels on all four sides, as of this writing, So if you place an image inside figure tags, be sure to set the margin to whatever size you want it to be if you don't want it to be 15 pixels.

Centering

By this point, there's probably a big question still remaining about images and alignment … how to center?! While there isn't a "center" property for images, there is a trick you can use to center an image on the page or within a section. The key lies in changing the way we refer to "centering" an element—in reality, what we're doing is making its left and right margins exactly equal.

First, we must tell the browser to display the image as a *block element.* In CSS, block elements will automatically fill the entire available space. So if an image becomes a block element, its margins will grow until they reach the edges of the browser window.

Next, if you tell the browser to make both the left and right margins the same, you will, in effect, center the image. The following is an example of the code you might use to center an image. First, the style sheet:

```
img.centered {display: block; margin-left: auto; margin-right: auto;}
```

This tells the browser to only apply the style to the centered class when it is used within an img tag.

Then, add the name of the class (in this case, it's "centered") to the img tag. No matter how wide (or narrow) the browser window is opened, the image remains centered horizontally.

Pulling It All Together

Now that we've looked at a few of the most commonly used style properties affecting images, let's pull it all together by reviewing a more complete style sheet for one of the examples used previously from Figure 8-8.

In this instance, the border-radius property is used to round the corners of the images, while the margin property is added to the figure element to control the amount of space between the floated images. Finally, the figure caption's text is made smaller and centered below the image. Figure 8-9 shows how the following code translates into a typical browser view.

```
<!doctype html>
<html>
<head>
<title>Fabric Banners from Nueva Imagen</title>
<style>
body {font-family: Tahoma, Geneva, sans-serif;}
figure {float: left; margin: 5px;}
figcaption {font-size: smaller; text-align: center;}
figure img {border-radius: 20px;}
</style>
</head>
<body>
<div id="bodyCopy">
<h1>Fabric Banners</h1>
<p>Nueva Imagen is a Nicaraguan-run ministry that helps women to
transition out of prostitution and into a new life. Money from the
sale of these banners goes directly to Nueva Imagen's discipleship
program, along with providing a small stipend to the women who are new
to the program.</p>
<p>You can use fabric banners for parties, above tables, above cribs,
or just for basic decorations in a room. Each fabric banner is hand-
sewn, double-sided, and hand-painted.  They vary in length depending
on the wording, but most are about 7-9 feet in length.  Each triangle
is 8 to 9 inches in height.  Prices vary depending on the fabric and
the length of the overall banner.</p>
```

```
<figure>
   <img src="christmas.jpg" alt="Merry Christmas Banner">
   <figcaption>"Merry Christmas" Banner</figcaption>
</figure>
<figure>
  <img src="itsaboy.jpg" alt="It's a Boy Banner">
  <figcaption>"It's a Boy" Banner</figcaption>
</figure>
<figure>
  <img src="names.jpg" alt="Names Banner">
  <figcaption>Names Banner</figcaption>
</figure>
</div>
</body>
</html>
```

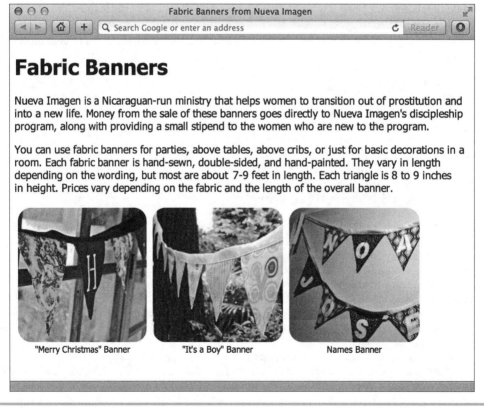

Figure 8-9 The images in this example are arranged and styled through a few key style sheet declarations.

Try This 8-2   Add an Image and Customize Image Characteristics

Returning to one of the web pages you've created, let's first add an image file, and then vary the characteristics of that image. Goals for this project include

- Specifying the height and width for an image

- Providing alternative text and a title for an image

- Linking an image to another web page

- Turning off the border for a linked image

- Aligning an image with the text around it

- Adding some buffer space around an image

1. Open your HTML editor and load one of the pages saved from a previous Try This.

2. Add the appropriate code to insert an appropriate image into the file.

3. Add the `height` and `width` attributes to the image code.

4. Add alternative text and a title to the image.

5. Add 10 pixels of buffer space around the image.

6. Link the image to another page and turn off the image's border.

7. Add another image to the page, making sure to specify the height, width, and alternative text.

8. Align the first image to the right of the text in that section.

9. Align the second image to the left of the text in that section.

10. Save the file.

11. Open your web browser and choose File | Open Page (or Open File or Open, depending on the browser you're using). Locate the file that you just saved.

12. Verify that all your changes were made as you expected. If you need to make additional changes, return to your text editor to do so. When you finish, save the file and switch back to the browser. Choose Refresh or Reload to preview the changes you just made.

You can customize the look and style of the images displayed in the foreground of your web pages in many ways. This project gives you practice with many image properties, including links, alignment, borders, and alternative text.

Use Images as Elements in the Background of a Web Page

Images have another role in a web page, which is in the background. Just as in a theatrical play, where actors may be moving in the foreground while scenery moves in the background, two levels of design also exist in a web page.

The old HTML specifications enabled you to add a single image to be used as the "scenery" in the background of your web page. This was accomplished using the background attribute of the `body` element, as in `<body background="picture.jpg">`. However, the W3C retired the background attribute in favor of using style sheets to specify backgrounds. The latter is done by adding the `background-image` property to a style declaration for the `body` element:

```
body {background-image: url("picture.jpg");}
```

One great advantage of the background property in style sheets is that it can be added to all sorts of page elements, from paragraphs to lists and table cells, using the same format shown for the `body` tag:

```
p {background-image: url("pattern.jpg");}
```

Several benefits arise from using an image in the background as opposed to the foreground:

- You can achieve a layered look in your designs this way, because an image in the foreground can actually be placed on top of the image in the background.

- Background images begin at the top of the page and run all the way to each of the four sides. By contrast, elements in the foreground are subject to borders on the top and left, similar to those that occur when you print something.

- Adding backgrounds to page elements (like navigation bars or footers) can be a great way to set that content apart from the rest of the page.

When you insert a background image with HTML, you need to remember a few other things:

- **All background images tile by default**   *Tiling* means background images repeat in the browser window as many times as needed to cover the whole screen.

- **You can only include one image in the background**   So, if you want to use two different patterns in your background, they need to be included in a single image file.

- **Text in the foreground must be readable on top of the background**   If you're using dark colors in your background, make sure the text on your page is much lighter. Likewise, try to avoid high-contrast backgrounds because they make it extremely difficult to read any text placed on top of them.

- **Background images should be small in file size**   This avoids a long download time. Take advantage of the fact that the browser repeats a background image and cut your image down as much as possible.

To help clarify these points, look at Figure 8-10. If I told you the darker bar on the left, as well as the word "Corinna" and the stars, are all in the background, could you imagine what the background image itself looks like when it isn't tiled? Figure 8-11 gives the answer.

Because the original image was only 1000 pixels wide but only 100 pixels tall, it appears to repeat more vertically than horizontally. Testing your pages on different screen sizes is important to ensure your background images are repeating as you expect.

You can force the background image to remain stationary by adding the `background-attachment` property to the page's style sheet. This property allows the background to stay in place (when set to *fixed*) or to move when the page is scrolled (when set to *scroll*). Similarly, you can even tell the browser whether or not to repeat your background image at all using the `background-repeat` property.

```
body {background-image: url("picture.gif");
     background-attachment: fixed;
     background-repeat: no-repeat;}
```

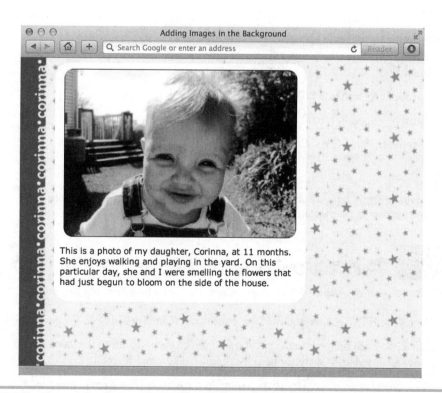

Figure 8-10   Here, a background image enables me to achieve a layered look because the photo in the foreground lies over the top of the image in the background.

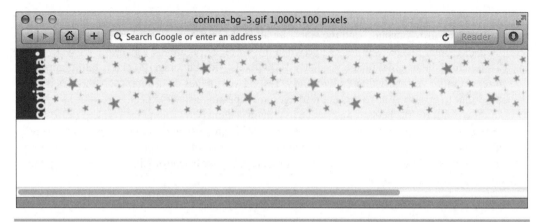

Figure 8-11 Before the image was tiled by the browser in Figure 8-10, it looked like this.

Possible values of the `background-repeat` property are

- **repeat**   Specifies the file should repeat both horizontally and vertically (which is the default)

- **repeat-x**   Specifies the file should repeat horizontally only

- **repeat-y**   Specifies the file should repeat vertically only

- **no-repeat**   Specifies the file should not repeat

TIP

You can find many images suitable for background tiles in the same clipart catalogs mentioned earlier in the chapter.

Try This 8-3   Add a Background Image

This final project in Chapter 8 gives you a chance to add a background image to your page.

1. Open your HTML editor and load the page saved from Try This 8-2.

2. Add a patterned image into the background of the page. (Refer to the stock image resources listed previously for help locating a background image.)

3. Make any changes necessary to the colors of the text on your page in order to ensure it remains readable against the new background.

4. Save the file.

5. Open your web browser and choose File | Open Page (or Open File or Open, depending on the browser you are using). Locate the file you just saved.

6. Preview the page to check your work. If you need to make changes, return to your text editor to do so. After making any changes, save the file and switch back to the browser. Choose Refresh or Reload to preview the changes you just made.

Adding an image in the background can add depth and appeal to your web pages when used wisely. This activity gives you practice using the background-image property with the body tag to add a background image.

TIP

Having trouble getting your background to display? If so, make sure the image file is located in the same directory as your HTML file. If it isn't, you need to specify the correct file location in the background-image property. For more tips, see Appendix C.

Extra Credit

Try reformatting the page you just completed using an internal style sheet. Some formatting possibilities might be to

- Specify that the background image should only repeat along the horizontal axis. You could also try repeating it only along the vertical axis.

- Specify that the background image should remain fixed at the top of the page and should not scroll with the page. Alternatively, you could specify that the background image should always be displayed at the top of the screen, even if the user has scrolled.

Chapter 8 Self Test

1. What does the src attribute do?

2. Why is it important to specify the height and width of images in web pages?

3. Which style sheet properties enable you to add blank space around images?

4. Which attribute must be added to an img tag to designate the image as a client-side image map?

5. Which two elements are used when defining a client-side image map's name and hot spots?

6. You are creating the code for a client-side image map, and one of the rectangular hot spots has the following coordinates: 0,0 (upper left); 50,0 (upper right); 50,50 (lower right); and 0,50 (lower left). Which are used in the following coords attribute?

```
<area shape="rect" coords="_____"       href="maryland.html">
```

7. Fill in the blank: The value of the `height` and `width` attributes is measured in _____.

8. Fix the following code:

```
<img href="contact.jpg">
```

9. Add the appropriate style declaration to use wallpaper.gif as a background for the web page code shown next. Note that the graphic is in the same folder as the HTML file.

```
body {                    }
```

10. What are the four possible values of the `clear` property (used to clear floats)?

11. Fill in the blank: The default value of the `border` property is ____ pixels for linked images and _____ pixels for nonlinked images.

12. True/False: You can achieve a layered look in your designs when an image in the foreground is placed on top of an image in the background.

13. What value must be used with the display property before you can center an image using the method discussed in this chapter?

```
img.centered {display:      ;
     margin-left: auto;
     margin-right: auto;}
```

14. Which attribute is used to add alternative text to an image?

15. Which statement is not true about background images?

A. All background images tile by default.

B. You can only include one image in the background.

C. Background images are added to web pages with the `background` tag.

D. Background images begin at the top of the page and run all the way to each of the four sides.

Chapter 9

Working with Multimedia

Key Skills & Concepts

- Understand How Plug-ins Are Used with Web Browsers

- Link to Different Types of Media from a Web Page

- Embed Different Types of Media into a Web Page

- Style Multimedia Content

On the Internet, the term *multimedia* is used to refer to presentations of various types of media, such as audio, video, text, graphics, or animation, which are integrated into a single file format. You may have seen multimedia presentations on news or weather sites, where they are used to display audio, video, and text to viewers. Other sites use multimedia to entertain viewers, often in the form of a cartoon or an animated story.

Many forms of multimedia enable visitors to interact with the presentations. For example, a visitor might be watching an animated story and then click the individual characters to learn more about them before continuing.

The Web itself is often considered multimedia because any web page can contain several different types of media files in it. By default, however, for many years web browsers were only capable of understanding HTML files, graphics files such as GIF and JPEG, and plain text documents (.txt). Any other file types needed to be handled through a plug-in, or helper application. Sometimes these types of controls came preinstalled in the browser, but other times they had to be downloaded by the user.

Thankfully, HTML5—and modern browsers that support it—gives us a built-in way to handle audio and video files without requiring the user to install anything. The caveat is that, as of this writing, the browsers have not yet caught up to this part of the standard and don't uniformly support the same file format. So while we still need to use helper applications for certain multimedia files, as well as for audio and video to be displayed in older browsers, things have gotten much easier in this realm. We'll go over the details of those new elements later in this chapter.

Understand How Plug-ins Are Used with Web Browsers

Until modern browsers uniformly support the popular multimedia formats, plenty of folks will still need help displaying audio and video files in certain browsers and on certain devices. A *helper application* is an additional piece of software or code that attempts to do something the browser cannot, whereas a *plug-in* (or an *ActiveX control,* as Microsoft calls theirs) extends the browser capabilities. If you thought of yourself as the browser, then a helper might be someone who mows your lawn for you, while a plug-in is a ride-on mower that helps you do it yourself. A plug-in enables the browser to do something itself, as opposed to the helper application performing the operation for the browser.

NOTE
ActiveX is a brand name used by Microsoft to reference its various technologies that offer added functionality to web browsers.

For example, if your web browser doesn't know how to display a certain type of video file, it first looks for a plug-in capable of doing so. If your web browser doesn't find a plug-in, it might prompt you to download one or look for a helper application loaded on the computer that could display the video. If the browser cannot find a suitable plug-in or helper application, and one isn't downloaded, then it won't be able to display the file. For this reason, I do not recommend including essential information in files requiring plug-ins or helper applications, unless you also provide an alternative text-only version.

Helpers are stand-alone programs, separate from your browser, that you can purchase for your computer. By contrast, plug-ins are usually free and can be easily downloaded from the Internet. In some cases, web browsers even come with certain plug-ins. When you download a plug-in, you should receive instructions on how to install it, if necessary.

Many times, the plug-in installs itself and you only need to close and reopen your web browser. Other times, you're asked to place the plug-in in the appropriate folder on your computer and then restart your browser. Once you agree to download a plug-in or ActiveX control, the browser downloads and installs the control, usually without relaunching the browser.

Identify the Installed Components

You can find out which plug-ins are installed under your browser in a few different ways. For example, the most rudimentary way to check for installed components is to look in the "plug-ins" directory in your browser's application folder. Firefox users can choose Tools | Add-Ons and then click the Plugins tab.

If you're using Internet Explorer, choose Internet Options from the Tools menu in your browser. Next, click the Programs tab, and then click the Manage Add-ons button to view a list of all add-ons (including ActiveX controls and plug-ins) used by Internet Explorer.

Recognize File Types, Extensions, and Appropriate Plug-ins

You may want to link or embed many different file types in your web pages, but Appendix E lists some of the more popular ones. Most file types can be "played" with at least one plug-in or helper application and, quite often, with more than one. If you want to be helpful to your visitors, list the plug-in or helper application they might use to open your files. You could also provide a link to download the appropriate plug-in.

For example, Flash, a file type requiring a plug-in, is popular enough that it ships with most browsers. Even so, you might have visited a web site and noticed a window pop-up saying something about "downloading the Flash player." Flash files enjoy widespread use because they're small (which translates as "quick to download!") and can include sound, video, interactivity, and animation. Another reason Flash is so popular is that the plug-in used to display Flash files is widely available on a large variety of platforms and browsers.

NOTE

Some plug-ins and helper applications aren't available for multiple computer systems and browsers. Refer to Appendix E at the back of the book for a list of file types, extensions, and descriptions.

When you're ready to include multimedia files in your HTML pages, consider how you want to include them. Do you want to *link* to them so that your visitors can choose whether to download them or view them now? Or do you want to *embed* them within your page, so they appear right within the web browser window? The rest of this chapter focuses on linking to and embedding several different types of multimedia.

Link to Different Types of Media from a Web Page

A link to a multimedia file is essentially the same as any other link. While embedding a file can sometimes be problematic (as discussed in the next section), a link to a file can be especially useful because links are understood by all web browsers. Figure 9-1 shows how the following code is displayed in a browser, while Figure 9-3 shows the result of clicking the video link.

```
<p>So what exactly do they do here? <a href="CompelledbyCompassion.m4v">Watch
this quick video</a> to find out.</p>
```

This is the phrase users can click to access the family video.

The name and location of the file are used as the value of the `href` attribute.

TIP

Including the proper file extension for your media file is important so that the browser and operating system can understand and display it. If you're unsure as to which file extension to use, check Appendix E in this book.

Clicking the link shown in Figure 9-1 would cause one of three things to happen, depending on how the system was set up:

- It may prompt the user to download the file and either view it now or save it for later (see Figure 9-2).

- If the browser recognizes the file as one it is set up to display automatically, it may take over and do just that (see Figure 9-3).

Knowing that many systems may handle your multimedia files differently, try to offer your visitors as much guidance and instruction as possible. For example, list the size of the file

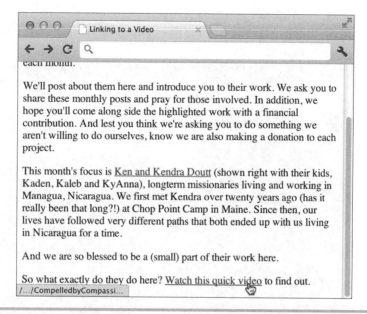

Figure 9-1 A link to a multimedia file is the same as any other link because it also uses the a tag and the `href` attribute.

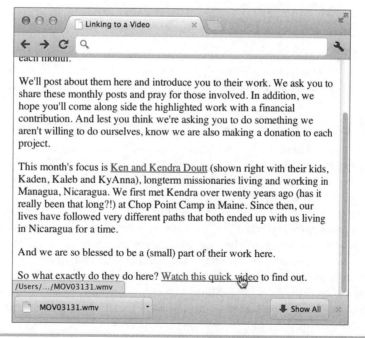

Figure 9-2 When the browser doesn't recognize a file type as one it should "play" within the browser, it may prompt the user to download the file.

Figure 9-3 When the link is clicked, the browser may be able to play the video itself if the appropriate plug-in or ActiveX control is installed.

you're asking them to download, so they can consider whether they want to wait for it to load to their system. In addition, provide alternative ways of getting the information, and include it within the multimedia files wherever possible.

Embed Different Types of Media onto a Web Page

When you embed multimedia files instead of linking to them, they appear right within the context of your page. As long as the appropriate plug-in or ActiveX control is installed on the user's computer, or the media file is supported natively, the file will load and play along with anything else that might be on that page.

The original method for embedding multimedia was to use the embed element. However, that was a proprietary tag created by Netscape. As a result, the W3C created its own object element as a method for embedding various types of media, from images to Flash movies and more. It was supported by version 3 (and later) of Internet Explorer, as well as all current versions of Mozilla-based browsers (such as Safari and Firefox).

Even though the object element finally brought some unity to the method by which media files were embedded, there lacked a built-in format for adding multimedia files to a web page.

Now, with HTML5, we have the addition of several new elements designed to natively handle the process of embedding audio and video:

- **\<audio\>**   Embeds audio content

- **\<video\>**   Embeds video content

- **\<source\>**   Specifies multiple sources for audio and video content

- **\<track\>**   Specifies text explanations for audio and video content

- **\<embed\>**   Specifies content to be played in older browsers

Start with the audio and video Elements

The development of these new elements means you can insert audio and video files almost as simply as image files. It all begins with the audio and video elements. Here, let's look at a basic example:

```
<video src="videoFile.mp4" controls preload></video>
<audio src="audioFile.mp3" controls preload></audio>
```

In this case, each element includes just three supportive attributes. First, the src attribute works the same as it does with the img element in that it identifies the source file to be displayed. The controls attribute, when present, tells the browser to make the audio or video controls visible to the user by default. The preload attribute, when included, requests the browser to preload the media file in an effort to reduce the chance users might have to wait for it to start even after pressing play.

Customize with Attributes

As with the majority of HTML elements, the customization happens with the attributes. The three from the previous example, as well as other commonly used attributes, are listed in Tables 9-1 and 9-2. The following code example shows how a few more of these attributes can be used to customize an embedded video:

```
<video src="videoFile.mp4" width="300" height="200" controls autoplay
poster="videoStill.jpg"></video>
```

NOTE
Most mobile browsers ignore the autoplay and preload attributes to avoid unsolicited downloads over cellular networks at the user's expense.

Specify Sources

The final step in the audio and video embed process is to specify a variety of file format options. But wait, you might say, I thought the audio and video elements were introduced to make things easier? That is certainly the plan, but as with any new feature, everyone has to get up to speed first.

Attribute	Value	Description
autoplay	n/a	When included, the audio will begin playing as soon as the content is loaded.
autobuffer	n/a	When included, the audio will begin buffering automatically, even if the file is not set to autoplay, to help the audio run smoothly when it is played.
controls	n/a	When included, the controls will be visible and accessible to users.
loop	n/a	When included, the audio will automatically begin again.
preload	n/a	When included, the browser will prepare the audio to play as soon as the page is loaded. (This attribute is ignored if autoplay is turned on.)
src	URL	Specifies the location of the file to embed.

Table 9-1 Attributes for the audio Element

Audio and video file formats are the big sticking point here. The current HTML5 draft does not specify exactly which file formats should be included, but leaves that up to browser developers. As luck would have it, the browser developers are not in agreement regarding which formats should be standard. So that brings us to codecs and containers.

Attribute	Value	Description
autoplay	n/a	When included, the video will begin playing as soon as the content is loaded.
autobuffer	n/a	When included, the video will begin buffering automatically, even if the file is not set to autoplay, to help the video run smoothly when it is played.
controls	n/a	When included, the controls will be visible and accessible to users.
height	Number of pixels	Specifies the height of the video's display area.
loop	n/a	When included, the video will automatically begin again.
preload	n/a	When included, the browser will prepare the video to play as soon as the page is loaded. (This attribute is ignored if autoplay is turned on.)
poster	URL	Specifies the location of a static image file to be displayed until the video starts.
src	URL	Specifies the location of the file to embed.
width	Number of pixels	Specifies the width of the video's display area.

Table 9-2 Attributes for the video Element

Codecs and Containers

In Chapter 8, you learned that JPEG offers file compression for still images. The method by which a file is compressed to lower file size is referred to as its *codec*. For many years, the most common video codec has been MPEG. Over the past decade and a half, the MPEG codec has been revised and refined, and additional codecs have been developed. Generally speaking, the newer codecs offer better compression and image quality, but are not as widely supported as the older codecs.

In addition to the codec, or compression method, we must deal with the *container format*. You might consider the container to be the wrapper, or packaging, of the audio or video content, as well as its codec. Sometimes, the codec and container have a particularly close relationship, but other times not.

To make things a bit more confusing, either the codec *or* the container name can be used as the file suffix. For instance, a file called movieFile.mov is simply a packaged file that happens to be in the QuickTime container format. But it could contain any number of different audio or video codecs with the content inside. Likewise, moviefile.mp4 uses the MPEG-4 codec, but could be packaged in a variety of different file containers.

So why haven't we standardized on a set of codecs and containers? The primary reason mostly has to do with money. (Doesn't it always?) More specifically, some codecs—such as H.264/MPEG4—are patent-protected and require licenses (and fees) to be used by developers. Other codecs—like the Ogg and WebM formats—do not require licenses to use. Because of that, many browser developers are pushing for the open formats to be adopted as standard. However, as of this writing, no official determination has been made by the W3C.

What that means to us, as web developers, is this: We typically must save our audio and video content in at least two different file formats (and sometimes more) in order to reach the widest possible audience. Table 9-3 outlines the most common codecs and containers (listed under the File Format column) and the corresponding browser support.

The big black hole, so to speak, of native audio support is in the Android browser. Because there are so many variants of that browser, it is almost impossible to specify exactly how many Android users will be able to hear these audio files. Because the market is so splintered, and the different options offer so little audio support, it is wise to offer alternative methods for these users to access your content. Flash is currently supported in Android browsers, although that support is expected to go away in favor of HTML5 codecs. Hopefully, the HTML5 support will be uniform by that time.

List Multiple Sources

To include multiple sources, we actually pull the source out of the audio or video element, instead listing it through its own source element. The following example shows three possible sources for a single instance of audio in a page. First, the browser is told to look for an .aac file. If the browser cannot play that first file, then it looks at the second source, and the third

File Format	File Type	Android	Chrome 9+	Firefox 15+	IE 9+	Opera 10+	Safari 3+
MPEG 4, MP3/ACC	Audio	?	Y	N	Y	Y	Y
Ogg, Vorbis/Opus	Audio	?	Y	Y	N	Y	Y
WAVE, PCM	Audio	?	N	Y	Y	N	Y
WebM, Vorbis	Audio	?	Y	Y	N	Y	Y
MPEG 4, H.264, MP3/ACC	Video	Y	Y*	N	Y	N	Y
Ogg, Theora, Vorbis	Video	Y	Y	Y	N	Y	Y**
QuickTime/MOV	Video	N	N	N	N	N	Y
WebM, VP8, Vorbis	Video	Y	Y	Y	Y	Y	Y**

* Google indicated it would remove support of these file formats from Chrome, but as of this writing they are still supporting them.
** Does not include iOS Safari support.

Table 9-3   Audio and Video File Format Support

source, in that order. As soon as the browser finds a file it can play, it stops searching and will not load any of the other source files.

```
<audio controls autoplay>
    <source src="audioFile.aac">
    <source src="audioFile.oga">
    <source src="audioFile.wav">
</audio>
```

TIP
Notice in Table 9-3 that if you provide media in both MPEG-4 and Ogg formats, you will reach a pretty wide audience among HTML5-supporting browsers.

Because files can be referenced by either their codec or container file extension, it's important to include the `type` attribute with the `source` element. This helps the browser decide whether it can play the media, without having to actually load the content.

```
<audio controls autoplay>
    <source src="audioFile.aac" type="audio/mp4">
    <source src="audioFile.oga" type="audio/ogg">
    <source src="audioFile.wav" type="audio/wav">
</audio>
```

If necessary, you can even include the codecs parameter inside of the `type` attribute to identify the exact version of the codec needed to play the file:

```
<source src="audioFile.aac" type="audio/mp4; codecs=mp4a.40.2">
```

Provide Fallback Options

If the browser is incapable of playing any of the specified formats, there are two more bits of code to add to help those users. First, you can include the `object` element, which was the preferred method of embedding audio and video prior to HTML5. This means any browser not supporting HTML5's video element can likely display the content using the `object` element. Then, for anyone else, a simple link to a text transcript can be included before the closing video tag.

```
<video controls>
    <source src="videoFile.mp4" type="video/mp4">
    <source src="videoFile.ogv" type="video/ogg">
    <object type="application/x-shockwave-flash"
            data="videoFile.swf"
            height="480"
            width="640"></object>
    Sorry, your browser doesn't support this video content.
    Here's a link to a <a href="transcript.txt">text transcript</a>.
</video
```

More About the object Tag

As mentioned, prior to HTML5 the `object` element was the preferred method of embedding audio and video. I'm including a brief review of that element here because it is still in use for non-HTML5–supporting browsers.

When you use the `object` tag, the `type` and `data` attributes are used to tell the browser what type of file you are embedding and where to locate that file:

```
<object type="application/x-shockwave-flash" data="movie.swf"
height="60" height="200">
```

Then, after the opening `object` tag, you add any properties you want to specify using the `param` tag (short for *parameters*). (Note that the `object` element enables you to specify the `height` and `width` attributes either in the `object` tag or in `param` tags, depending on the plug-in employed.)

```
<param name="movie" value="movie.swf">
<param name="BGCOLOR" value="#ffffff">
```

Finally, you close the `object` tag.

```
</object>
```

Table 9-4 lists some commonly used attributes for the `object` element. Note that some of these attributes work only with certain file formats. When using the object element to embed multimedia, I recommend checking the developer documentation for the particular media type.

TIP

Whenever you embed audio within a web page, it's always considered good practice to display at least some portion of the controls. This lets visitors turn off the sound or adjust the volume as they see fit.

Java Applets

You can also use the `object` tag to embed Java applets in your web page. *Java applets* are mini-applications (which is where we get the term *applet*) written in the Java programming language that can run within your browser window. Web developers use these mini-applications to do things that aren't easily accomplished through HTML or other means.

Attribute	Value	Description
autoplay	true false	Defines whether the file immediately starts playing when the page is loaded.
controller	true false	QuickTime movies only. Turns on the movie controller.
controls	console playbutton pausebutton smallconsole stopbutton volumelever	Specifies the style of the controller displayed in the web page. Used mostly for audio files.
height	Number of pixels	Specifies the height of the window (video/animation) or controller (sound).
loop	true false # (number of times)	Defines how a file repeats. True tells the browser to loop the file infinitely. False specifies to never loop. Alternatively, you can specify the exact number of times it should loop.
name	*Name*	Gives a (case-sensitive) name to the file so that it can be referenced by a script or other method.
standby	*Text to be displayed*	Specifies text to be displayed while the object is loading.
type	MIME type	Specifies the type of file being embedded, which then defines the plug-in needed.
volume	Number between 0 and 100	Specifies the volume of the sound file.
width	Number of pixels	Specifies the width of the window (video/animation) or controller (sound).

Table 9-4 Commonly Used Attributes for the `object` Element

TIP

You can learn much more about embedding Flash files by visiting an online tutorial, such as **www.w3schools.com/flash**.

Java applets can be used to add functionality to your web pages, whether through a real-time clock, a mortgage calculator, a stock ticker, or an interactive game.

TIP

Visit **http://docs.oracle.com/javase/tutorial/deployment/applet/** to learn more about developing Java applets.

The following is an example of how to embed these applets using the `object` element:

```
<object type="application/x-java-applet" height="300" width="400">
   <param name="code" value="Test">
   <param name="archive" value="Test.jar">
   <param name="codebase" value="http://www.test.com/test/">
   This text will display if the Java plug-in doesn't run.
</object>
```

Add Text Tracks

In recent years, there has been an increased initiative to ensuring all multimedia content is made accessible to nontraditional users. One example of this might be including captions for audio and video content. HTML5 has introduced the track element for just that purpose.

NOTE

As of this writing, the track element is only supported by IE 10+ and Chrome 18+. However, it only works in Chrome 18 if the `track` element is enabled by the user from the chrome://flags options page. (Type **chrome://flags** in the browser's address bar and scroll to find the "Enable <track> element" section.)

When placed inside an `audio` or `video` element, track tags provide links to text-based files in one or more languages. Those files can contain any of the following five kinds of tracks, which are specified inside the kind attribute. Table 9-5 lists possible values of the kind attribute, as well as the other attributes for the track element.

Here's a code example showing tracks for subtitles in two different languages:

```
<video src="videoFile.m4p">
    <track kind="subtitles" src="EnglishSubtitles.vtt" srclang="en"
default label="English Subtitles"></track>
    <track kind="subtitles" src="SpanishSubtitles.vtt" srclang="sp"
label="Spanish Subtitles"></track>
</video>
```

Attribute	Value	Description
default	n/a	Specifies, when used, that this track should be used by default (unless the user's browser preferences indicate otherwise).
kind	captions chapters descriptions metadata subtitles	Identifies the type of text track.
label	*text*	Identifies the track's title.
src	*URL*	Specifies the location of the track file.
srclang	*language_code*	Defines the language of the track. (This attribute is required if the kind is set to subtitles.)

Table 9-5 Attributes for the `track` Element

WebVTT Tracks

Web Video Text Tracks, or WebVTT for short, are the new standard for multimedia track files. Essentially, a track file is a series of cues, which are each composed of a time stamp and the text to be displayed onscreen. Here's an example of what a small portion of a WebVTT file might look like:

```
WEBVTT
00:00:01.000 --> 00:00:06.000
OK, here's some winter fetch with Rocky!

00:00:16.000 --> 00:00:20.000
Come on back now, here Rocky!
```

Figure 9-4 shows how the first bit of text translates when displayed in Chrome. Note it is not possible to test tracks like this locally on your computer. In other words, you must upload them to a live web server in order to test the captions. Eventually, when this element garners wider browser support, users will be able to select between the available language tracks.

In the meantime, the formatting of the time stamp is extremely important and must follow this format: *hours:minutes:seconds.milliseconds,* where hours, minutes, and seconds each have two digits and milliseconds has three.

TIP

Here's a site where you can validate your WebVTT file to make sure it is formatting correctly: **http://quuz.org/webvtt**. And for more on writing WebVTT files, visit **http://dev.w3.org/html5/webvtt**.

Figure 9-4 Contents of this English subtitles track when displayed in Chrome

Use embed for Non-native Multimedia Content

The expectation is that most of your multimedia content can be handled through the audio and video elements in HTML5. But for those instances where you must include content not supported in that way, we have the embed element. This new element works well for content requiring an external helper application or plug-in, such as Adobe Flash.

```
<embed src="flashFile.swf" type="application/x-shockwave-flash"
width="600" height="400">
```

In this example, the embed tag includes all four of the attributes listed in Table 9-6 to help the browser appropriately display the media file. Because the embed element is empty, there is no need to include a closing tag.

Attribute	Value	Description
height	*pixels*	Defines the height of the media content.
src	URL	Defines the location of the media content.
type	MIME type	Defines the type of file being embedded.
width	*pixels*	Defines the width of the media content.

Table 9-6 Attributes for the embed Element

Style Multimedia Content

Because the new methods for adding multimedia content are native HTML5 elements, they can be styled with CSS the same way other page elements can. For example, we can use styles to change the opacity of a video, add borders, or even change the look and feel of the controls.

Figure 9-5 shows a sample custom controller from the Safari Developer Library. To see what it might look like to pull something like this off, check out **http://developer.apple.com/ library/safari/#samplecode/HTML5VideoPlayer/Introduction/Intro.html#//apple_ref/doc/ uid/DTS40008930**.

Even if you're not quite ready to tackle a full-scale player overhaul, there are plenty of quick and easy style changes you can make to help your media files integrate into your site's

Figure 9-5 This video controller has been styled with CSS to match the look and feel of the rest of the web site.

design. For example, you could add some padding and margin space and then enclose the video inside a border, as I did in the following illustration.

```
video { width: 300px; border: 5px solid #666 ; border-radius: 10px;
padding:10px; margin: 25px; }
```

You can also play around with some new CSS styles not yet fully functional, but nevertheless exciting. In August 2012, the W3C released a new draft for applying filters to HTML elements. (Read more here: **https://dvcs.w3.org/hg/FXTF/raw-file/tip/filters/index.html**.) This means you could change the hue and saturation of a video, for instance, through the browser without having to go back and re-render the actual video footage. Figure 9-6 shows an example of the result of using the following code to do just that:

```
<!doctype html>
<html>
    <head><title>Web Filter Test</title>
    <style>
        video {float: left;width: 50%;}
        .filtered {-webkit-filter: hue-rotate(180deg)
saturate(200%);}
    </style>
</head>
<body>
<video src="winter-fetch.m4v"></video>
<video src="winter-fetch.m4v" class="filtered"></video>
</body>
</html>
```

Figure 9-6 The hue and saturation of this video have been altered through the use of a CSS filter style. (The image on the right is mostly yellow in blue, while the one on the left is normal.)

Even though this screen capture makes it look like CSS filters are ready to use, I'm afraid we still have a little way to go yet in terms of browser support. During testing, I found the video controller disappeared when a filter was applied to the video, even with the controls set to display. So if you decide to experiment with CSS filters—which I certainly suggest doing— just be sure to thoroughly test your files in a variety of end-user situations before making them live for the general population.

Try This 9-1 Add Multimedia to a Web Page

Now you're going to create a link to a video file. You can use any video file just for practice. Try searching your computer for video files to see what you have available. If you cannot find anything on your personal computer, find your favorite YouTube video and click the link to embed the video. Then, follow the directions to use YouTube's code to embed the video in your page. For extra credit, try to adjust their code to use the HTML5 elements discussed in this chapter.

1. Open your text or HTML editor and then one of the pages saved from a previous Try This exercise.

2. Add a video file to the page in the most appropriate location.

3. Float the video to the left of the text content around it.

4. Add ten pixels of margin space to the right of the video.

5. Save the file.

6. Open your web browser and choose File | Open Page (or Open File or Open, depending on the browser you're using). Locate the file you just saved. Make sure the link works and the movie plays.

7. If you need to make changes, return to your text editor to do so. After making any changes, save the file and switch back to the browser. Choose Refresh or Reload to preview the changes you just made.

Multimedia can add a lot of interest to a web page. This project gave you practice embedding a multimedia file. Because multimedia support varies so widely, be sure to test your page in a variety of browsers and situations before making it live for the general public.

Chapter 9 Self Test

1. What's the difference between a plug-in and a helper application?

2. Which element does the W3C recommend for embedding video in a web page?

3. How can users determine which plug-ins are installed on their computers, and how they can download new plug-ins?

4. What are two ways to include multimedia files in a web site?

5. True/False: Clicking a link to a sound file automatically downloads the file and saves it for later listening.

6. What are two ways to specify the height and width of multimedia files embedded with the `object` tag?

7. Fix the following code:

```
<embed href="sillyme.mov" height="100" width="50">
```

8. Add the appropriate code here to link to wendy.mov. Note that the movie is in the same folder as the HTML file.

```
<html>
<head>
   <title>Home Movie</title>
</head>
<body>
<                         >View my home movie!<      >
</body>
</html>
```

9. Which attribute can cause a video to play even before the user clicks the play button?

10. Which element can be used to provide subtitles for a video?

11. True/False: A link to a multimedia file is the same as any other link because it also uses the a element.

12. What is the purpose of the `poster` attribute?

13. Which element tells the browser where to find the actual audio or video content?

14. Which element is used to add Flash files to a web page coded with HTML5?

Chapter 10

Creating Lists

Key Skills & Concepts

- Use Ordered Lists in a Web Page
- Use Unordered Lists in a Web Page
- Use Definition Lists in a Web Page
- Combine and Nest Two or More Types of Lists in a Web Page
- Style Lists

Lists are everywhere—on your refrigerator, in schoolbooks, next to the telephone, on bills, and in all sorts of other documents. That's why there's a special set of tags just for creating lists. This chapter focuses on the three different types of lists possible in HTML:

- Ordered lists
- Unordered lists
- Definition lists

Lists are especially useful in web pages to draw attention to short pieces of information. Keep that in mind when you create your lists, and try to include short phrases, instead of long sentences, in each list item.

Use Ordered Lists in a Web Page

An *ordered list* is one in which each item is preceded by a number or letter. For example:
My favorite fruits are:

1. raspberries

2. strawberries

3. apples

If you want to create the previous list on a web page, you should use an ordered list. Here's what the HTML code would look like:

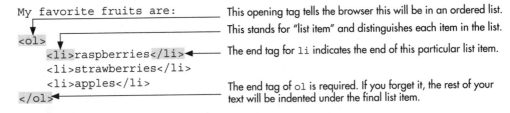

```
My favorite fruits are:
<ol>
    <li>raspberries</li>
    <li>strawberries</li>
    <li>apples</li>
</ol>
```

This opening tag tells the browser this will be in an ordered list.

This stands for "list item" and distinguishes each item in the list.

The end tag for li indicates the end of this particular list item.

The end tag of ol is required. If you forget it, the rest of your text will be indented under the final list item.

NOTE
While it's not required, I indent the list items to make seeing the structure of the list easier.

Notice I didn't include any numbers in my list. This is because I used the `ol` element to tell the browser this is an ordered list. When browsers see ordered lists, they know to place a number in front of each list item.

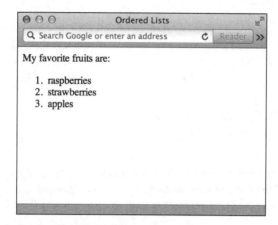

The default type of ordered list uses Arabic numbers, but you can use the `type` attribute to change that. Table 10-1 identifies the different types of ordered lists you can create with the `type` attribute.

To change the type of ordered list, add the `type` attribute and its value to the opening `ol` tag:

```
<ol type="I">
    <li>Introduction</li>
    <li>Understanding the Medium</li>
    <li>Basic Page Structure</li>
</ol>
```

Type Attribute Value	Numbering Style	Example
1	Arabic numbers	1, 2, 3,...
a	Lowercase alphabet	a, b, c,...
A	Uppercase alphabet	A, B, C,...
i	Lowercase Roman numerals	i, ii, iii,...
I	Uppercase Roman numerals	I, II, III,...

Table 10-1 Ordered List Types

Here, I changed the type to "I," which tells the browser to place uppercase Roman numerals in front of each list item. So the previous code would create a list like the following:

I. Introduction

II. Understanding the Medium

III. Basic Page Structure

You can also specify the starting number or letter for an ordered list with the `start` attribute. The default for the starting number is 1. To change this, add the `start` attribute to your `ol` tag:

```
<ol type="a" start="3">
    <li>Color</li>
    <li>Working with Text</li>
    <li>Working with Links</li>
</ol>
```

Even though the value of the `type` attribute may be something other than Arabic numerals, the value of the `start` attribute is always an integer. So, in the previous example, `start="3"` actually tells the browser to start the list with the third letter because `type="a"`.

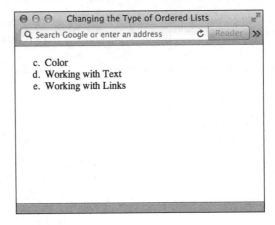

If you want to change an individual value—for example, if you want to make the third item in the list use the letter *g*—you can add the `value` attribute to the specific `li` tag:

```
<ol type="a" start="3">
    <li>Color</li>
    <li>Working with Text</li>
    <li value="7">Working with Links</li>
</ol>
```

As with the `start` attribute, the `value` attribute is always an integer. The browser looks at the value of the third list item and changes it to *g* because the type is *a.*

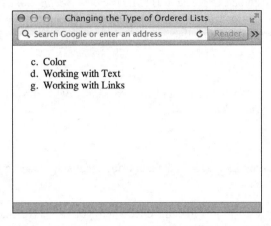

You can also reverse the order completely by adding the reversed attribute to your opening `ol` tag. In this case, the list would be ordered 3, 2, 1 instead of the default 1, 2, 3.

```
<ol reversed>
    <li>Color</li>
    <li>Working with Text</li>
    <li>Working with Links</li>
</ol>
```

Use Unordered Lists in a Web Page

The second type of list is similar to the first, except *unordered lists* don't use numbers or letters. As the name suggests, unordered lists don't rely on order for importance. These lists use bullets to precede each list item. The following is an example of an unordered list:

- Red

- Green

- Blue

You still use the `li` element to identify each item in the list, but instead of beginning with the `ol` element, unordered lists are contained within the `ul` element:

```
<ul>
    <li>red</li>
    <li>green</li>
    <li>blue</li>
</ul>
```

Aside from that, the code used to create the first two types of lists is the same.

Use Definition Lists in a Web Page

The third type of list you can create in HTML is called a *definition list*. As its name suggests, you might use a definition list to show terms and their definitions. For example, in the following list, the term is listed on the first line and then the definition is on the line below the term:

W3C

    The World Wide Web Consortium was created in 1994 to develop standards and protocols for the World Wide Web.

HTML

    Hypertext Markup Language is the authoring language used to create documents for the World Wide Web.

A definition list works just like this one, where you use HTML tags to identify the terms and definitions for each of the list items. The dl element sets up the definition list, while the dt element contains the definition term, and the dd element is used for the actual definition data.

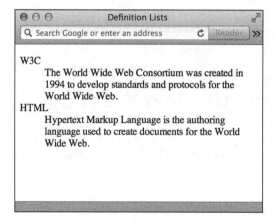

The code to create the page shown in the preceding illustration looks like this:

```
<dl>
  <dt>W3C</dt>
    <dd>The World Wide Web Consortium was created in 1994 to develop
standards and protocols for the World Wide Web.</dd>
  <dt>HTML</dt>
    <dd>Hypertext Markup Language is the authoring language used to
create documents for the World Wide Web.</dd>
  </dl>
```

You can use more than one dd for each dt if you need to; the browser will just simply indent each line below the dt.

Combine and Nest Two or More Types of Lists in a Web Page

You can also use another list inside itself or even one type of list inside another type of list. Each time you use a list inside another list, you are *nesting* lists. Perhaps the best example for nested lists is an outline like those created for a term paper.

I. Introduction

II. Part 1

    A. Description

    B. Examples

        1. Reference One

        2. Reference Two

III. Part 2

IV. Summary

Can you imagine what the HTML code would look like for the preceding outline? The best solution would be to use a series of nested ordered lists as shown in the following illustration and code:

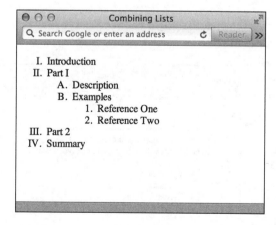

```
<ol type="I">
<li>Introduction</li>
<li>Part I
    <ol type="A">
        <li>Description</li>
        <li>Examples
```

```
            <ol type="1">
                <li>Reference One</li>
                <li>Reference Two</li>
            </ol>
        </li>
    </ol>
</li>
<li>Part 2</li>
<li>Summary</li>
</ol>
```

As I mentioned before, you can also nest one type of list inside another type. For example, you could include a bulleted list inside a definition list to give further clarification to a definition description. Look at the following illustration and code to see what I mean:

```
<dl>
<dt><b>Morning</b></dt>
    <dd>Corinna wakes up around 7:00.</dd>
    <dd>Change her diaper and dress her.</dd>
    <dd>Feed her breakfast. Some of her favorites are:
        <ul>
            <li>Waffles</li>
            <li>Oatmeal</li>
            <li>Cereal</li>
            <li>Fruit</li>
        </ul>
    </dd>
</dl>
```

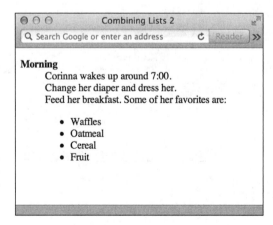

TIP

The most important thing to remember when nesting lists is always to confirm that you have closed each list. If you notice a section of your nested list is indented more than it should be or continues within the list above it, try drawing semicircles from each of the list's opening and closing tags. If any of the circles cross or don't have an ending spot, you may need to recheck your work for errors.

Try This 10-1 Use Lists on Your Web Page

In this project, you create a web page listing your company's products and/or services. Goals for this project include

- Using an ordered list in a web page

- Using an unordered list in a web page

1. Open your text/HTML editor and create a new file entitled **services.html**.

2. Type all the HTML tags needed for a basic web page.

3. Specify a white background color and that the entire page should use the Verdana font.

4. Add the necessary content to describe your site's services, making sure to include at least one ordered and unordered list for practice.

5. Format the top headline as a Level 1 header.

6. Add any other formatting you think is appropriate.

7. Save the file.

8. Open your web browser and choose File | Open Page (or Open File or Open, depending on the browser you're using). Locate the file sessions.html that you just saved. Make sure the file appears as you intended.

9. If you need to make changes, return to your text editor to do so. After making any changes, save the file and switch back to the browser. Choose Refresh or Reload to preview the changes you just made.

Ordered and unordered lists can be great ways to draw attention to important information on your page. This project gave you practice using each type of list in preparation for using them on your own web pages.

TIP

Is the text after your list indented? If so, check to make sure you closed your lists with the proper ending tag (`</ol>` or `</ul>`). For more tips, see Appendix C.

Style Lists

While there is no style sheet property for actually *creating* lists—that's done with HTML, as you just learned—there are three properties that can be particularly useful in formatting lists. Table 10-2 provides details. Note that all three properties can only be used to format *lists* and no other HTML elements.

Customize the Bullets

For example, suppose you wanted to create a list on a web page in which each item was preceded by an image of a star. You could add an image tag to the beginning of each item in a definition list to achieve this sort of thing, such as with the following code:

```
<dd><img src="star.gif" width="12" height="12" alt="star">The World
Wide Web Consortium was created in 1994</dd>
```

But what if you had 20 items in your list? Adding that long img tag to every list item would be tedious. A more efficient alternative is to switch to an unordered list (one with bullets, by default) and use a style sheet in the header of your page to change the regular bullet to the image of your choice. The following code and illustration show how this might work:

```
<style>
li {list-style-image: url(star.gif);}
</style>
```

Sample Property and Value	Description	Possible Values
list-style-image: url (bullet.gif)	Changes the appearance of the bullet by replacing it with an image.	Specify the location of the image (URL).
list-style-position: inside	Identifies the indentation of additional lines in list items.	Can be inside (lines after the first one are not indented) or outside (all lines in the item are indented). Default is outside.
list-style-type: decimal	Changes the appearance of the bullet or characters at the beginnings of each list item.	Can be none (no bullets), disc, circle, square, decimal (numbers), lower-roman (lowercase Roman numerals), upper-roman (uppercase Roman numerals), lower-alpha (lowercase letters), upper-alpha (uppercase letters), decimal-leading-zero (01., 02., and so on). Default is disc for unordered lists and decimal for ordered lists.

Table 10-2 *Style Sheet Properties for Formatting Lists*

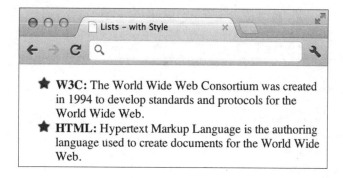

TIP

For the best results, choose images that are about the same height as the text in each list item.

Customize the Spacing

As you know, the HTML list tags indent each list item by default. Unfortunately, the exact amount of that indentation does vary a bit according to the browser. Thankfully, there are CSS properties for adjusting the indent. Two properties—margin and padding—in particular affect the spacing around each item in your list, and around the list in general.

When attached to the ul or ol tag, the margin property affects the space around the entire list. But when it is used with the li tag instead, the margin property alters the space around each individual list item.

The padding property dictates the amount of buffer space around the text in the list item, before the edge of the list item is reached. Take a look at the following illustrations to help visualize how this works (first, I'll show you a visual representation of a list with some extra spacing, then the code used to create that example).

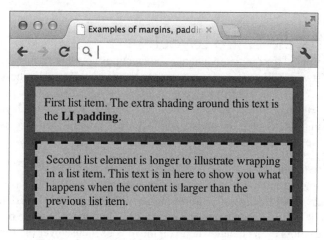

```
     lists-padding.html
lists-padding.html  ×

Code   Split   Design    Live Code  ⌨ ⬚    Live View   Inspect  ⬆⬇ ⊕  Multiscreen ▾ ⬚ C  Title: Examples of margins, pa

1   <!doctype html>
2   <html>
3   <head>
4   <title>Examples of margins, padding, and borders</title>
5   <style>
6   ul {
7       background: green;             /* Background color of the list container is green */
8       margin: 12px 12px 12px 12px;
9       padding: 3px 3px 3px 3px;
10      font: Verdana, Arial, Helvetica, sans-serif;/* No borders set */
11          }
12  li {
13      color: black;                  /* Text color is black */
14      background: #ccc;              /* Background color of content and padding is gray */
15      margin: 12px;
16      padding: 12px;                 /* 12px padding on all sides */
17      list-style: none;              /* No glyphs before a list item *//* No borders set */
18          }
19  li.withborder {
20      border-style: dashed;
21      border-width: medium;          /* Sets border width on all sides */
22      border-color: black;
23  }
24  </style>
25  </head>
26  <body>
27  <ul>
28    <li class="style1">First list item. The extra shading around this text is the <strong>LI padding</strong>.</li>
29    <li class="withborder style1">Second list element is longer to illustrate wrapping in a list item. This text is in
     here to show you what happens when the content is larger than the previous list item.</li>
30  </UL>
31  </BODY>
32  </HTML>
33

<head> <style>                                                    2K / 1 sec  Unicode 6.0 UTF-8
```

It is important to note that whenever you alter the spacing around your lists and list items, you must test your pages in a variety of browsers just to make sure everything displays as intended. Some older versions in particular have trouble properly displaying lists with altered spacing.

Customize the Entire Layout

What if you wanted to completely change the layout of your list so that it no longer looked like the typical list with bullets and indentations? In the past, web page authors have used tables (such as those created in word processing programs or spreadsheets) to hold each "item" in an irregular list. But style sheets provide a method of easily changing the layout of a list, whether that means simply removing the bullets and indents or going so far as to switch the whole thing from vertical to horizontal.

Vertical Navigation

Probably the most common reason for playing with the layout of a list is to use it as a navigation bar. Consider the navigation bar shown in Figure 10-1. It certainly doesn't look like a list; in fact, it looks more like a bunch of graphical buttons. There are borders separating the links, and the colors even change when you move your mouse over the links.

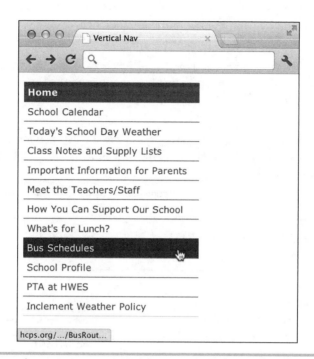

Figure 10-1 CSS made it easy to turn a boring list into a stylish navigation bar.

The actual HTML code used to create that list is shown next:

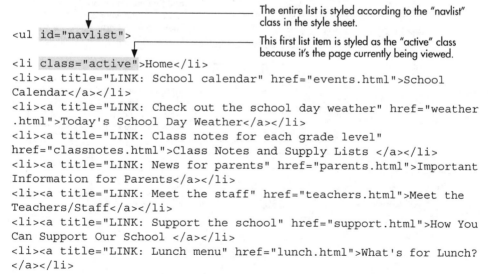

The entire list is styled according to the "navlist" class in the style sheet.

This first list item is styled as the "active" class because it's the page currently being viewed.

```
<ul id="navlist">

<li class="active">Home</li>
<li><a title="LINK: School calendar" href="events.html">School
Calendar</a></li>
<li><a title="LINK: Check out the school day weather" href="weather
.html">Today's School Day Weather</a></li>
<li><a title="LINK: Class notes for each grade level"
href="classnotes.html">Class Notes and Supply Lists </a></li>
<li><a title="LINK: News for parents" href="parents.html">Important
Information for Parents</a></li>
<li><a title="LINK: Meet the staff" href="teachers.html">Meet the
Teachers/Staff</a></li>
<li><a title="LINK: Support the school" href="support.html">How You
Can Support Our School </a></li>
<li><a title="LINK: Lunch menu" href="lunch.html">What's for Lunch?
</a></li>
```

```
<li><a title="LINK: Bus routes" href="bus.html">Bus Schedules</a></li>
<li><a title="LINK: School profile" href="profile.html">School
Profile</a></li>
<li><a title="LINK: PTA" href="pta.html">PTA at HWES</a></li>
<li><a title="LINK: Inclement weather news" href="snow.html">Inclement
Weather Policy</a></li>
</ul>
```

Notice how the HTML for the list looks the same as the lists previously created in the beginning of this chapter. In fact, every bit of the formatting is achieved through the style sheet, which looks like this:

This style declaration specifies that all the text on the page should display in the Verdana font at 10 points.

```
<style>
body {
    font-family:Verdana, Arial, Helvetica, sans-serif;
    font-size: 10pt;
}
```

```
#navlist {
    width: 250px;
    padding-left: 0;
    margin-left: 0;
    border-bottom: 1px solid #cccccc;
}
```

This defines the characteristics of the navlist section of the page, specifying the width of the buttons (250 pixels) and the bottom edge.

```
#navlist li {
    list-style: none;
    margin: 0;
    border-top: 1px solid #666666;
    line-height: 200%;
}
```

This defines how each list item within the navlist section should appear, by removing the bullets and indentation and then adding a border of separation between each item. The line-height property allows for some breathing room around each item.

```
#navlist li a {
    color: #990000;
    display: block;
    padding-left: 5px;
    text-decoration: none;
}
```

This defines how each link within those list items should be formatted. The display: block line is important to ensure the background color runs the entire length of the button.

```
#navlist li a:hover {
    color: #ffffff;
    background-color: #333333;
}
```

This defines the rollovers for each link in the list, changing the text color and the background color.

```
.active {
        background-color: #990000;
        color: #ffffff;
        font-weight: bold;
        padding-left: 5px;
        }
    </style>
```

This defines how the button should appear when it lists the currently displayed page.

Horizontal Navigation

What if you wanted to display the navigation bar horizontally across the page instead of vertically down the page? The reason lists run down the page by default is that they are block-level elements in HTML. As mentioned previously, block-level elements automatically fill the available space.

With that in mind, we can easily make a list display horizontally by specifying it should be displayed as an *inline* element instead of a block-level element with `display: inline`. Figure 10-2 shows a very basic unordered list, with a style sheet applied to turn it into a horizontal navigation bar. The list code looks like the following:

```
<ul id="navlist">
<li class="active">Home</li>
<li><a title="LINK: About Us" href="aboutus.html">About Us</a></li>
<li><a title="LINK: Services" href="services.html">Services</a></li>
<li><a title="LINK: Clients" href="clients.html">Clients</a></li>
<li><a title="LINK: Contact Us" href="contactus.html">Contactus</a>
</li>
</ul>
```

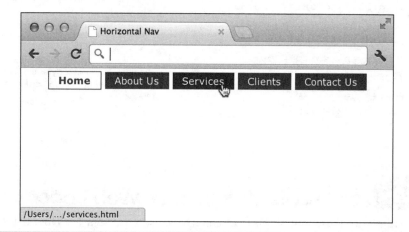

Figure 10-2 Changing the list from *block-level* to *inline* allows the items to run horizontally across the page.

And the style sheet looks like this:

```
<style type="text/css">
body {
    font-family:Verdana, Arial, Helvetica, sans-serif;
    font-size: 10pt;
    }
#navlist {
    margin: 0;
    padding: 0;
    text-align: center;
    }
#navlist li {
    list-style: none;
    display: inline;
    }
#navlist li a {
    color: #fff;
    background-color: #900;
    padding: .2em 1em;
    text-decoration: none;
    }
#navlist li a:hover {
    color: #ffffff;
    background-color: #333333;
    }
.active {
    border: 1px solid #900;
    color: #900;
    font-weight: bold;
    padding: .2em 1em;
    }
</style>
```

Here, I turn off the bullets and tell the browser to display the list inline (one after another, horizontally across the page).

This specifies how the links in each list item should look.

This specifies how the colors should change when the user rolls over each link in the list item.

The final declaration styles the "active" button by giving it a red border and bold, red text.

Try This 10-2 Style Lists Within Your Web Page

In this project, we'll use style sheets to customize the lists created in Try This 10-1. Goals for this project include

- Stylizing the bullet in an unordered list
- Creating an inline list for navigational purposes

1. Open your text or HTML editor and return to the file saved from the previous project.

2. Replace the Roman numerals in the ordered list with a graphical button, such as those included at **http://www.prodraw.net/button**. (HINT: Try using `ol>li` as your selector to tell the browser only to use the star for list items *within the ordered list* on your page, not *all the list items* on the page.)

3. If you don't already have one, add a new content division for the navigation.

4. Create an unordered list in that division, with at least three list items that make sense for your site. Here are some suggestions:

   - Home

   - About Us

   - Our Services

5. Link "Home" to the index.html page you've created.

6. Link the others to their corresponding pages. (If they haven't yet been created, simply create a placeholder link.)

7. Specify that "Our Services" should use the "active" class in your style sheet.

8. Add the appropriate style declarations to your style sheet to make the list in the navigation division display as a horizontal navigation bar.

9. Turn off the underlines for the links in the navigation bar.

10. Continue adding style sheet properties to format the list items with a one-pixel, solid, black border.

11. Create a class called "active" and give that class a gray background color.

12. Save the file.

13. Open your web browser and choose File | Open Page (or Open File or Open, depending on the browser you're using). Locate the file you just saved. Make sure the file appears as you intended.

14. If you need to make changes, return to your text editor to do so. After making any changes, save the file and switch back to the browser. Choose Refresh or Reload to preview the changes you just made.

Style sheets make it very easy to turn simple lists into elegant navigation bars. This project gave you practice working the various style sheet properties used to do just that.

Chapter 10 Self Test

1. What's the difference between an unordered list and an ordered list?

2. Which element is used to enclose list items in both ordered and unordered lists?

3. You created an unordered list with four list items. All the content following the fourth list item that should be normal text is indented under the list. What is the most likely cause of this problem?

4. Which HTML attribute changes the numbering style of a list?

5. True/False: You can use more than one dd element for each dt element.

6. Which HTML attribute changes the starting letter or number for a list?

7. Fill in the blank: When displayed in a browser, each item in an unordered list is preceded by a(n) _____ by default.

8. Fix the following code:

```
<dl>
  <dd>HTML</dd>
  <dt>Hypertext Markup Language is the authoring language used
to create documents for the World Wide Web.</dt>
  </dl>
```

9. Add the appropriate code to turn the following text into an ordered list:

```
<html>
<head>
   <title>My favorite fruits</title>
</head>
<body>
      My favorite fruits, in order of preference, are:
      Raspberries
      Strawberries
      Apples
</body>
</html>
```

10. Fill in the blank: The dl element stands for _____.

11. True/False: When you nest unordered lists, the bullet style remains unchanged.

12. What value is used with the display property to change a list from vertical to horizontal?

13. How can you change a list from using Arabic numbers to lowercase letters?

14. Which CSS property is used to replace the standard bullet in a list with an image?

Chapter 11

Using Tables

Key Skills & Concepts

- Understand the Concept and Uses of Tables in Web Pages

- Create a Basic Table Structure

- Format Tables Within Web Pages

- Format Content Within Table Cells

At this point in the book, you've made it through the majority of the basic tags used to create web pages. The next few chapters deal with content that can sometimes seem a bit more complicated than tags for lists and links. Don't worry, though, because even the pros struggled with these concepts when they first start (myself included).

Understand the Concept and Uses of Tables in Web Pages

Although you might not recognize the terminology, you have undoubtedly seen tables in other printed or electronic documents. In fact, throughout the course of this book, I've used tables to give order to certain sections that might otherwise be confusing. Quite simply, a *table* is a section of information, broken up into columns and/or rows of blocks, called *cells*.

Those of you who use Microsoft Word may be familiar with a menu item in that program called Table that enables you to create tables just like those used in web pages. Microsoft's word processor isn't the only one with tables. Most word processors are capable of letting you format content in tables.

TIP

When considering whether or not to use a table in a web page, first think of how you'd present that same information in a standard word processing program. If you'd use a table in the word processor, you likely should use one in your web page as well. If not, consider another method of presenting that information in your web page.

Another form of a table, either printed or electronic, is the spreadsheet. Along these lines, you might think about a table as a large piece of grid paper, where you get to decide the size of the cells that will hold the information.

To make decisions about how large or small your cells and table should be, you need to do a little planning. Even though HTML tables are created in digital documents, the best way to plan out tables is to use a pencil and paper when you're first learning. As you become more familiar with the structure of a table, you may be able to plan it in your head without first drawing it.

Let's first consider what a table would look like for a simple tic-tac-toe game.

1. Draw a large box on your piece of paper.

2. Divide that box into three columns and three rows.

3. Place an *X* or an *O* in each of the boxes, leaving no boxes empty.

Following these steps will probably get you a piece of paper with a drawing similar to mine.

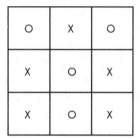

Now, imagine you want to translate this tic-tac-toe game into a web page. How would you do that? You've already learned that in HTML, you cannot simply tab over to the next column and type an *X* as you might in a spreadsheet application. You can, however, use a table to lay out the tic-tac-toe game's structure.

Create a Basic Table Structure

First, decide how large you want your table, or in this case, how large you want your tic-tac-toe game. Remember, pixels are the units of measure on the screen; inches or centimeters won't get you far in HTML. In the beginning, it'll probably be useful for you to write out your measurements on your drawings. Don't worry, though. Nothing you're doing now is set in stone. You'll be able to make changes later as needed.

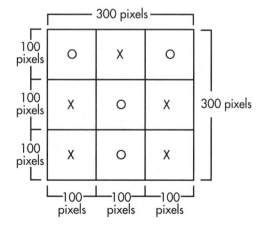

After planning out the dimensions of the table, it's time to get started working on the table structure in HTML.

Table Structure

You need to know about four basic table tags, as described next:

`<table>` `</table>`	The `table` element is a container for every other tag used to create a table in HTML. The opening and closing `table` tags should be placed at the beginning and end of your table.
`<tr>` `</tr>`	The `tr` element stands for table row. The opening and closing `tr` tags surround the cells for that row.
`<td>` `</td>`	The `td` element stands for table data and holds the actual content for the cell. There are opening and closing `td` tags for each cell in each row.
`<th>` `</th>`	The `th` element stands for table header. An optional tag used instead of the `td` tag, this tag defines a cell containing header information. By default, the content in header cells is bolded and centered.

With these tags in mind, you can create both basic and complex table structures according to your needs. Say you want to create a basic table structure, such as the following:

Popular Girls' Names	Popular Boys' Names
Emily	Jacob
Sarah	Michael

Your code might look like that shown next:

```
<table>
<tr>
    <th>Popular Girls' Names</th>
    <th>Popular Boys' Names</th>
</tr>
<tr>
    <td>Emily</td>
    <td>Jacob</td>
</tr>
<tr>
    <td>Sarah</td>
    <td>Michael</td>
</tr>
</table>
```

NOTE

While you're not required to indent your td or th tags, I did so here to help you differentiate between table rows and cells.

Opening and closing `table` tags surround the entire section of code. This tells the browser that everything inside these tags belongs in the table. And there are opening and closing `tr` tags for each row in the table. These surround `td` or `th` tags, which, in turn, contain the actual content to be displayed by the browser.

NOTE

Some browsers show a border around each cell by default. I discuss more about borders in the section titled "Borders and Margins."

Cell Content

You can include nearly any type of content in a table cell that you might include elsewhere on a web page. This content should be typed in between the opening and closing td tags for the appropriate cell. All tags used to format that content should also be included between the td tags.

TIP

Want to include a blank cell with no content? Type the code for a nonbreaking space ( ) between the opening and closing td tags, and your cell will appear blank. If you have a lot of blank cells, you could add empty-cells: show; to the style declaration for your table tag.

If we return to our tic-tac-toe game, the following is the markup for that table:

```
<table>
<tr>
    <td>O</td>
    <td>X</td>
    <td>O</td>
</tr>
<tr>
    <td>X</td>
    <td>O</td>
    <td>X</td>
</tr>
<tr>
    <td>X</td>
    <td>O</td>
    <td>X</td>
</tr>
</table>
```

If you were to create a basic HTML page with this code, save it, and preview it in your browser, you'd see something like the following:

By default, the size of each cell is only as large or as small as the content of the cell. (We'll talk about changing the size of the cell shortly.) If you typed three *X*s or *O*s in each cell and added a sentence in the center cell, the table would change to look like that shown next:

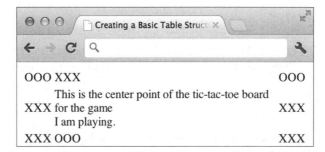

After a certain number of characters, the browser may *wrap* the content. This means it stops printing on that line and continues on the next line. This usually doesn't occur until the table runs up against another element within the page or hits the edge of the window. The default point at which the content wraps varies according to the browser.

Text

You can customize the text within each cell using the elements you learned in previous chapters. For example, you can use the `strong` element to add emphasis and make the text within a cell bold:

```
<table>
<tr>
    <td>OOO</td>
    <td>XXX</td>
    <td>OOO</td>
</tr>
<tr>
    <td>XXX</td>
    <td>This is the center point of the <strong>tic-tac-toe board</strong> for
the game I am playing.</td>
    <td>XXX</td>
</tr>
```

This text is made bold by using the `strong` tag in the cell.

```
<tr>
    <td>XXX</td>
    <td>OOO</td>
    <td>XXX</td>
</tr>
</table>
```

Enclosing the words "tic-tac-toe board" in the center cell with the opening and closing versions of the `strong` element tells the browser to add emphasis to the text and make it bold.

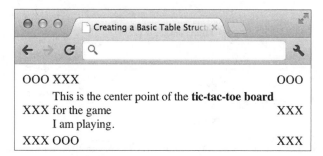

If you want to make all the text in every cell take on the same characteristics, the best solution is to use a style sheet with the `td` tag as the selector. For example, the style sheet in the following example can be placed between the opening and closing `head` tags to change the face and size of text within all the cells created by `td` tags throughout the entire page:

```
<style>
td {font-family: verdana;
    font-size: 10pt;}
</style>
```

Images

You can also add images to any of the cells in your HTML tables. To do so, add the image reference (using the `img` element) inside the cell in which you want it to appear. In the following example, I used a graphic of an *O* instead of text wherever the *O* appeared in the game board:

```
<table>
<tr>
    <td><img src="images/o.gif" alt="O" width="19" height="19"></td>
    <td>XXX</td>
    <td><img src="images/o.gif" alt="O" width="19" height="19"></td>
</tr>
<tr>
    <td>XXX</td>
    <td><img src="images/o.gif" alt="O" width="19" height="19"></td>
    <td>XXX</td>
</tr>
```

```
<tr>
    <td>XXX</td>
    <td><img src="images/o.gif" alt="O" width="19" height="19"></td>
    <td>XXX</td>
</tr>
</table>
```

When viewed in the browser, the image *O*s appear where the text *O*s used to appear, as shown next:

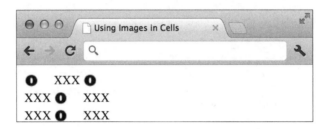

You can also combine text, images, and other types of media (such as animation, sound, and video) within table cells by drawing on many of the elements discussed in previous chapters. The key is determining which pieces go in which cells.

Format Tables Within Web Pages

You may have noticed by now that all the text in a table appears aligned to the left side of each cell. This, and many other features of a table, can be easily customized with your style sheet.

Borders and Margins

Tables, by nature of their design, have internal and external borders. By default, most browsers set the border size to zero, making them invisible. However, borders can be quite useful for tables of statistical information, for example, where it's necessary to see the columns to understand the data better. The key is understanding the three attributes related to the use of these borders.

TIP

When a table with borders is viewed in a text-based browser (i.e., a browser set to display plain text only, with no extra formatting or images), the borders are represented as dashes for the horizontal borders and as pipes (|) for the vertical borders.

The border Attribute

Even if you ultimately want your table borders to be invisible, a great way to see how your table is shaping up while you're building it is to turn on all the table borders temporarily. You can do so by adding the `border` attribute to the opening `table` tag and specifying a value of 1:

```
<table border="1">
```

Changing the border size to 1 for my tic-tac-toe table lets you see more clearly where each cell begins and ends because it turns on all the internal and external borders. The border attribute accepts values of 0 and 1 to turn the borders off or on, respectively.

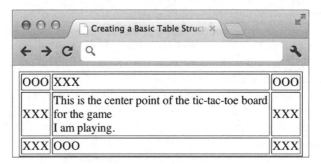

Border Properties

You can also use the border properties in a style sheet to format the borders of your tables, specifically the border-width, border-style, and border-color properties. See Chapter 3 for details.

The latest version of the CSS specification also provides an additional style sheet property to alter table spacing in web pages. Specifically, the border-collapse and border-spacing properties are useful when you need to eliminate or customize the space between the cells. The border-collapse property might be used in either of the following two ways:

- **border-collapse: collapse**   Turns off all the space between the cell borders.
- **border-collapse: separate**   Maintains the space between the cell borders.

When the border-collapse property is set to separate, you then use the border-spacing property to specify exactly how much space should be included:

```
table {border-collapse: separate; border-spacing: 10px 5px;}
```

In this code example, I've told the browser to maintain space between the cell borders, and then specified exact dimensions for that space. If two units are included—as they were here—then the first identifies the horizontal space and the second identifies the vertical space. When only one unit is listed, it is used for both the horizontal and vertical space measurements.

Spacing Properties

You can also use the padding and margin properties with style sheets to format the spacing in and around table cells. Note that entire tables can be styled with both the padding and margin properties, while individual cells can include padding, but no margins. Refer to Chapter 3 for details.

Width and Height

When I first introduced tables, I mentioned planning out the size of your tables ahead of time. This is particularly important if the table you are creating needs to fit within a predetermined amount of space on your page. When adding tables to your pages, it is considered good practice to specify the size of the table with the `height` and `width` style sheet properties. If you don't specify them in your code, the browser chooses the size based on the amount of content within each cell and the amount of available space in the window, which means it may or may not display the table as you expect.

Let's say I want to include that tic-tac-toe game in my web page, but I only had an available space on my page that measured 200 pixels wide by 200 pixels high. Because tables have a tendency to "grow" according to the amount of content in them, I might want to restrict the height and width of my table to avoid it growing out of that 200 × 200–pixel area I designated for it. I could do so by specifying the dimensions in my style sheet. Provided there was only one `table` element on my page, I could even use `table` as my selector:

```
table {width: 200px; height: 200px; border: 3px solid black;}
```

> **NOTE**
>
> If there were multiple tables on my page, I could style each one independently by adding the `class` attribute to each opening `table` tag and then styling the classes uniquely in my style sheet.

In this case, I would specify an *absolute size* for my table, one that shouldn't change if the browser window were larger or smaller.

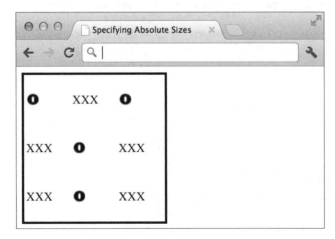

On the other hand, if I didn't care about the exact measurements of my table, but I only wanted it to take up 50 percent of the window and no more, I could use a percentage in the value of those attributes:

```
table {width: 50%; height: 50%; border: 3px solid black;}
```

This is called *relative sizing* because I'm not specifying absolute pixel dimensions but, instead, sizes that are relative to the browser window opening. Compare the next two illustrations to see how, with relative sizing, the table size varies according to the window size.

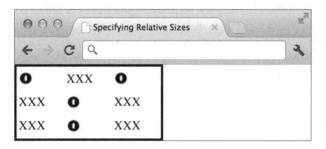

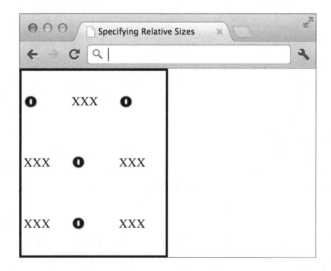

Ask the Expert

Q: Wait! When I try that, my table doesn't fill 50 percent of the screen vertically, only horizontally!

A: If you're following along by typing these code examples into your own HTML editor and then viewing the pages in your own browser, you may have hit a snag when trying to duplicate my example of a table set to 50 percent of the browser window's height. Never fear—there is an explanation for this problem, and it lies in how your browser actually defines what 100 percent of the height is.

(continued)

You see, when you specify that the table should be 50 percent, most browsers read that as "50 percent of the parent object." In this case, the parent object is the HTML page itself. Because HTML pages aren't *block-level* elements, they don't automatically fill all the available space. This causes a dilemma if you want your table to fill half the screen, especially when the browser thinks the "screen" stops as soon as your page content does.

The solution is to add a simple bit of code to your style sheet to force the browser to behave like a block-level element, or rather to fill the entire browser window, regardless of the amount of content visible:

```
html, body {
    height:100%;
    margin: 0;
    padding: 0;
    border: none;
    }
```

Once you've done that, the `height:50%` declaration will actually work on your `table` tag!

Basic Alignment

As discussed in Chapter 8, you can use the `float` property to cause an image, or in this case a table, to be aligned to the right or left of any surrounding text. If only one table exists on the page, you can even use the `table` element as your selector, like this:

```
table {float: right;}
```

The following illustration shows our tic-tac-toe table aligned to the right of the window, with text flowing around it on the left. The complete source of the page is also listed here to give you a better idea how the style sheet affects the table formatting.

```
<html>
<head>
<title>Floating Tables</title>
<style>
body {font-family: verdana;}
table {width: 200px;
      height: 200px;
      border: 3px solid black;
      float:right;}
td {border: 3px solid black;
      text-align: center;}
</style>
</head>
<body>
<table>
```

```
<tr>
    <td><img src="images/o.gif" alt="O" width="19" height="19"></td>
    <td><img src="images/x.gif" alt="X" width="19" height="19"></td>
    <td><img src="images/o.gif" alt="O" width="19" height="19"></td>
</tr>
<tr>
    <td><img src="images/x.gif" alt="X" width="19" height="19"></td>
    <td><img src="images/o.gif" alt="O" width="19" height="19"></td>
    <td><img src="images/x.gif" alt="X" width="19" height="19"></td>
</tr>
<tr>
    <td><img src="images/x.gif" alt="X" width="19" height="19"></td>
    <td><img src="images/o.gif" alt="O" width="19" height="19"></td>
    <td><img src="images/x.gif" alt="X" width="19" height="19"></td>
</tr>
</table>
<h1>Tic-Tac-Toe</h1>
<p>There are many places online where you can play tic-tac-toe, either
by yourself or with other web users. Visit <a href="http://dir.yahoo
.com/Recreation/Games/Puzzles/Tic_Tac_Toe/">Yahoo Games</a> for a list
of some hot tic-tac-toe games.</p>
<p>A game like this one, in which no one wins, is often called a cat's
game. There are many theories as to why it is called that, but my
personal favorite is this: In many other games it is called a scratch
game when no one wins. Since cats scratch, you can see where the
phrase "cat's game" might have originated.</p>
</body>
</html>
```

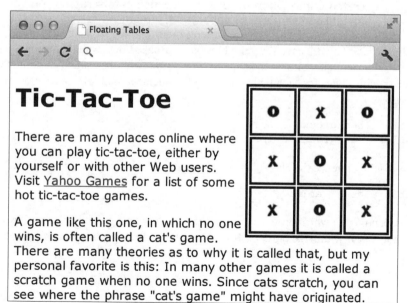

Colors

To change the background color of an entire table, you can add the `background-color` property to your style sheet, using the `table` tag as the selector. The following example shows how this might look in an internal style sheet, supposing the table you're formatting is the only table on the page:

```
table {background-color: #999;}
```

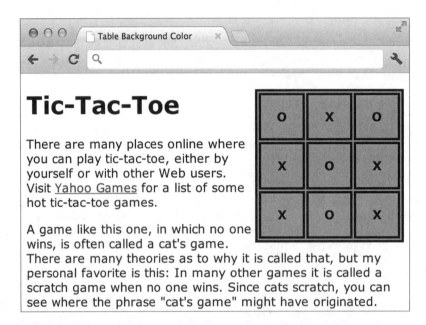

But what if you did have several tables on your page? Be aware that using the preceding code would cause all tables on the page to be rendered with the same background color. To create specific styles for each table on a page that included multiple tables, you might use classes:

```
.table1 {background-color: #999;}
.table2 {background-color: #333;}
```

Then, you'd reference the class name (without the period) from the opening `table` tag, as in

```
<table class="table1">
```

Depending on which browser renders the table, the background color you specify may or may not appear within the borders. Test your pages in multiple browsers to be sure.

Background Images

The background-image property can be added to your style sheet to apply an image to the entire table background. The background-image property works the same when applied to a table as it does applied to other web page objects. This means it automatically repeats from left to right, top to bottom. However, you can use the other background properties discussed in Chapter 8 (such as background-repeat and background-attachment) to change the repeating options if desired.

Adding a background image is one way you could achieve a textured or patterned table background, as shown in Figure 11-1. This only requires a small repeating image, such as the following:

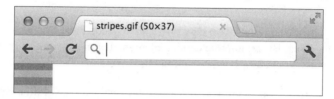

and a bit of code added to your style sheet:

```
table {background-image: url('images/stripes.gif');}
```

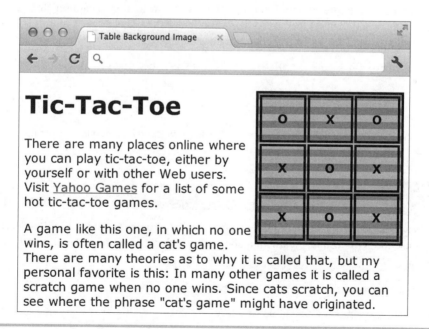

Figure 11-1 The background-image property can be applied to the table to produce a patterned effect.

Captions

The `caption` element enables you to specify captions for your tables. This isn't an attribute of the `table` element; it's a stand-alone element used after the opening `table` tag but before the first table row. Here is the first portion of the table markup:

```
<table border="3" align="right" bgcolor="#999">
<caption>This is a "cat's game" of tic-tac-toe.</caption>
<tr>
    <td>O</td>
    <td>X</td>
    <td>O</td>
</tr>
```

Opening and closing `caption` tags surround the actual text you want to display as a caption for the table. By default, the caption is aligned at the top-center of the table. Two CSS properties are useful in changing the caption alignment:

- **text-align** Use this to adjust whether the text is aligned left, right, or center on whichever side it is placed.

- **caption-side** Use this to specify on which side the caption should be placed (top, right, bottom, or left).

With those properties in mind, can you figure out how to align a caption along the bottom edge of a table and then set the text to be right-aligned along that edge? Figure 11-2 shows a visual example, and the following code provides the answer:

```
caption {text-align: right; caption-side: bottom;}
```

TIP

You can also use additional formatting properties to draw more attention to a caption, such as making it bold or different colors.

Try This 11-1 Create a Basic Table

Tables are particularly useful for allowing customers to compare products and/or services. You'll use the skills you just learned to add such a table to a web page. Goals for this project include

- Creating a basic table structure

- Adding text content to the table structure

- Formatting the table

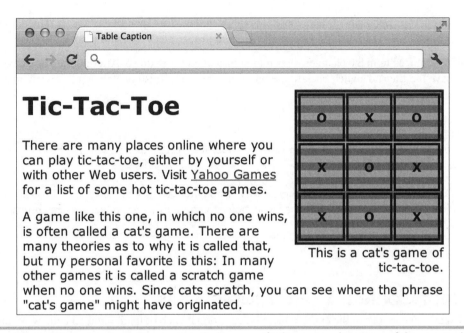

Figure 11-2   The `caption` element is styled to specify the exact alignment of the text in the caption.

1. Open your text or HTML editor and locate a page where it would be appropriate to add a table of services or products.

2. Create the table on the page, using the following table as a guideline. Note the first row is a table header row.

Features	Product 1	Product 2	Product 3
Feature 1	x		x
Feature 2		x	x
Feature 3	x	x	x

3. Specify a border size of 1.

4. Add a Level 1 headline above the table, as well as a brief paragraph explaining its purpose.

5. Save the file.

(continued)

6. Open your web browser and choose File | Open Page (or Open File or Open, depending on the browser you're using). Locate the file you just saved. Make sure it appears as you want.

7. If you need to make changes, return to your text editor to do so. After making any changes, save the file and switch back to the browser. Choose Refresh or Reload to preview the changes you just made.

NOTE

Is your table missing when you try to view the page? If so, check to make sure you have closed your `table` tag (`</table>`). For more tips, see Appendix C.

Tables are used in a wide variety of ways throughout the digital and print industries. This project gave you practice creating a basic table structure, using a product/service comparison chart as the basis for your table.

Format Content Within Table Cells

Just as you can format the entire table, you can format each of the individual cells within the table. This means changing the alignment, width, height, and background colors, as well as restricting line breaks and spanning content across multiple columns or rows.

Alignment

If you refer to the table you created in Try This 11-1, you may notice the alignment appears different for some of the cells, depending on how much content is in each cell and how wide the browser window is open. For example, the cells in the first row might contain text that is centered, while the remaining cells in the other rows might be left-aligned.

To change vertical and horizontal alignment, you can add the `text-align` property for horizontal alignment or the `vertical-align` property for vertical alignment to the `tr`, `th`, or `td` tags.

- **tr** Adding the `text-align` or `vertical-align` properties to the opening `tr` tag causes the alignment you specify to take effect for all the cells in that row.

- **td, th** Adding the `text-align` or `vertical-align` properties to an opening `td` or `th` tag causes the alignment you specify to take effect for only that cell.

Table 11-1 lists the possible values for these two properties when used in tables.

NOTE

The default values for the `text-align` and `vertical-align` properties are left and middle, respectively. For header cells (using the `th` tag), however, the horizontal alignment defaults to center instead of left.

Property	Possible Values
text-align	left right center *string* (for example, text-align: '.' would tell the browser to align along the period, which could be useful for a column of monetary values)
vertical-align	baseline (aligns baselines of element and parent) sub (subscript) super (superscript) top (aligns top of element with tallest part of the line) text-top (aligns top of element with parent's font) text-bottom (aligns top of element with parent's bottom) bottom (aligns bottom of element with lowest part of the line) middle (aligns midpoint of element with baseline plus half the height of the letter "x" of the parent) *percentage* (relative to the element's line-height value)

Table 11-1 Text Alignment Options for Tables

If you want to align all the cells in your table in a similar manner, it's easy to use the td tag as the selector in your style sheet in the following manner:

```
td {text-align: center;}
```

But what if you wanted each column of cells to be aligned differently? You could create three classes:

```
.left {text-align: left; vertical-align: top;}
.right {text-align: right; vertical-align: bottom;}
.center {text-align: center; vertical-align: middle;}
```

and then reference each class from within the appropriate td tag. Figure 11-3 shows the result of this type of style sheet when applied to our tic-tac-toe board.

```
<tr>
    <td class="left">O</td>
    <td class="center">X</td>
    <td class="right">O</td>
</tr>
```

Width and Height

Earlier in the chapter, you used the width and height properties to identify the size of the entire table. You can also specify the size of individual cells by adding those properties to your td or th tags.

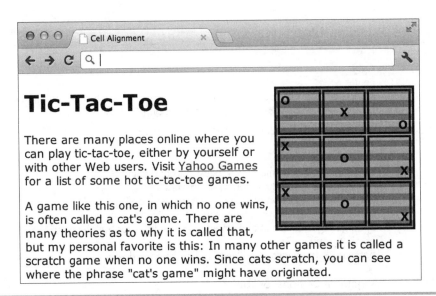

Figure 11-3 Three different classes were created to align the cells of this table in three different ways.

TIP

This can be particularly useful if you want to have columns that are the same size, because most browsers won't make columns the same size when the width is left unspecified.

You may remember that the value of these two attributes can be dictated by either a pixel length or a percentage. This is the same regardless of what element is being sized. However, use caution when mixing pixel values with percentages because you might get unpredictable results in different browsers.

Look at the table in the following example. Although the table itself has a width set to 100 percent of the window opening, none of the cells have width dimensions. This leaves the decision about how wide each cell should be up to the browser.

If I want to make all three of the columns the same width, regardless of what size the browser window is, I could specify in my style sheet that each `th` tag should be one-third of the overall table width:

```
th {width: 33%;}
```

Then, each of the following cells in that column will have the same width (and/or height). An exception to this rule might be when one cell contains an extremely long string of text without spaces, such as "abcdefghijklmnopqrstuvwxyz." In this case, the browser may have to make that cell larger, as necessary, to accommodate the long string of text.

It isn't necessary to place `width` properties in every cell in a column—only the first one. Also, if you set the width two columns, the third will simply use the remaining available space. In the end, I recommend testing your pages in multiple browsers to verify that the table appears as you intended.

```
⊖ ○ ⊖   📄 Forcing Cell Widths          ×

←  →  C   🔍

| Age         | Height  | Weight        |
| Birth       | 19.5"   | 7 lbs. 9 oz.  |
| 6 months    | 25"     | 17 lbs. 8 oz  |
| 12 months   | 29.5"   | 22 lbs. 5 oz. |
```

Cell Padding

While table cells don't have margins (at least not by CSS standards), they do have padding. This means if you want to have some buffer space around the content of your cells (padding), you can add the padding property to your style sheet declaration.

Using the padding property for tables is the same as using it for other HTML elements, as was discussed in previous chapters. So, if you wanted to add 10 pixels of padding around each cell, the style sheet might look like this:

```
td {padding: 10px;}
```

```
⊖ ○ ⊖   📄 Cell Padding          ×

←  →  C   🔍

| Age         | Height  | Weight        |
|             |         |               |
| Birth       | 19.5"   | 7 lbs. 9 oz.  |
|             |         |               |
| 6 months    | 25"     | 17 lbs. 8 oz  |
|             |         |               |
| 12 months   | 29.5"   | 22 lbs. 5 oz. |
```

Can you imagine how you might achieve 10 pixels of padding only on the top and bottom edges of each cell? There are a couple of ways to do it, but I like to simply specify the padding in pairs, where the first number lists the top and bottom padding, and the second number lists the left and right padding. Check it out:

```
td {padding: 10px 0;}
```

Colors

While adding the `background-color` property to a table style declaration lets you change the color for the entire table, using this property with the `tr`, `td`, or `th` tag lets you specify the color of a single row or cell:

```
tr {background-color: green;}
```

Coloring rows or columns in a table with different hues can be a great way to make the table more readable, particularly if it's a long table. Style sheets make it easy to create such patterns through the use of classes. Consider the table shown in Figure 11-4. If you had to add the style declarations to each row in the table, it could become quite cumbersome as the table grew to include more rows. Instead, create the two classes in your internal or external style sheet:

```
.hilite {background-color: #ccc;}
.lolite {background-color: #999;}
```

and then reference each one in alternating rows of your table.

TIP

When naming classes, stick with names that reference the purpose of the class, as opposed to the style of the class. For example, avoid a name like "bluerow" and "orangerow" because these would become confusing if you ended up changing the colors of the rows. Instead, try "hilight" and "lolite" for alternating color rows like these.

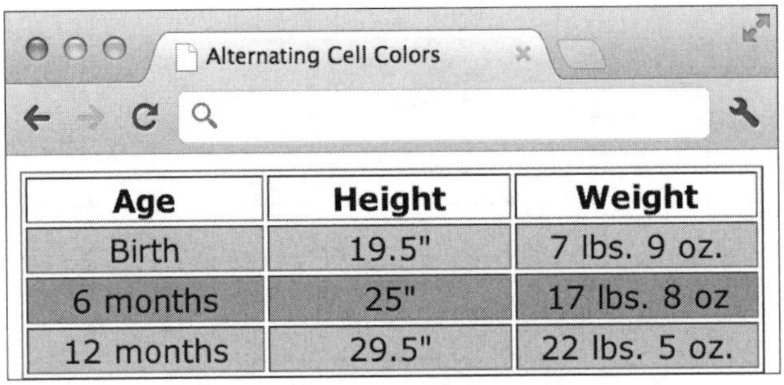

Figure 11-4 Style sheets and classes make it easy to create rows of alternating colors like these.

```
<tr class="hilite"><td>Birth</td>
   <td>19.5"</td>
   <td>7 lbs. 9 oz.</td>
</tr>
<tr class="lolite"><td>6 months</td>
   <td>25"</td>
   <td>17 lbs. 8 oz</td>
</tr>
<tr class="hilite"><td>12 months</td>
   <td>29.5"</td>
   <td>22 lbs. 5 oz.</td>
</tr>
```

NOTE

When you include background colors for both individual cells and the entire table, the background color of the table may also show through in between the cells (in the border). However, this does vary somewhat from browser to browser. My advice to you on this topic is to test your pages in a wide number of settings to make sure you're happy with how they look under each different browser.

Prohibit Line Breaks

At times, you might have content in a cell that needs to be kept on a single line. In cases like this, you can use the white-space property with a value of "nowrap" to tell the browser to try and keep all the content in that cell on a single line if possible. (This might not be possible if the browser window is so small that the content cannot be rendered across a single line.) The style sheet might look like the following:

```
td.nowrap {white-space: nowrap;}
```

while the only change to the HTML table is the addition of the class reference:

```
<td class="nowrap">This content won't wrap.</td>
```

Spanning Columns

So far in this chapter, you have only worked with tables in a grid-like fashion where an equal number of cells is in each row and column. While this is the default, you can add an attribute to an opening td or th tag to cause it to merge with another cell below it, as shown here:

These two cells have been merged so the content from the first cell flows into the second.		3
4	5	6

To accomplish this, use the `colspan` attribute. By default, each cell is set to *span,* or to go across, only one column. Using the `colspan` attribute enables you to change that, so that a cell spans two or more columns. The following HTML shows how you might code the preceding table:

```
<table border="1">
<tr>
    <td colspan="2">These two cells have been merged so the content
from the first cell flows into the second.</td>
    <td>3</td>
</tr>
<tr>
    <td>4</td>
    <td>5</td>
    <td>6</td>
</tr>
</table>
```

Span Rows

Just as you can merge cells across two or more columns, you can merge cells across two or more rows. The attribute used to do so is `rowspan`.

If you take the table used in the preceding section and merge the two cells on the right (#3 and #6) into one, the table might look like that shown next.

These two cells have been merged so the content from the first cell flows into the second.		These two cells have been merged so the content from the top one flows into the bottom one.
4	5	

Here you have two cells in the first row merged, while the third cell from the first row is merged with the third cell from the second row. Here is the HTML used to create this table:

```
<table border="1">
<tr>
    <td colspan="2">These two cells have been merged so the content
from the first cell flows into the second.</td>
    <td rowspan="2">These two cells have been merged so the content
from the top one flows into the bottom one.</td>
</tr>
<tr>
    <td>4</td>
    <td>5</td>
</tr>
</table>
```

The rowspan attribute can be used by itself in a td tag to cause a cell to merge with the cell below it, or it can be combined with the colspan attribute to cause a cell to merge with both the cell below it and the one next to it.

Although the colspan and rowspan attributes give web developers a lot of power to build creative table structures, they add a degree of complexity to tables that's often difficult to grasp. Don't worry—everyone struggles with these concepts at first. If you have trouble, go back to using your pencil and paper to plan out your table structure before you type a single key.

TIP

If you have a picture in your mind of the final output of your table, draw that first. Then, go back and add the table or grid structure around the picture, placing each piece into a cell or a group of cells. This is also one of the places where a visual HTML editor may come in handy because it enables you to see the table while you're creating it.

Additional Formatting Techniques for Tables

HTML has additional tags geared toward helping web developers build more user-friendly tables. These tags and attributes enable you to group rows and/or columns so that the browser more clearly understands the purposes of each element.

Group Rows

Three tags in particular are used to group rows within tables:

- **thead** table header
- **tfoot** table footer
- **tbody** table body

When you use these tags, the browser is able to differentiate between the header and footer information and the main content of the page. The benefit here is that when a user views a page containing a long table, the header information is repeated at the top of each page or screen view of the table, even if the table is printed. This helps users avoid wondering what column three was supposed to hold, when they are looking at page four, and the title of column three was only listed on page one.

While these three tags are never required, when they are used, each must contain at least one table row, as defined by the tr tag. In addition, if you include a thead and/or a tfoot, you must also include at least one tbody. So, a table layout using these three tags might look like this:

```
<table>
<thead>
<tr>
```

```
    <th>Age</th>
    <th>Height</th>
    <th>Weight</th>
</tr>
</thead>
<tfoot>
<tr>
    <td colspan="3">Data taken from the Corinna Research Society</td>
</tr>
</tfoot>
<tbody>
<tr>
    <td>Birth</td>
    <td>19.5 inches</td>
    <td>7 lbs. 9 oz.</td>
</tr>
<tr>
    <td>6 m.</td>
    <td>25 inches</td>
    <td>17 lbs. 8 oz.</td>
</tr>
<tr>
    <td>12 m.</td>
    <td>29.5 inches</td>
    <td>22 lbs. 5 oz.</td>
</tr>
</tbody>
</table>
```

An additional benefit of using these tags is that it helps make styling the table easier. For example, suppose you wanted to format the data rows of your table in one way, the header in a different way, and the footer in yet another fashion. As long as the thead, tbody, and tfoot tags are in place, you only need to reference those tags in your style sheet to do so. Figure 11-5 shows how the preceding code would be viewed in a browser when the following style sheet is also included:

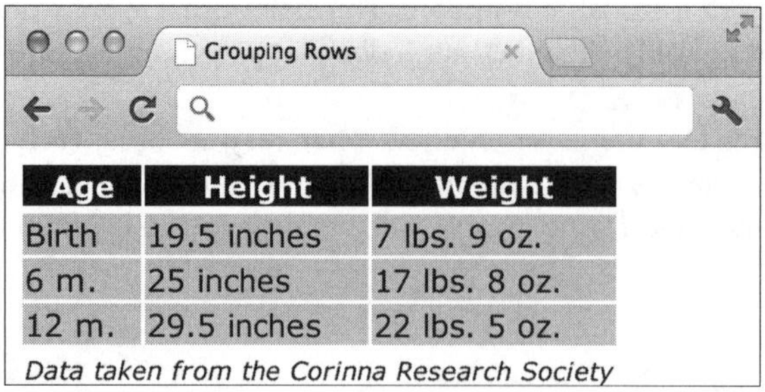

Figure 11-5 When you use the thead, tbody, and tfoot tags, styling table rows becomes a snap.

```
body {font-family: verdana;}
thead {background-color: black;
    color: white;}
tbody {background-color: #ccc;}
tfoot {font-size: 10pt;
    font-style: italic;}
```

Group Columns

Along the same lines, you can group columns together with the col and colgroup elements. Browsers that understand these tags can then render the table incrementally, instead of all at once. This causes long tables to load more quickly than they might otherwise. In addition, using colgroups enables you to apply styles and characteristics to entire sections of columns, as opposed to doing so individually.

TIP

Simply stated, the colgroup and col elements are ways to pass information about structure and style on to the browser in the beginning of the table in order to help render it.

The opening and closing colgroup tags enclose one or more columns in the group and can dictate how those columns should be rendered. This means you can use the colgroup tag as a selector in your style sheet to format all the columns in that group the same way. You can also add the span attribute to this tag to tell the browser how many columns should be included in the group.

NOTE

If you had both colgroups and theads, the colgroups would be placed before the theads in your table structure.

In this example, the first colgroup contains five columns, while the second colgroup contains two columns. You can see the colgroup tags are placed at the top of the table, before all the table rows and table cells.

```
<table border="1">
<colgroup span="5" id="group1"></colgroup>
<colgroup span="2" id="group2"></colgroup>
<tr>
    <td>
```

Each colgroup in this example also has an ID assigned: group1 and group2. If you make formatting specifications in the corresponding ID style declaration, they take effect for all the columns in that group. If you need to alter the width or alignment of specific columns in the group, you then only have to make the change once in the style sheet. The following shows what a style sheet might look like to make all the columns in group1 50 pixels in width, while those in group2 are 25 pixels wide:

This tells the browser to look for a `colgroup` with an ID name of group1 and then apply the corresponding style to it.

```
colgroup#group1 {width:50px;}
colgroup#group2 {width:25px}
```

In this next example, there are two groups of columns in a table about adventure trips at a summer camp. In this case, the colgroups aren't set up to handle width as much as background colors. The first group contains two columns, one for each of the camp sessions available. The second group contains three columns for the information about trips offered during each session. The session columns are styled with different background colors. In addition, two classes are created to handle capitalization and text alignment styling.

```
<style>
body {
    font-family: verdana;
    background-color: white;
    }
th {
    background-color: black;
    color: white;
    padding: 4px;
    }
td {
    padding: 4px;
    }
#first {
    background-color: #999;
    }
#second {
    background-color: #ccc;
    }
.center {
    text-align: center;
    }
.uppercase {
    text-transform: uppercase;
    }
</style>
</head>
<body>
<table border=1>
<table rules="rows" frame="box">
    <colgroup id="sessions">
        <col id="first">
        <col id="second">
```

```
        </colgroup>
        <colgroup id="trip-details">
            <col id="type">
            <col id="duration">
            <col id="location">
</colgroup>
<tr class="uppercase">
    <th colspan="2">Sessions</th>
    <th colspan="3">Trip Details</th>
</tr>
<tr>
    <th>1st</th>
    <th>2nd</th>
    <th>Type</th>
    <th>Duration</th>
    <th>Location</th>
</tr>
```

The table then continues with the rest of the cell data. You can see how it all turned out visually in the following illustration.

SESSIONS		TRIP DETAILS		
1st	2nd	Type	Duration	Location
X		Canoeing	2 days	Kennebec River
X		Canoeing	4-5 days	Allagash River
	X	Canoeing	4 days	Moose River
X	X	Kayaking	2 days	Kennebec River
X	X	White Water Rafting	1 day	Kennebec River
X		Biking	3 days	Acadia National Park
	X	Mountain Biking	3 days	Carrabasset Valley
	X	Hiking	3 days	Baxter State Park
X		Hiking	3 days	Mount Washington
X	X	Sightseeing	3 days	Quebec City
X	X	Fishing	1 day	Maine Coast
	X	Whale Watching	1 day	Maine Coast
X	X	Sailing	2 days	Maine Coast

NOTE

As of this writing, the only aspects of cols or colgroups that can be styled are borders, background, width, and visibility. Unfortunately, this means you can't use a colgroup to adjust the alignment of all the cells in that column (wouldn't that be nice!). The only way to do that is to add a class to each cell you want to style, and then use the text-align property with that class in your style sheet.

Whether used in the colgroup or col tag, column width can be specified as demonstrated in Table 11-2.

Value	Description	Example
pixels	Sets the width of each column in pixel dimensions.	colgroup {width: 50px;} col {width: 20px;}
percentages	Sets the width of each column in percentages, relative to the size of the entire table.	colgroup {width: 50%;} col {width: 10%;}

Table 11-2   Setting the Column Width

Try This 11-2   Format Cell Content

Returning to the services page you began in Try This 11-1, let's format some of the individual cells and add a horizontal rule that spans the entire width of the table. Goals for this project include

- Changing the alignment of content within table cells

- Causing a cell to span across multiple columns

1. Open your text or HTML editor and open the file used in Try This 11-1.

2. Create two column groups—one for the feature column, and one for the product columns.

3. Assign IDs to each column so that you can reference them from your style sheet.

4. Style the first column to have a colored background.

5. Style the second column group to have a different colored background.

6. Style the table header rows to have a very dark background color with white (or very light) text.

7. Add a four-pixel padding to the table cells for a bit of buffer space around the content.

8. Adjust the border to display only the outside box around the table and the horizontal lines between each row (but not the vertical lines between the columns).

9. Save the file.

10. Open your web browser and choose File | Open Page (or Open File or Open, depending on the browser you're using). Locate the file you just saved. Make sure the file appears as you intended it.

11. If you need to make changes, return to your text editor to do so. After making any changes, save the file and switch back to the browser. Choose Refresh or Reload to preview the changes you just made.

NOTE

Feel free to experiment with other types of formatting as you see fit for your particular table design.

Although somewhat complex in nature, these formatting techniques help you build more creative tables than might otherwise have been possible. In addition, formatting techniques such as adjusting alignment, colors, and sizes are ways to draw attention to cell content. This project gave you practice working with many of these features.

Chapter 11 Self Test

1. What is the difference between the `td` and `th` elements?

2. The `td` and `th` elements are contained within which other table tag (aside from the `table` tag itself)?

3. How do you force a cell's contents to display along a single line?

4. What should be the value of the border attribute to turn on a table's borders?

5. True/False: You cannot use other HTML tags between opening and closing `td` tags.

6. Fill in the blank: The _____ property affects the space around the content of each individual table cell.

7. Fix the following code:

```
<table>
<td>HTML</td>
<td>Hypertext Markup Language is the authoring language used to
create documents for the World Wide Web.</td>
</table>
```

8. What are two types of measurements you can use to identify a table's width?

9. Add the appropriate code to cause this table to fill the entire browser window, regardless of the user's screen size.

```
<html>
<head>
   <title>A Big Table</title>
<style type="text/css">
</style>
</head>
<body>
<table>
```

```
<tr>
  <td>X</td>
  <td>X</td>
  <td>O</td>
</tr>
</table>
</body>
</html>
```

10. Fill in the blank: You can add the _____ property to your style sheet to change the background color of the whole table.

11. True/False: To add a caption to a table, you use the `caption` attribute in the opening `table` tag.

12. If you include a `thead` or a `tfoot` group in your table, you must also include which other group?

13. Which CSS property (and value) is used to align all the text in a cell to the right?

14. True/False: If you had both `colgroups` and `theads` in a single table, the `colgroups` would be placed before the `theads` in your table structure.

Chapter 12

Creating Forms

Key Skills & Concepts

- Understand the Concept and Uses of Forms in Web Pages

- Create a Basic Form

- Validate the Form Content

- Provide a Way for Your Form to Be Processed

One of the best features of the Web is its capability to enable new forms of communication and have them connect with other methods already in existence. Online forms are popular ways of facilitating such communications. For example, forms allow web site visitors to comment on a site, order a product, communicate with friends via social media, and register for a service. This chapter discusses how to create forms such as these and use them effectively on your web site.

Understand the Concept and Uses of Forms in Web Pages

The most basic purpose of any form is to collect information. When you register to vote, you fill out a form specifying your name, address, birth date, and political party affiliation. The form is collected and processed. The same concept holds true with online forms—they are filled out, collected, and processed. For example, Figure 12-1 shows a page with a form for people to post an item for sale on Craigslist.

Just as paper forms must have once been written, typed, or otherwise created, online forms need to be coded. This can be accomplished with HTML alone or by combining HTML with other technologies. For the purposes of this chapter, we will use HTML to create our forms.

Create a Basic Form

Even the most basic forms have the same structure. This includes opening and closing `form` tags, input controls, and processing methods. The `form` element surrounds the entire form, just as the `html` element surrounds the entire HTML document.

```
<form>
 ... content goes here ...
</form>
```

First, let's discuss *input controls*, or ways for users to enter data. For example, for you to enter your name on a form, there must be a space for you to do so. This space is what I'm

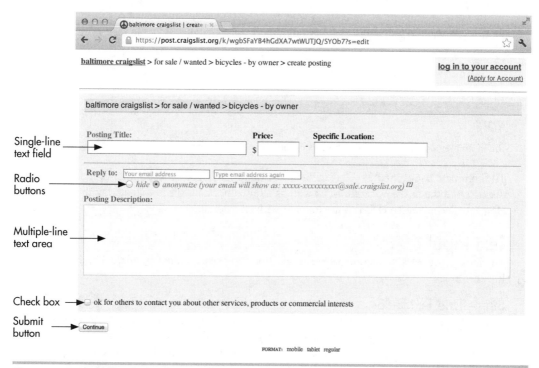

Figure 12-1   Online forms have a variety of uses, from sending messages to searching for keywords.

referring to when I use the phrase *input control* or simply "control." Figure 12-1 contains some of the following input controls:

- Text inputs
- Check boxes
- Radio buttons
- Select menus
- File selects
- Buttons (submit buttons, reset buttons, and push buttons)
- Hidden controls

Because most controls are created with an `input` element, the actual description of which control you want to include is made through the `type` attribute, as in the following example:

```
<form>
   <input type="checkbox">
</form>
```

NOTE
The input element is empty, which means it doesn't require a closing tag.

The complete list of input types is included in Table 12-1. The most popular of these are then discussed in the next few sections, as well as a few other controls not created with the input element. Those new to HTML5 are marked with an asterisk.

Text Input
The most basic text-input controls are single-line text boxes (called *text fields*) and multiple-line text areas.

Single-Line Text Fields
The single-line text field is actually the default type for input controls, which means you don't even have to specify the type attribute because without it the input element defaults to a plain text field. This control is a space, resembling a box, that can contain a single line of text. Usually, text fields are preceded by descriptive text telling the user what to enter in the box. For example:

```
<form>
   Please enter your first name: <input><br>
   Please enter your last name: <input>
</form>
```

As the following illustration shows, text fields are single-line white spaces that appear slightly indented into the page. Unless you specify otherwise with the `size` attribute, text fields are usually 20 characters in length.

Input Type	Description
<input type="button">	Clickable button
<input type="checkbox">	Check box
<input type="color"> *	Color selection tool
<input type="date"> *	Date selection tool (day, month, and year)
<input type="datetime"> *	Date and time selection tool (with time zone control)
<input type="datetime-local"> *	Date and time selection tool for local time only
<input type="email"> *	Email field
<input type="file">	File selection tool (with a Browse... button)
<input type="hidden">	Hidden input field
<input type="image">	Clickable image
<input type="month"> *	Month and year selection tool
<input type="number"> *	Number input field
<input type="password">	Password field
<input type="radio">	Radio button
<input type="range"> *	Number input field with slider
<input type="reset">	Reset button
<input type="search">	Search field
<input type="submit">	Submit button
<input type="tel"> *	Telephone number field
<input type="text">	Single-line text field (default)
<input type="time"> *	Time selection tool (no time zone support)
<input type="url"> *	URL field
<input type="week"> *	Week and year field (no time zone support)

Table 12-1 Types of Controls Added with the input Element

NOTE
The sizes of text fields are specified in characters. However, it ultimately depends on the default font size in the viewer's browser. This means even though you might specify a text field to be 25 characters in length, it may appear larger or smaller on someone else's system, depending on how that person's browser is set up.

Any of the attributes listed in Table 12-2 can be added to this and other `input` elements to customize the control. We'll cover more of these attributes in the next few sections, but first we need to talk about the most important one—and the one *every* input control needs—name. To process all the controls in your form, each one must be identified with a name. For example, when the form is processed, you could tell it to take whatever the user entered in the control you named "FirstName" and print that text at the top of an email message.

TIP

Blank spaces between words in the values of some attributes can cause problems in HTML and other coding methods. To avoid such problems when using the `name` attribute, many developers like to run any phrases together, capitalizing the first letter in each word. For example, instead of using "Middle Initial" as the value of your `name` attribute, use "MiddleInitial." Just remember, these values are case-sensitive, which means whenever you reference that control later, you must also capitalize the first letter of each word. In addition, be sure to use unique names to avoid confusion when the form is processed.

```
<form>
Please enter your first name: <input name="FirstName">
<br>
Please enter your last name: <input name="LastName">
</form>
```

The other attributes are optional. For example, you can use the `size` attribute to specify the length of the text field in characters, while the `maxlength` attribute enables you to limit the number of characters that can be entered in that box. For example, if you created a text field where users can enter their ZIP code in the following format: xxxxx-xxxx, you could specify a `maxlength` of ten characters.

Every control has an initial value and a current value. An *initial value* is an optional value you specify for a control when you code the form, while a *current value* is whatever the user entered that is then processed with the form. For example, if most users will enter a certain value for a field, you might use the `value` attribute to prepopulate that field with the default answer. You may be tempted to use the value attribute to send instructions to the user, but if you do and the user doesn't enter any data, then the initial value you entered is sent along when the form is processed.

```
<input name="FirstName" value="Enter your first name here">
```

When the page is viewed, however, users who need to change the value will have to erase it before entering their information. So, if you're intending to give users a hint but let them enter a unique value, the placeholder attribute is a better option.

```
<input name="FirstName" placeholder="Enter your first name here">
```

Attribute	Value(s)	Description
autocomplete	on off	Defines whether the autocomplete feature of the browser should be enabled.
autofocus	n/a	When used, tells the browser to place the cursor inside this control as soon as the page is loaded.
form	Form_ID	Identifies one or more forms to which the control belongs.
max	Number or date	Identifies the maximum allowed value.
maxlength	Number	Specifies the maximum number of characters that can be entered in the text field by the user.
min	Number or date	Identifies the minimum allowed value.
multiple	n/a	When used, specifies the user can enter more than one value.
name	Name	Identifies the control so that it's correctly handled when the form is processed. This information isn't displayed when the form is viewed through a browser. In most cases, the value of the name attribute should be the same as the value of the id attribute. This consistency will make it easier to format and style the input controls later. (The one exception occurs with radio button and check boxes, which we'll discuss shortly.)
pattern	RegularExpression	Defines a set pattern against which the control's value is checked when the form is submitted.
placeholder	Text	Defines the text present in the field before it is clicked (which can be used as a hint to the user).
readonly	n/a	When used, the control cannot be changed by the user.
required	n/a	When used, the control must be completed by the user in order for the form to be submitted.
size	Number	Specifies the length of the text field in characters.
step	Number	Used with the min and max attributes to identify the incremental values accepted.
title	Text	Required when pattern is used. Indicates the "tool tip" instructional text to tell the user what type of pattern is expected.
value	Value	Defines what text, if any, should be present within the text field when it's initially displayed on the page.

Table 12-2 Attributes for Text Fields

In this case, as soon as the user puts the cursor in the text box, the placeholder text disappears, allowing a new value to be easily entered.

Text Fields for Passwords

HTML also enables you to create single-line text fields for passwords. The main difference is that password text fields show text that's entered as bullets instead of straight text.

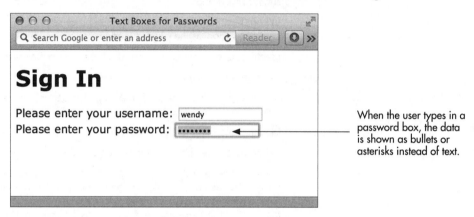

When the user types in a password box, the data is shown as bullets or asterisks instead of text.

You use `password` as the value of the `type` attribute in your `input` element to create this type of control. The following is an example of the code for the preceding illustration:

```
<form>
Please enter your username: <input name="UserName"><br>
Please enter your password: <input type="password" name="Password">
</form>
```

Although this may seem as if it adds a level of security to your page, it's merely a way to prevent those looking over the user's shoulder from seeing a password. The actual password is not encrypted in any way when the form is processed, and therefore, this control shouldn't be implemented as the only means of security for pages with passwords.

Text Fields for Search Boxes

Using the search input type identifies an otherwise normal text field as one that contains search terms.

```
<input type="search" name="search" placeholder="Enter search terms
here…" size="50">
```

Supporting browsers round the corners of the box to set it apart from regular text boxes.

In addition, after the user starts typing, a small cancel icon (usually in the shape of an x) appears to the right side of the search field. This allows the user to quickly clear the box and start over as needed.

american bulldogs

Multiple-Line Text Areas

When it's necessary to allow your web site visitors to enter more than a single line of text, use a text area instead of a text field. Unlike most other form input controls, a *text area* uses the `textarea` tag instead of the `input` element.

```
<form>
We welcome your thoughts and opinions about our products.<br>
<textarea name="Comments"></textarea>
</form>
```

To specify the size of the text area, use the `cols` and `rows` attributes:

- The `cols` attribute identifies the visible width of the text area, based on an average character width.

- The `rows` attribute identifies the visible height of the text area, based on the number of text lines.

Because the sizes of the `rows` and `cols` attributes relate to the character width in the browser, the actual size of the text area may differ, depending on the user's settings. Scroll bars may appear when users attempt to enter more data than can be displayed in the visible text area.

While you can use the placeholder attribute to specify hints to users, you don't use the `value` attribute in this tag to create an initial value that prints within the text area. Instead, include any text you want to print within the text area between the opening and closing `textarea` tags. Figure 12-2 shows how the following code might be displayed in a browser:

```
<form>
We welcome your thoughts and opinions about our products.<br>
<textarea name="Comments" cols="30" rows="5">Type your comments
here.</textarea>
</form>
```

TIP

You can control whether scroll bars appear on your text area with the CSS `overflow` property. For example, setting `overflow: scroll` forces scroll bars to appear, while `overflow: auto` leaves it up to the browser to decide based on the amount of text entered.

Radio Buttons

Radio buttons are small, round buttons that enable users to select a single option from a list of choices. This is accomplished with the `input` element and a value of `radio` in the `type` attribute. You might use radio buttons to allow those interested in receiving more information the option of choosing to do so via email, phone, fax, or regular mail. When the user selects one of the options by selecting the radio button, the circle is filled in with a black dot.

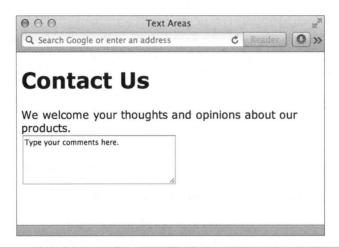

Figure 12-2 Text areas enable users to enter more than a single line of text. Any text you enter between the opening and closing `textarea` tags is used as the initial value of the text area.

TIP

Radio buttons are particularly useful for questions requiring a yes or no answer.

The `name` and `value` attributes are especially important to radio buttons because they help to make sure the data is processed correctly. Consider the following HTML code used to create the illustration shown next:

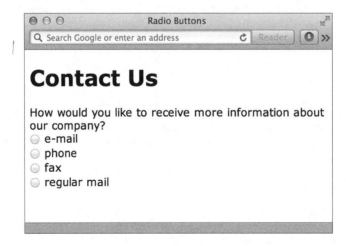

```
<form>
How would you like to receive more information about our company?<br>
<input type="radio" name="ContactMe" value="email"> email<br>
<input type="radio" name="ContactMe" value="phone"> phone<br>
<input type="radio" name="ContactMe" value="fax"> fax<br>
<input type="radio" name="ContactMe" value="mail"> regular mail<br>
</form>
```

Notice the `name` attributes contain the same value for all four options. This ensures these four controls are linked together when the form is processed. Because the type of control is *radio*, the browser knows only one option can be selected. If you make a mistake and use different names for each of the options, the user will be able to select multiple buttons.

When the form is processed, it locates the selected option (meaning it looks for whichever radio button the user selected) and transmits that option's `value` along with its `name`. If I selected the radio button next to the word *fax*, the appropriate name and value would be transmitted: ContactMe – fax. You can see how using words and phrases that actually mean something can be important.

If you want to set one of the radio buttons to be selected by default when the page is initially loaded, use the `checked` attribute in the `input` tag. Users can select a different option if they want.

```
<input type="radio" name="ContactMe" value="fax" checked> fax<br>
```

Check Boxes

Check boxes are similar to radio buttons in that they don't let users enter any data; they can only be clicked on or off. However, check boxes let the user select more than one choice from a list of options. For example, you might use check boxes to give users the option to select which services they would like to receive more information about. When a check box is selected, a small *x* or a check mark typically appears in the box, depending on the browser.

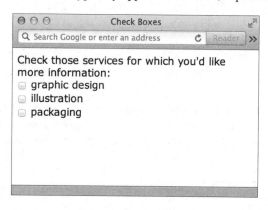

To include a check box in your online form, use the `input` tag and `type` attribute with a value of `checkbox` (note that check box is one word when used as an HTML value). Just as with radio buttons, the values of the `name` attributes for all the options should be the same. Use the `value` attribute to identify what is different about each option, as in the following example:

```
<form>
Which services are you interested in?<br>
<input type="checkbox" name="Services" value="graphic design"> graphic design<br>
<input type="checkbox" name="Services" value="illustration"> illustration<br>
<input type="checkbox" name="Services" value="packaging"> packaging
</form>
```

When the form is processed, the values of any check boxes selected by the user will be transmitted to the server along with the value of the `name` attribute. So, in the preceding example, if I selected the check boxes next to "graphic design" and "illustration," the appropriate name and values would be transmitted: Services – graphic design, illustration.

Use the `checked` attribute any time you want a check box to be selected by default when the page is loaded. Users can uncheck that box if they want.

```
<input type="checkbox" name="Services" value="packaging" checked> packaging
```

Date and Time Inputs

HTML5 brings us several new input controls, including six from Table 12-1 that help with date and time fields:

- date
- datetime
- datetime-local
- month
- time
- week

As of this writing, Google Chrome, Opera, and Safari on an iOS device are the only browsers that support any of these new controls, and Opera is the only one that supports all six. Take a look at Figure 12-3 to see how Opera displays these controls, coded like this:

```
<form>
What is your birthday?<br>
<input type="date"><br><br>
When would you like your service to begin?<br>
<input type="datetime"><br><br>
Please specify the date and time of the meeting:<br>
```

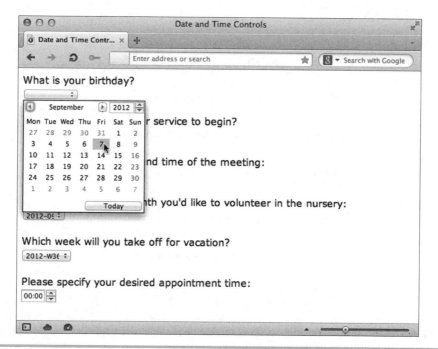

Figure 12-3   Opera is able to show user-friendly date and time pickers for these types of input controls.

```
<input type="datetime-local"><br><br>
Please specify which month you'd like to volunteer in the nursery:<br>
<input type="month"><br><br>
Which week will you take off for vacation?<br>
<input type="week"><br><br>
Please specify your desired appointment time:<br>
<input type="time"><br>
</form>
```

Thankfully, the good news is these new input controls degrade quite gracefully. In other words, in browsers without support for the new HTML5 input controls, the fields simply display as default single-line text fields. So even if your users cannot use a handy month or date picker, they can still enter the month or date by typing it in the text field (as they likely would have prior to HTML5), as shown in Figure 12-4.

Other Number Inputs

Prior to HTML5, there was no way in HTML to differentiate between text fields and number fields. Developers often had to resort to using something like JavaScript to achieve similar results. The number and range input types change all that.

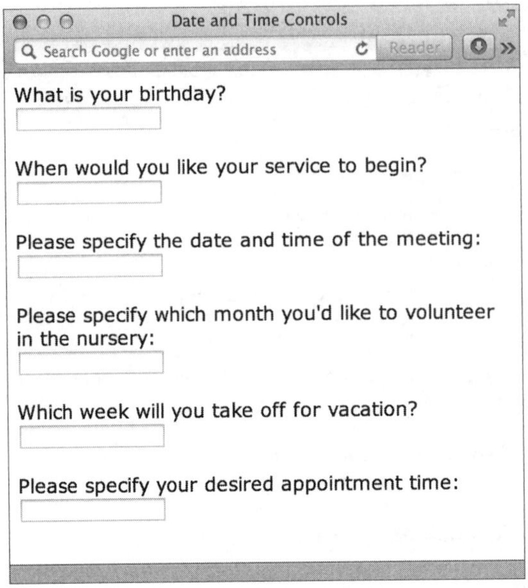

Figure 12-4 Safari 6 on a desktop system simply displays these controls as default text fields.

The number input type can be used to simply designate a text box as a number field, or you can customize it a bit with the addition of a few other attributes, like this:

```
<input type="number" min="0" max="12" step="2" value="8">
```

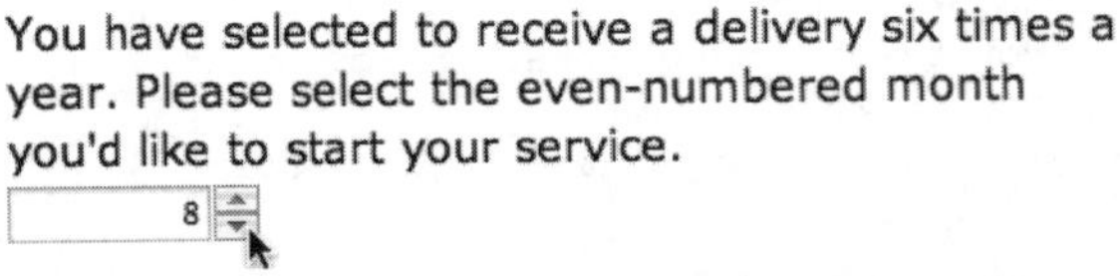

In this example, the `min` attribute designates the minimum possible value, while the `max` attribute identifies the maximum possible value. Then, because the step value is set to 2, only even-numbered options between 0 and 12 are possible. The starting value is 8.

The range control type is similar, in that it accepts the min, max, and step attributes, but different because it displays the input field as a slider. The following illustration shows how this code displays in Opera.

```
Please rate our service (10 is the best!): <br>
1<input type="range" min="1" max="10" step="1" value="5">10
```

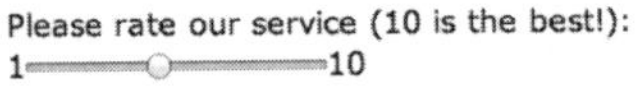

NOTE

As with the date and time inputs, those using browsers that don't support these number inputs will simply see standard text fields. So make sure your explanations are thorough enough for all users to know how to answer the question or request, even with older browsers.

Contact Methods

Three other input controls have been added in HTML5 to help identify certain types of contact methods. While the email, url, and tel input types don't change the way the form fields display in desktop browsers, they do offer great help to mobile users with supporting operating systems (as of this writing, only Apple mobile devices support these features). For example, the following code displays what appears to be three basic text boxes in most browsers:

```
<input name="email" type="email">
<input name="website" type="url">
<input name="phone" type="tel">
```

But when those same form fields are encountered in Safari on the iPhone, the keyboard changes to help the user enter the desired content. Compare Figures 12-5, 12-6, and 12-7 to see how the keyboard updates according to the input type.

The at symbol appears when the user encounters a field designated as an email input control.

Figure 12-5   Keyboard adjusted to help user input email addresses

These options appear when a user encounters a field designated as a website input control.

Figure 12-6   Keyboard adjusted to help user input web addresses

Figure 12-7   Keyboard adjusted to help user input phone numbers

Color Selectors

The final new type of input type I want to discuss in this section gives us the ability to add color pickers to our forms. Suppose you were creating a site for a t-shirt designer. You might use these color input fields to allow customers to select the shirt and ink colors for their designs, like this:

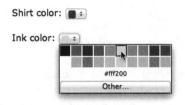

```
Shirt color: <input name="ShirtColor" type="color"><br><br>
Ink color: <input name="InkColor" type="color"><br><br>
```

NOTE

Browsers that don't yet support the color input type simply display the default text box.

As of this writing, many modern browsers don't yet support the color input type. The previous illustration shows how Opera supports color pickers. Chrome also supports color inputs, but relies on the operating system to actually select the color. As you can see in the next illustration, clicking the color box in Chrome on the Mac reveals the Apple color picker.

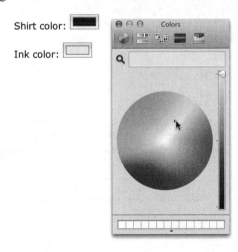

Select Menus

Whenever you want to let users select from a long list of options, you might consider using a select menu instead of check boxes or radio buttons. Select menus are lists that have been compressed into one or more visible options, similar to those menus you find at the top of other software applications.

NOTE

Menus may appear differently depending on which browser or computer system is used.

Also called *drop-down menus*, this type of menu enables users to click an option initially visible, and then pull down to reveal additional options. Unless a number greater than 1 is specified in the `size` attribute, only a single option is visible when the page loads. This option is accompanied by a small arrow, signifying that the menu expands. When the `size` attribute is 2 or more, that number of choices is visible in a scrollable list. Figure 12-8 shows two select menus. The first one uses the default size of 1, while the second is set to `size=3`.

The `select` element is used to create the menu initially, while `option` tags surround each item in the menu. A menu asking users to choose their favorite color might be coded like the following:

```
<form>
Please choose your favorite color:
<select name="FavoriteColor" size="3">
    <option value="blue">blue</option>
    <option value="red">red</option>
    <option value="yellow">yellow</option>
    <option value="green">green</option>
    <option value="other">other</option>
    </select>
</form>
```

NOTE

If you don't use the `value` attribute with each `option` tag, the text displayed in the menu will be transmitted as the option's value when the form is processed. Based on my experience, I recommend using the `value` attribute whenever possible to avoid confusion when the form is processed.

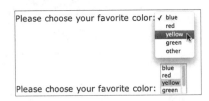

Figure 12-8 The `size` attribute enables you to specify how many options in your select menu are visible at once.

By default, users can select one item from the list. If you'd like them to be able to choose more than one option, add the `multiple` attribute to your opening `select` tag. The way users select more than one menu item depends on their computer system. For example, Macintosh users hold down the COMMAND key when clicking, while Windows users hold down the SHIFT key (or the CONTROL key to select noncontiguous choices in the list) and click.

```
<select name="FavoriteColors" size="3" multiple>
```

In addition, you can specify any item to be already selected when the page is loaded by adding the `selected` attribute to that item's opening `option` tag. Users can select a different menu item if they choose.

NOTE

Don't specify more than one item as `selected`, unless you also let users choose more than one option by adding the `multiple` attribute to the `select` tag.

```
<option value="red" selected>red</option>
```

Submenus

The `optgroup` element is used to divide long menus into categories of submenus. The `label` attribute is employed along with the `optgroup` element to give the submenu a name. The following is an example of how to create submenus with `optgroup` tags, followed by a visual representation of how one browser displays them:

```
<form>
Please choose the time and day that is best to reach you.
<select name="TimeDay">
<optgroup label="Monday">
    <option value="Monday AM">Monday AM</option>
    <option value="Monday PM">Monday PM</option>
</optgroup>
<optgroup label="Tuesday">
    <option value="Tuesday AM">Tuesday AM</option>
    <option value="Tuesday PM">Tuesday PM</option>
</optgroup>
</select>
</form>
```

Please choose the time and day that is best to reach you.

Disable Form Elements

When you want to restrict a user's input for a specific element, you might use one of two attributes:

```
readonly
disabled
```

The `readonly` attribute can be added to input controls so that users cannot change the values. For example, in the following code, the phrase `ww1234` is displayed in the text field but cannot be changed by the user. If you try to type in a text field that has been set to `readonly`, an alert is displayed or heard, but otherwise, no change exists in the appearance of the box.

```
Your username: <input value="ww1234" name="UserName" readonly>
```

The `disabled` attribute works essentially the same way, except input controls that are disabled also appear in gray or faded text to reduce their importance in the form. You cannot click in a text field that has been set to `disabled`.

```
Your username: <input value="ww1234" name="UserName" disabled>
```

While these attributes can be useful for sending data the user can't edit, there's actually a better way to do that. Keep reading to see what I mean.

Hidden Fields

Depending on the type of form you are creating, you may need to include a hidden field. For example, many teachers create several versions of a test to avoid having students look over their classmate's shoulder and cheat. In cases like this, you might make a special mark on the test identifying to which answer key it belongs. On web forms, these special marks are called *hidden fields*.

A hidden field is data attached to, and processed with, a form that cannot be seen or changed by the user. You can use as many hidden fields in your form as you'd like, using `input` tags with `type` attributes set to `hidden`.

```
<input type="hidden" name="TestVersion" value="3">
<input type="hidden" name="Creator" value="Wendy Willard">
```

TIP

This is also how you pass information from one form to the next when you start to build multipage forms.

File Uploads

Some online forms might require that a file be transmitted along with any data from the form. For example, you might provide the option for potential employees to submit a photo along with a job application being filled out online. This can be accomplished by using `type="file"` with the `input` element.

By giving your control a name, you can reference it when the form is processed.

`<input type="file" name="PhotoUpload">`

This tells the browser to expect a file input from the user.

NOTE

Check with your site's system administrator before adding file uploads to your web form because some hosts do not permit users to upload files through the web browser for security reasons. In addition, even if file uploads are permitted on your site's system, some adjustments to the host computer may need to be made.

For document uploads, most browsers display a text field followed by a button typically labeled Browse. By clicking the button, users can locate the file they want to send with the form on their computers. After they do so, the browser prints the location and name of the file in the text field provided.

Choose File   christmas.jpg

You can increase the size of the text field by adding the `size` attribute to the `input` tag. Because many file locations may be long, you might want to specify a size of 30 to 40 characters.

`<input type="file" name="PhotoUpload" size="40">`

In addition, HTML5 added the multiple attribute to file uploads. Using this attribute lets the browser know it's okay for the user to select multiple files to upload:

`<input type="file" name="PhotoUpload" size="40" multiple>`

Buttons

Buttons enable users to interact with a form. For example, to tell the browser you're finished filling out a form and are ready to process it, you might click a button labeled Submit. You can create three types of buttons with HTML:

- **Submit buttons**   Used to process a form
- **Reset buttons**   Used to reset a form
- **Other buttons**   Serve any alternative needs for buttons in a form

You can use the `input` or `button` tag to create any of these buttons. Because the `input` element is the preferred method for adding buttons *to forms*, I suggest you use that. In either

Type of Button	Description	HTML	Browser View
Submit	When clicked, this button processes the form.	`<input type="submit" value="Submit">` or `<button type="submit">Submit </button>`	Submit
Reset	When clicked, this button resets all the form's fields back to their initial values.	`<input type="reset" value="Reset">` or `<button type="reset">Reset</button>`	Reset
Button	When clicked, an action or event is triggered, based on a predefined script or function. (This usually involves some scripting language beyond basic HTML, such as JavaScript.)	`<input type="button" value="Verify Data">` or `<button type="button">Verify Data</button>`	Verify Data

Table 12-3 Types of Buttons

case, add the `type` attribute and appropriate `value` to identify which button you are creating (see Table 12-3).

TIP
On the PC, these buttons are displayed as rectangles with squared-off edges by default.
On the Mac, these buttons have rounded edges.

Formatting with the button Element
You may be wondering why I'd even mention the `button` element when the `input` element is more popular. Well ... while the `input` and `button` elements both create a basic gray `button` with text inside, the button element has additional formatting possibilities. You may have noticed in Table 12-3 that, unlike the `input` element, which doesn't have a closing tag, the `button` element has both opening and closing tags. This enables you to enter text, images, and other HTML that will be placed on the button when viewed in the browser.

For example, if I include an `img` element between the opening and closing `button` tags, that image would be displayed in the center of the button when viewed in the browser.

```
<button type="submit" name="Submit" value="Submit">
<img src="savenow.gif" width="106" height="47" alt="Save Now!">
</button>
```

By default, most browsers display a gray background with a black border around buttons created in this fashion. This means by default, using the preceding code, that button might look like this in the browser:

If you want your images to appear seamlessly on the button, use that same gray as your image's background color or make the image's background transparent. Or, change the background color and turn off the border in your style sheet.

```
button { background-color: white; border: none; }
```

Graphical Buttons with the input Element

You can also use an image as a button with the `input` tag by changing the type to `image`, as in the following example. The `src` attribute is then required to specify where to find the image. Likewise, you also should add the `alt` attribute to allow for a text description to display when the image does not.

```
<input type="image" src="savenow.gif" name="Submit" alt="Send Message">
```

Graphical buttons created with the `input` tag are different from those created with the `button` tag because they aren't naturally placed on a button in the browser. Instead, they're surrounded by a border, just like what's around any other linked image by default. You can use style sheets, as needed, to turn off that border.

Try This 12-1   Create a Basic Form

All web sites should contain some way for visitors to contact the business or organization. Otherwise, it's like having an advertisement in the phone book that doesn't list your phone number! This could be accomplished through a simple email link, a listed phone number, or even a *Contact Us* form. In this project, you create a *Contact Us* form for your practice site. The goals for this project include

- Creating a basic form
- Using several different input controls in the form
- Creating submit and reset buttons

(continued)

1. Open your text or HTML editor and create a new file entitled **contactus.html**.

2. Type all the HTML tags needed for a basic HTML page.

3. Type opening and closing `form` tags.

4. Create input controls that allow visitors to request information about products and services for this company. Be sure to include ways for the company representative to reach the user, such as through a phone number and/or email address.

5. Save the file.

6. Open your web browser and choose File | Open Page (or Open File or Open, depending on the browser you're using). Locate the file contactus.html, which you just saved. Make sure the file appears as you intended it. Note: Nothing will happen when you try to "submit" your form, but don't worry—we address processing forms in the next section. For now, we're focusing on creating the form itself.

7. If you need to make changes, return to your text editor to do so. After making any changes, save the file and switch back to the browser. Choose Refresh or Reload to preview the changes you just made.

TIP

Do your text fields, select menus, and other controls appear? If not, check to make sure you closed your `form` tag (`</form>`). For more tips, see Appendix C.

Online forms are a great way to get customer feedback. In addition, forms make it easy for your visitors to ask questions about products and services. This project gave you practice working on a basic form.

Validate the Form Content

Prior to HTML5, the only way to validate form content involved scripting or programming beyond basic HTML. This pushed it beyond the realm of many new or novice developers. Thankfully, HTML5 brings us the required and pattern attributes.

This eight-letter word—*required*—may seem inconsequential at first glance, but is actually quite powerful in supported browsers. Simply adding it to an input control will prevent the form from being submitted if that particular field is left empty.

```
<input type="email" name="Email" required>
```

As an added bonus, when used in conjunction with a specialized text field like email, supporting browsers will prompt the user to enter the appropriate content before proceeding.

If you're practicing these elements and attributes alongside me, you may have noticed the browser indicated the field was invalid in some way, to identify the problem area to the user. You can adjust the color, shape, or other characteristic of the input control—both when it is valid and when it is invalid—with a few special selectors. For instance, in the following code snippet, all input controls will carry a two-pixel, solid gray border. When the cursor is present inside the form field—with the `:focus` pseudo-selector—the border changes to green. When the form is submitted within the required fields—with the `:invalid` pseudo-selector—the border changes to red.

```
input {border: 2px solid gray;}
input:focus {border: 2px solid green;}
input:invalid {border: 2px solid red;}
```

We'll look at this a bit more in the next chapter.

Using Patterns

One of the most frustrating aspects of forms can be the incomplete data received when the form is submitted. We'll talk a little later about validating that content to help prevent the submission of incomplete data, but first let's consider one of the new HTML5 attributes that is applicable to this conversation.

NOTE

The `pattern` attribute works with the following types of input controls: text, search, url, tel, email, and password.

The `pattern` attribute allows us to specify those characters deemed acceptable for a particular text input field. For instance, suppose you coded a form with credit card fields. How useless is it to receive a completed form that is missing one of the numbers in the credit card field? We can use the `pattern` attribute to indicate exactly how many numbers are required, like this:

```
<input pattern="[0-9]{16}" title="Enter your 16-digit credit card
number, without any spaces or dashes." name="CreditCard">
```

The accepted value of the `pattern` attribute is a valid *regular expression*. In the preceding example, the first part of the pattern, [0-9], tells the browser to only accept numbers between zero and nine. The second part, {16}, specifies the total length of the required characters.

Regular expressions—or *regexp* in JavaScript terminology—are somewhat cryptic-looking character strings that specify an expected pattern. There are tons of different options available, depending on exactly what you're looking to describe. For an excellent resource on writing regular expressions for your patterns, check out **www.html5pattern.com**.

The following illustration shows how Chrome handles a situation when the user input doesn't match the requested pattern.

It's important to note that the tool tip only displays when the user enters incorrect data and attempts to submit the form. If the field is left blank, the pattern is not checked. So to prevent users from submitting a form with a blank field, add the `required` attribute to the `input` tag, like this:

```
<input pattern="[0-9]{16}" title="Enter your 16-digit credit card
number, without any spaces or dashes." name="CreditCard" required>
```

With both the `pattern` and `required` attributes, the browser will prevent the form from being submitted unless a valid text string is entered in the corresponding field.

Provide a Way for Your Form to Be Processed

The phrase *processing method* refers to what happens to the form after the user enters all the data and clicks the Submit button. Is it emailed to the site's administrator or stored in a database? Or perhaps it's written to another web page on the site, such as what occurs with a guest book or bulletin board. Many possibilities exist, which ultimately depend on the purpose of the form.

Inside the opening `form` tag, you need to tell the browser how to process your form. This is accomplished through the `action` attribute (which is required), as well as the `method` and `enctype` attributes (which are optional).

The action Attribute

The `action` attribute gives the location where the form's information should be sent. This can be in the form of either an email address:

```
<form action="mailto:name@emailaddress.com">
```

or the URL of a CGI script:

```
<form action="../cgi-bin/form.cgi">
```

While the easier way to process a form is to have the data sent to an email address, I don't recommend this method. Because no official specification exists for using email to process forms in HTML, the results achieved with this method vary according to the browser. In fact, many browsers don't support this method at all. Perhaps the best use of this might be testing your forms before implementing a CGI script.

TIP

You might think of a CGI program as being similar to the mail carrier for your post office. This person picks up your mail and transports it to and from the post office. Some mail carriers drive trucks, while others drive cars or walk. Regardless of how they get there, they all take mail to the post office and bring mail back to you. In like manner, CGI scripts, regardless of which language they are written in, transfer information to and from the server.

CGI stands for *Common Gateway Interface* and refers to a program that sends information to and from the server. This program, also called a *script*, can be written in several different scripting languages such as ASP, PHP, or CFM. The oldest and most common of these languages is Perl, because of its ease of use and the large number of people who are able to write it.

CGI scripts must reside on your server (the computer hosting your web pages for everyone on the Web to access) in directories with special settings that allow them to be *executed*, or run. For this reason, using a CGI script requires you to talk to the company that hosts your web site about whether it supports CGI scripts and, if it does, how to implement them. Most hosting companies receive questions about CGI scripts quite often and have pages of information on their web sites dedicated to the subject. When in doubt, visit your host company's web site or call to see what your next step should be.

NOTE

One reason some hosting providers don't allow CGI scripts on their servers is that they can infringe on the site's security. If your hosting provider doesn't let you use a CGI script, don't worry. Several services are set up to host these scripts and process your forms for you. Check with your own hosting provider for referrals, or search Google for a list of companies providing these types of services.

What Does a CGI Script Look Like?

Just because a CGI script cannot be written in HTML, that doesn't mean you can't learn how to write one. As I mentioned before, I don't consider myself a computer programmer and I didn't study computer science in school. I can understand and write basic Perl scripts to process my HTML forms, though.

While creating CGI scripts (whether in Perl or another language) is beyond the scope of this book, Figure 12-9 shows what a CGI script written in Perl looks like. By showing this, I hope to give you an idea of what happens to the form data after a user clicks the Submit button.

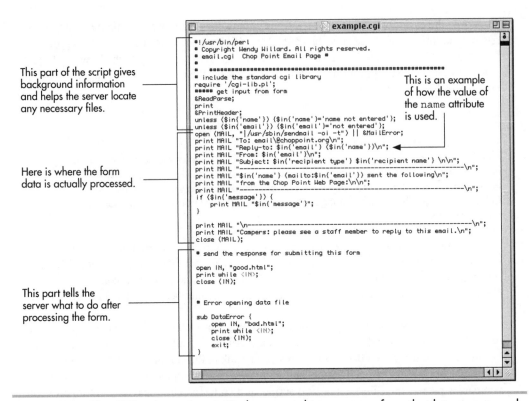

This part of the script gives background information and helps the server locate any necessary files.

This is an example of how the value of the name attribute is used.

Here is where the form data is actually processed.

This part tells the server what to do after processing the form.

```perl
#!/usr/bin/perl
# Copyright Wendy Willard. All rights reserved.
# email.cgi  Chop Point Email Page #
#
#  =========================================================
# include the standard cgi library
require '/cgi-lib.pl';
##### get input from form
&ReadParse;
print
&PrintHeader;
unless ($in{'name'}) ($in{'name'}='name not entered');
unless ($in{'email'}) ($in{'email'}='not entered');
open (MAIL, "|/usr/sbin/sendmail -oi -t") || &MailError;
print MAIL "To: email\@choppoint.org\n";
print MAIL "Reply-to: $in{'email'} ($in{'name'})\n";
print MAIL "From: $in{'email'}\n";
print MAIL "Subject: $in{'recipient type'} $in{'recipient name'} \n\n";
print MAIL "-----------------------------------------------------\n";
print MAIL "$in{'name'} (mailto:$in{'email'}) sent the following\n";
print MAIL "from the Chop Point Web Page:\n\n";
print MAIL "-----------------------------------------------------\n";
if ($in{'message'}) {
    print MAIL "$in{'message'}";
}

print MAIL "\n-----------------------------------------------------\n";
print MAIL "Campers: please see a staff member to reply to this email.\n";
close (MAIL);

# send the response for submitting this form

open IN, "good.html";
print while <IN>;
close (IN);


# Error opening data file

sub DataError {
    open IN, "bad.html";
    print while <IN>;
    close (IN);
    exit;
}
```

Figure 12-9 This CGI script, written in Perl, was used to process a form that lets parents and friends email kids at camp.

Where Can I Get a CGI Script?

Literally thousands of free CGI scripts are available on the Web, and thousands of others are available for small fees. First, check with your hosting provider for referrals. Your provider might even have some scripts on hand for you to use that are already set up to work on their systems.

If you need to find your own scripts, try searching Google or looking at some of these sites:

● **www.javascriptsource.com/forms**

● **www.tectite.com**

● **www.hotscripts.com**

Pay attention to the documentation offered with each script because it should tell you how to customize the script for your needs and how to install it on your server.

The method and enctype Attributes

The two other attributes you'll probably use in the opening `form` tag are `method` and `enctype`. The `method` attribute tells the browser how to send the data to the server. There are two common values for this attribute: `get` and `post`.

TIP
For help deciding which method or enctype to use, consult your hosting provider or the creator of your CGI script.

The `get` method takes all the data submitted with the form and sends it to the server attached to the end of the URL. For example, say the script location is **http://www.yoursite .com/cgi-bin/form.cgi**, and the only data from the form is the user's name (in this case, we'll use `wendy`). If the method was set to `get`, here's what would be sent to the server when the user clicked the Submit button:

```
http://www.yoursite.com/cgi-form.cgi?name=wendy
```

This method works best for searches where a small amount of information must be transferred to the server, such as the keywords you are searching for. For more comprehensive forms, the `post` method can be used. Instead of attaching the information to the URL of the script, the information is sent directly to the location of the script file. (However, there are limitations on file size, depending on where the data is going and how the server is set up. Check with your system administrator for more information if file size becomes an issue.)

The `enctype` attribute, short for *encoding type*, tells the browser how to format the data when the `method` attribute is set to `post`. The default value is `application/x-www-form-urlencoded`. Because this should work for most of your `forms`, you needn't include the `enctype` attribute in your `form` tag unless you want to change the value.

For example, if you are allowing users to upload files with your form, you need to change the `enctype` to `multipart/form-data`, as in the following example:

```
<form action="myscript.cgi" method="post" enctype="multipart/form-data">
```

Chapter 12 Self Test

1. Fill in the blank: _____ tags must surround all web forms.

2. Name four types of text input controls in HTML web forms.

3. Which attribute names an input control so that it's correctly handled when the form is processed?

4. Which input control is most useful for questions requiring a simple yes or no answer?

5. True/False: Radio buttons are small, round buttons that enable users to select a single option from a list of choices.

6. Fill in the blank: The _____ attribute identifies the visible width of a text area based on an average character width.

7. Fix the following code so that users can enter multiple lines of data into the comment box, which should measure 30 characters wide by 5 lines tall:

```
Enter your comments here:
<input size="30,5"></input>
```

8. How do you cause three options in a select menu to be visible at once?

9. Add the appropriate code to create a single-line text field in which, upon entry of data, all contents are displayed as bullets or asterisks in the browser. Name the field "secret."

```
Please enter your secret word:
<                               >
```

10. Fill in the blank: _____ tags surround each item in a select menu.

11. Add the appropriate code to create a place where users can upload a graphic file from their personal computers to the web server. Name the field "upload."

```
Please select the file to upload:
<                               >
```

12. Which attribute is added to the `form` tag to give the location where the form's information should be sent?

13. Which attribute and value are added to the `form` tag to tell the browser to take all the data submitted with the form and send it to the server attached to the end of the file's URL?

Chapter 13

Formatting and Styling Forms

Key Skills & Concepts

- Apply Tables to Forms

- Make Forms More User-Friendly

- Style Forms for Layout

- Style Forms for Client-Side Validation

In the previous chapter, you learned the basics of setting up a form on a web page. As you might have guessed, you can use many of the formatting techniques discussed in other chapters to format and style those forms. For example, to add a line break in between a text input field and its label, you could simply add the br element:

```
First Name:<br> <input name="FirstName">
```

But what if you wanted to add line breaks in between all of a form's input controls and labels? Sure, it's possible to add br elements like this throughout the whole form, but what if you change your mind later and then need to remove them all? Thankfully, there are much better ways to format and style forms. Let's take a look at some of the options.

Apply Tables to Forms

If you refer to the form you created in the last chapter's Try This, you may notice the text fields are scattered through the page. If, instead, you want to have all the text fields lined up in a column, you could use a table to format your form.

When using a table to lay out a form, you will probably place each individual element in its own table cell. Perhaps the labels for the form (telling people what information to enter) might be placed in cells in the first column, while the input controls (text fields, and so forth) might be placed in the second column.

```
<form action="..." method="post">
<table>
<tr>
    <td>First Name</td>        ← This text label is in a cell
                                  by itself in the first column.
    <td><input name="FirstName"></td>
</tr>
                                  This cell in the second column contains only
<tr>                              the input control for the user's first name.
    <td>Last Name</td>
    <td><input name="LastName"></td>
</tr>
```

```
<tr>
    <td>Mailing Address</td>
    <td><input name="AddressLine1"></td>
</tr>
<tr>
    <td> </td> ◄──── This cell is empty.
    <td><input name="AddressLine2"></td> ◄──── This text field is a second line for
                                                users to enter their mailing addresses.
</tr>  The two columns are merged for this row to allow the Submit
<tr>  and Reset buttons to flow freely at the bottom of the table.
    <td colspan="2"><input value="Send Form"><input type="reset"
value="Start Over"></td>
</tr>
</table>
</form>
```

Using a table like this enables you to achieve a more uniform look in your forms. Notice in the following illustration how all of the text fields line up vertically, regardless of how long or short the preceding text is.

While a table can definitely help give structure to your forms, it is not always the most user-friendly way to do so. First, let's look at a few ways to make forms more user-friendly in general. Then, we'll review a few other ways to structure forms that don't require the use of tables.

TIP
Because determining where each text label and input control should be placed can initially be confusing, I recommend you first create the form itself before placing it into a table. As with any table, it may help to plan the form on paper before coding.

Make Forms More User-Friendly
One of the goals in formatting and styling forms is to make them easier to understand and complete. Forms have become such an integral part of the Web; we cannot ignore opportunities to make them better. Whether you're creating a simple contact form, a search tool, or a complex job application, it's important to spend adequate time and energy to make your form as user-friendly as possible.

Set Tab Order and Keyboard Shortcuts

Chapter 7 discussed changing the tab order and adding keyboard shortcuts for links using the `tabindex` and `accesskey` attributes. You can also use these attributes to format input controls in a form. Remember, the tab index begins at 0, not 1.

This attribute causes the text field to become active after the user presses the TAB key three times.

```
Enter your first name (alt-f):
<input name="FirstName" tabindex="2" accesskey="f">
```

This allows the text field to become active when the user types F and presses another key (ALT on the PC, COMMAND on the Mac).

Refer to Chapter 7 for details on using either of these two attributes.

Ask the Expert

Q: I used a table to lay out my web page and placed a form for searching in one cell. When I did so, however, I noticed a lot of extra space in that cell, which I can't seem to delete by adjusting the padding or margins. What's going on?

A: Unfortunately, this is a common problem. The root of the problem lies in understanding what kind of tag the `form` tag is. As outlined in Chapter 2, tags in HTML usually fall into one of two categories: block elements or inline elements. *Block elements,* like `form` and `table`, are used for structure and layout on a page, while inline elements are employed to alter the appearance of text. For example, `strong`, an inline element, is used to make text bold, but it doesn't alter the location of the text. Block elements do alter the location of text or other items on a page, and by default, many of them force a line break within the page. This means that wherever you place the `form` element, a blank line is also inserted.

Q: Yes, but isn't there any way around that?

A: The easiest way to fix this is to turn off the margins of your form with CSS. Using the `form` tag as your selector, add `margin:0` and `padding:0` to the style declaration to reset both values and remove any extra space. If this is a big problem on your page, a better option is to use style sheets instead of tables to lay out your form. This is discussed more in the latter part of this chapter, in the section titled "Use Styles and Fieldsets to Eliminate the Table Layout."

Include Labels

Whenever you include descriptive text before an input control, you are labeling it for users, helping them to understand what type of information they should enter. To link the label and the associating control formally, you can use the `label` element and the `id` attribute. Each `label` can only be attached to one control. Also, it's worth mentioning that when labels are used with check box and radio button fields, clicking the label actually checks or unchecks the selected box or button.

This gives the label a name so that it
can be referenced by the input control.

```
<label for="birthday">When is your birthday?  (MM/DD/YY)</label> <input
type="date" name="BirthDate" id="birthday" size="8">
```

This references the appropriate label.

NOTE

As of this writing, the use of either the `label` element or the `id` attribute doesn't change the way the page appears in a graphical browser.

This formal labeling process was new to HTML in version 4.01. Since then, it's become an important technique for linking labels and controls, particularly to ensure your page is accessible to all users. The reason for this is that when tables are used, controls and their labels are often separated across table cells. This can be especially troublesome for nonvisual browsers when they try to link controls with the appropriate label.

```
<form action="..." method="post">
<table>
<tr>
    <td><label for="fname">First Name</label></td>
    <td><input name="FirstName" id="fname"></td>
</tr>
<tr>
    <td><label for="lname">Last Name</label></td>
    <td><input name="LastName" id="lname"></td>
</tr>
</table>
</form>
```

There are a lot of different opinions regarding the best place for form field labels. The most common three options are

- **Top-aligned**   Where the form field item is placed just below its text label
- **Left-aligned**   Where the form field is placed to the right of the text label, but left-aligned on the page

- **Right-aligned** Where the form field is placed to the right of the text label, but then right-aligned on the page

Of these, studies have shown that top-aligned form labels offer the best readability for users, so much so that they increase the likelihood users will actually complete the form. However, this type of vertical layout does increase the overall height of the form, which can sometimes cause other usability concerns. So in situations where height is an issue, right-aligned labels are the next best choice. In the end, you must balance all of the various usability factors to determine the best course of action for your particular forms.

Group-Related Controls

While the `label` element is used to attach names to controls formally, the `fieldset` element enables you to group sets of labels and controls. Grouping input controls with these elements can be a great alternative to using tables for form layouts. For example, if you had an employee application form with three distinct sections, such as Schooling, Work Experience, and Skills, you could use `fieldset` tags to group all the labels and controls under these headings. The `legend` tags then give a caption to the group, if you want to include one.

```
<form action="form.php" method="post">
<fieldset>
  <legend>Schooling</legend>
  <p>High School: <input name="HighSchool"><br>
  College: <input name="College"></p>
</fieldset>
<fieldset>
  <legend>Work Experience</legend>
  <p>Current Job: <input name="CurrentJob"><br>
  Previous Job: <input name="PreviousJob1"><br>
  Previous Job: <input name="PreviousJob2"></p>
</fieldset>
<fieldset>
  <legend>Skills</legend>
  <p>Skill 1: <input name="Skill1"><br>
  Skill 2: <input name="Skill2"><br>
  Skill 3: <input name="Skill3"></p>
</fieldset>
</form>
```

Most browsers supporting the `fieldset` element add boxes around each group and place the caption from the `legend` tag in the outline of the box as a headline.

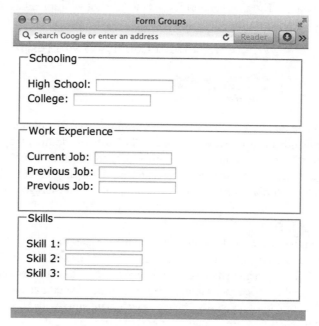

Add Data Lists

What if you want to provide a list of options for the user, but also want to allow custom options to be entered? Or suppose you asked users to enter the name of their city, but couldn't include options for every single city out there. You might include the most popular city names in a data list for a text field, like this:

```
Where in Harford County do you reside?<br>
<input name="city" list="HarCoCities">
  <datalist id="HarCoCities">
    <option value="Abingdon">Abingdon</option>
    <option value="Aberdeen">Aberdeen</option>
    <option value="Bel Air">Bel Air</option>
    <option value="Belcamp">Belcamp</option>
    <option value="Churchville">Churchville</option>
    <option value="Darlington">Darlington</option>
    <option value="Edgewood">Edgewood</option>
    <option value="Fallston">Fallston</option>
    <option value="Forest Hill">Forest Hill</option>
    <option value="Havre de Grace">Havre de Grace</option>
    <option value="Joppa">Joppa</option>
    <option value="North Harford">North Harford</option>
  </datalist>
```

Then, when the user starts typing a city name, matching values from your data list will display as selectable options. Browser support for data lists is not widespread as of this writing. But, the following illustration shows how this is supported in Chrome on the Mac.

Where in Harford County do you reside?

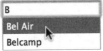

Data lists like this are great for making forms more user-friendly, because they reduce the amount of typing that is necessary to complete the form. In addition, they help the data entry to be more uniform, such as without spelling errors or capitalization issues.

The key to matching up your data list with the corresponding input control is this: Make sure your input tag's list attribute matches the value of the id attribute assigned to the datalist element.

Show Progress

HTML5 introduces two new elements to handle the measurement of various aspects of your forms: progress and meter. Let's take a look at how these work.

The key difference between these two elements has to do with the type of measurements described. While the progress element marks a measurement that is changing, such as one that is on a path or part of a process, the meter element simply identifies measurements, regardless of whether they are changing or part of a process.

There are six attributes for the `meter` element, the first three of which are also used for `progress`:

- **`value`** Marks the starting or default measurement

- **`min`** Identifies the minimum allowed measurement (default is 0)

- **`max`** Identifies the maximum allowed measurement (default is 1, or 100%, depending on the content)

- **`low`** Specifies the low end of the measurement range (cannot be lower than the `min` value)

- **`high`** Specifies the high end of the measurement range (cannot be higher than the `max` value)

- **`optimum`** Identifies the optimal value, somewhere between the `min` and `max` values

With this information in mind, let's consider a few real-world examples. Suppose you wanted to show the progress of a file upload inside of a form. The progress element is perfect for this situation. The basic HTML for this example is super easy, and could be something as simple as this:

```
<input type="file" name="PhotoUpload"><progress value="0"
max="100">Waiting to start</progress>
```

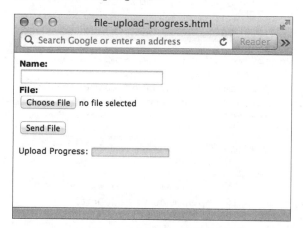

What's much trickier is getting the progress bar to actually update as the file is being uploaded. That bit of interactivity requires some scripting beyond HTML, typically with JavaScript. Read over Chapter 14, and then when you're ready to tackle some JavaScript, check out the following online tutorials about scripting progress bars:

- Using the HTML5 Progress Tag **www.htmlatoms.com/basic/using-the-html5-progress-tag**

- Mozilla Demos the New 'Progress' HTML5 Element **news.softpedia.com/news/Mozilla-Demos-the-New-HTML5-Element-in-Firefox-6-204713.shtml**

- HTML5 Progress Bar – jsFiddle **www.jsfiddle.net/wmichaelgreen/Gj6Pv/**

Other examples of uses for the progress element include showing the strength of a password and indicating progress in a multistep or multipage form.

NOTE

While these two elements are often used within forms, you can actually use them to show progress and measurements in other parts of your pages as well. This means it's safe to include them even if you don't have a form on your page.

The `meter` element is used not so much to show progress, but to show a measurement in relationship to a defined range. For example, you might use it to show the percentage of responders who selected a particular option on a form.

```
Which candidate do you support?<br>

<input type="radio" name="candidate" value="Big Bird" id="candidate-
option1"> <label for="candidate-option1">Big Bird <meter min="0"
max="50" value="30"></meter></label><br>

<input type="radio" name="candidate" value="Bugs Bunny" id="candidate-
option2"> <label for="candidate-option2">Bugs Bunny <meter min="0"
max="50" value="40"></meter></label><br>

<input type="radio" name="candidate" value="Rudolph" id="candidate-
option3">  <label for="candidate-option3">Rudolph <meter min="0"
max="50" value="20"></meter></label><br>

<input type="radio" name="candidate" value="Micky Mouse"
id="candidate-option4"> <label for="candidate-option4">Micky Mouse
<meter min="0" max="50" value="10"></meter></label>
```

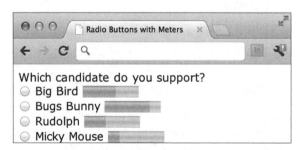

In addition to the `min`, `max`, and `value` attributes, the `high`, `low`, and `optimum` attributes can help provide visual clues about the measurement. For instance, consider a thermometer to gauge a child's fever. While the official `min` and `max` might be 90° and 106°, adding a `high` of 104° and a `low` of 96° might help parents see when there is perhaps cause for concern. In this situation, an `optimum` value would be 98.6°. If we used all these numbers within a `meter` element and added an initial value of 104.1, supporting browsers would color the bar yellow, so as to indicate it is above the target high.

Child's temperature of 104.1: ▓▓▓▓▓▓

Here's what the corresponding code might look like:

```
Child's temperature of 104.1:
<meter value="104.1" max="106" high="104" low="96" min="90"
optimum="98.6">104.1</meter>
```

With both the `progress` and `meter` elements, any text included between the opening and closing tags will only display in browsers that do not support meters and progress bars. As of this writing, there are still some modern browsers that don't offer support, so be sure to thoroughly test your pages when using these elements.

TIP

The `progress` and `meter` elements each require some level of scripting to truly be functional and interactive in web pages. Check out **www.basewebmaster.com/html/ html5-form-elements.php** for a very basic set of examples and then read Chapter 14 for more on JavaScript.

Other examples of uses for the `meter` element include showing user ratings, indicating relevance in search results, and giving a total score on a test or quiz.

Assist Your Users

There are a few final comments I'd like to make about making forms more user-friendly before we close this section:

- **Mark required fields**   When you specify form fields as required in the code, don't forget to let the user know. Clearly indicate those fields are, well, *required* so a user doesn't waste time trying to submit a form before it's complete. Note if 8 out of 10 fields are required, it makes more sense to mark the optional fields and then specify—in the instructions for the form—that all other fields are required.

- **Explain yourself**   Make it clear *why* the form itself is necessary to help the user understand why he is being asked to provide his information.

- **Make text labels readable**   Web designers are known for preferring smaller font sizes and faces, but web forms are not appropriate places to test out our latest favorites. Stick with standard web fonts of at least 11 pixels in colors that stand out well against the background.

- **Avoid adding links to external content within the form**   No one likes having to re-enter content. If you provide distracting links within a form that then take the user somewhere else without first finishing the form, he risks having to re-enter the content later. If you absolutely must include a link inside the form, force that content to display in another browser window or tab, so as not to lose the user's current place in the form.

- **Don't ask for information you don't need**   Many business owners want to capture as much information as possible from their user base. This is understandable, but maintaining said information can get risky. You don't want to be responsible for storing, and safeguarding, your users' personal information if you don't need it. This means, for example, if you don't plan to call your users, you don't need their phone numbers. In addition, many users stop filling out long forms when they get to information they either don't find relevant or simply don't want to give.

- **Likewise, safeguard the information you do request** If you gather personal information about users through web forms, you better have a safe way to store it. Here's what is not safe: simply having the form data emailed to you and then stored in your inbox. Using Secure Sockets Layer (SSL) encryption is a good option, but does require some additional setup. Check out **www.sslshopper.com/article-how-to-make-a-secure-login-form-with-ssl.html** for some tips.

- **Match the button's importance level to its weight** Have you ever accidentally clicked the Reset or Cancel button in a form, only to lose all of your work? This occurs when a form designer gives equal visual importance to all the buttons, so much so that the user can't quickly distinguish between them. To solve this problem, change the style of less important buttons (or lose them altogether if possible) to clearly indicate the primary actions on the form.

TIP

For more tips on making forms usable, check out this great resource: **http://uxdesign.smashingmagazine.com/2011/11/08/extensive-guide-web-form-usability**.

Style Forms

Most of the form tags you learned can also be altered with style sheets. This means you could quite easily turn all of your text boxes green if you wanted to. It also means you can finally do away with those boring white and gray form elements! And because the form tag is a block-level element (just like the p tag), you can even style your entire form to have a particular background color or border.

To further illustrate this point, consider Figures 13-1 and 13-2. The first figure shows a basic HTML form, created with the tags discussed in this chapter and the previous one, that has been placed in a table. The HTML used to create this form is shown next.

```
<form action="..." method="post" id="salesform">
<table>
<tr><td width="50%">Name:</td>
<td width="50%"><input name="name" size="25"></td>
</tr>
<tr><td>Company:</td>
<td><input name="company" size="25"></td>
</tr>
<tr><td>Preferred contact method:</td>
<td><select name="contact-type"><option value="Email">Email</option>
<option value="Phone">Phone</option></select></td>
</tr>
<tr><td>Email address/phone number:</td>
```

```
<td><input size="25" name="contact-method"></td>
</tr>
<tr><td>Identify whether this is your first time here:</td>
<td><input type="radio" name="first-visit" value="yes" class="radio">
Yes, this is my first visit<br>
<input type="radio" name="first-visit" value="no" class="radio"> No,
I've been here before</td>
</tr>
<tr><td>Select those products you're considering:</td>
<td><input type="checkbox" name="products" value="Photoshop">
Photoshop<br>
<input type="checkbox" name="products" value="Illustrator">
Illustrator<br>
<input type="checkbox" name="products" value="Acrobat"> Acrobat<br>
<input type="checkbox" name="products" value="InDesign"> InDesign</td>
</tr>
<tr><td>Commments/questions:</td>
<td><textarea cols="25" rows="5" name="comments"></textarea></td>
</tr>
<tr>
<td colspan="2">When finished, click this button to transmit your
information to our sales team: <input type="submit" name="Submit"
value="Submit" id="submit"></td>
</tr>
</table></form>
```

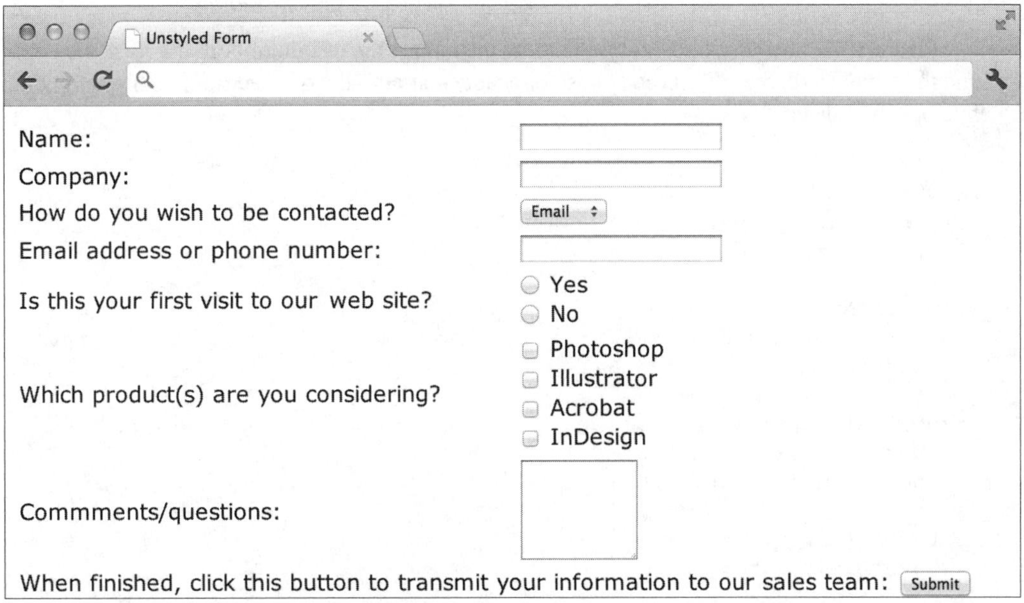

Figure 13-1 This is our very basic HTML form (inside a table) before CSS.

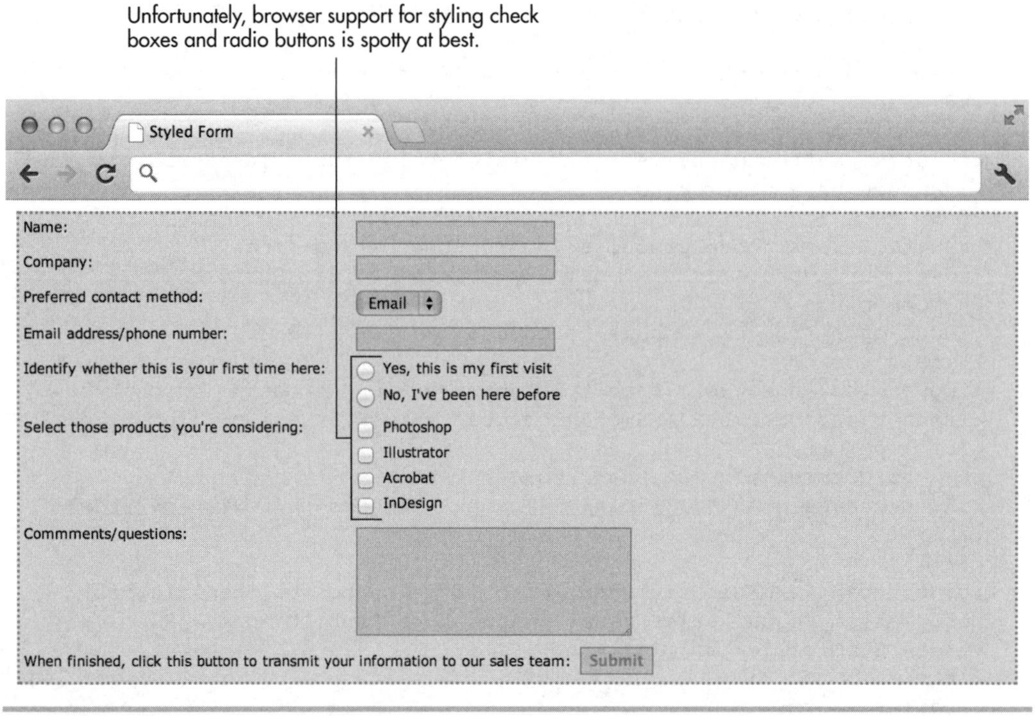

Unfortunately, browser support for styling check boxes and radio buttons is spotty at best.

Figure 13-2 This is the same HTML code with a style sheet applied.

Figure 13-2, however, adds a style sheet to customize the design of both the form elements and the table. Here, the HTML code has not changed at all—the only addition is the following internal style sheet:

```
<style>
body {
    font-family: verdana;
    font-size: 10px;
}
form#salesform {
    border: 2px dotted #F60;
    background-color: #fde6a2;
}
input, select, textarea {
    border: 1px solid #F60;
    background-color: #FC3;
}
textarea {
    overflow: auto;
    padding: 5px;
}
```

```
td {
    vertical-align: top;
}
#submit {
    color: #F60;
    font-weight: bold;
}
</style>
```

TIP

The key to styling forms (or any other page element for that matter) is in properly preparing the HTML code before you even begin the style sheet. Depending on your needs, this may mean adding `id` attributes to each form element so that they can be referenced later. Or perhaps using the `colgroup` tag to enable easy access to each column (for styling purposes).

Use Styles and Fieldsets to Eliminate the Table Layout

What if you wanted to take your style sheet one step further and use it to lay out the entire form, and even eliminate the need to use a table for layout? Not only is this a great option, it actually can make the design and maintenance of forms much easier. Consider the same form used in the previous section, this time coded without any table tags:

```
<form action="..." method="post" id="salesform">
<fieldset>
    <legend>Contact Information</legend>
    <label for="name">Name:</label>
        <input name="name" size="25" id="name">
    <label for="company">Company:</label>
        <input name="company" size="25" id="company">
    <label for="contact-type">Preferred contact method:</label>
        <select name="contact-type" id="contact-type">
        <option value="Email">Email</option>
        <option value="Phone">Phone</option>
        </select>
    <label for="contact-method">Email address/phone number:</label>
        <input size="25" name="contact-method" id="contact-method">
</fieldset>

<fieldset>
    <legend>New Customer?</legend>
    <label for="first-visit">Identify whether this is your first time
here:</label>
        <input type="radio" name="first-visit" value="yes"
class="radio"> Yes, this is my first visit<br>
        <input type="radio" name="first-visit" value="no"
class="radio"> No, I've been here before
</fieldset>
```

```
<fieldset>
    <legend>Product Interest</legend>
    <label for="products">Select those products you're considering:
</label>
        <input type="checkbox" name="products" value="Photoshop">
Photoshop<br>
        <input type="checkbox" name="products" value="Illustrator">
Illustrator<br>
        <input type="checkbox" name="products" value="Acrobat">
Acrobat<br>
        <input type="checkbox" name="products" value="InDesign">
InDesign
</fieldset>

<fieldset>
    <legend>Message</legend>
    <label for"comments">Please enter your comments/questions here:
</label>
    <textarea cols="25" rows="5" name="comments"></textarea>
</fieldset>

<label for="Submit">When finished, click this button to transmit your
information to our sales team:</label>
<input type="submit" name="Submit" value="Submit" id="submit">
</form>
```

Figure 13-3 shows the preceding table as coded, without any styling. While there is a little bit of structure, just from the `fieldset` tags, much of the content runs together across the screen. To prevent this, you could specify that the labels for each form element be displayed as block elements. You might remember this causes the browser to fill the screen horizontally with the element in question. So in the case of our form field labels, it forces the form field after each label to drop down to the line below. Compare Figures 13-3 and 13-4 to see what I mean. The following is the complete style sheet used to display the styled form.

```
<style>
body {
    font-family: verdana;
    font-size: 10px;
}
form#salesform {
    border: 2px dotted #F60;
    background-color: #fde6a2;
    padding: 10px;
}
input, select, textarea {
    border: 1px solid #F60;
    border-radius: 10px;
    background-color: #FC3;
    clear: both;
}
```

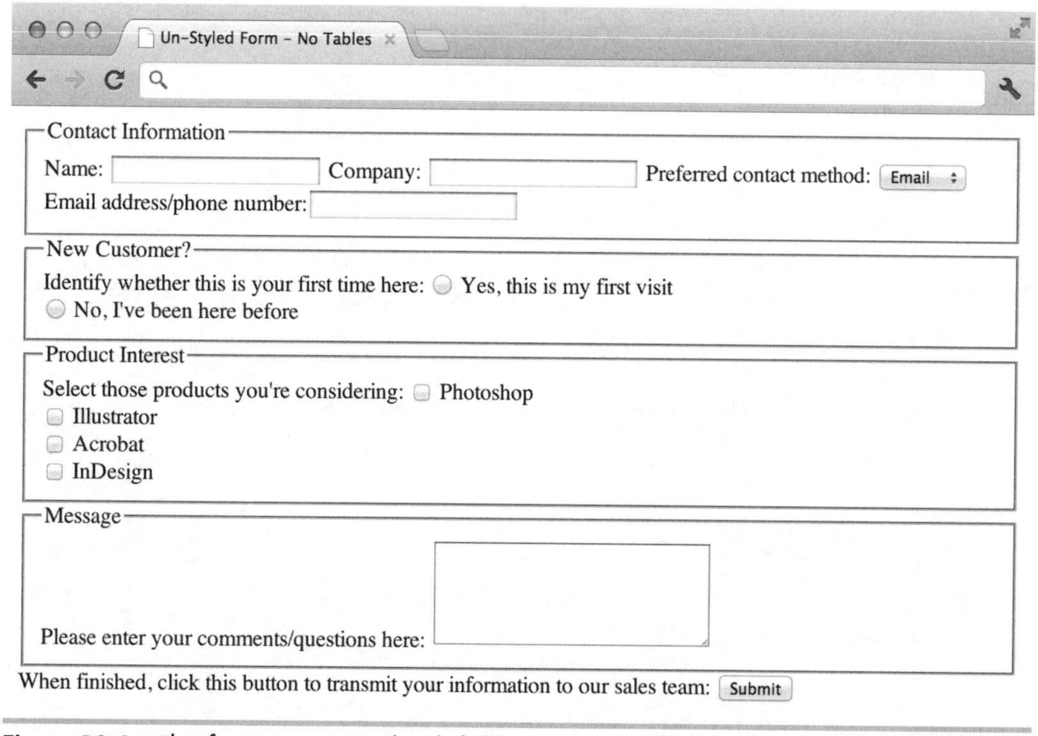

Figure 13-3 This form was created with fieldsets instead of tables. Even though it's a bit jumbled now, a style sheet will make this form shine.

```
textarea {
    overflow: auto;
    padding: 5px;
}
input#submit {
    color: #F60;
    font-weight: bold;
}
label {
    padding-top: 10px;
    display: block;
    font-weight: bold;
}
legend {
    font-size: 14pt;
    font-weight: bold;
    color: #F60;
}
fieldset {
```

```
        border-width: 1px 0px 0px 0px;
        border-style: solid none none none;
        border-color: #F60;
        margin-bottom: 10px;
    }
    </style>
```

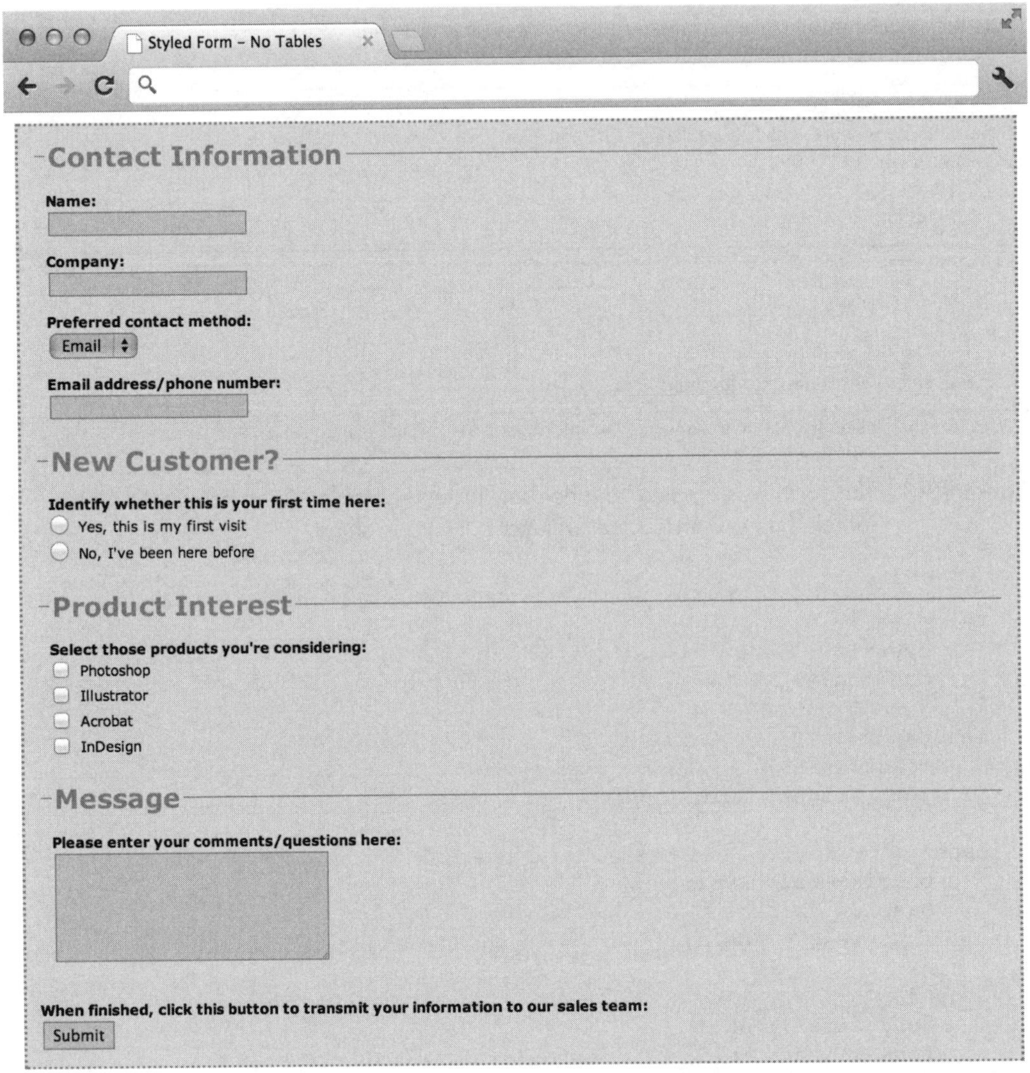

Figure 13-4   After the style sheet is added to this form, the content becomes more legible and organized.

As you can see, by comparing the table-based form with the fieldset/style-based form, you can achieve somewhat similar results with the two different types of coding methods. However, the latter—when combined with style sheets—is easy to code and maintain, and offers significantly more customization options. For more help with creating functional and stylish web forms, check out **http://wufoo.com/gallery**. This online sample gallery has tons of downloadable forms and style sheets to help get you started.

Use Styles for Client-Side Validation

In the previous chapter, I outlined a few ways to help ensure your forms are completed properly before being submitted by the user. In this section, I want to take that one step further to show how you can use CSS to clarify any errors or missing data so the user understands why the form isn't complete.

As I mentioned previously, we use the new `required` attribute to let the browser know a form field must be completed before the form can be submitted. I also told you it's possible to use the `pattern` attribute to further ensure the *right kind of content* is entered into the form field. But how is the user to know exactly which fields are missing or incorrect? This is where client-side (meaning *in the browser*) validation comes into play.

Consider the following bit of code used to create a basic "contact us" form:

```
<form action="form.php">
<fieldset>
    <legend>Contact Us</legend>
    <p>All fields are required, as indicated by the red icons.</p>
    <label for="name">Name:</label>
    <input name="name" type="text" size="30" id="name" taborder="1"
required>
    <label for="email">Email:</label>
    <input type="email"  taborder="2" size="30" name="email"
id="email" required>
    <label for="comments">Message:</label>
    <textarea cols="25" rows="5" name="comments" required></textarea>
    <br><br>
    <input type="submit" name="Submit" value="Submit" id="submit">
</fieldset>
</form>
```

As you can see by the code, all three fields are required. Next, let's add some style declarations to help the user understand what is required. Let's tackle the rules for the invalid fields first.

The `input:required:invalid` selector tells the browser to look for input controls that are required, but currently *invalid*. By default, all required fields are considered invalid by the browser until the user enters at least one character. In this case, I'm telling the browser to add a small red icon inside the field's background to indicate the field is invalid. I also add a red box shadow.

```
input:required:invalid, textarea:required:invalid {
    background: #fff url(invalid.png) no-repeat 98% center;
    box-shadow: 0 0 5px #d45252;
    border-color: #b03535;
}
```

Now, let's use the `input:required:valid` selector to identify a CSS rule for all required fields after they are valid. We'll change the icon to a green check mark to indicate the data is valid. And because the browser understands what constitutes a valid email address, it will not turn the icon green for the email field until data in the proper email format has been entered (email@domain.com).

```
input:required:valid, textarea:required:valid {
    background: #fff url(valid.png) no-repeat 98% center;
    box-shadow: 0 0 5px #5cd053;
    border-color: #28921f;
}
```

Take a look at Figure 13-5 to see this client-side form validation in action. If you want to try it yourself, here's the complete code I used:

```
<!doctype html>
<html>
<head>
    <title> Form with Client-Side Validation </title>
<style>
body {
    font-family: verdana;
```

Figure 13-5 The browser recognizes the email field has not been properly completed in this example.

```
            font-size: 11px;
            }
    input, textarea {
        border: 1px solid #aaa;
        box-shadow: 0px 0px 3px #ccc, 0 10px 15px #eee inset;
        border-radius: 2px; padding:4px;
        }
    input:focus, textarea:focus {
        background: #fff;
        border: 1px solid #555;
        box-shadow: 0 0 3px #aaa;
        }
    textarea {
        overflow: auto;
        padding: 5px;
        }
    input#submit {
        color: #555;
        font-weight: bold;
        }
    label {
        padding-top: 10px;
        display: block;
        font-weight: bold;
        }
    legend {
        font-size: 14pt;
        font-weight: bold;
        color: #555;
        }
    fieldset {
        border: 1px solid #555;
        border-radius: 4px;
        margin-bottom: 5px;
        }
    input:invalid, textarea:invalid {
        background: #fff url(invalid.png) no-repeat 98% center;
        box-shadow: 0 0 5px #d45252;
        border-color: #b03535; }
    input:required:valid, textarea:required:valid {
        background: #fff url(valid.png) no-repeat 98% center;
        box-shadow: 0 0 5px #5cd053;
        border-color: #28921f;
        }
    </style>
    </head>
    <body>
    <form action="#">
```

```
<fieldset>
    <legend>Contact Us</legend>
    <p>All fields are required, as indicated by the red icons.</p>
    <label for="name">Name:</label>
    <input name="name" type="text" size="30" id="name" taborder="1"
required>
    <label for="email">Email:</label>
    <input type="email"  taborder="2" size="30" name="email"
id="email" required>
    <label for"comments">Message:</label>
    <textarea cols="25" rows="5" name="comments" required></textarea>
    <br><br>
    <input type="submit" name="Submit" value="Submit" id="submit">
</fieldset>
</form>
</body>
</html>
```

This is just the tip of the iceberg in regard to form validation. Check out these resources to learn more:

- A List Apart's Forward Thinking Form Validation   **www.alistapart.com/articles/ forward-thinking-form-validation**

- Form Field Validation Styles From CSS   **http://blog.ngopal.com.np/2012/04/09/form- field-validation-styles-from-css**

- IBM Developer Works' Example Form Field Validation   **https://www.ibm.com/ developerworks/mydeveloperworks/blogs/bobleah/entry/html5_example_form_ validation_and_form_elements141?lang=en**

- HTML5 Form Field Validation with CSS3 from GirlieMac! Blog   **http://girliemac.com/ blog/2011/11/28/html5-form-field-validation-with-css3**

Try This 13-1 Format the Form

Returning to the Contact Us page created in Try This 12-1, use additional formatting techniques to achieve a more uniform appearance of the labels and controls. Goals for this project include

- Grouping form elements with the `fieldset` and `legend` tags

- Styling the form

- Adding the `method` and `action` attribute to the `form` tag

1. Open your text or HTML editor and open the file entitled contactus.html from Try This 12-1.

2. Group related controls into fieldsets.

3. Use `label` elements to associate each form control with its text description.

4. Add a style sheet to format the page in a similar fashion as was discussed previously in the final section of the chapter. (Feel free to adjust the colors, fonts, and so on, according to your tastes.)

5. Add the `action` and `method` attributes to the opening `form` tag. For testing purposes, you can have the results mailed to your e-mail address, or simply use a fake address for a CGI script. Set the `method` to `post`.

6. Save the file.

7. Open your web browser and choose File | Open Page (or Open File or Open, depending on the browser you're using). Locate the file contactus.html you just saved. Make sure the file appears as you intended it.

8. If you need to make changes, return to your text editor to do so. After making any changes, save the file and switch back to the browser. Choose Refresh or Reload to preview the changes you just made.

Many of the additional formatting techniques used with forms help to make them more efficient and accessible. This project gave you practice using some of those techniques to make an existing form more user-friendly.

Chapter 13 Self Test

1. True/False: The `fieldset` element is used to divide long select menus into categories of submenus.

2. Add the appropriate attribute and value to allow users to press the F key to access this input control:

   ```
   <input name="FirstName"                >
   ```

3. Add the appropriate attribute and value to set this input control as the first in the tab order:

   ```
   <input name="FirstName"                >
   ```

4. Which tags and attribute should be placed around the following descriptive text to indicate that the text belongs to the birthday input control?

   ```
   <                >When is your birthday? (MM/DD/YY)</        >
   <input type="date" name="BirthDate" id="birthday" size="8">
   ```

5. What CSS selector would you use to create a style sheet rule for all invalid required form fields created with the input element?

6. What CSS selector would you use to create a style sheet rule for all valid required form fields created with the textarea element?

7. Which attribute is used to specify the ideal value in a meter element?

8. Which element is used to indicate progression in a multistep process?

9. Which element is used to signify a relationship between a measurement and its range?

10. Which element is used to add suggested data to input fields to help a user complete a form?

Chapter 14

Beyond Static HTML

Key Skills & Concepts

- Understand the Concept and Uses of JavaScript and HTML5 APIs in Web Pages

- Understand the Purpose of the Following New HTML5 Features: Multitasking, Storage, Offline, Geolocation, Canvas

While HTML enables you to create static, or unchanging, web pages, tools like JavaScript extend the capabilities of HTML, enabling you to create dynamic pages, which either change or react to users' input. The combination of JavaScript and cascading style sheets (CSS) gives us what's commonly called Dynamic HTML, or DHTML.

Taking it one step further, the W3C has added one key element and several specifications for *application programming interfaces*—or APIs—that allow HTML to work in conjunction with other tools like JavaScript. The understanding and use of the canvas element and those APIs can get pretty complex pretty quickly. So this section is not intended to teach you everything about the canvas, JavaScript, or the HTML5 APIs.

Moreover, this chapter gives a brief introduction into the how and why of the HTML5 canvas, as well as how JavaScript works with HTML, and then focuses on the presentation of a few typical examples of using dynamic content in a web page. If this whets your appetite for basic web scripting and you want to learn more, don't miss the great additional resources listed at the end of the chapter.

Understand the Concept and Uses of JavaScript and HTML5 APIs in Web Pages

Contrary to what its name implies, JavaScript is not the same as Java. Sun Microsystems created the Java programming language, while Netscape developed JavaScript. Unlike Java, which can run on its own as a mini-application, *JavaScript* is built into web browsers and cannot stand on its own. Essentially, it's just a set of statements, or scripts, that are instructions for the browser. As such, JavaScript is built into all modern web browsers. However, users can turn off support for JavaScript from within their personal browser. This means you should use caution when relying on JavaScript to transfer important information to users.

NOTE

In 2012, Google released a *stand-alone,* high-performance JavaScript engine, called V8, with its Chrome browser. Check out **http://code.google.com/p/v8** if you're interested in learning more.

When you write JavaScript, it's actually placed right within the HTML on your page. This means you can learn JavaScript from your favorite web sites, just as you can with HTML, by viewing the HTML source from within the browser.

But, before you can do that, you have to know what JavaScript looks like and where to look for it. The following is a basic example:

```
<html>
<head>
    <title>My Web Page</title>
<script type="text/javascript">
    document.write("I can write JavaScript!");
</script>
</head>
<body>
</body>
</html>
```

The opening and closing `script` tags are HTML, while everything in between them is written in JavaScript. This is an important distinction because JavaScript is quite different from HTML in several ways:

- JavaScript is case-sensitive; some forms of HTML are not.

- In JavaScript, quotes are required; in some forms of HTML, quotes are optional.

- JavaScript has a distinct format that must be adhered to; most forms of HTML are forgiving about spacing and formatting.

- JavaScript is considered to be a programming language, whereas HTML is called a markup language.

Given those restrictions, troubleshooting JavaScript can be a bit tricky. Whenever you copy a script from a web site or a book, be sure to copy it exactly as written, unless otherwise specified. For example, placing a line break in the middle of the previous example could produce an error when the page is viewed in a browser.

```
<script type="text/javascript">
    document.write("I can write JavaScript!
");
</script>
```

This misplaced line break can cause browsers to display an error when the page is viewed.

Troubleshoot JavaScript

If you are using a modern browser, you likely have a great way to troubleshoot your JavaScript right within the browser. For example, in Firefox you can choose Tools I Web Developer I Error Console to display any error information associated with recent web browsing. (If you've visited any web sites recently, chances are good you'll see plenty of errors, as I did when I took this screen capture!)

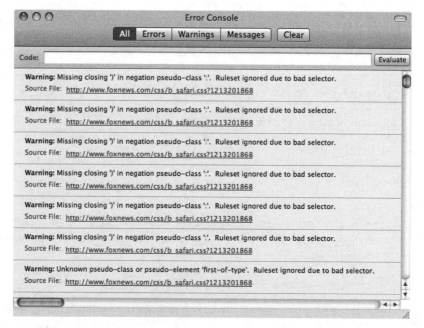

You can use this console to view errors on your pages, or even to test strings of code, by typing them into the console and clicking Evaluate.

In Google Chrome, choose View | Developer | JavaScript Console. Safari users can choose Develop | Show Error Console. In Opera, choose View | Developer Tools | Error Console.

If you're using Internet Explorer, you've probably seen a small warning icon displayed in the bottom-left corner of the browser at one time or another. This occurs when a page displays with errors. (You may even see a statement such as "Done, but with errors on page" along the bottom edge of the browser window.) Click the icon to the left of the statement to reveal information about the error(s).

TIP

Firefox users can download a great add-on called Firebug from **https://addons .mozilla.org/en-US/firefox/addon/1843**. This popular tool allows you to edit, view, and troubleshoot not only JavaScript, but also CSS and HTML in live web pages.

Terminology

You should learn several new terms before you use any JavaScript. The following examines the most common.

NOTE

Many web sites and other books contain the official JavaScript specifications. Refer to the section "Learn More" at the end of this chapter for details.

Objects and Methods

To understand these terms, let's first look back at the preceding example and identify the pieces.

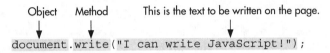

```
document.write("I can write JavaScript!");
```

NOTE

Semicolons can be omitted on single-statement lines like this, but *must* be included on all lines with multiple statements. I made it a habit to always include them when I was first learning to avoid forgetting them when they were required.

In this example, `document` is a JavaScript object. Quite simply, an *object* is anything that can be manipulated or changed by the script. In this case, the object `document` tells the browser the code directly following it refers to the HTML document itself.

Objects can have *methods,* which are actual things that happen to the objects (in this case, a document is written to). For example, the object "car" might have a method called "drive." Along those lines, what other methods might you imagine for the car object? (How about "clean" or "park"?) Methods are followed by a set of parentheses containing any specific instructions on how to accomplish the method. In the previous example, the text inside the parentheses is written within the current document.

Certain JavaScript methods can work together with HTML5 to extend the capabilities of your web pages. For example, the getCurrentPosition() method finds the geographic location of the user. This can be particularly useful when performing actions like showing restaurants near the user or displaying a custom weather forecast. We'll look more specifically at these types of methods later in the chapter.

Properties

Just as an object, such as a car, has features (tires, brakes, and so forth) in the real world, JavaScript objects can have *properties.* This is useful if, for example, you want to manipulate a specific section of a document. Objects and properties are separated by periods. When you want to specify the *value* of a property, such as the color of the background, you add the value after the property, as in the following example:

```
document.body.style.backgroundColor="#333333";
```

This changes the `background-color` property in the page's style sheet to gray.

NOTE

An object can even have a property that is, in itself, another object. For example, `document.location.href` includes a `document` object, its `location` (an object itself and a property of `document`), and an `href` (a property of `location`).

Variables, Operators, and Functions

In JavaScript, a *variable* is something you specify for your own needs. You might think of variables as labels for changeable values used within a single script. To define a variable, type **var**, followed by the one-word name of the variable:

```
var VotingAge;
```

TIP

Remember, JavaScript is case-sensitive. If you capitalize a letter when you first define a variable, you must also capitalize that letter every time you refer to it.

An *operator* does something, such as a calculation or a comparison between two or more variables. The symbols used to do this (listed in Table 14-1) should look familiar because they are also used in simple mathematics. One place you can use operators is in defining values of variables, as in the following example.

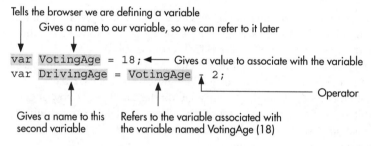

Likewise, a *function* is a group of commands to which you give a name so that you can refer to the group later in the page. To create a function, type **function**, followed by the

Operator	Description	Operator	Description
+	Adds	-	Subtracts
*	Multiplies	/	Divides
++	Adds one	--	Subtracts one
=	Sets value	==	Is equal to
<	Less than	>	Greater than
<=	Less than or equal to	>=	Greater than or equal to
!=	Is not equal to	||	Or
&&	And		

Table 14-1　JavaScript Operators

function name and a set of parentheses. Then, type the commands that are part of the function below the name and enclosed in curly brackets. This is shown in the following example:

```
function functionName()
{
    commands go here
}
```

You can't use just any name for a variable or a function, because there's a list of reserved words that have a special meaning in either JavaScript or Java. If you use one of these words (shown in Table 14-2) as a function or a variable, users may encounter errors when viewing your pages.

Event Handlers

By contrast with the other terms discussed here, *event handlers* needn't be placed within the opening and closing `script` tags. These pieces of JavaScript can actually be embedded within HTML to respond to a user's interaction and make a page dynamic. For example, placing the event handler `onclick` within a tag (`<a>`) causes the event to occur when the user clicks the link. So, if I wanted to change the page's background color when a link was clicked, I could use the following code:

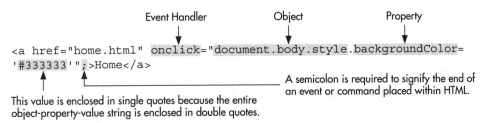

abstract	break	boolean	byte
case	char	comment	continue
default	delete	do	double
else	export	false	final
float	for	function	goto
if	implements	import	in
instanceOf	int	interface	label
long	native	new	null
package	private	protected	public
return	switch	synchronized	this
throws	transient	true	typeof
var	while	with	void

Table 14-2   Common Reserved JavaScript Words

Event Handler	Specifies Action to Occur...
onabort	...when the user stops loading the current page
onblur	...when the user moves away from an object (such as a browser window)
onchange	...when the user changes an object
onclick	...when the user clicks an object
onfocus	...when the user brings an object (such as a browser window) to the foreground
onload	...when an object is fully loaded
onmousedown	...when the user presses the mouse button down over an object
onmouseover	...when the user moves the cursor over an object (such as an image or text)
onmouseout	...when the user moves the mouse away from an object (such as an image or text)
onmouseup	...when the user releases the mouse button after clicking an object
onselect	...when the user selects an object (such as a check box or another form field)
onsubmit	...when the user submits a form

Table 14-3   Common Event Handlers in JavaScript

Table 14-3 lists popular event handlers, but is just a few of the many possible. Check out **www.w3schools.com/html5/html5_ref_eventattributes.asp** for a list of all event handlers in HTML5.

Ask the Expert

Q: What is AJAX and how does it relate to JavaScript?

A: AJAX officially stands for asynchronous JavaScript and XML. However, since the term was first coined, its explanation has evolved somewhat so that XML is no longer required. In essence, AJAX is JavaScript that accomplishes tasks by working with the server behind the scenes, so as to not interfere with the rest of the page. In addition, because it works in the background, it doesn't require the page to be reloaded when something changes. AJAX is not a new programming language, but rather a different way to use existing technologies. To learn more, check out the Mozilla Developer Network's AJAX section: **https://developer.mozilla.org/en-US/docs/AJAX**.

JavaScript Logic

Given that scripts are essentially a set of instructions to the browser, you can often read them logically as a series of commands. For example, in the following script, I am telling the browser to write one thing if the user has Internet Explorer and something else if the user doesn't have IE:

This part of the script checks if the browser's name is Microsoft Internet Explorer. Notice the two equal signs (meaning "is equal to").

```
<script type="text/javascript">
if (navigator.appName == "Microsoft Internet Explorer") {
   document.write("The Magic 8-ball says: Your browser is Internet Explorer.");
}
else {
   document.write("The Magic 8-ball says: Your browser is not Internet Explorer.");
}
</script>
```

This is what the browser is supposed to do if it is IE.

This is what the browser is supposed to do if it is not IE.

These types of *if … then* statements are called *conditionals* and tell the browser to do one thing if *x* is true, and to do something else if *x* is false. Notice the actual instructions on what to do are included within curly brackets: {}. The spacing here is important because it should be consistent. As with HTML and CSS coding, there are several different spacing methods a developer can use. I recommend you pick one and stick with it to avoid confusing yourself, or others who might need to maintain the code. I prefer to keep the opening curly bracket on the same line as the `if` or `else`. The closing curly bracket is then on a line by itself, after the instructions end. In addition, all statements (instructions) end with semicolons. The following is a simple example of the layout:

```
if (something) {
   do this;
}
else {
   do this;
}
```

It could also appear in the following form, which, although less common, easily splits the conditions from each other:

```
if (something)
  {
   do this;
  }
else
  {
   do this;
  }
```

We've just scratched the surface of a very complex topic. For more information, refer to the resources listed at the end of this chapter.

New and Notable

HTML5 introduces several new features that allow it to work more seamlessly with JavaScript. In this section, we'll take a quick look at those features and the benefits they offer.

Multitasking

JavaScript was intended to work on a single task at a time. Given the extensive opportunities JavaScript affords web developers, it is now being pushed to do more. HTML5 brings us something to help JavaScript handle multiple tasks at once.

Appropriately named, these *Web Workers* can handle several different JavaScript activities without slowing down the page display or causing errors. Here's a brief example of how a Web Worker is invoked:

```
var worker = new Worker('script.js');
```

In this instance, a new Worker is created to handle the contents of an external JavaScript file named script.js. You can learn much more about Web Workers here: **www.html5rocks .com/en/tutorials/workers/basics**.

Storage

For many years, the only way to store information about a user's experience on your web site was through the use of *cookies*. Even aside from some concerns over privacy, cookies continue to cause headaches for many web developers, due to their tendency to slow down traffic, their inability to transmit data securely, and their limited storage capabilities.

Thankfully, HTML5 introduces two new storage mechanisms: *local storage* and *session storage*. Local storage has no official size limit, although the W3C has made some recommendations regarding the limitation of disc space. (As of this writing, the topic was still being discussed. Refer to **http://dev.w3.org/html5/webstorage/#disk-space** for more information.) It is conceivable, however, that local storage could be used to store the contents of a user's webmail inbox, for example. And, because it is not limited to a single session or site visit, the data doesn't have to be transmitted each time the user accesses it. This saves both download time and speeds up general access to the content.

By contrast, session storage is intended to provide a temporary place for the browser to store critical information for a page's script. And because the session storage is tied to a particular instance of the browser window, web developers can actually allow users to run a script in multiple browser windows at the same time, which wasn't possible with cookies. This can be quite helpful if you want to make two different transactions at the same web site in two different browser windows, such as might be the case if you're searching for airfare to different airports at the same time. Check out the HTML5Rocks resources for additional information: **www.html5rocks.com/en/features/storage**.

Offline

In conjunction with the storage capabilities I just discussed, the ability to *cache* applications in HTML5 means we could effectively take the Web offline. Lest you think this sounds counter-intuitive, consider the following scenarios:

- **Gaming** Instead of having to download games that are then stored on one particular desktop computer, users can download an instance of the game to play online (if connected) as well as offline (when the Internet connection is not accessible) on whatever device is readily available. Because session information can also be stored locally, the user can pick up where he left off in mere seconds.

- **Calendaring** Users could track tasks or make other changes to an "offline" calendar that are then queued to "publish" all at once when reconnected.

- **Image editing** When users want to upload images, either to a social media site like Facebook or an online photo storage tool like Flikr, they often need to perform a certain amount of basic editing—like rotating, cropping, adding a frame, adding titles, and so on—to the images first. An offline app could handle all of those features and then queue the images for publishing when back online.

These are just a few very brief examples where HTML5's offline features can really benefit both the developer and the user. For much more on these concepts check out **www .html5rocks.com/en/features/offline**.

Ask the Expert

Q: I've heard it said that HTML5 is a Flash-killer. Why?

A: As you've learned, HTML5 has built-in methods for handling audio and video. In a few minutes, you'll also read about the canvas element, which enables us to add illustration, animation, and interactivity right within the HTML page. All of these features remove the need for an external application, like Flash, to display them to site users. And because HTML5 can be uniformly supported across a variety of browsers without the need for a helper application, it is better suited to reaching desktop and mobile users alike. In other words, sites built with HTML5 and its related technologies are more likely to be supported by a larger audience, regardless of what type of device is used. So while many developers have created Flash and non-Flash versions of their apps, they can now create an HTML5 version to serve both audiences.

Geolocation

One of the most popular new APIs of HTML5 is its built-in capacity to handle geolocation. Or, to say it more plainly, developers love that they can access a user's geographical location and use it in their pages. How is this information used? You've probably already encountered plenty of instances but perhaps didn't realize exactly what was happening.

Figure 14-1 shows how the browser requests permission before retrieving the user's location. If you've ever been prompted by a similar alert, either in your desktop browser or on a mobile device, you've seen geolocation in use.

The browser typically seeks to identify your location through one of several possible avenues. Mobile users are found either by pulling the longitude and latitude coordinates from your device's GPS, or triangulating based on Wi-Fi or cell IDs. Desktop user locations are typically identified by interpreting geographical data from IP addresses or Wi-Fi signals. Although none of these methods are foolproof, they are usually pretty close.

After the user's location has been identified, we can perform a variety of tasks, everything from simply displaying the location on the screen to retrieving job listings within a ten-mile radius and displaying each one's typical commute. Check out a few more ideas here: **https://developers.google.com/maps/location-based-apps**. We'll take a look at a sample script in the following section.

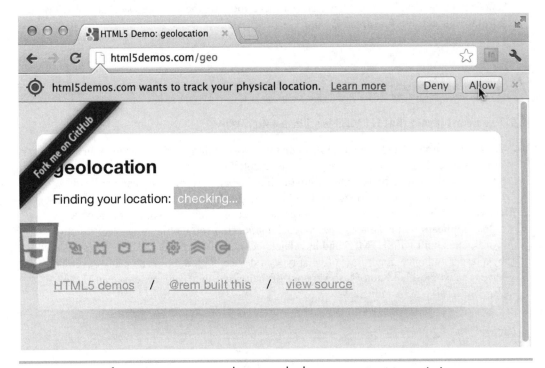

Figure 14-1 Before retrieving a user's location, the browser requests permission.

Canvas

Prior to HTML5, there was no built-in method for adding stuff like animation and interactivity to your web pages. Sure, you could create all sorts of scripts and multimedia with external applications and then link to them, but developers craved a way to create such interactivity right from within the HTML page so they could manipulate that data on the fly and in response to a user's interaction. This is where the new canvas element comes in.

By adding one simple line of code to your pages, you open them up to a whole new world of coding. Let me show you what I mean:

```
<canvas id="myCanvas" width="600" height="400"></canvas>
```

This tells the browser to open a blank canvas, named *myCanvas,* with a width of 600 pixels and a height of 400 pixels. That is the easy part. It's what comes next that means you'll need a bit more training to fully take advantage of this powerful new element.

NOTE

When you don't specify otherwise, the canvas size defaults to 300 pixels in width and 150 pixels in height.

Suppose you wanted to do something really simple, like draw a rectangle and then fill it with a solid color. In HTML5, you can create your blank canvas and then use JavaScript to dictate how to display that shape. After the `canvas` element is created, here's what the script might look like to draw a blue rectangle in the upper-left quarter of the canvas:

```
<script type="text/javascript">
window.addEventListener('load', function () {
    var elem = document.getElementById('myCanvas');   ◄─── First, we have to tell
    if (!elem || !elem.getContext) {                        the browser which
        return;                                             part of the page we're
    }                                                       editing. In this case,
    var context = elem.getContext('2d');   ◄─── Next, we invoke the 2d context.   it's the element whose
    if (!context) {                                                               ID is "myCanvas."
        return;
    }
    context.fillStyle = 'blue';        ┐ Last, we specify the color
    context.fillRect(0, 0, 300, 200);  ┘ and size of the shape.
}, false);
</script>
```

In essence, this little script tells the browser to locate the myCanvas element, switch to the 2d context, and then draw a blue rectangle. With canvas, the word *context* refers to whether we're working with a two- or three-dimensional drawing space. Because there is no fully functioning and fully supported three-dimensional context yet, as of this writing, 2d is the context in use by the majority of canvas users.

The size of the rectangle is dictated by the dimensions listed in the context.fillRect() statement. In this case, I told the browser to start the shape at the top-left corner of the canvas (as indicated by the 0 and 0 starting dimensions) and then finish 300 pixels across and 200 pixels down. The result is shown in Figure 14-2.

After the shape has been created, there are tons and tons of things we can do to it. For example, JavaScript includes an API for adding shadows to shapes. In the following example, I've changed the box color to yellow and added a gray drop shadow behind it:

```
context.shadowOffsetX = 5;
context.shadowOffsetY = 5;
context.shadowBlur    = 4;
context.shadowColor   = 'rgba(0, 0, 0, 0.5)';
context.fillStyle = 'yellow';
context.fillRect(0, 0, 300, 200);
```

You may have noticed the various descriptions of the shape are actually listed before the shape's dimensions. If we were to translate this into plain English, it would be like saying the adjectives before the noun. In other words, you provide the shape's characteristics prior to declaring the shape itself.

The Shadow API has four possible properties:

- **shadowOffsetX**   Sets the horizontal offset

- **shadowOffsetY**   Sets the vertical offset of the shadow

Figure 14-2   JavaScript is used to draw this blue rectangle on the page.

- **shadowBlur**   Assigns the amount of blur on the shadow in pixels

- **shadowColor**   Specifies the shadow color (in the same way CSS colors are specified)

In this case, the shadow color is black (0, 0, 0 in RGB), and 50 percent transparent (listed as 0.5 for the RGB's alpha channel), as shown in Figure 14-3.

This is just one of many, many JavaScript APIs you can use to draw on your new HTML5 canvas. After drawing a variety of lines and shapes, you can then use other APIs to manipulate those pieces, either as a result of the user's interaction, or simply based on a time sequence. If JavaScript and the canvas element interest you, I encourage you to pursue the additional resources listed at the end of the chapter to learn more. In the meantime, check out these great examples of what developers are doing right now with the new `canvas` element:

- True 8-bit Color Cycling with HTML5   **www.effectgames.com/demos/canvascycle**

- The Cloth Simulation   **www.andrew-hoyer.com/andrewhoyer/experiments/cloth**

- The Wilderness Downtown (an Interactive Film)   **www.thewildernessdowntown.com**

- The Fish Bowl   **http://ie.microsoft.com/testdrive/Performance/FishBowl/Default.html**

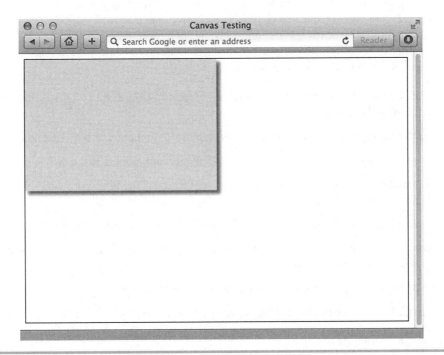

Figure 14-3   The Shadow API enables us to add drop shadows like this to canvas elements.

Sample Scripts

The next few sections include sample scripts for you to try in your web pages. Remember, these are provided as examples only purely to get you started with JavaScript. They might not work in every situation. Because it's beyond the scope of this book to teach you JavaScript at the same level you've learned HTML, please refer to the additional resources at the end of this chapter for more help.

Add the Current Date and Time

The most basic way to add the current date and time to a web page is shown in the following script. Once you learn more about JavaScript, you can customize this script. For example, you might tell the browser to print only the month and day, or to print the month, day, and year in 00/00/00 format.

Place this script within the body of your web page wherever you want the date to appear:

```
<script type="text/javascript">
    document.write(new Date());
</script>
```

Format a New Window

While you learned in previous chapters that you could use the `target` attribute to load links into another browser window, you cannot control the size and style of that browser window with standard HTML. Instead, you can use JavaScript to open the window and then specify settings such as how large or small that window should be and whether the scroll bars are present.

Some of the characteristics you can specify include

- **`toolbar=yes or no`** Turns the browser toolbar—Back, Stop, Reload, and so on—on or off in the new window.

- **`location=yes or no`** Turns the browser location bar on or off in the new window.

- **`status=yes or no`** Turns the browser status bar on or off in the new window.

- **`menubar=yes or no`** Turns the browser menus—File, Edit, View, and so on—on or off in the new window.

- **`resizeable=yes or no`** Specifies whether users can resize the new window.

- **`scrolling=yes, no or auto`** Allows or prevents scrolling, or leaves it up to the browser to decide as needed.

- **`width=#`** Specifies the width of the new window in pixels.

- **`height=#`** Specifies the height of the new window in pixels.

Instructions and Script

Place this script in the header of your page (between the opening and closing `head` tags). The bolded text highlights pieces of the script you should customize.

In the beginning of the script, we see `function NewWindow(link)`. This part identifies the function we use to open the new window so we can reference it later. The end of the script—`MonthWindow.focus()`—brings the window named MonthWindow to the front of the screen.

This defines the characteristics of the new window. When typed in your text/HTML editor, these should be contained on a single line without any breaks.

```
<script type="text/javascript">
function NewWindow(link) {
var MonthWindow = window.open(link, 'Month', 'toolbar=no,location=no,
status=yes,menubar=no,resizeable=yes,scrollbars=yes,width=200,height=200');
MonthWindow.focus();
}
</script>
```

Even though it is misspelled, it is actually the proper way to write it! (The correct spelling is ignored by most browsers.)

Then, in the body of your page, reference the function created in the previous script from within the appropriate link. You can use the following code to load other links in `NewWindow`, simply by changing the URL listed in the parentheses:

This tells the browser to perform the function called `NewWindow`.

This gives the location of the page to load in the new window.

```
<a href="javascript:NewWindow('january.html');">January</a><br>

<a href="javascript:NewWindow('february.html');">February</a><br>
```

If you want to give users the option of closing the window easily, you can add the following code to the bottom of the page that's loaded into the new window:

```
<a href="javascript:window.close();">Close Window</a>
```

NOTE
If you try this script and run into trouble, check the security settings in your browser. Some browsers block new windows from being opened by default.

Create a Dynamic Navigation Bar
In Chapter 6, I mentioned how you can actually have hidden layers of content within your web page. While the layers can be created and hidden with CSS, you use JavaScript to make them visible when a user interacts with the web page. The most common use of this in web pages is for dynamic navigation bars, where a submenu or drop-down menu appears after you click a link, providing additional link choices without refreshing the HTML page itself.

These dynamic navigation bars can become extremely complex, but the core concept is relatively simple, and that's what this section discusses—a bare-bones method for invoking submenus. For more on how to make your navigation bar "bigger and better," refer to the resources section at the end of this chapter. Figures 14-4 and 14-5 show this nav bar in action, and the code used to accomplish this task is included in the following section.

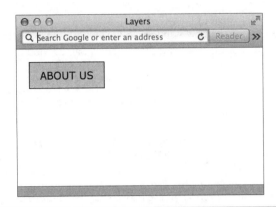

Figure 14-4 This shows the navigation button before it's been clicked.

Instructions and Script

Place this JavaScript in the header of your page between the opening and closing head tags. The bolded text highlights pieces of the script you should customize.

```
<script type="text/javascript">
function showLayer() {
    document.getElementById("aboutus-sub").style.visibility="visible";
}
function hideLayer() {
    document.getElementById("aboutus-sub").style.visibility="hidden";
}
</script>
```

Replace this with the name of the layer whose visibility you're altering.

Replace this with the name of the layer whose visibility you're altering.

Figure 14-5 This shows how the hidden layer is made visible after I clicked the About Us button.

Next, adjust your style sheet to format the visible navigation button/link and the hidden submenu. Be sure to set the positioning so that the submenu displays below the top menu. What follows is the style sheet I used to create the menus shown in Figures 14-4 and 14-5.

```
body {
    font-family: verdana;
}
#aboutus {
    position: absolute;
    top: 20px;
    left: 20px;
    width: 100px;
    padding: 10px;
    text-align: center;
    background-color: #ccc;
    border:1px solid black;
    cursor: pointer;        ◄——————— This changes the cursor to a pointer to
}                                    help indicate that the content is linked.
#aboutus-sub {
    position: absolute;
    visibility: hidden;     ◄——————— I set the visibility to hidden so that the submenu
    top: 60px;                        is not visible when the page first loads.
    left: 20px;
    width: 100px;
    padding: 0px 10px;
    text-align: center;
    background-color: #333;
    color: #fff;
    border: 1px solid #999;
    cursor: pointer;
}
ul {
    padding: 0px;
    margin: 0px;
}
li {
    list-style: none;
    padding: 5px 0px;
    border-bottom: 1px dashed white;
}
li a {
    color: #fff;
    text-decoration: none;
}
.last {
    border: 0px;
}
```

The final piece to this code is the actual HTML for the content, which is placed between the opening and closing body tags:

The onclick JavaScript event handler tells the browser to display the "aboutus-sub" layer when the user clicks anywhere within the "aboutus" content area.

```html
<div id="aboutus" onclick="showLayer('aboutus-sub');">ABOUT US</div>
<div id="aboutus-sub">
<ul><li><a href="history.html">History</a></li>
    <li><a href="location.html">Location</a></li>
     <li class="last"><a href="team.html">Team</a></li>
</ul>
</div>
```

Display a User's Location on a Map

In this practice script, we'll display the user's location within Google Maps. There are three main components to finding a user's location on a map. First, we must check for browser support. Second, we read the user's location. Last, we access a mapping tool like Google Maps to display the location.

Instructions and Script

Before we can get to any of the embedded JavaScript, we need to link to the external Google Maps API, like this:

```html
<script src="http://maps.google.com/maps/api/js?sensor=true"></script>
```

In this case, we are telling the browser to use sensing techniques (such as a GPS locator) for determining the user's location. If you did not want to use a sensor, simply change the end part of the URL to sensor=false.

NOTE

This basic API is free for personal use. If you end up wanting something a bit more customized or complex, or if you need to use the API for a business, check Google's guidelines for licensing details: **https://developers.google.com/maps/documentation/business/guide**. You likely just need to register your business and receive a custom application key to use it legally.

After that, we need to add some internal scripting to determine whether the user's browser supports geolocation. If browser support exists, we start laying the groundwork for what's to come.

```javascript
if (navigator.geolocation) {
        var timeoutVal = 10 * 1000 * 1000;
        navigator.geolocation.getCurrentPosition(
            displayPosition,
```

```
        displayError,
        { enableHighAccuracy: true, timeout: timeoutVal,
maximumAge: 0 }
        );
}
```

For browsers that don't support geolocation, we let them know:

```
else {
    alert("Geolocation is not supported by this browser");
}
```

Now, we get to the real meat of the JavaScript. While we told the browser to run the `displayPosition` function if it supported geolocation, here is where we identify what should happen when the `displayPosition` function is run. This is where we identify the user's location and display it on the map. After that, the map options are set, such as the zoom level and how it is centered.

```
function displayPosition(position) {
    var pos = new google.maps.LatLng(position.coords.latitude,
position.coords.longitude);
    var options = {
        zoom: 10,
        center: pos,
        mapTypeId: google.maps.MapTypeId.ROADMAP
        };
    var map = new google.maps.Map(document.getElementById("map"),
options);
    var marker = new google.maps.Marker({
        position: pos,
        map: map,
        title: "You are here"
        });
}
```

Then, we need to also explain the `displayError` function for some basic error handling:

```
function displayError(error) {
    var errors = {
        1: 'Permission denied',
        2: 'Position unavailable',
        3: 'Request timeout'
        };
    alert("Error: " + errors[error.code]);
}
```

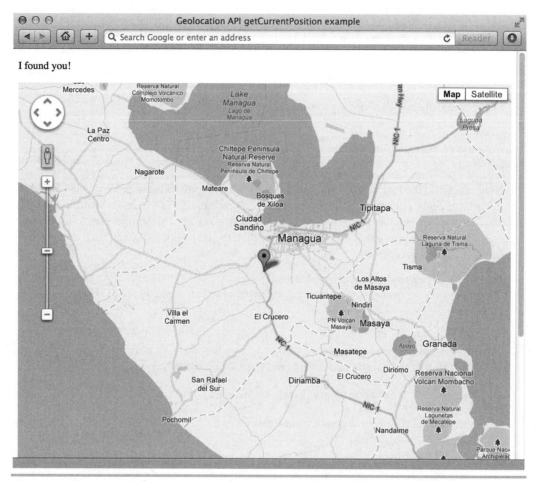

Figure 14-6 Our sample script causes the browser to display the user's location in a Google Map.

After that, we can add a tiny bit of CSS to make the map fill the screen and a single line of text to tell the user, "I found you!" Here's how the code looks all together. (See Figure 14-6 for a screen shot of the final product.)

```
<!doctype html>
<html>
<head>
<title>Geolocation Example</title>
<style>
    #map { width:100%; height:800px; }
</style>
```

```html
<script src="http://maps.google.com/maps/api/js?sensor=true"></script>
</head>
<body>
<p>I found you!</p>
<div id="map"></div>
<script>
    if (navigator.geolocation) {
        var timeoutVal = 10 * 1000 * 1000;
        navigator.geolocation.getCurrentPosition(
            displayPosition,
            displayError,
            { enableHighAccuracy: true, timeout: timeoutVal, maximumAge: 0 }
        );
    }
    else {
        alert("Geolocation is not supported by this browser");
    }
    function displayPosition(position) {
        var pos = new google.maps.LatLng(position.coords.latitude,
position.coords.longitude);
        var options = {
            zoom: 10,
            center: pos,
            mapTypeId: google.maps.MapTypeId.ROADMAP
        };
        var map = new google.maps.Map(document.getElementById("map"), options);
        var marker = new google.maps.Marker({
            position: pos,
            map: map,
            title: "You are here"
        });
    }
    function displayError(error) {
        var errors = {
            1: 'Permission denied',
            2: 'Position unavailable',
            3: 'Request timeout'
        };
        alert("Error: " + errors[error.code]);
    }
</script>
</body>
</html>
```

As mentioned previously, this really is just the tip of the iceberg regarding what is possible. If it's inspired you to want to do more with JavaScript, HTML, and CSS, don't miss the section "Learn More" at the end of this chapter.

Use JavaScript to Launch
a New Browser Window

JavaScript can add much to a web site that wouldn't otherwise be possible with HTML. Many
of the popular JavaScript techniques used on the Web make a site seem more dynamic. In this
project, we use JavaScript to launch a new browser window from a link on one of your site's
pages. The goal for this project is to use JavaScript to launch and control a new browser window.

1. First, locate your business or organization on Google Maps (**maps.google.com**). Copy the
   address of the page from the top of the browser window so you can link to it.

2. Then, open one of the pages already completed in your text or HTML editor.

3. Add the necessary JavaScript to the header of the page to set up a function for launching a
   new browser window.

4. Name the window **MapWindow**.

5. Title it **'Map'**.

6. Turn the menu bar, the status bar, the toolbar, and the location off in the new window.

7. Set the scrolling to `auto`.

8. Format the new window to be 500×500 pixels in size.

9. Create a link to the Google Maps page you identified in Step 1 somewhere within the text.
   Using JavaScript, specify that the link should open in the MapWindow.

10. Save the file.

11. Open your web browser and choose File | Open Page (or Open File or Open, depending on
    the browser you're using). Locate the file you just saved. Click the link to verify that the
    linked page opens in a new browser window with the appropriate customizations.

12. If you need to make changes, return to your text editor to do so. After making any changes,
    save the file and switch back to the browser. Choose Refresh or Reload to preview the
    changes you just made.

TIP

Do you get an error or see nothing in the new browser window? Make sure the link to
Google Maps is correct. If you receive other errors, try comparing your code against
the following example, or using your browser's JavaScript console for troubleshooting.

```
<!doctype html>
<html>
<head>
<title>About Us</title>
<script type="text/javascript">
```

```
function NewWindow(link) {
var MapWindow =
window.open(link,'Map','toolbar=no,location=no,status=no,menubar=no,
resizeable=yes,scrollbars=auto,width=500,height=500');
MapWindow.focus();
}
</script>
```

This entire section should be on one line, without any hard returns, or it will "break" the script.

Here's an example of what the code for your Google Maps link might look like:

```
<a href="javascript:NewWindow('google maps link here');">Find Us</a>
```

Although JavaScript isn't the same as HTML, the two can be used together to make web pages more dynamic in nature. This project gave you a chance to practice one JavaScript technique—controlling browser windows.

Learn More

While I didn't expect this chapter would teach you everything you need to know about JavaScript or the new HTML5 APIs, I hope it gave you a basic understanding of what types of things these scripts can do. If you'd like to learn more, many sources of additional information are available on this topic. The following section lists some of the most popular.

Also, the sites listed here offer many free scripts that you may borrow and use on your own site. This is considered perfectly normal, so long as you give credit to the original author(s) in your code.

Online References and Scripts

- **HTML5Studio**   Access demos of the latest and greatest of HTML5, JavaScript, and CSS3 (**http://studio.html5rocks.com**).

- **HTML5 Canvas Element Guide**   Learn the history of this exciting new element and the basics of how to use it in your pages (**http://sixrevisions.com/html/canvas-element/**).

- **Canvas Tutorial**   This tutorial, from the Mozilla Developers Network, covers all you need to know to get started with the canvas element (**https://developer.mozilla.org/en-US/docs/Canvas_tutorial**). It also includes links to some helpful examples.

- **SitePoint.com**   This site contains DHTML and JavaScript articles (**www.sitepoint.com/subcat/javascript**), as well as a whole blog about this stuff (**www.sitepoint.com/tag/html5-dev-center**).

- **Web Reference JavaScript Articles**   This web site (**www.webreference.com/programming/javascript**) includes tutorials, tips, and reviews of tools.

- **Mozilla Developer Center**   This section of the Mozilla Developer Center (**https://developer.mozilla.org/en-US/docs/HTML/HTML5**) is specifically geared toward anyone developing with HTML5 and includes helpful documentation and support communities.

- **javascripts.com** You can find thousands of free scripts and information about how to use them.

- **The Code Player** Prefer to learn visually? Check out these video tutorials for all things related to HTML5, JavaScript, and CSS3 (**http://thecodeplayer.com**).

NOTE

Always look for the most recent references you can find when working with JavaScript and HTML. The reason is this: Older scripts were written for older browsers and may or may not be valid today. Often, those older browsers required web developers to use special workarounds, called hacks, in their JavaScripts and HTML. Many of those hacks are no longer necessary, and in some cases they can even "break" in modern browsers.

Chapter 14 Self Test

1. Fill in the blank: JavaScript is case-_____.

2. Name two ways JavaScript differs from standard HTML.

3. What is an API?

4. Fill in the blank: In the following code, _____ is the JavaScript object. `document .write("This is a text!");`

5. True/False: A plus sign (+) is an example of a JavaScript variable.

6. When placed within the header of an HTML file, which opening and closing tags surround all JavaScripts?

7. Fill in the blank: Objects can have _____, which are actual things that happen to the objects, such as "write" in the following statement: `document.write("I can write JavaScript");`.

8. What term is given to an aspect of JavaScript that you specify for your own needs, which is used as a label for a changeable value?

9. Fill in the blank: A(n) _____ is a group of commands to which you give a name so that you can refer to it later in the script.

10. Which aspect of JavaScript is embedded within the page's HTML and responds to a user's interaction?

11. How are conditionals used in JavaScript?

12. What does the following JavaScript do when added to an a tag on a web page? `onClick="document.body.style.backgroundColor='green'"`

13. How do you specify that a new browser window should not have any scroll bars?

14. What punctuation ends all JavaScript statements?

15. What does `onFocus` do when used in JavaScript?

Part III

Going Live

Chapter 15

Publishing Pages

Key Skills & Concepts

- Select Possible Domain Names for Your Site

- Determine the Most Appropriate Type of Hosting for Your Site

- Prepare Your Site for Its Public Debut

- Upload Your Site to a Host Computer

- Test Your Site

- Publicize Your Web Site

Throughout the course of this book, you've created and viewed web pages on your personal computer. At some point you'll undoubtedly want to show your web pages to other people. To do that, your site must be transferred, or *uploaded,* to a host computer with 24-hour access to the Internet, where it has a suitable URL. Then, to drive traffic to that site, you need to consider submitting your site to search engines and using other marketing techniques.

Select Possible Domain Names for Your Site

Before diving into the actual meat of this chapter, I want to mention domain names briefly. Many people underestimate the power of a guessable and memorable domain name. While it may seem logical to its business owners to purchase a domain name using a shortened version of the business name, this is probably not the first thing a potential customer would guess.

TIP

There are probably thousands of places online where you could research and register a domain. A couple of options include **www.networksolutions.com** and **www.godaddy.com**.

Consider my friend's online tutoring business. The name onlinemathtutor.com would be my first guess, but because that is already taken, I might try onlinemathinstructor.com, onlinemathmaster.com, or even something like skypememath.com. If more than one of those were available, you might even register both. Purchasing multiple domain names is an inexpensive way to bring in some additional customers and build your brand identity online. Whenever appropriate, you might also purchase the same domain name ending with different extensions, such as onlinemathmaster.com and onlinemathmaster.net.

Determine the Most Appropriate Type of Hosting for Your Site

Many different options are available for those who want to publish a site on the Internet. For the purposes of this chapter, I group these options into two categories: personal site hosting and business site hosting.

Personal Site Hosting

When you want to publish a personal web site but you aren't concerned about having your own domain name (such as wendywillard.com), you have a wide range of free options available. For example, all the following sites offer free web space for personal sites to anyone who asks for it. Your site's address might be something like this: www.hostcompany.com/wendywillard. If you currently have an email account with any of these, you're already halfway there.

- Webs (**www.webs.com**)
- Google Sites (**sites.google.com**)
- Weebly (**www.weebly.com**)
- Yola (**www.yola.com**)

Because these sites are largely targeting beginners, they make uploading and maintaining your web pages a breeze. Most use web-based tools to do so, meaning you don't even need any additional software.

Blogs

The previous list of suggestions for personal web sites includes companies that provide space on their servers for anyone wishing to upload web pages (although some do offer the option to install additional features, like blogs). But what about those who are looking to "journal" online and don't want to bother creating custom web pages for that purpose? There are many

Ask the Expert

Q: What are the valid characters for a domain name, and how long can a domain name be?

A: According to Network Solutions (**www.networksolutions.com**), you can use letters and numbers. You can also use hyphens, although they may not appear at the beginning or end of your web address. Spaces or other characters like question marks and exclamation marks are never allowed.

Your complete domain name (including the extension—such as .com, .edu, .net, .org, .biz, .tv, or .info) can be up to 67 characters long. Remember, "www" isn't included in the domain name you register, so you needn't count those characters. Having said that, shorter is better … most of us have trouble remembering ten-digit phone numbers (555-555-5555)!

sites offering free blogs, where you can journal, vent, gossip, or simply share to your heart's content—with little to no HTML knowledge required.

As a bonus, if you can handle coding some HTML (which of course you can, since you're reading this), you'll be able to tailor your blog to your specific needs. The following two sites are the most popular free blogging tools online. Both offer tutorials to help you get started, as well as tons of templates for customizing the look of your blog.

- Google's Blogger (**www.blogger.com**)

- Wordpress (**www.wordpress.com**)

While all of these sites offer free hosting to anyone who requests it, remember to check first with your current *Internet service provider (ISP)*. ISPs frequently throw in some free web space with Internet access. If none of these free options suits your purposes, or if you need to register your own domain, move on to the next section about business site hosting.

Even if you don't want to use your site for journaling or more traditional blogging, you should still consider using a tool like Wordpress. To understand why, consider just a few of the key benefits of building a site with blogging software:

- **Easy to build**   There are thousands of Wordpress themes, as well as add-on features, available for free or minimal cost. The basic process looks like this: arrange for hosting, install Wordpress, select a theme, customize theme, add content, install add-ons, customize add-ons, publish site. Using a tool like Wordpress actually minimizes the amount of hand-coding a developer has to do.

- **Easy to maintain**   Tools like Wordpress store your site's content separately from its design, which is referred to as its *theme*. This makes maintenance of both the content and design simple and straightforward. In fact, I often build sites in Wordpress and then transfer them to clients—which typically includes someone who doesn't know HTML—to maintain.

If you are at all interested in using a blogging tool as the basis for your next web development project, I highly suggest checking out these online resources to learn more:

- **http://codex.wordpress.org/New_To_WordPress_-_Where_to_Start**

- **http://learn.wordpress.com/get-started/**

- **http://wordpress.tv/**

NOTE

Before you sign up with any ISP, be sure to check the terms of service to verify your site fits within the confines of the ISP's requirements. For example, the majority of ISPs prohibit sites distributing pornography or illegal copies of computer software. In addition, free ISPs usually limit the amount of space and/or bandwidth you can use. Finally, if you change ISPs, you'll need to locate a new host. I mention these only to point out that restrictions do exist and you'd be wise to review all terms and details carefully to avoid incurring unexpected fees.

Business Site Hosting

On the business side, your options vary from onsite to dedicated offsite to shared. In the case of *onsite hosting,* your business purchases a server, its software, and a dedicated Internet connection capable of serving your site to web users 24 hours a day, 365 days a year. For small businesses, this isn't a viable option because it requires expensive start-up costs and on-staff information technology (IT) talent.

For the majority of small to mid-size businesses, *offsite hosting* is the most cost-effective and popular solution. This can be on either a *shared* or a *dedicated* server. While a shared server can be significantly less expensive than one dedicated to your needs, it may not be possible in all situations. For example, if your site runs custom web applications, requires a high level of security, or needs a large amount of space, a dedicated server is preferred.

Many service levels, and therefore, many price levels, exist within shared offsite hosting. For this reason, be wary of comparing apples to oranges. When you are considering two or more hosting providers, look closely at the fine print to be sure they offer similar services before making a final decision solely on price.

The following are some questions to ask when you look for business hosting:

- How much space on the server will I receive? How much extra do I have to pay if I go over that space?

- How much traffic can my site generate over a month? What are some average traffic rates for some similar sites you host? How much extra will I pay if the site generates more traffic than allowed?

- Is multimedia streaming supported? If so, how much traffic is supported for any given event, and at what point will the system overload? What are procedures for dealing with excess traffic?

- How many email accounts will I receive with this account?

- Can I use my own domain name(s) (as opposed to www.hostcompany.com/mybusiness)? Will you help me register my domain (if you haven't already registered one)? Will you charge extra if I have multiple domain names for a web site? If so, how much more?

- What kind of access will I have to my web site? For example, is FTP (File Transfer Protocol) access available for uploading files?

- What kind of support do you offer? (For example, if I need help adding password protection to my site, will you help me?) What hours is your support staff available?

- Can I load additional applications (blogging software, database tools, e-commerce tools, and so forth) onto the server? What requirements or restrictions do you have regarding those? Are additional costs involved?

- What additional services do you offer? (For example, can you also host my online store and, if so, how much would it cost me in addition to my current fees?)

- How many Internet connections do you have? (The more connections a host has, the better chance your site has of staying "live" if one connection goes down.)

- How often do you perform backups? How easy is it for me to gain access to a backup if I need one?

- What are the start-up costs? What are the monthly costs? Are there any guarantees?

- Do you offer a service to measure statistics for my site, such as how many people have visited? If so, can I see an example?

- Can you provide references?

Here are a few of my favorite business hosting options:

- Site5 (**www.site5.com**)

- Yahoo! (**http://smallbusiness.yahoo.com**)

- HostMonster (**www.hostmonster.com**)

- Dream Host (**www.dreamhost.com**)

- BlueHost (**www.bluehost.com**)

- Weebly (**www.weebly.com**)

- Webs (**www.webs.com**)

In the end, you'll probably get the best ideas about which hosting provider to use by asking friends or business associates.

Prepare Your Site for Its Public Debut

Before you upload your site to a host computer and submit it to search engines, tidying it up a little is best. Consider the following dos and don'ts.

Do

- **Make sure all your images have alternative text**   Directories and engines can't see the images—they only "look" at the alternative text for descriptions.

- **Give your pages descriptive 5- to 13-word titles, using keywords from the page** Search engines look at the titles of your pages and often use them to list your site. So "Page 2" would definitely not entice as many visitors as, say, "Lawn Care Products for Sale."

- **Repeat keywords throughout the page**   On a page entitled "Lawn Care Products for Sale," you should include those same words in the headlines, body text, and alternative text for images on the page. This increases the relevancy of the page when someone searches for those words.

Don't

- **Stray from the topic**   If a page is about lawn care products, don't include information about your favorite links or television shows on that same page. Extraneous information only weakens the relevancy of your pages because search engines typically show pages with the most relevant information at the top of the results list.

- **Repeat keywords too many times**   Search engines are known for dropping sites from their listings because of suspected spamming—a word repeated too many times on a page is a big red flag for spamming. Be realistic and honest. Use the words whenever they seem appropriate and you'll be fine.

- **Use irrelevant keywords just to draw in people**   Don't include keywords that aren't appropriate for your site. Users will get annoyed and complain, causing your site to be dropped from the search engine altogether.

Update Meta Content

There are a variety of HTML elements used in the head section of a page to pass along information to the browser. For example, you can use `meta` tags to aid search engines in identifying your content. `meta` tags are hidden instructions about your page, such as a description and keywords.

NOTE

Be aware that some search engines ignore `meta` tags altogether. For this reason, they shouldn't be relied on as the "be all and end all" of preparing your site.

These tags should be added to each page on your site between the opening and closing `head` tags. The following is an example of how `meta` tags might be used first to specify the character set, then to list the description and keywords for a page selling handmade children's clothing:

```
<head>
    <title>Wendy's Handmade Children's Clothing For Sale</title>
    <meta charset="UTF-8">
    <meta name="description" content="We sell handmade children's
clothing for boys and girls, sizes 6-12. Our children's clothing -
pants, shirts, dresses, and more - is made to last generations.">
    <meta name="keywords" content="kids children clothing clothes
handmade pant shirt suit dress skirt">
</head>
```

Customize the content of the latter two tags to identify a description that properly explains the purpose of your site in a sentence or two (20 to 40 words is a good place to start) and keywords that parallel what users will probably search for. Because most users search for words in lowercase, you can avoid using capital letters in your keywords. The number of keywords you can use varies somewhat according to the search engine or directory; make sure your most important keywords are listed first because many limit the contents of your keywords to 900 characters.

TIP

There are many other types of meta tags you can use. Check out **www.html-5.com/ metatags** for a more detailed list of the options available.

Troubleshoot the Code

Testing pages on a variety of different computer environments is a whole lot easier with the addition of validation and inspection tools built into all the modern browsers. For example, to find them in Firefox, select Tools | Web Developer.

Web Search	⌘K		
Downloads	⌘J		
Add-ons	⇧⌘A		
Set Up Sync...			
Web Developer	▶	Web Console	⌥⌘K
Page Info	⌘I	Inspect	⌥⌘I
		✓ Responsive Design View	⌥⌘M
Start Private Browsing	⇧⌘P	Debugger	⌥⌘S
Clear Recent History...	⇧⌘⌫	Scratchpad	⇧F4
		Style Editor	⇧F7
		Page Source	⌘U
		Error Console	⇧⌘J
		Get More Tools	

NOTE

In IE9+, press F12 to reveal the developer tools. In all other modern browsers, you can simply right-click (or control-click on the Mac) any page element and choose Inspect Element.

There you will find everything from a console for identifying page errors and a tool for editing page styles, to a code inspector and a preview of how different browser window sizes affect your designs. The latter —called Responsive Design View in the Web Developer menu and shown in Figure 15-1—helps you get an idea how your pages might be visible on small mobile devices, medium tablets, and large-screen desktop monitors.

Firefox's Inspector tool is accessible either from the Tools | Web Developer menu, or simply by right-clicking a particular page element and choosing Inspect Element. The result

Figure 15-1   Firefox's Responsive Design View helps you preview pages in different window sizes.

will look something like Figure 15-2, where everything except that element is dimmed, with the related HTML code shown at the bottom and the corresponding styles to the right. (Note: Either of those can be toggled on or off as needed.)

The reason these tools are so robust is this: You can actually turn various styles on and off to see how they affect the page display. In Figure 15-3, I toggled off the text-transform: uppercase declaration for the top menu, and the browser immediately updated the display to change the case of the letters. This can make sure work of troubleshooting a nasty bug you just can't figure out.

TIP

Want to learn more about Firefox's Web Developer tools? Check out **www.howtogeek .com/105320/how-to-use-firefoxs-web-developer-tools**.

Figure 15-2 Firefox's Inspector puts robust testing tools right at your fingertips.

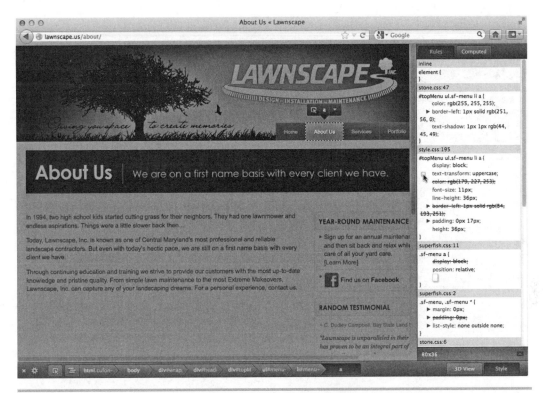

Figure 15-3 Here, the text-transform option has been toggled off, causing the links to switch to lowercase.

Figure 15-4 shows how Chrome arranges its inspection tools. Even though they display a tad bit differently than Firefox's, they function the same.

Validate the Code

Along with troubleshooting your pages, it's a good idea to run them through a validator. Tools like the one located at **validator.w3.org** compare your code against the official HTML specification to look for errors or missteps. Because those errors can lead to pages being misinterpreted—and poorly displayed—by browsers, it's important to fix anything that doesn't validate.

When you validate your pages, the tool actually compares it to whichever HTML spec you've specified as being used in your page. How does it know? That's where the doctype identifier comes into play. Remember this little line of code?

```
<!doctype html>
```

Figure 15-4 Chrome's Inspector makes it super easy to troubleshoot your page elements.

Including that at the top of every HTML file you create tells the browser to compare your code against the HTML5 spec. Leaving that out is not only illegal in HTML terms, but will ultimately prevent your page from being validated.

Preview on Mobile Devices

As the statistics on mobile web use rise almost daily, it's important for us to plan for and test our sites in various mobile environments. But what if you don't own all those different mobile devices your site visitors might use? In addition to the resources listed in the previous section, there are a variety of other mobile-specific options available to help:

- iPadPeek (**www.ipadpeek.com**) gives you a preview of how your page might display on an iPad, iPod, or iPhone simply by changing the viewing space and using an appropriate frame around your page display.

- Mobilizer (**www.springbox.com/mobilizer**) is a downloadable tool that shows a preview of your web site when viewed on several different mobile phones. Figure 15-5 shows the White House web site previewed through Mobilizer on the iPhone 4 and a Blackberry.

- Opera's Mobile Emulator (**www.opera.com/developer/tools/mobile**) is another downloadable tool for emulating mobile web browsing on a desktop computer. The difference is Opera also offers additional testing and troubleshooting tools that can be paired with its Mobile Emulator. This makes Opera an ideal environment for developing mobile-friendly web sites. Figure 15-6 shows the White House web site previewed through this emulator on Samsung Galaxy X and Kindle Fire tablets.

- Finally, Adobe's entry into the mobile site development arena is called Shadow (**www .adobe.com/shadow**). It is both a downloadable tool and a Chrome extension. It's worth noting that Shadow does require you to actually have the mobile device on which you want to test. Instead of showing you what a live site might look like on a mobile device, Shadow syncs your browsing on a desktop computer and all mobile devices on the same network that have the Shadow app installed. In fact, you can make edits in Chrome's inspection tool and check out the results of those edits immediately in any paired mobile device.

TIP

For more on making sites mobile-friendly, check out **www.html5rocks.com/en/mobile/ mobifying**.

Figure 15-5 Mobilizer enables you to preview a web site on several different mobile phones.

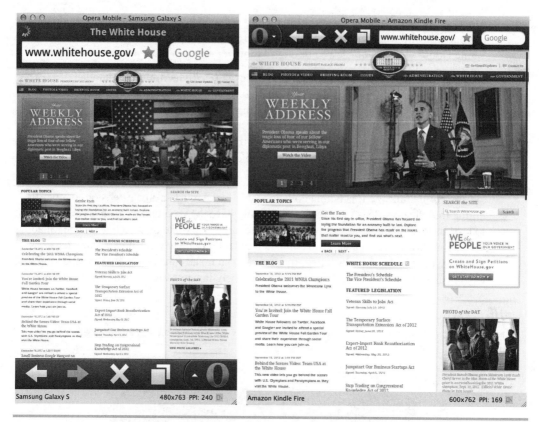

Figure 15-6 Opera's Mobile Emulator offers previews of many tablet and phone environments.

Preview in Other Browsers

Just as it's important to know what your site looks like on mobile devices, it's also worthwhile to check it on other desktop computers. (Remember: Alternative browsers, operating systems, and monitors can all cause a page to display differently.) But it's not necessary to own a bunch of different computers to do so, thanks to a few pieces of software.

Here are a few of my favorite tools for previewing sites in other browsers:

- Browsercam (**www.browsercam.com**)
- Browsershots (**www.browsershots.com**)
- Adobe Browser Lab (**browserlab.adobe.com**)

Of those three, Adobe's Browser Lab is the only one accessible from both inside Dreamweaver as well as from within the browser. In Figure 15-7, you can see an example

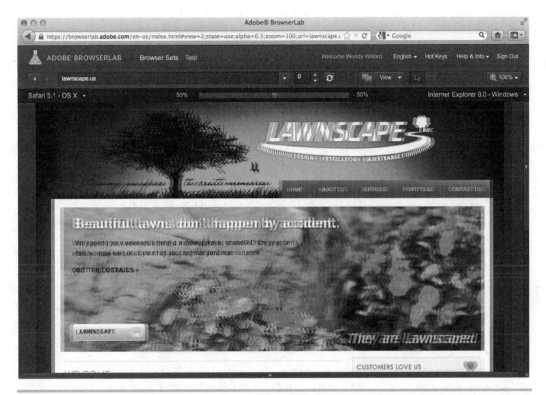

Figure 15-7 Opera's Mobile Emulator offers previews of many tablet and phone environments.

of the onion skin feature, which lets you preview how a page looks in two different browser scenarios—in this case, Safari 5.1 on Mac OS X is shown beneath IE 9.0 in Windows—at the same time. Here, you can see how the dimensions of the layout are slightly off from one user scenario to the other. However, because the alignment issues from one browser to the other do not prevent the page content from being read and understood, it doesn't concern me.

Upload Your Site to a Host Computer

After your site is finished and you're ready to make it "live," or accessible by visitors on the Web, it's time to transfer the pages to the host computer. You can use File Transfer Protocol (FTP) programs to do so.

The concept of using an FTP program is similar to moving things around on your own personal computer. The key difference is instead of moving files from one folder to another on your computer, you're actually moving them from one folder on your computer to another folder on a different computer.

Just as you can change settings and information about who has access to view or edit a file on your own computer, you can also make these changes on a host computer. For information about how these settings might work, checking with your ISP or host company is best.

Depending on what type of computer you have and who's hosting your site, you may use one of many different types of desktop FTP programs. Or you might use an FTP tool that comes with your HTML editor, such as the built-in FTP capabilities with Adobe Dreamweaver. The next sections outline a few popular options.

Desktop FTP Programs

Just about all of the HTML editors discussed previously include some method of FTP. But if you'd prefer a stand-alone tool, there are tons and tons of desktop FTP programs (just Google *FTP program* to see what I mean). Some are free; many are not. One of the most popular cross-platform free FTP programs is FileZilla. It is available for download from **www.filezilla-project.org**. The following overview outlines how to use this particular tool, but the basic steps are the same, regardless of which FTP program you select.

After the program is downloaded and installed, double-click the app's icon to get started. To begin, you must choose which computer you want to access. If you want to upload your files to your web server, enter that computer's information in the spaces provided at the top of the screen (Host, Username, Password) before clicking Quickconnect.

NOTE

You should receive all the necessary information when you sign up for hosting service. If you're unsure, check your host company's web site or call its customer support line for assistance.

If your connection is successful, FileZilla displays the company you're accessing, referred to as the *Remote Site,* in the right window. The files on your local computer are visible in the left window.

You can transfer files between these two computers in a couple of different ways. The simplest transfer method is to double-click the file you want to transfer. To be more specific with your actions, you can right-click (CTRL-click on the Mac) the file and select from one of the available options (Figure 15-8).

You can also navigate through the directory structure of either computer by clicking the folder names to expand or condense them. Right-click (CTRL-click on the Mac) to quickly add a new folder or to delete an existing one.

TIP

You can transfer files in two different ways: ASCII or binary. HTML and text files should be transferred in ASCII mode, while graphic, multimedia, and most other file types should be transferred in binary mode. FileZilla (and most FTP programs) uses the "auto" mode by default, whereby the program tries to determine the best transfer method for each file type.

These are the folders located on the local computer.

These are the files located within the "NannyDee" folder on the local computer.

These are the folders on the remote computer.

These are the files located within the "www" folder on the remote computer.

Status notes are printed in this space.

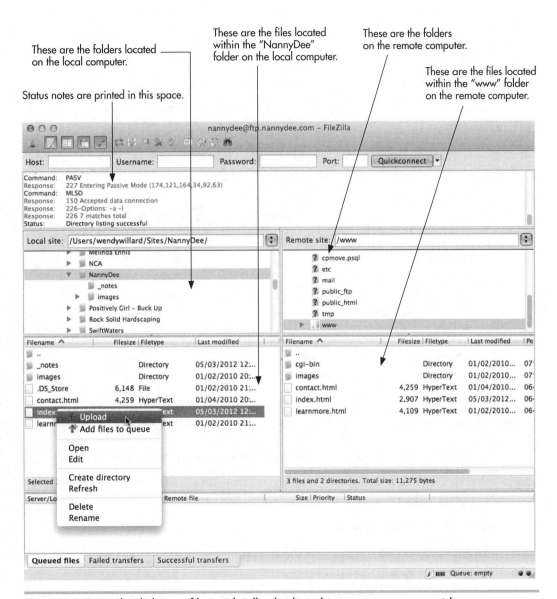

Figure 15-8   Right-clicking a file in FileZilla displays this context menu, providing access to download the file or perform other necessary actions.

That covers the most basic method of FTP—the transfer of files from one computer to another. If you have an FTP site you plan to visit often, you can store that server's login information in FileZilla's Site Manager to save you time (see Figure 15-9). To access the Site Manager, click the first button in the upper-left corner of the main FileZilla window. When

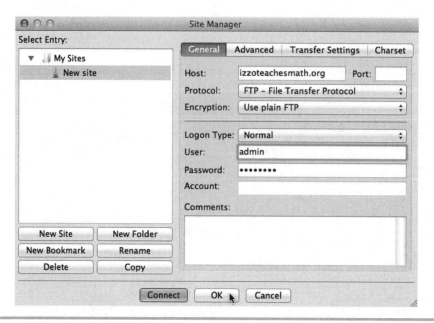

Figure 15-9 Use FileZilla's Site Manager to store usernames and passwords for frequently accessed FTP sites.

the Site Manager displays, choose New Site and add the necessary login information before clicking OK to save the information or Connect to save and also connect to the remote site immediately.

For more information about using FileZilla, visit **www.filezilla-project.org**. Or, if you prefer, try one of these other great FTP programs:

- CoffeeCup Free FTP (**www.coffeecup.com/free-ftp**)—Windows

- SmartFTP (**www.smartftp.com**)—Windows

- FTP Voyager (**www.ftpvoyager.com**)—Windows

- WS-FTP (**www.ipswitch.com**)—Windows

- YummyFTP (**www.yummyftp.com**)—Mac

- Fetch (**www.fetchsoftworks.com**)—Mac

- VicomsoftFTP (**www.vicomsoft.com**)—Mac

- Transmit (**www.panic.com**)—Mac

Web-Based FTP

If you are using a free service to host your web page, you probably have FTP capabilities through that company's web site. This is called *web-based FTP* because you don't need any additional software to transmit the files—in fact, you transmit the files right from within your web browser.

Even if your host company doesn't offer web-based FTP, if you use the Firefox web browser, you have an even better option. While I typically use the built-in FTP capabilities in Dreamweaver, since that's my preferred HTML development tool, I sometimes have a need for file transfer outside of Dreamweaver. If so, I use a powerful Firefox add-on called FireFTP.

To install FireFTP (or another web-based FTP tool for Firefox), open Firefox and visit **https://addons.mozilla.org**. Search for FTP. Locate the FTP app you want to add, and click the corresponding Add To Firefox button.

After the FTP app is installed, you can locate it under the Tools menu in Firefox. Similarly to how the previously discussed FTP programs function, FireFTP displays your local files on the left and the remote files on the right. Take a look at Figure 15-10 to see what I mean.

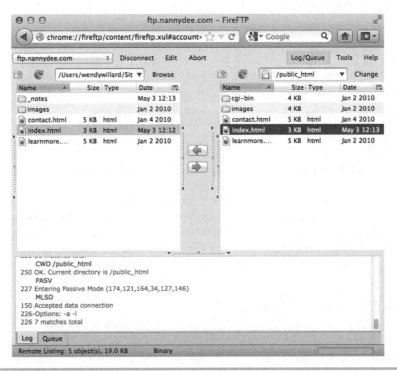

Figure 15-10 Web-based FTP is a super easy way to upload your files to a web server.

Test Your Published Site

After your site is uploaded to the server, you'll want to run through each page once more in order to verify everything transferred as expected. In addition, test to make sure all the links work and images appear.

Once you've made a cursory check, it's time to check for cross-browser and cross-platform consistency. Throughout the book, I have mentioned the importance of checking your pages in multiple browsers and on multiple computer systems to make sure they appear as you intended. Earlier in this chapter, I mentioned a few tools to help you test in a variety of potential user situations. However, if you weren't able to do so before for whatever reason, now's your last chance.

After your site is uploaded to the host computer, you should run through each page *once more* to verify that everything transferred as expected. Then, consider the following notes:

- Do all the page titles accurately reflect the content? If you bookmark them, do the titles work to help the user remember the page and its content?

- Does the text content display in an easily readable fashion?

- Do all the images display as intended?

- Do all the other media elements display and function as intended?

- Do all the links function as expected?

- Turn off the image display in your browser. Do all images contain alternate text explanations that accurately reflect their content?

- Does the layout flow as expected no matter the size of the browser window?

TIP

Finding errors? Remember to check out Appendix C in regard to troubleshooting.

Even if you don't have more than one type of computer or browser, now that your pages are live, you can ask friends or family to test them for you. Have them record what type of browser they're using, what size monitor they have, what size screen resolution they're using, and what computer operating system they're running. That way, when they report bugs or errors on your pages, you'll have help in determining the problem.

Publicize Your Web Site

After your site is live, you can begin submitting its URL to search engines. The process typically involves entering the URL of your web site and, perhaps, a contact e-mail address. You should look for a link labeled "Add URL" or "Add a Site." Your listing typically appears within a few days, but it may take as long as a week or so.

The different types of search engines vary greatly according to how they index your site. Because most give results based on how relevant pages are to search terms, you might rank 10th on one day or 1,000th on another. Another key aspect to keeping your site in the top of the search engines is to make it popular. Unfortunately, this may seem a bit like the chicken-and-egg syndrome.

TIP

A great way to find out where you should list your site to increase its popularity is to check your competition. If you enter **link:*competitor.com*** into Google (where *competitor* .*com* is replaced with the URL of your competitor's web site), you can see all the sites that link *to* your competitor. Chances are good that if you want to acquire some of those customers from the competition, you could benefit by having links from those same sites.

Your site needs to be clicked in the search results to become "popular" by search engine standards, but if your site is at the bottom of the search list because it's new, few people may ever find it to click it! This is why paid ads on search engines are such a big deal these days. Ever searched on Google and seen little ads appear on the right side that seem to be selling exactly what you searched for? These businesses are doing just that—they pay to "sponsor" certain search terms. So a summer camp might pay to appear each time a user searches for "summer camp" in Google. Theoretically, you'll only need to pay for these ads for a short time, provided they work and get people to click your web site link. Ideally, once your site becomes popular in Google, it will naturally rise to the top of the search results. Check out **adwords.google.com** to learn more.

NOTE

Unfortunately, you can't just click your own site's link a thousand times to increase its popularity in Google. The search engine not only records the number of times a link is clicked, but also the computer's address from which it was clicked. It will ignore any links clicked from your computer if it identifies potential fraud. Sorry!

One of the most common questions I receive from web site owners is this: *How can I increase my page's ranking in the search engines?* The answers to that question vary widely according to who's being asked. Search engine optimization (SEO) has become a niche market, and companies and consultants who specialize in SEO are hired to assist throughout the development of a web site.

As I mentioned previously, on the Web, content is king. So when trying to increase your site's ranking in a search engine, first and foremost you must review your content. Next, when you have intriguing, meaningful, quality content, it's time to advertise and promote your content to encourage others to link to it. Earning links from other web sites not only increases your traffic, but also betters your search engine ranking.

TIP

Always remember that search engine optimization doesn't happen overnight! It requires patience and diligent work to be successful.

Because the ins and outs of SEO can be difficult to navigate, I typically recommend businesses hire an SEO expert. When looking for an SEO consultant, consider the following:

- Be skeptical of firms that send you emails stating they visited your site and noticed you're "not listed in the top search engines." These are usually scams.

- Avoid agencies that claim they can make your site #1 on any particular search engine. This is simply not possible.

- Thoroughly research the companies being considered. Using a search engine is a great place to start.

- You're paying for their time, *not* placement costs. Reputable search engines do not accept money to increase your listing. Having said that, it is acceptable to incur temporary advertising fees if you choose to advertise on a search engine (such as with Google AdWords).

Finally, a few links to help you get started with SEO:

- Search Engine Land (**www.searchengineland.com**)

- The Official Google Analytics Blog (**analytics.blogspot.com**)

- Web Analytics Demystified (**www.webanalyticsdemystified.com**)

NOTE

Because many search engines have their own sets of rules and guidelines, reading through any tips or help files they provide before submitting your site is important. For example, on some sites, if you submit your site too often, they actually remove it from their listings altogether.

Marketing Tips

In addition to submitting your site to search engines and search directories, you can do many other things to promote your web site on- and offline:

- **Exchange links with related sites**   Consider asking sites with related content for links in exchange for a link to their site from yours. Don't forget about organizations you belong to, like your local chamber of commerce or an industry association. These are great places to exchange links. Another place you can exchange links is with a group of related sites, called a *web ring*. Visit **www.webring.com** for some examples.

- **Create newsworthy content**   Everyone loves free publicity, and with the thousands of media outlets both on- and offline, you should be able to get a little publicity yourself. If you have an interesting product or a new twist on an old idea, tell someone! Email news agencies, send out a press release, write to your local paper, contribute to an association's newsletter ... and don't forget to plug your web site.

- **Use your customers and tell everyone you know**   Give out free pins, bumper stickers, pens, or anything with your web site address to your existing customers. If your services and products are good, they'll have no problem telling others about them. In addition, spread the word through industry events where you can network and sell your business.

- **Don't forget traditional advertising**   If you have stationery, add your web site address. If you already run radio or print ads, include your web site address. Consider running a special ad promoting your new or revamped web site.

- **If you have the budget, consider paid online advertising**   Banner ads and paid listings in directories can be beneficial if targeted toward the right audience. Sometimes a less-expensive alternative might be to sponsor a related nonprofit web site. For example, if you sell school supplies, consider sponsoring a nonprofit homework help site. Another alternative is to sponsor free email or Internet service providers. But by and large, the best bang for your buck these days is likely either Google ads (**adwords.google.com**) or Facebook ads (**ads.facebook.com**). And because users provide demographic information when they sign up for a Facebook account, you can target specific users with your advertising.

- **Most important, create useful content**   If your site is boring or otherwise useless, people won't come and they won't help you promote it. While the best marketer for your business is a satisfied customer, the best marketer for your competition is a dissatisfied one.

Make the Site Live!

As a final step in creating your web site, research possible hosting solutions. Refer to the beginning of the chapter for links and tips on finding personal and business hosting.

TIP

If you simply want to test the pages you created to learn HTML in this book, I suggest signing up for a free site with one of the hosts mentioned at the beginning of this chapter.

After selecting a hosting provider, use an FTP program to transfer your web site to the server. Test the pages in several browsers and on different computer systems to confirm you successfully created and uploaded your web site. For practice, try making a change to one of the pages after viewing it live. Then, reupload the page and choose Refresh or Reload in your browser to review the change.

If appropriate, add your site to search engines and search directories, and continue with other marketing techniques. Remember, promoting your web site is an ongoing task and requires frequent maintenance.

Congratulations! If you've successfully uploaded your pages to a server and made them live, you certainly should be proud. Keep practicing what you've learned, and you'll surely be on your way to creating some stellar web sites.

Chapter 15 Self Test

1. Fill in the blank: ISP stands for _____.

2. Including the extension, what is the limit for characters in a domain name?

3. Which type of business hosting is used when your business purchases its own server, software, and a dedicated Internet connection capable of serving your site to web users 24 hours a day, 365 days a year?

4. Mobilizer is a tool that allows you to preview your pages in what type of user situation?

5. True/False: Some search engines ignore `meta` tags.

6. Why is it important to include the following line of code at the start of all your HTML pages?

   ```
   <!doctype html>
   ```

7. Where are `meta` tags placed within a web page?

8. True/False: All search engines use the same set of standards for indexing web pages.

9. Fill in the blanks: When testing a web site, you should test for cross-_____ and cross-_____ consistency.

10. What does FTP stand for?

Chapter 16

HTML for Email

Key Skills & Concepts

- Determine Whether HTML Email Is Appropriate for Your Needs
- Don't Send Spam
- Identify the Necessary Tools for the Task
- Code for Email Readers, Not Web Browsers
- Test, Test, Test

The year 2013 marks 14 years since the first edition of *HTML: A Beginner's Guide* was written. Throughout the bulk of those years, the rise of CSS has had the biggest impact on web designers and developers (and ultimately on web users). Perhaps the second most important change for web designers is the widespread support of HTML and CSS by email readers.

Indeed, at the end of the twentieth century your email inbox was a lot less colorful (and most likely a lot less full). HTML emails bring color, images, formatting, and much more interactivity than their plain-text counterparts. While most companies still provide plain-text emails to customers who request them, the vast bulk of business marketing and advertising email now sent is HTML-based.

NOTE
Because the bulk of HTML email is sent from businesses, this chapter focuses on creating HTML emails for marketing and advertising purposes.

For the web designer, this brings a whole new avenue of work opportunities, as well as new headaches. Why? Because an HTML email is essentially just a web page. So if you can design and code web pages, you can design and code HTML email.

The reason for the headaches is this: Support for HTML and CSS is growing among email readers, but it still lags behind on many fronts. In fact, coding HTML for email in 2013 is a bit like coding HTML for web browsers was a decade ago—which means you'll spend a lot of time testing, and testing, and testing, and revising and testing some more.

Email Standards Project

At the beginning of this book, I discussed the W3C and its role in creating web standards. In November 2007, a group of people got together to form the Email Standards Project. This organization works with email client developers and the design community to improve web standards support and accessibility in email.

Over the past five years, the folks behind the Email Standards Project have talked with Yahoo!, Google (Gmail), and IBM (Lotus Notes) about improving their respective email clients. While this is undoubtedly a slow process, there is great hope among the design community that this organization will help bring the same level of consensus that the W3C brought on the web browser front.

You can download the Email Standards Project's "Acid Test" to see exactly how they tested each email client. You can also view the results of their tests, and learn more about the movement, at **www.email-standards.org**.

Determine Whether HTML Email Is Appropriate for Your Needs

Before we jump into the details of coding HTML emails, we need to have a brief conversation about whether it is appropriate for you or your project. To make that determination, consider the following pros and cons.

The Purpose of Email Is to Communicate

At the end of the day, we use email to communicate with each other. While there certainly are many forms of communication, email has traditionally used written language to communicate. All email readers allow users to read written text. This is the most basic requirement of any email reader.

When you start styling that text with color and other formatting, you stop relying on the written word to communicate your message. Suppose, for example, you received an email from a friend. In that email your friend listed the menu for a bridal shower you were helping to throw next weekend, and then included the following line at the bottom: "Thanks for helping with the party! I highlighted the items I still need. Can you help with any of them?"

If your email program is set to read email as text-only, there won't be any highlighted text in that email. In instances like this, the communication method moves from the written language only to include visual clues like highlighting. Before you make the decision to send HTML emails, you need to determine the specific message of the emails being sent and whether or how any extra formatting will affect that message.

The End-User Display Is Unknown

Unlike web browsers, which have become much more uniform in their display and support of HTML, email readers are plentiful and vastly different from one another. Consider all the ways you read email. If you have a Yahoo!, Hotmail/Live Mail, or Gmail account, you probably read your email in a web browser.

But, you still have the option to read your email in a stand-alone email program like Outlook or MacMail. And if you are like a growing number of people, you might also check your email on a mobile phone like a Blackberry or iPhone. I just named off seven different ways to read an email, and I'm only getting started!

It is virtually impossible to know how your HTML emails will display when read by the end user. Testing in as many of the popular email readers as possible is certainly important, but ultimately you must make smart design decisions that ensure the widest possible audience can still glean the message being communicated. Keep this in mind when deciding whether HTML is the best delivery method for a particular email.

Plain-Text Email Is Safer and Smaller

Due to the proliferation of HTML email spam, the simple truth is that plain-text email is more likely to actually get to the reader. This may mean that the most important email communication with a customer—such as receipts—should be kept in plain text.

For example, many email readers block images and attachments from unknown senders or suspected spammers. One reason this happens is that anything attached to an email is capable of harboring viruses and other malicious code. Also, when you send HTML email with images stored on a web server, you can tell whether an email was opened by simply reviewing the site's access logs to see if the images were displayed. This allows spammers to differentiate between active email addresses and bad email addresses.

In fact, HTML emails are more likely to be tagged as spam simply for having embedded images. That means your beautifully designed HTML email may end up in a customer's spam bucket and eventually in the trash without the customer even knowing it.

Another reason HTML email might not make it to the target destination is size. If you get a little crazy with large images and hefty attachments, you can cause someone's email system to slow down drastically or even crash.

But ... HTML Email Marketing Works

Now that I've given you several reasons HTML email might not be appropriate, I must state the obvious: HTML email can definitely be more appealing. Let's face it, most of us react more quickly to an image of a double-dip chocolate ice cream cone on a hot summer day than we might to those words mixed in with other text in a crowded paragraph. As the saying goes, "a picture is worth a thousand words."

The simple truth is that when done right, HTML email marketing works. Here are a few of the reasons:

- **Cost effective** Advertisers who used to rely on expensive print-mail campaigns are largely embracing HTML email as an efficient way to get their message in front of customers more quickly and less expensively. While design costs might be similar, the cost of sending a thousand emails is significantly less than the cost to print and snail-mail a thousand postcards to customers.

- **Targeted** While most companies do target certain ZIP codes when sending snail-mail ads, email advertising allows you to target very specific demographics and behaviors. For example, suppose you are a customer of a certain grocery store who has recently started offering delivery. Being interested in the service, you viewed a page on a company's web site describing this new service, but you never actually purchased it. Because you were logged in to your account with this company at the time you viewed the delivery page, they decide to send you a targeted email ad offering free delivery on your next order. Such targeted emails tend to be highly successful.

- **Timely**   Email advertisements can be sent within seconds of certain events. Wake up to a snow day? Why not send a special "snow day savings" email to parents of elementary school students? Customers could be reading your HTML email (and making purchasing decisions) before a snail-mail equivalent even reaches the printer.

- **Fosters relationships**   Companies have long known that loyal customers are often the best ones. If you can keep a customer happy, you stand a good chance at keeping her a customer. Email—particularly HTML email with some interactivity—provides an effective tool for building and maintaining customer relationships.

At the end of the day, you can measure the success of any email marketing campaign with the right software. Businesses can tell how many people opened the messages, what links were clicked, who saw which versions (HTML or plain text), and even the revenue each generated. So it is relatively easy to stop sending out campaigns that aren't working, and to try something new.

Don't Send Spam

Before you start writing your HTML emails, you must know about the audience. From a legal standpoint, the most important thing to know about your audience is whether you have permission to contact them in this manner and for this purpose. In addition, you must always provide a reliable method for users to *opt-out,* or stop receiving your mail. In short, spam is *any mail sent without the permission of the recipient.*

Email the Right People

So how do you gain permission from recipients? Here are a few guidelines in that regard:

- You can send email to current customers. Most people consider anyone who has purchased from you within the last two years to be a "current" customer.

- You can send email to people who request information from you, either in person or online. Keep in mind that you can only send them email about relevant topics. In other words, if someone responds to a job posting on a company's web site but isn't hired, you can't start sending him marketing email about your products.

This means you can't harvest email addresses off email forwards or those found on the Internet. Just because I post my email address on my personal web site, that doesn't mean I want to receive marketing email from any business who visits my web site.

While it might be very tempting to send mass emails to strangers in the hopes that one might become a new customer, it is much more effective to target people who have already expressed an interest in your business or product.

TIP

If you're working with a business that is unsure whether their marketing list is legal, consider checking the guidelines presented by email marketing giant Campaign Monitor: **www.campaignmonitor.com/guides/permission**.

Always Provide a Way to Opt Out

Federal guidelines require you to always provide a way for someone to tell you he no longer wishes to receive your emails. At a bare minimum, this means you must provide a valid return address to which users can send a "please remove me" email. Most reputable email systems offer efficient unsubscribe mechanisms that allow recipients to opt out through an online form linked from all emails.

Federal guidelines further require you to keep such unsubscribe methods available for at least 30 days after emails are sent. After receiving an unsubscribe request, companies have 10 days to stop sending the recipient email.

Adhere to Other FTC Rules

To avoid your email being considered spam, you also must use legitimate headers and subject lines. In other words, you can't send an email with a subject of "FREE delivery on your next order" unless the offer is valid and indeed available to recipients. The from and reply-to email addresses must also be active.

Your company's business name and physical mailing address must also be visible in the email.

TIP

Check out **business.ftc.gov/documents/bus61-can-spam-act-compliance-guide-business** for more information about the Federal Trade Commission's CAN-SPAM laws.

Identify the Necessary Tools for the Task

Now that we've discussed why you might send HTML email, let's move on to how. You've already learned that you can type HTML code in just about any text editor, but in order to be viewed by a web browser, it must be saved with a certain file extension (such as .html). Similarly, you can type HTML code into an email, but it will just look like a bunch of code unless you send it through the proper channel.

Send Live Web Pages with a Personal Email Account

As I mentioned, an HTML email is really just a web page. Have you ever wanted to email a web page to someone? The method depends on your email software. If you have Apple's Safari browser, you simply navigate to the page you want to send and choose File | Mail Contents Of This Page. Next, the page will display in an email in MacMail. Simply address it and send it off!

New Window	⌘N
New Tab	⌘T
Open File...	⌘O
Open Location...	⌘L
Close Window	⇧⌘W
Close All Windows	⌥⇧⌘W
Close Tab	⌘W
Save As...	⌘S
Mail Contents of This Page	⌘I
Mail Link to This Page	⇧⌘I
Open in Dashboard...	
Import Bookmarks...	
Export Bookmarks...	
Print...	⌘P

You can also use Internet Explorer 7+ to send a web page via email. If you use the web-based Hotmail/Live Mail, choose Page | Email With Windows Live. If you don't use web-based email, but have Outlook or some other email software installed and set up on your system, choose Page | Send By Email. (This option is grayed out if you don't have an email account currently set up on your system.)

These methods are useful when you want to share a web page with family or friends. However, you wouldn't use these methods to send out mass business email for several reasons. First, most Internet service providers (ISPs) limit the amount of bandwidth you can use on a daily or monthly basis. Sending lots and lots of HTML email will likely have your ISP hounding you pretty quickly. In addition, sending bulk email through your business or personal server runs you the risk of having *all* your email blocked as spam.

Using an Email Service Provider

The best method for sending bulk HTML email is to use an email service provider (ESP). Similar to an Internet service provider, an ESP handles all aspects of bulk email delivery, from managing the recipient lists (both subscribe and unsubscribe features) to tracking the number of times each email is opened and clicked.

Just as there are hundreds of ISPs out there, you also have your choice from quite a few ESPs. As a freelancer, I have used a fair number of ESPs for different businesses. Each has its pros and cons, depending on the business and its audience.

When researching ESPs, here are a few things to look for:

- Contact management tools to handle your subscriber list

- Email creation tools to help format and lay out the content

- Email sending tools to help you test your emails

- Design services to help with graphic design and creative support

- Email reporting tools to help you track things like click-throughs, opens, and conversions

- Ease of use

- Support

As with any software, I encourage you to try before you buy. ESPs typically charge either a monthly fee or per-email/per-recipient fees (or a combination of both). Many also offer rebranding tools to allow designers to create their clients' emails, and then give the clients the tools to send and manage them. A few of the most popular ESPs include

- Blue Hornet (**www.bluehornet.com**)

- Campaign Monitor (**www.campaignmonitor.com**)

- Constant Contact (**www.constantcontact.com**)

- Emma (**www.myemma.com**)

- iContact (**www.icontact.com**)

- Lyris (**www.lyris.com**)

- MailChimp (**www.mailchimp.com**)

NOTE

If you are considering sending bulk mail, run (don't walk) toward these ESPs as fast as you can. I strongly discourage you from using your personal email account and email software to send *any* amount of bulk mail. The risks are just too great, and the benefits too small to justify it.

Code for Email Readers, Not Web Browsers

I'm now going to tell you a few things about HTML that apply only when you're coding HTML for email. For instance, because of the inconsistency of support for HTML5 and CSS3 among email readers, I'm actually going to suggest you use HTML tables for reliable layout! Gasp! While I would never suggest you use HTML tables to lay out an entire web page (as we used to before the rise of CSS), I am suggesting you use tables to lay out complex designs for email. I know it's a bit backward and awkward, but bear with me for a few minutes.

The most important differences in coding for email readers instead of web browsers are outlined in the following sections. But before we delve into those, we first need to determine exactly which email readers we're talking about.

According to Campaign Monitor (**www.campaignmonitor.com**), the top three email clients used in 2011 were Outlook, iOS devices, and Hotmail, with Apple Mail and Yahoo! Mail quite close behind. When we look at consumer recipients, the top three clients remain the same, but change in market share. Refer to Tables 16-1 and 16-2 for the complete lists.

Business Email Client	Market Share
Outlook Outlook 2003 and earlier Outlook 2007	36% 29% 7%
Hotmail/Live Mail	33%
Yahoo! Mail	14%
Gmail	6%
MacMail	4%
Windows Live Mail	3%
Thunderbird	2.4%
iPhone	1.3%
Lotus Notes	0.2%
AOL Mail	0.1%

Table 16-1 The Top Ten Email Clients Used by Business Recipients *(Source: fingerprintapp .com/email-client-stats)*

Ultimately, you must determine which email clients to target in terms of your project's desired audience. And just as with traditional web pages, you must test as much as possible within your target email clients. As a designer who frequently creates HTML email for clients, I have email accounts set up in all the top five email clients specifically to use for testing HTML email.

Now, on to the recommendations.

Consumer Email Client	Market Share
Yahoo! Mail	29%
Outlook Outlook 2003 and earlier Outlook 2007	27% 14% 13%
Hotmail/Live Mail	25%
MacMail	4%
Gmail	4%
Comcast	3%
AOL Mail	3%
Thunderbird	2%
Windows Live Mail	2%
iPhone	1%

Table 16-2 The Top Ten Email Clients Used by Consumer Recipients *(Source: fingerprintapp .com/email-client-stats)*

Absolute Paths

You must use absolute paths for all links and images. Remember Chapter 7, where I gave you the option of using either absolute or relative pathnames for links? Because your email is downloaded and displayed on the reader's system, you need to make sure all images are stored on a web server and referenced with complete, absolute URLs (i.e., those that start with http://). Likewise, all links to other web pages or content need to include the http://.

Images

There are three key points I'd like to make about using images in HTML email.

You Can't Rely on Images to Transfer Your Message

Image blocking is much more common in email readers than web browsers, so you need to provide text-only methods for readers to access your information. This doesn't just occur when images are placed in the trash or spam bucket. In fact, some email programs (such as Outlook, AOL, and Gmail) have default settings blocking images in email from unapproved senders.

Figure 16-1 shows how an email from an unknown sender shows up in my Gmail inbox by default. After receiving emails like this, the user can tell Gmail to display the images in a single email or always display images in emails sent by this sender (making Sears a "trusted sender").

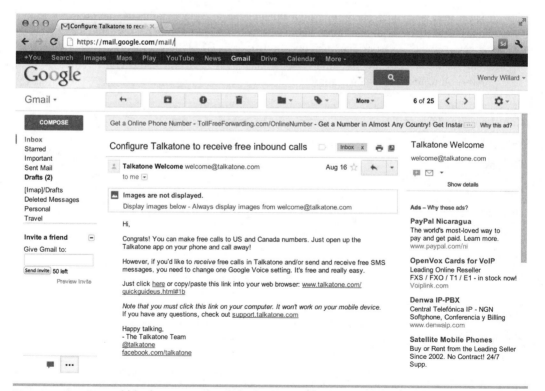

Figure 16-1 Gmail blocks images by default in email from unapproved senders.

Web-Based Client	Default Image Display	Trusted-Sender Image Display	Renders ALT Contents
Hotmail	OFF	Y	N
Yahoo! Mail (New)	OFF	Only if changed in spam settings	Y
Gmail	OFF	Y	N
AOL Webmail	OFF	Y	Y

Table 16-3 Image Blocking in Web-Based Email Clients

Tables 16-3, 16-4, and 16-5 cover the default settings in popular email clients, courtesy of Campaign Monitor, as of this writing. Refer to **www.campaignmonitor.com** for up-to-date resources of this nature.

Now that you know what you're up against, here are a few steps you can take to help ensure your emails still work if the images are blocked:

● Always include alternative text so that those email readers that do recognize it still show something in place of any blocked images.

● Always provide an alternative way of viewing the information. This may be plain-text content or a link to view the email in a web browser instead.

● Always include every image's height and width values in the img tag. This allows the email reader to leave the appropriate amount of space as a placeholder so that your entire layout isn't compromised.

● Always test your emails with images turned off so that you know what to expect.

Desktop Client	Default Image Display	Trusted-Sender Image Display	Renders ALT Contents
Outlook 2007	OFF	Y	Replaces ALT contents with security message
Outlook 2003	OFF	Y	Y
Outlook for Mac 2011	OFF	Y	Y
Outlook Express	ON	N	Y
Windows Live Hotmail	OFF	Y	Y
Apple Mail	ON	N	N
Thunderbird	OFF	Y	Y
AOL Desktop	OFF	Y	N
Lotus Notes	ON	Y	Y

Table 16-4 Image Blocking in Desktop Email Clients

Mobile Client	Default Image Display	Trusted-Sender Image Display	Renders ALT Contents
iPhone/iPad	ON	Y	N
Android default	OFF	Only if changed in spam settings	Y
Android Gmail	OFF	Y	N
Windows Mobile 7	OFF	Y	Y
Blackberry OS6	OFF		

Table 16-5   Image Blocking in Mobile Email Clients

All Images Must Be Stored on a Live Web Server

I know I already mentioned this a few pages back, but I can't stress how important this is. In order for images referenced in an HTML email to display once they are downloaded by the recipient, they must be stored on a live web server and referenced with an absolute URL. So, your images will *not* work if your code looks like this:

```
<img src="news-headline.gif">
```

Where should you store your images? These are the two most common scenarios:

- Create a folder on your company's web server to house all email files. In this case, your image references might look like: `<img src="http://www.mycompany.com/email/images/news-headline.gif">`.

- Store the images on your ESP's web server. Many ESPs offer space to their clients to house all email-related files. If you go this route, your image references might look like: `<img src="http://files.myesp.com/8897678432/43278953489.gif">`.

Images Should Be Small in File Size

While many people have significantly increased the speed at which they connect to the Internet, email bandwidth is a whole different ball game. Most people do not have an unlimited amount of email storage space. If you send large HTML email, you risk bogging down your recipient's email, or, worse yet, filling up her inbox.

Tables for Layout

You should use tables for structuring content. If you need to create columns in your email (such as are common with email newsletters), the only widely supported method of doing so is HTML tables.

TIP

When it comes to HTML for email, simple layouts are best. Complex page designs are not only more difficult to achieve successfully in HTML for email, but they are also less likely to be appreciated by users. Always remember how quick you typically check your inbox, and recognize your customers are devoting the same amount of time—not much—to reading their email.

I know, I know … anyone who has been around the web industry for any number of years likely thought table-based layout was a thing of the past. Indeed, so did I! Up until the advent of Outlook 2007, things actually looked promising, and most designers expected to be using CSS for email layout by that time.

But unfortunately, Microsoft built Outlook 2007 to use the Microsoft Word rendering engine for displaying HTML emails instead of Internet Explorer. When this news was announced, there was a ton of uproar among those who code HTML email. If you've ever actually viewed a web page inside of Microsoft Word, you probably are already groaning.

Here are the major issues with Outlook 2007:

- No background images in divs or table cells
- No background colors in nested tables or divs
- No support for the `float` or `position` properties in CSS
- Very poor support for `padding` and `margins`

The third bullet point—no support for the `float` or `position` properties—is what causes us to need tables for layout again. Those two CSS properties free us from using tables for pages viewed in web browsers. Without either of them, we must resort to the "old-fashioned" method of putting all the page content within table cells.

TIP

Refer to Chapter 11 for a refresher on using tables. For specific tips related to using tables for email design, check out **www.campaignmonitor.com/resources/will-it-work/guidelines**.

Compare Figures 16-2 and 16-3 to see an example of how a table-based layout might work for an HTML email. Figure 16-2 shows the layout in "Expanded Tables mode" in Dreamweaver, which allows you to see which pieces of the design are in which cells. Figure 16-3 shows the final, completed layout with the table border hidden.

NOTE

Always define the width of your table cells when using them for layout in HTML email to ensure your layout stays as you intend it to.

Figure 16-2 With Dreamweaver's Expanded Tables mode, you can easily see which pieces of the design go where.

Inline CSS

All CSS should be inline. This essentially means when you are coding HTML for email, you can ignore what I told you in the first few chapters about internal and external style sheets, because many email readers ignore those. As a refresher, here's an example of an inline style:

```
<p style="font-family:verdana;color:red;">
```

Check out Tables 16-6, 16-7, and 16-8 to see how the popular email clients stack up when it comes to internal, external, and inline style sheet support.

Figure 16-3   After the table borders are hidden and the view is returned to normal, the layout is seamless.

	Outlook 2011 (Mac)	Outlook '07/'10	Outlook '03/ Express/Mail	Windows Live Mail	Apple Mail 4	Entourage 2008	Notes 6/7	Lotus Notes 8.5	AOL Desktop 10	Thunderbird 2
`<style>` in `<head>`	Y	Y	Y	Y	Y	Y	N	Y	Y	Y
`<style>` in `<body>`	Y	Y	Y	Y	Y	Y	N	Y	Y	Y
`<link>` in `<head>`	Y	Y	Y	Y	Y	Y	Y	Y	Y	Y
`<link>` in `<body>`	Y	Y	Y	Y	Y	Y	N	Y	Y	Y

Table 16-6   CSS Support Among Desktop Email Clients

	Windows Live Hotmail	Yahoo! Mail (New)	Gmail	AOL Mail
<style> in <head>	Y	Y	N	Y
<style> in <body>	Y	Y	N	Y
<link> in <head>	N	N	N	N
<link> in <body>	N	N	N	N

Table 16-7 CSS Support Among Web-Based Email Clients

	iPhone iOS / iPad	Blackberry	Android Default	Android Gmail	Windows Mobile	HP webOS
<style> in <head>	Y	Y	Y	N	N	Y
<style> in <body>	Y	Y	Y	N	N	Y
<link> in <head>	Y	Y	Y	N	N	Y
<link> in <body>	Y	Y	Y	N	N	Y

Table 16-8 CSS Support Among Mobile Email Clients

Ask the Expert

Q: In previous chapters, you discussed creating fixed-width vs. liquid pages. How does that argument apply to HTML email?

A: While I encourage you to use flexible (liquid) page layouts whenever possible on the Web, HTML emails are a bit different. In fact, if you receive any amount of business email, you've probably already determined that most are fixed-width instead of liquid. This is due in part to the reliance on tables for layout (CSS more easily adapts to varying page sizes). But also, HTML emails are displayed within email readers, with lots of other elements fighting for screen space. Most people have a list of mailboxes, then mail within those boxes, plus other navigation, all surrounding the actual email. Therefore, it is recommended that you not design HTML emails wider than about 600 pixels.

When it comes to height, you must consider how much of your email needs to be visible in the "preview pane." This is the part of the email that is visible by default before the recipient decides to click and read more. Some research shows the average preview pane to be around 300 to 500 pixels tall. Keeping in mind how quickly people scan their inboxes, it is wise to place the most appealing and compelling aspects of your email in the top portion that is viewable in the preview pane.

In addition, consider including a brief line of text at the very top of your email that gives an overview of what's included. This is particularly important for Gmail users, who only see the first line of text in their preview pane. A reasonable example might be: IN THIS ISSUE: Upcoming Car Shows, How to Save on Insurance, Car Seat Safety, and more….

As you probably noticed, Gmail is the real reason I suggest using only inline styles. No currently available version of this popular web client supports internal or external styles.

No Shorthand

While you're steering clear of internal and external style sheets to reach the widest possible audience, you should also avoid all CSS shorthand. Instead, write out every complete style declaration. For example, while it is perfectly acceptable to write:

```
<p style="font:verdana 10px bold;">
```

this type of shorthand is not very well supported by email clients. So, you'll need to write each individual property and value, as in:

```
<p style="font-family:verdana;font-size:10px;font-weight:bold;">
```

Reference Guide to CSS Support in Email Clients

Campaign Monitor, a fabulous ESP and wonderful resource for all things HTML email, is part of the Email Standards Project. As such, they have a ton of information about CSS support among the most popular email readers. I've included (with permission) some of their most recent research, as of this writing. For updates, refer to **www.campaignmonitor.com/css/** and **www.email-standards.org/clients/**.

First, Table 16-9 lists the most common CSS properties and how they are supported by common desktop email clients. Next, Table 16-10 compares the support of those same CSS properties, but this time among popular web-based email clients. Then, Table 16-11 runs through mobile email client support. I encourage you to consult these tables (and their online counterparts) when deciding how to best code your HTML emails for your target audience.

Interactivity and Multimedia in HTML Email

After you've designed a few HTML emails for someone, they'll likely start to ask about adding more "pizzazz" to those emails. Thus, the question always comes up about including video, Flash, and forms in HTML email.

Video in Email

Video is not common in email, largely due to security concerns and lack of widespread support. As with all multimedia, you must first consider whether it's warranted and accepted by your target audience before even worrying about how to add it.

Thankfully, some testing has been done to determine exactly what support does exist. (Refer to **www.campaignmonitor.com/videoinemail** for the complete test results.) But unfortunately, the results aren't pretty: The only email tool that supports any sort of video in email is Apple Mail. As of this writing, the only reliable way to include any sort of motion graphics in an email is with an animated GIF. And, there is no support for sound at all in any email reader. So in short, you cannot realistically add video to your HTML emails.

	Outlook 2011 Mac	Outlook '07/'10	Outlook '03/Express/Mail	Windows Live Mail	Apple Mail 4	Entourage 2008	Notes 6/7	Lotus Notes 8.5	AOL Desktop	Thunderbird
background-color	Y	Y	Y	Y	Y	Y	N	Y	Y	Y
background-image	Y	N	Y	Y	Y	Y	N	N	Y	Y
background-position	Y	N	Y	Y	Y	Y	N	N	Y	Y
background-repeat	Y	N	Y	Y	Y	Y	N	N	Y	Y
border	Y	Y	Y	Y	Y	Y	N	Y	Y	Y
border-collapse	Y	Y	Y	Y	Y	Y	Y	Y	Y	Y
border-radius	Y	N	N	N	Y	Y	N	N	N	N
border-spacing	Y	N	N	N	Y	Y	N	N	N	Y
bottom	Y	N	Y	Y	Y	Y	N	Y	Y	Y
caption-side	Y	N	N	N	N	N	N	N	N	Y
clear	Y	N	Y	Y	Y	Y	N	Y	Y	Y
clip	Y	N	Y	Y	Y	Y	N	N	Y	Y
color	Y	Y	Y	Y	Y	Y	Y	Y	Y	Y
cursor	Y	N	Y	Y	Y	Y	N	Y	Y	Y
direction	Y	N	Y	Y	Y	Y	N	Y	Y	Y
display	Y	N	Y	Y	Y	Y	Y	Y	Y	Y
empty-cells	Y	N	N	N	Y	Y	N	N	N	Y
float	Y	N	Y	Y	Y	Y	N	Y	Y	Y
font-family	Y	Y	Y	Y	Y	Y	Y	Y	Y	Y
font-size	Y	Y	Y	Y	Y	Y	Y	Y	Y	Y
font-style	Y	Y	Y	Y	Y	Y	Y	Y	Y	Y
font-variant	Y	Y	Y	Y	Y	Y	N	Y	Y	Y
font-weight	Y	Y	Y	Y	Y	Y	Y	Y	Y	Y
height	Y	N	Y	Y	Y	Y	N	Y	Y	Y

left	Y	Y	Z	Y	Y	Y	Y	Y	Y
letter-spacing	Y	Y	Z	Y	Y	Y	Y	Y	Y
line-height	Y	Y	Z	Y	Y	Y	Y	Y	Y
list-style-image	Y	Z	Z	Y	Y	N	Y	Y	Y
list-style-position	Y	Z	Z	Y	Y	N	Y	Y	Y
list-style-type	Y	Z	Y	Y	Y	Y	Y	Y	Y
margin	Y	Y	Y	Y	Y	Y	Y	Y	Y
opacity	Y	Z	Z	N	Y	N	N	Z	Y
overflow	Y	Z	Z	Y	Y	N	Y	Y	Y
padding	Y	*	Y	Y	Y	N	Y	Y	Y
position	Y	Z	Y	Y	Y	Y	Y	Y	Y
right	Y	Z	Y	Y	Y	Y	Y	Y	Y
table-layout	Y	Y	Y	Y	Y	Y	Y	Y	Y
text-align	Y	Y	Y	Y	Y	Y	Y	Y	Y
text-decoration	Y	Y	Y	Y	Y	Y	Y	Y	Y
text-indent	Y	Y	Y	Y	Y	Y	Y	Y	Y
text-shadow	Y	Z	N	Y	Y	N	Y	N	N
text-transform	Y	Y	Y	Y	Y	Y	Y	Y	Y
top	Y	Z	Y	Y	Y	Y	Y	Y	Y
vertical-align	Y	Z	Y	Y	Y	Y	Y	Y	Y
visibility	Y	Z	Y	Y	Y	Y	Y	Y	Y
white-space	Y	Y	N	Y	Y	N	Y	N	Y
width	Y	*	Y	Y	Y	N	Y	Y	Y
word-spacing	Y	Z	Y	Y	Y	Y	Y	Y	Y
z-index	Y	Y	Y	Y	Y	Y	Y	Y	Y

Table 16-9 CSS Property Support Among Desktop Email Clients

	Windows Live Hotmail	Yahoo! Mail (New)	Gmail	AOL Mail
background-color	Y	Y	Y	Y
background-image	N	Y	Y	Y
background-position	N	Y	N	Y
background-repeat	N	Y	N	Y
border	Y	Y	Y	Y
border-collapse	Y	Y	Y	Y
border-radius	N	N	N	*
border-spacing	Y	Y	Y	Y
bottom	Y	N	N	Y
caption-side	Y	Y	Y	Y
clear	Y	Y	Y	Y
clip	N	N	N	Y
color	Y	Y	Y	Y
cursor	Y	Y	N	Y
direction	Y	Y	Y	N
display	Y	Y	Y	Y
empty-cells	Y	Y	Y	Y
float	Y	Y	N	Y
font-family	Y	Y	Y	Y
font-size	Y	Y	Y	Y
font-style	Y	Y	Y	Y
font-variant	Y	Y	Y	Y
font-weight	Y	Y	Y	Y
height	Y	Y	Y	Y
left	N	N	N	Y
letter-spacing	Y	Y	Y	Y
line-height	Y	Y	Y	Y
list-style-image	N	Y	N	Y
list-style-position	N	Y	N	Y
list-style-type	Y	Y	Y	Y
margin	*	Y	Y	Y
opacity	Y	N	N	Y

Table 16-10   CSS Property Support Among Web-Based Email Clients (*continued*)

	Windows Live Hotmail	Yahoo! Mail (New)	Gmail	AOL Mail
overflow	N	N	N	Y
padding	Y	Y	Y	Y
position	Y	N	N	Y
right	Y	N	N	Y
table-layout	Y	Y	Y	Y
text-align	Y	Y	Y	Y
text-decoration	Y	Y	Y	Y
text-indent	Y	Y	Y	Y
text-shadow	Y	Y	Y	*
text-transform	Y	Y	Y	Y
top	Y	N	N	Y
vertical-align	Y	Y	Y	Y
visibility	Y	Y	N	Y
white-space	Y	Y	Y	Y
width	Y	Y	Y	Y
word-spacing	Y	Y	Y	Y
z-index	N	N	N	Y

Table 16-10 CSS Property Support Among Web-Based Email Clients

Flash

I'm afraid the results aren't any better for Flash lovers. In fact, Apple's MacMail is the only email client to offer native support for Flash files. While you can include a "fallback" image when embedding Flash files in normal web pages, for browsers to display when the Flash player isn't available, most email clients won't even let you do that.

So again, you cannot realistically add Flash to your HTML emails.

Forms

Imagine sending out an invitation via email. Wouldn't it be nice to embed a form inside that email so guests could simply click "yes" or "no" and then hit the Submit button to reply? While the concept sounds great, email clients haven't quite caught up yet.

Although most of the email clients tested by Campaign Monitor do display forms correctly (all except Outlook 2007), only about half allow the form to be functional. Those email clients that do allow functioning forms include Yahoo! Mail (the new version only), Gmail, MacMail, Thunderbird, Penelope (aka Eudora 8), Outlook Express, Windows Live Mail, Lotus Notes 8, and Entourage. Among the notables left off that list are AOL, Hotmail, and Outlook (both 2003 and 2007).

	iPhone / iPad	Blackberry	Android Default	Androis Gmail	Windows Mobile 7	HP webOS 2
background-color	Y	Y	Y	Y	Y	Y
background-image	Y	Y	Y	N	N	Y
background-position	Y	Y	Y	N	N	Y
background-repeat	Y	Y	Y	N	N	Y
border	Y	Y	Y	Y	Y	Y
border-collapse	Y	Y	Y	Y	Y	Y
border-radius	Y	N	Y	N	N	Y
border-spacing	Y	Y	Y	Y	N	Y
bottom	Y	Y	Y	N	N	Y
caption-side	N	*	Y	Y	*	Y
clear	Y	Y	Y	Y	Y	Y
clip	Y	Y	Y	N	N	Y
color	Y	Y	Y	Y	Y	Y
cursor	Y	N	N	N	N	N
direction	Y	Y	Y	Y	Y	Y
display	Y	Y	Y	N	N	Y
empty-cells	Y	Y	Y	Y	Y	Y
float	Y	Y	Y	Y	Y	Y
font-family	Y	Y	Y	Y	Y	Y
font-size	*	N	Y	Y	Y	Y
font-style	Y	Y	Y	Y	Y	Y
font-variant	Y	Y	Y	Y	Y	Y
font-weight	Y	Y	Y	Y	Y	Y
height	Y	Y	Y	Y	Y	Y
left	Y	Y	Y	N	N	Y
letter-spacing	Y	Y	Y	Y	Y	Y
line-height	Y	Y	Y	Y	Y	Y
list-style-image	Y	Y	Y	N	N	Y
list-style-position	Y	Y	Y	N	Y	Y
list-style-type	Y	Y	Y	N	Y	Y
margin	Y	Y	Y	Y	Y	Y

Table 16-11 CSS Property Support Among Mobile Email Clients (*continued*)

	iPhone / iPad	Blackberry	Android Default	Androis Gmail	Windows Mobile 7	HP webOS 2
opacity	Y	Y	Y	N	N	Y
overflow	Y	*	*	*	N	*
padding	Y	Y	Y	Y	Y	Y
position	Y	Y	Y	N	N	Y
right	Y	Y	Y	N	N	Y
table-layout	Y	Y	Y	Y	Y	Y
text-align	Y	Y	Y	Y	Y	Y
text-decoration	Y	Y	Y	Y	Y	Y
text-indent	Y	Y	Y	Y	Y	Y
text-shadow	Y	Y	Y	Y	N	N
text-transform	Y	Y	Y	Y	Y	Y
top	Y	Y	Y	N	N	Y
vertical-align	Y	Y	Y	Y	Y	Y
visibility	Y	Y	Y	N	N	Y
white-space	Y	Y	Y	Y	Y	Y
width	Y	Y	Y	Y	Y	Y
word-spacing	Y	Y	Y	Y	Y	Y
z-index	Y	Y	Y	N	N	Y

*Support varies or is not consistent

Table 16-11   CSS Property Support Among Mobile Email Clients

Given this information, your best bet is to link to a form displayed in a web browser until email clients offer more widespread support.

Test, Test, Test

After you've coded your HTML email, the fun really begins. While we've come to the point where web pages that work in Firefox and Internet Explorer are considered "safe" for the Web at large, HTML email still requires extensive testing in multiple clients.

Thankfully, many ESPs offer services to make this process easier. For example, Campaign Monitor provides screenshots to show how your email will look in more than 15 of the most popular email clients, including the potential problem areas like Outlook 2007 and Lotus Notes, plus mobile clients too. Visit **www.campaignmonitor.com/testing** to learn more. Figures 16-4, 16-5, and 16-6 show how the same test email displays differently depending on the email client. These screenshots are samples taken using Campaign Monitor's testing tool.

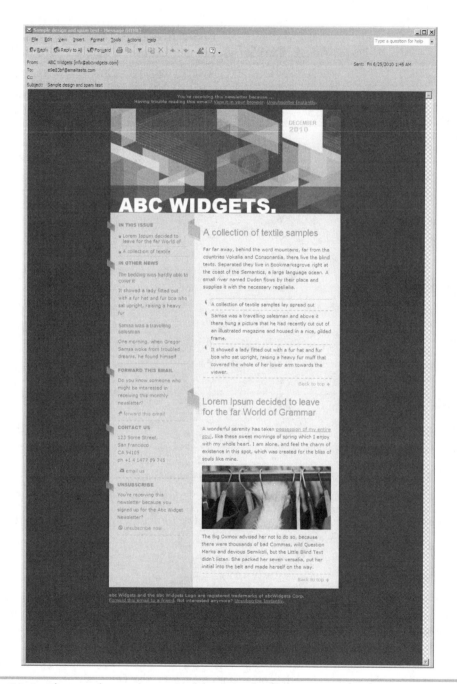

Figure 16-4 The sample email as it displays in Outlook XP

Figure 16-5   The sample email as it displays on a Blackberry

Another great option is a stand-alone testing tool like Litmus. Billing itself as the "advanced testing tool for web professionals," Litmus offers testing for both standard web pages and HTML email. Litmus' basic account offers unlimited email and page tests per month. Additional fee-based options allow spam filter tests and email analytics. Visit **http://litmusapp.com** for details.

Spam Test

One of the unique aspects you can test is the likelihood of your email being flagged as spam. Many of the popular ESPs offer this testing with their email messaging services. (If yours does not, there are other tools you can use. For example, the Email Spam Test at **www.emailspamtest.com** is a free service from Blink Campaign.)

SpamAssassin is the most widely used spam filter to process email received by ISPs. If your email gets blacklisted by SpamAssassin, you'll have a hard time getting your content in front of any of your subscribers. Refer to **spamassassin.apache.org** to learn more.

Figure 16-6 The sample email as it displays through web mail in Gmail

Wondering what might cause an email to be flagged as spam? Here are just a few of the many reasons SpamAssassin might give you a higher "spam score." (And in this case, higher is not better.)

- HTML link text says "click here" (I warned you in Chapter 6 not to do this!)

- A WHOLE LINE OF YELLING DETECTED

- Messages that include "Dear Friend" or "Dear (Name)"

- Message that contains "call" or "dial" or "toll free" followed by 800, 888, 877, 866, 855, 844, 833, or 822 (for example, "Call 1-877-555-5555 for your offer now!")

- Messages with the phrase "risk free" and other spam keywords

- HTML title contains "Untitled" (always title your web pages, even if they're being emailed!)

TIP

Want to know more about how spam filters work? Check out **www.mailchimp.com/ resources/guides/how-to-avoid-spam-filters**.

Try This 16-1   Design an HTML Email

Why not give your HTML skills a real test by putting them in front of some good old-fashioned email readers? This project asks you to create an HTML email advertising the new web site you've created. The goals for this project are

- Coding an HTML page for email readers, not web browsers

- Testing an HTML page in an email reader

NOTE

This project requires you to upload your test email to a live web server. If you don't currently have access to a web server, check with your ISP (which may provide space on its site free to customers), school, or business. You will be unable to test an HTML email without access to a live web server because all images in HTML email must be stored on the Internet in order to be accessed by email readers. Alternatively, you could sign up for an account with one of the ESPs listed previously in this chapter.

1. Open your text or HTML editor and create a new HTML page.

2. Add graphics and text created throughout the course of this book to advertise the new web site you set up. Be sure to use full, absolute paths when referencing images and other links.

TIP

In the case of HTML email, less is more. So I suggest using a few key images, and perhaps a screenshot of the new web site, mixed with a brief paragraph explaining the new features of the site.

3. Format the content to display in the most popular email readers, as discussed previously in this chapter.

4. Make sure all the images and some highlighted text link to the new site.

5. Save the file.

6. Upload your saved file to a live web server.

7. Open Safari on the Mac or IE on the PC.

8. Enter the address of the file you just uploaded in the address box in the browser.

9. In Safari, choose File | Mail Contents Of This Page. In IE, choose Page | Send By Email if you have an email account set up in Outlook, or choose Page | Email With Windows Live if you use a web-based email tool. Enter a few different email addresses to send test messages of your HTML email.

10. If you need to make changes, return to your text or HTML editor to do so. After making changes, save the file, reupload it, and switch back to the browser. Choose Refresh or Reload to preview the changes, and then repeat Step 9.

HTML email is a whole different breed. While web browsers are fairly uniform in their display of HTML pages, email readers still have a long way to go to reach this point. Designing HTML email involves lots of patience as you design, test, and redesign. This project gave you a glimpse into that process using a sample marketing email for the company or organization of your choice.

Ready for more practice? I encourage you to sign up for a free test account with one of the ESPs mentioned in this chapter. Then, try re-creating your sample marketing email using their web-based creation tools. Each ESP offers different options, but all provide the messaging services necessary to send bulk HTML email safely and securely.

Chapter 16 Self Test

1. True/False: The W3C maintains a special specification for HTML email.

2. Fill in the blank: _____ is any email sent without the permission of the recipient.

3. What is the difference between an ISP and an ESP?

4. Fill in the blank: You must use _____ paths for all images and links in HTML email.

5. Why should you avoid relying on images to translate key messages in HTML email?

6. Which type of style sheets should be used for all HTML email?

    A. Inline

    B. Internal

    C. External

    D. Linked

7. Why must we rely on tables for column-based layout in HTML email?

8. Which methods of adding interactivity to HTML email are widely supported by email readers? (Select all that apply.)

    A. Flash

    B. Video

    C. Forms

    D. None of the above

9. True/False: It is acceptable to use CSS shorthand in HTML email.

10. Why should you avoid using background images in tables in HTML email?

Part IV

Appendixes

Appendix A

Answers to Self Tests

Chapter 1: Getting Started

1. What is a web browser?

A web browser is a software program that runs on your computer and enables you to view web pages.

2. What does HTML stand for?

HTML stands for Hypertext Markup Language.

3. Identify the various parts of the following URL:
http://www.mcgrawhill.com/books/webdesign/favorites.html
_____://_____/_____/_____/_____

The various parts of the URL are as follows: protocol://domain/folder/folder/file

4. What is WYSIWYG?

WYSIWYG is the acronym for what-you-see-is-what-you-get. It refers to the idea that, for example, instead of typing code to cause a certain bit of text to be bold, you simply click a button that makes it bold.

5. Fill in the blank: The version of HTML currently under development is _____.

The version of HTML currently under development is HTML5.

6. What is the program Adobe Dreamweaver used for?

Dreamweaver is a WYSIWYG web page development and editing tool.

7. What is one of the three most popular web browsers?

Internet Explorer, Google Chrome, and Firefox are the most popular web browsers, as of early 2013.

8. Fill in the blank: When you type a URL into your web browser, you send a request to the _____ that houses that information.

When you type a URL into your web browser, you send a request to the web server that houses that information.

9. What does the acronym "URL" stand for?

URL stands for uniform resource locator.

10. What organization maintains the standards for HTML?

The World Wide Web Consortium (W3C) maintains the standards for HTML.

11. How can you give your site's visitors visual clues as to where they are in your site's structure?

The following list is not exhaustive; you may come up with plenty of other good ideas.
A. Highlight the current section on the navigation bar.
B. Repeat the page name in the page title at the top of the browser window.
C. Include the page name in the filename.
D. Include an appropriate headline on the page.

12. **Fill in the blank: Good practice is to include a standard _____ on all pages for consistency and ease of use.**

Good practice is to include a standard <u>navigation bar</u> on all pages for consistency and ease of use.

13. **Fill in the blank: Selling products and recruiting potential employees are examples of web site _____.**

Selling products and recruiting potential employees are examples of web site <u>goals</u>.

14. **Fill in the blank: Before you can begin developing your web site, you must know a little about the site's target _____.**

Before you can begin developing your web site, you must know a little about the site's target <u>audience</u>.

15. **If your site represents a new company or one that doesn't already have information about its client demographics, where might you look for information?**

Look to the competition. Chances are good that if your competition has a successful web site, you can learn from them about your target audience.

Chapter 2: Page Setup

1. **What file extensions do HTML files use?**

HTML uses the .htm or .html file extension.

2. **The following line of HTML code contains errors. What is the correct way to write this line:**

```
<p This is a paragraph of text p>
<p>This is a paragraph of text</p>
```

3. **At the very least, which tags should be included in a basic HTML page?**

A basic HTML page should include the following tags: `!doctype`, `html`, `head`, `title`, and `body`.

4. **Identify the tag name, attribute, and value in the following line of HTML code:**
```
<a href="page.html">
```

Here, `a` is the tag name, `href` is the attribute, and `page.html` is the value.

5. **Fill in the blank: HTML5 is case-_____.**

HTML5 is case-<u>insensitive</u>.

6. **Which option is *not* acceptable for an HTML filename?**
   A. myfile.html
   B. my-file.html
   C. my file.html
   D. my1file.html

C. The name **my file.html** is not an acceptable HTML filename.

7. **What is the named character entity used to add a copyright symbol to a web page?**

   The sequence © is the named character entity used to add a copyright symbol to a web page.

8. **You just created a web page, and you're previewing it in a web browser when you notice an error. After fixing the error and saving the web page, which button should you click in the browser to view the changes made?**

   Use the Refresh or Reload button to view the changes you have made.

9. **The tags in the following line of code aren't nested properly. Rewrite the code so the tags are nested properly: `<p><strong><em>Hello World!</p></strong></em>`**

   ```
   <p><strong><em>Hello World!</em></strong></p>
   ```

10. **How can you rewrite the following text so that it doesn't display when the page is viewed in a browser?**

    ```
    <!-- Hide Me! -->
    ```

11. **Which two options will the browser ignore when they are coded in a web page?**
    A. `<p>`
    B. A tab
    C. `<br>`
    D. `<br><br>`
    E. Single space with the SPACEBAR
    F. Double space with the SPACEBAR

    Answers B and F are correct. The browser will ignore the intent of both a tab and a double space made with the SPACEBAR and turn them each into a single space when they are coded in a web page.

12. **Fill in the blank: The p tag is an example of a _____ tag because it contains sections of text.**

    The p tag is an example of a <u>container</u> (or <u>block-level</u>) tag because it contains sections of text.

13. **The following line of HTML code contains errors. What is the correct way to write the code: `< img src = " photo.jpg " >`?**

    ```
    <img src="photo.jpg">
    ```

14. **What symbols must start and end all HTML tags?**

    Left and right angle brackets (< >) must start and end all HTML tags.

Chapter 3: Style Sheet Setup

1. **What file extension is used for external CSS files?**

   .css

2. **The following line of HTML code contains errors. What is the correct way to write this line?**

   ```
   h2 {font-family: verdana;}
   ```

3. *font-family*, *font-size*, and *color* are all examples of what in CSS?

They are all examples of CSS properties.

4. Update the following code to reference the URL of the following background image: *images/ background.jpg*.

```
body {background-image: url(images/background.jpg);}
```

5. Fill in the blank: CSS <u>properties</u> alter specific attributes of a selector.

6. The second two numbers in a six-digit hexadecimal code refer to which color?

The second two numbers in a six-digit hexadecimal code refer to green.

7. Which element is used as a CSS selector when you want to change the color of a page's links?

The a element is used as a CSS selector when you want to change the color of a page's links.

8. Which element is used as a CSS selector when you want to change the background color of a page?

The body element is used as a CSS selector when you want to change the color of a page background.

9. Which takes precedence when there are conflicting style declarations?

A. A style applied to all p tags
B. A style applied with an ID selector
C. A style applied to the body element
D. A style applied with a class selector

Answer B is correct.

10. Which takes precedence when there are conflicting style declarations?

A. An inline style
B. An internal style sheet
C. An external style sheet
D. A browser default style sheet

Answer A is correct.

Chapter 4: Working with Text

1. Which file format has become a standard in electronic document delivery because of its ease of use, reliability, and stability?

PDF (Portable Document Format) has become a standard in electronic document delivery.

2. Why should you avoid underlining text on a web page?

Linked text is underlined by default, so it might be confusing to see linked and nonlinked text both underlined on a page.

3. What is a reasonable range for column widths on web pages?

Two hundred to 400 pixels is a reasonable range for web page column widths.

4. What are three key things to consider when designing a printable version of a web page?

When designing a printable version of a web page, consider size, color, and reference.

5. Name four possible values of the font-size CSS property.

Possible values of the font-size CSS property include point sizes (12pt, 14pt, and so on), pixel sizes (10px, 12px, and so on), em sizes (24em, 36em, and so on), and keywords (such as xx-small, x-small, small, medium, and so on).

6. What is the default characteristic of text marked with the del element?

It is rendered in the strikethrough style.

7. What is the default characteristic of text marked with the mark element?

It is rendered in the strikethrough style.

8. Fill in the blank: You use the _____ property in CSS when specifying the font name in which the text should be rendered.

You use the font-family property in CSS to specify the font name in which the text should be rendered.

9. When you specify a font size in ems, that size is relative to what?

The size is relative to the height of the font in general.

10. Fill in the blank: The process of providing a backup font name in the font-family property is also referred to as _____.

The process of providing a backup font name when specifying fonts is also referred to as cascading.

Chapter 5: Page Structure

1. What is the purpose of the br element?

The <br> element is used to add a line break.

2. What happens when you code three p elements in a row?

The browser uses only the first element and ignores the others.

3. List two style sheet properties used for text alignment.

The CSS properties text-align and vertical-align are used for text alignment.

4. How is the div element different from the article element?

The div element is a generic container for page content, whereas the article element is designated for content available for syndication.

5. Which element—head or header—goes inside the body of an HTML document?

The header element goes inside the body of an HTML document.

6. True/False: The `blockquote` tag indents text on both the left and right sides.

True.

7. True/False: You can only use one `header` element in each page.

False.

8. Using #introduction indicates the style named *introduction* was applied to an element using which HTML attribute?

`<section id="introduction">`

9. What is the primary difference between the `article` and `section` elements?

Both are container elements, but the `section` element is used for thematically related content, whereas the `article` element is used for syndicated content.

10. Which CSS property is used to specify the buffer space around a content box inside of the box's border?

The `padding` property adds buffer space around the content box, but inside the box border.

11. Which CSS property is used to specify the buffer space around a content box outside of the box's border?

The `margin` property adds buffer space around the content box, but outside the box border.

Chapter 6: Positioning Page Elements

1. Fill in the blank: _____ positioning takes an element out of the normal page flow and positions it in a particular place on the page.

Absolute positioning takes an element out of the normal page flow and positions it in a particular place on the page.

2. Which property determines whether a layer is hidden or visible?

The `visibility` property determines whether a layer is hidden or visible.

3. Which two properties are set in the `body` element to ensure all browsers use the same "starting point" for page layout?

The `padding` and `margin` properties can be set in the `body` element to ensure all browsers use the same "starting point" for page layout.

4. According to the default W3C specifications, if you had a box that was 150 pixels wide with 10 pixels of padding on all four sides and a 2-pixel border all the way around, what would be the total horizontal space used by the box?

174 pixels (150 pixels wide + 10 pixels left padding + 10 pixels right padding + 2 pixels left border + 2 pixels right border)

5. **Which HTML element is used to create generic sections of content to be formatted with style sheets?**

   The `div` element is used to separate content into formatting areas.

6. **Fill in the blank: The _____ attribute identifies the medium for which a particular external style sheet should be used.**

   The `media` attribute identifies the medium for which a particular external style sheet should be used.

7. **Add the appropriate code so the content area has a 20-pixel margin around the top, right, and left sides but a 5-pixel margin around the bottom.**

   ```
   #content {                              }
   ```

   The correct code:

   ```
   #content {padding: 20px 20px 5px 20px;}
   ```

8. **Which HTML element can be used to reference an external style sheet?**

   The `link` element can be used to reference an external style sheet.

9. **Add the appropriate code to import a style sheet called design.css.**
   ```
   <style>

   </style>
   ```

   The correct code is
   ```
   <style>
       @import "design.css";
   </style>
   ```

10. **Fill in the blank: _____ positioning is the default type of positioning.**

    Static positioning is the default type of positioning.

11. **True/False: Relative positioning adjusts an element's location on the page relative to itself.**

    True.

12. **Add the appropriate code to place the content area 50 pixels from the left edge of the browser and 150 pixels from the top edge.**

    ```
    #content {                        }
    ```

    The correct code:
    ```
    #content {left: 50px; top: 150px;}
    ```

13. **Which property is used to specify an element's stacking order on the page?**

    The `z-index` property is used to specify an element's stacking order on the page.

14. **True/False: When adjusting an element's stacking order on the page, lower values take precedence over higher values.**

    False. The element with the highest value is placed on "top."

Chapter 7: Working with Links

1. **What does the `href` attribute do?**

   The `href` attribute gives the location of the content to which you are linking.

2. **Which of these can be classified as a relative link?**
   A. `<a href="../email.html">`
   B. `<a href="http://www.yahoo.com/email.html">`
   C. `<a href="/email.html">`
   D. `<a href="http://email.yahoo.com">`

   Answers A and C are relative.

3. **What must be installed and activated on a user's machine to take advantage of an email link in a web site?**

   To take advantage of an email link in a web site, the user must have an email program, such as Microsoft Outlook or Apple Mail, installed and active. Email links like these may not work if the visitor uses only a web-based email service such as Gmail or Hotmail.

4. **How do you tell the browser to launch a link in a new window?**

   Add the `target` attribute to the a tag.

5. **Which style sheet selector enables you to change the color of the links on your page after someone has clicked them?**

   The `a:visited` selector enables you to change the color of the links on your page after someone has clicked them.

6. **In Windows, what must users type to highlight the following link?**
   `<a href="contact.html" tabindex="2" accesskey="t">Contact Me</a>`

   Windows users must type ALT-T to highlight the link shown.

7. **Fill in the blank: After successfully using the TAB key to highlight a link, you must press the _____ key to actually visit that link.**

   After successfully using the TAB key to highlight a link, you must press the <u>RETURN</u> or <u>ENTER</u> key to actually visit that link.

8. **Fix the following code: `< ahref="contact.html" >Contact Me</a>`**

   The correct code is `<a href="contact.html">Contact Me</a>`.

9. **Add the appropriate code so that this link enables users to email you at your personal email address: `<    > Email Me </ >`**

   The answer should be similar to this (with your email address):
   `<a href="mailto:name@emailaddress.com">Email Me</a>`

10. **Which tag links to a section within the current page?**
    A. `<a href="page1">Page 1</a>`
    B. `<a href="#page1">Page 1</a>`
    C. `<a href="*page1">Page 1</a>`
    D. `<a href="page1.html">Page 1</a>`

    Answer B links to a section within the current page.

11. **Which common phrase should always be avoided when naming links?**

    The phrase *Click here* should always be avoided when naming links.

12. **Fill in the blank: By default, all linked text is _____.**

    By default, all linked text is <u>underlined</u>.

13. **True/False: A dot-dot-slash tells the browser to go up a level in the directory structure before looking for a file.**

    True.

14. **Which links to a section named *Intro* within the web page named genealogy.html?**
    A. `<a href="genealogy.html">Intro</a>`
    B. `<a href="genealogy.html#intro">Intro</a>`
    C. `<a href="genealogy.html#Intro">Intro</a>`
    D. `<a href="genealogy.html=Intro">Intro</a>`
    E. `<a href="genealogy.html=intro">Intro</a>`

    Answer C links to a section named *Intro* within the web page named genealogy.html.

15. **What does `_blank` do when used as the value of the `target` attribute?**

    It causes the browser to open the link in a new unnamed browser window.

Chapter 8: Working with Images

1. **What does the `src` attribute do?**

   The `src` attribute gives the location of the image you're adding to the page with the `img` tag.

2. **Why is it important to specify the height and width of images in web pages?**

   It is important to specify the height and width of images in web pages because this information enables the browser to continue displaying the rest of the page without having to wait and calculate the size of its images.

3. **Which style sheet properties enable you to add blank space around images?**

   The CSS properties `margin` and `padding` enable you to add blank space around an image.

4. **Which attribute must be added to the img tag to designate the image as a client-side image map?**

   The usemap attribute must be added to the img tag to designate the image as a client-side image map.

5. **Which two elements are used when defining a client-side image map's name and hot spots?**

   The map and area elements are used when defining a client-side image map's name and hot spots.

6. **You are creating the code for a client-side image map, and one of the rectangular hot spots has the following coordinates: 0,0 (upper left); 50,0 (upper right); 50,50 (lower right); and 0,50 (lower left). Which are used in the coords attribute: <area shape="rect" coords="_____" href="maryland.html">?**

   The correct code, using the upper-left and lower-right coordinates, is <area shape="rect" coords="0,0,50,50" href="maryland.html">.

7. **Fill in the blank: The value of the height and width attributes is measured in _____.**

   The value of the height and width attributes is measured in pixels.

8. **Fix the following code: <img href="contact.jpg">**

   The correct code is shown here: <img src="contact.jpg">

9. **Add the appropriate style declaration to use wallpaper.gif as a background for the web page code shown next. Note that the graphic is in the same folder as the HTML file.**

   body {background-image: url("wallpaper.gif");}

10. **What are the four possible values of the clear property (used to clear floats)?**

    Left, right, all, and none are the possible values of the clear property.

11. **Fill in the blank: The default value of the border property is ____ pixels for linked images and _____ pixels for nonlinked images.**

    The default value of the border property is 1 pixel for linked images and 0 pixels for nonlinked images.

12. **True/False: You can achieve a layered look in your designs when an image in the foreground is placed on top of an image in the background.**

    True.

13. **What value must be used with the display property before you can center an image using the method discussed in this chapter?**
    img.centered {display: ;
     margin-left: auto;
     margin-right: auto;}

    The correct code is img.centered {display:block; margin-left: auto; margin-right: auto;}

14. **Which attribute is used to add alternative text to an image?**

`alt` is used to add alternative text to an image.

15. **Which statement is not true about background images?**
A. All background images tile by default.
B. You can only include one image in the background.
C. Background images are added to web pages with the `background` tag.
D. Background images begin at the top of the page and run all the way to each of the four sides.

Answer C is correct, or in this case, Answer C is the only statement that isn't true about backgrounds. Background images are added to a web page with the `body` tag and `background` attribute, not the `background` tag.

Chapter 9: Working with Multimedia

1. **What's the difference between a plug-in and a helper application?**

A plug-in helps the browser display a file, whereas the helper application does it for the browser.

2. **Which element does the W3C recommend for embedding video in a web page?**

The `video` element is recommended by the W3C for embedding video in a web page.

3. **How can users determine which plug-ins are installed on their computers and/or download new plug-ins?**

Most users can look in the plug-ins directory within their browser's application or program folder. For example, Firefox users can choose Tools | Add-Ons and then click the Plugins tab. Internet Explorer users choose Internet Options from the Tools menu in the browser, and then click the Programs tab and the Manage Add-Ons button to view a list of all add-ons.

4. **What are two ways you can include multimedia files in a web site?**

You can include multimedia files in a web site by linking to them or embedding them.

5. **True/False: Clicking a link to a sound file automatically downloads the file and saves it for later listening.**

False.

6. **What are two ways to specify the height and width of multimedia files embedded with the `object` tag?**

You can specify the height and width either in the `object` tag itself or in `param` tags nested between the opening and closing `object` tags.

7. **Fix the following code:**
```
<embed href="sillyme.mov" height="100" width="50">
```

The correct code is `<embed src="sillyme.mov" height="100" width="50">`.

8. **Add the appropriate code here to link to wendy.mov. Note that the movie is in the same folder as the HTML file.**

```
<html>
<head>
 <title>Home Movie</title>
</head>
<body>
<        >View my home movie!<   >
</body>
</html>
```

The correct code is

```
<html>
<head>
 <title>Home Movie</title>
</head>
<body>
<a href="wendy.mov">View my home movie!</a>
</body>
</html>
```

9. **Which attribute can cause a video to play even before the user clicks the play button?**

   `autostart`

10. **Which element can be used to provide subtitles for a video?**

    `track`

11. **True/False: A link to a multimedia file is the same as any other link because it also uses the a element.**

    True.

12. **What is the purpose of the `poster` attribute?**

    The `poster` attribute is used to indicate the static image to display while a video is loading.

13. **Which element tells the browser where to find the actual audio or video content?**

    `source`

14. **Which element is used to add Flash files to a web page coded with HTML5?**

    The W3C recommends using the `embed` element to add Flash files in HTML5.

Chapter 10: Creating Lists

1. What's the difference between an unordered list and an ordered list?

An unordered list's items are not listed in a particular order, whereas an ordered list's items are. In addition, an unordered list's items are preceded by bullets, whereas an ordered list's items are preceded by numbers or letters.

2. Which element is used to enclose list items in both ordered and unordered lists?

The `li` element is used to enclose list items in both ordered and unordered lists.

3. You created an unordered list with four list items. All the content following the fourth list item that should be normal text is indented under the list. What is the most likely cause of this problem?

A missing closing tag, such as `</ul>`, is most likely the cause of the problem.

4. Which HTML attribute changes the numbering style of a list?

The `type` attribute changes the numbering style of a list.

5. True/False: You can use more than one dd element for each dt element.

True.

6. Which HTML attribute changes the starting letter or number for a list?

The `start` attribute changes the starting letter or number for a list.

7. Fill in the blank: When displayed in a browser, each item in an unordered list is preceded by a(n) _____ by default.

When displayed in a browser, each item in an unordered list is preceded by a <u>bullet</u>, by default.

8. Fix the following code:
```
<dl>
 <dd>HTML</dd>
 <dt>Hypertext Markup Language is the authoring language used to
create documents for the World Wide Web.</dt>
</dl>
```

The correct code is
```
<dl>
 <dt>HTML</dt>
 <dd>Hypertext Markup Language is the authoring language used to
create documents for the World Wide Web.</dd>
</dl>
```

9. Add the appropriate code to turn the following text into an ordered list:
```
<html>
<head>
```

```
  <title>My favorite fruits</title>
</head>
<body>

My favorite fruits, in order of preference, are:

Raspberries

Strawberries

Apples

</body>
</html>
```

The correct code is

```
<html>
<head>
 <title>My favorite fruits</title>
</head>
<body>
My favorite fruits, in order of preference, are:
 <ol><li>Raspberries</li>
 <li>Strawberries</li>
 <li>Apples</li>
 </ol>
 </body>
 </html>
```

10. **Fill in the blank: The dl element stands for _____.**

The dl element stands for <u>definition list</u>.

11. **True/False: When you nest unordered lists, the bullet style remains unchanged.**

False.

12. **What value is used with the display property to change a list from vertical to horizontal?**

Use display: inline to change a list from vertical to horizontal.

13. **How can you change a list from using Arabic numbers to lowercase letters?**

To change a list from using Arabic numbers to lowercase letters, you can use type="a".

14. **Which CSS property is used to replace the standard bullet in a list with an image?**

The list-style-image property is used to replace the standard bullet in a list with an image.

Chapter 11: Using Tables

1. What is the difference between the `td` and `th` elements?

The `td` element is used for standard table cells, whereas the `th` element is used for cells containing header information. By default, the contents of `th` elements are made bold and centered.

2. The `td` and `th` elements are contained within which other table tag (aside from the `table` tag itself)?

The `td` and `th` elements are contained within the `tr` tag.

3. How do you force a cell's contents to display along a single line?

Use the `white-space` property in your style sheet, with a value of `nowrap`, to force a cell's contents to display along a single line.

4. What should be the value of the `border` attribute to turn on a table's borders?

Add `border="1"` to the opening `table` tag.

5. True/False: You cannot use other HTML tags between opening and closing `td` tags.

False.

6. Fill in the blank: The _____ property affects the space around the content of each individual table cell.

The <u>padding</u> attribute affects the space around the content of each individual table cell.

7. Fix the following code:
```
<table>
<td>HTML</td>
<td>Hypertext Markup Language is the authoring language used to
create documents for the World Wide Web.</td>
</table>
```

The correct code is
```
<table>
<tr>
<td>HTML</td>
<td>Hypertext Markup Language is the authoring language used to
create documents for the World Wide Web.</td>
</tr>
</table>
```

8. What are two types of measurements you can use to identify a table's width?

Pixels and percentages identify a table's width.

9. **Add the appropriate code to cause this table to fill the entire browser window, regardless of the user's screen size.**

```
<html>
<head>
 <title>A Big Table</title>
</head>
<body>
<table>
<tr>
 <td>X</td>
 <td>X</td>
 <td>O</td>
</tr>
</table>
</body>
</html>
```

The correct code is

```
<html>
<head>
    <title>A Big Table</title>
</head>
<body>
<table width="100%">
<tr>
    <td>X</td>
    <td>X</td>
    <td>O</td>
</tr>
</table>
</body>
</html>
```

10. **Fill in the blank: You can add the _____ property to your style sheet to change the background color of the whole table.**

    You can add the <u>background-color</u> property to your style sheet to change the background color of the whole table.

11. **True/False: To add a caption to a table, you use the `caption` attribute in the opening `table` tag.**

    False. You use the `caption` element, which stands on its own, in between the opening and closing `table` tags.

12. **If you include a `thead` or a `tfoot` group in your table, you must also include which other group?**

    If you include a `thead` or `tfoot` group in your table, you must also include `tbody`.

13. **Which CSS property (and value) is used to align all the text in a cell to the right?**

    Use `text-align: right` to align all text in a cell to the right.

14. **True/False: If you had both `colgroups` and `theads` in a single table, the `colgroups` would be placed before the `theads` in your table structure.**

    True.

Chapter 12: Creating Forms

1. **Fill in the blank: _____ tags must surround all web forms.**

    `form` tags must surround all web forms.

2. **Name four types of text input controls in HTML web forms?**

    Single-line text boxes (text fields) and multiple-line text areas are two types of text input in HTML web forms. Additional types include those for email addresses, URLs, dates, time, passwords, telephone numbers, and searches.

3. **Which attribute identifies an input control so that it's correctly handled when the form is processed?**

    The `name` attribute identifies an input control so that it's correctly handled when the form is processed.

4. **Which input control is most useful for questions requiring a simple yes or no answer?**

    The radio button is most useful for questions requiring a simple yes or no answer.

5. **True/False: Radio buttons are small, round buttons that enable users to select a single option from a list of choices.**

    True.

6. **Fill in the blank: The _____ attribute identifies the visible width of a text area based on an average character width.**

    The `cols` attribute identifies the visible width of a text area based on an average character width.

7. **Fix the following code so that users can enter multiple lines of data into the comment box, which should measure 30 characters wide by 5 lines tall.**
    ```
    Enter your comments here:
    <input size="30,5"></input>
    ```

    The correct code is
    ```
    Enter your comments here:
    <textarea cols="30" rows="5"></textarea>
    ```

8. **How do you cause three options in a select menu to be visible at once?**

   Use `<select size="3">`.

9. **Add the appropriate code to create a single-line text field in which, upon entry of data, all contents are displayed as bullets or asterisks in the browser. Name the field "secret".**
   Please enter your secret word:
   `<        >`

   The correct code is
   Please enter your secret word:
   `<input type="password" name="secret">`

10. **Fill in the blank: _____ tags surround each item in a select menu.**

    `option` tags surround each item in a select menu.

11. **Add the appropriate code to create a place where users can upload a graphic file from their personal computers to the web server. Name the field "upload."**
    Please select the file to upload:
    `<        >`

    The correct code is
    Please select the file to upload:
    `<input type="file" name="upload">`

12. **Which attribute is added to the `form` tag to give the location where the form's information should be sent?**

    The `action` attribute gives the location where the form's information should be sent.

13. **Which attribute and value are added to the `form` tag to tell the browser to take all the data submitted with the form and send it to the server attached to the end of the file's URL?**

    The `method="get"` attribute and value tell the browser to take all the data submitted with the form and send it to the server attached to the end of the file's URL.

Chapter 13: Formatting and Styling Forms

1. **True/False: The `fieldset` element is used to divide long select menus into categories of submenus.**

   False. The `optgroup` element is used to divide long select menus into categories of submenus.

2. **Add the appropriate attribute and value to allow users to press the F key to access this input control:**

   `<input name="FirstName" accesskey="f">`

3. **Add the appropriate attribute and value to set this input control as the first in the tab order.**

   `<input name="FirstName" taborder="0">`

4. **Which tags and attribute should be placed around the following descriptive text to indicate that text belongs to the birthday input control?**

```
<label for="birthday">When is your birthday? (MM/DD/YY)</label>
<input type="date" name="BirthDate" id="birthday" size="8">
```

5. **What CSS selector would you use to create a style sheet rule for all invalid form fields created with the input element?**

```
input:required:invalid
```

6. **What CSS selector would you use to create a style sheet rule for all valid form fields created with the `textarea` element?**

```
textarea:required:valid
```

7. **Which attribute is used to specify the ideal value in a `meter` element?**

```
optimum
```

8. **Which element is used to indicate progression in a multistep process?**

```
progress
```

9. **Which element is used to signify a relationship between a measurement and its range?**

```
meter
```

10. **Which element is used to add suggested data to input fields to help a user complete a form?**

```
datalist
```

Chapter 14: Beyond Static HTML

1. **Fill in the blank: JavaScript is case-_____.**

   JavaScript is case-<u>sensitive</u>.

2. **Name two ways JavaScript differs from standard HTML.**

   JavaScript is case-sensitive; standard HTML is not. In JavaScript, quotes are required; in standard HTML, quotes are optional. JavaScript has a distinct format that should be adhered to; standard HTML is more forgiving about spacing and formatting.

3. **What is an API?**

   An API, or application programming interface, allows HTML to work in conjunction with other tools like JavaScript.

4. **Fill in the blank: In the following code, _____ is the JavaScript object.**
   ```
   document.write("This is a text!");
   ```

   In the following code, <u>document</u> is the JavaScript object.

5. **True/False: A plus sign (+) is an example of a JavaScript variable.**

   False.

6. **When placed within the header of a web page, which opening and closing tags surround all JavaScripts?**

   Use `script` tags around all JavaScripts when placed within the header of a web page.

7. **Fill in the blank: Objects can have _____, which are actual things that happen to the objects, such as `write` in the following statement: `document.write("I can write JavaScript");`.**

   Objects can have <u>methods</u>, which are actual things that happen to the objects.

8. **What term is given to an aspect of a JavaScript you specify for your own needs as a label for a changeable value?**

   Variable is a term given to an aspect of a JavaScript you specify for your own needs as a label for a changeable value.

9. **Fill in the blank: A(n) _____ is a group of commands to which you give a name so that you can refer to it later in the script.**

   A <u>function</u> is a group of commands to which you give a name so you can refer to it later in the script.

10. **Which aspect of JavaScript is embedded within the page's HTML and responds to a user's interaction?**

    Event handlers are embedded within the page's HTML and respond to a user's interaction.

11. **How are conditionals used in JavaScript?**

    JavaScript uses *if ... then* statements called conditionals to tell the browser to do one thing if *x* is true and something else if *x* is false.

12. **What does the following JavaScript do when added to an tag on a web page? `onClick="document.body.style.backgroundColor='green'"`**

    It changes the background color of the document when the user clicks the link.

13. **How do you specify that a new browser window should not have any scroll bars?**

    Add `scrolling=no` to the JavaScript.

14. **What punctuation ends all JavaScript statements?**

    A semicolon (;) ends all JavaScript statements.

15. **What does `onFocus` do when used in a JavaScript?**

    It specifies that an action should occur when the user brings an object (such as a browser window) to the foreground.

Chapter 15: Publishing Pages

1. **Fill in the blank: ISP stands for** _____.

   ISP stands for <u>Internet service provider</u>.

2. **Including the extension, what is the limit for characters in a domain name?**

   The character limit in a domain name is 67, not including "www."

3. **Which type of business hosting is used when your business purchases its own server, software, and a dedicated Internet connection capable of serving your site to web users 24 hours a day, 365 days a year?**

   Onsite hosting requires your business to purchase a server, software, and a dedicated Internet connection capable of serving your site to web users 24/7.

4. **Mobilizer is a tool that allows you to preview your pages in what type of user situation?**

   Mobilizer allows you to preview your pages on web-enabled mobile phones.

5. **True/False: Some search engines ignore `meta` tags.**

   True.

6. **Why is it important to include the following line of code at the start of all your HTML pages?**

   ```
   <!doctype html>
   ```

   It's important to include this line of code so the browser knows which version of HTML your page uses.

7. **Where are `meta` tags placed within a web page?**

   All `meta` tags are placed between the opening and closing `head` tags.

8. **True/False: All search engines use the same set of standards for indexing web pages.**

   False.

9. **Fill in the blanks: When testing a web site, you should test for cross-_____ and cross-_____ consistency.**

   When testing a web site, you should test for cross-<u>browser</u> and cross-<u>platform</u> consistency.

10. **What does FTP stand for?**

    FTP stands for File Transfer Protocol.

Chapter 16: HTML for Email

1. **True/False: The W3C maintains a special specification for HTML email.**

   False. The Email Standards Project maintains those recommendations.

2. Fill in the blank: _____ is any email sent without the permission of the recipient.

Spam is any email sent without the permission of the recipient.

3. What is the difference between an ISP and an ESP?

An ISP provides Internet access to customers, while an ESP provides bulk messaging services.

4. Fill in the blank: You must use _____ paths for all images and links in HTML email.

You must use absolute paths for all images and links in HTML email.

5. Why should you avoid relying on images to translate key messages in HTML email?

You should avoid relying on images to translate key messages in HTML email because so many email readers block images by default.

6. Which type of style sheets should be used for all HTML email?

A. Inline
B. Internal
C. External
D. Linked

A. Inline is the correct answer.

7. Why must we rely on tables for column-based layout in HTML e-mail?

We must rely on tables for column-based layout in HTML email because of the lack of widespread support of CSS for layout among email readers.

8. Which methods of adding interactivity to HTML email are widely supported by email readers? (Select all that apply.)

A. Flash
B. Video
C. Forms
D. None of the above

D. None of the above is the correct answer.

9. True/False: It is acceptable to use CSS shorthand in HTML email.

False.

10. Why should you avoid using background images in tables in HTML email?

You should avoid using background images in tables in HTML email because Outlook 2007 does not support them.

Appendix B

HTML/CSS
Reference Table

This resource serves as a reference table for the tags and properties learned in this book. It is organized alphabetically, with HTML tags and CSS properties included together for easy comparison. Because the scope of this book is at a beginner's level, I decided not to discuss a few elements and properties. If you come across something not listed here or in the index, try visiting an online reference library such as the following:

- **webdesign.about.com/od/html5tags/l/blhtml5reference.htm**
- **html5doctor.com/element-index/**
- **www.w3schools.com/tags/default.asp**

NOTE
The latest version of the HTML specifications can be found on W3C's web site at **www.w3.org**.

Generic Attributes

The following groups of attributes can be used by a large number of tags in HTML. In the rest of the tables in this appendix, a code is listed in the attribute column on a particular tag if it accepts any of the following groups of generic attributes:

- Core attributes (*core) provide rendering and accessibility information to elements.
- Event handlers (*events) provide a way of triggering an action when an event occurs on a page. Note: Not all event handlers are listed.
- International attributes (*intl) provide a way of rendering documents using multiple language or character sets.

Group Type: Core

Attribute	Uses
accesskey	Assigns a keyboard shortcut to the element.
class	Assigns a text label to an element, to allow it to be referenced in a style sheet.
contenteditable*	Specifies whether content is editable.
contextmenu*	Specifies the context menu (accessed by right-clicking in the browser) for the element.
draggable*	Specifies if an element is draggable.
dropzone*	Identifies what happens to an element (copied, moved, or linked) when it is "dropped" in the browser.
hidden*	Identifies an element that is hidden from view.
id	Assigns a unique identifier to an element.

Attribute	Uses
spellcheck*	Identifies whether an element should have its content spell-checked.
style	Gives instructions on how to render an element.
tabindex	Assigns the tab order of an element.
title	Gives a brief description of an element.

*New in HTML5

Group Type: Events

Attribute	Applies To	Uses
onabort	media element (audio, video, images, objects)	Triggers an event to occur when the element is aborted.
onafterprint*	page or window	Triggers an event after the page is printed.
onbeforeprint*	page or window	Triggers an event before the page is printed.
onbeforeunload*	page or window	Triggers an event before the page is closed.
onblur	form element	Triggers an event when an element loses focus.
oncanplay*	media element	Triggers an event when the content is loaded and ready to play.
oncanplaythrough*	media element	Triggers an event when the content is able to be played all the way through without pausing to load more content.
onchange	form element	Triggers an event when the value of an element is changed.
onclick	user action	Triggers an event when the element is clicked.
oncontextMenu*	form element	Triggers an event when an element's context (right-click) menu is engaged.
ondblclick	user action	Triggers an event when the element is double-clicked.
ondrag*	user action	Triggers an event when an element is dragged.
ondragend*	user action	Triggers an event when an element finishes being dragged.
ondragenter*	user action	Triggers an event when an element is dragged into a valid drop target.
ondragleave*	user action	Triggers an event when an element is dragged away from a drop target.
ondragover*	user action	Triggers an event when an element is dragged over a valid drop target.
ondragstart*	user action	Triggers an event when an element starts being dragged.

Attribute	Applies To	Uses
ondrop*	user action	Triggers an event when an element is being dropped.
ondurationchange*	media element	Triggers an event when the length of the media changes.
onemptied*	media element	Triggers an event when the media is suddenly unavailable.
onended*	media element	Triggers an event when the media finishes playing.
onerror*	page or window	Triggers an event when an error occurs.
onfocus	form element	Triggers an event when an element receives focus.
onformchange*	form	Triggers an event when a form is changed.
onforminput*	form	Triggers an event when a form receives user input.
onhaschange*	page or window	Triggers an event when the page has changed.
oninput*	form element	Triggers an event when a form element receives user input.
oninvalid*	form element	Triggers an event when an element is invalid.
onkeypress	keyboard	Triggers an event when a key is pressed and released immediately.
onkeydown	keyboard	Triggers an event when a key is pressed and held down.
onkeyup	keyboard	Triggers an event when a key that was pressed is now released.
onload	page or window	Triggers an event when the page finishes loading.
onloadeddata*	media element	Triggers an event when the media element is loaded.
onloadedmetadata*	media element	Triggers an event when the media element's meta data is loaded.
onloadedstart*	media element	Triggers an event when the media element first begins to load.
onmessage*	page or window	Triggers an event when the browser displays an alert or message.
onmousedown	user action	Triggers an event when the pointer is pressed down over an element.
onmouseup	user action	Triggers an event when the pointer is released over an element.
onmouseover	user action	Triggers an event when the pointer is passed over an element.
onmouseout	user action	Triggers an event when the pointer moves away from an element.
onmousewheel*	user action	Triggers an event when the mouse wheel is being rotated.
onoffline*	page or window	Triggers an event when the page goes offline.
ononline*	page or window	Triggers an event when the page comes online.

Attribute	Applies To	Uses
onpagehide*	page or window	Triggers an event when the page is hidden.
onpageshow*	page or window	Triggers an event when the page becomes visible.
onpause*	media element	Triggers an event when the media element is paused.
onplay*	media element	Triggers an event when the media element starts playing.
onplaying*	media element	Triggers an event while the media element is playing.
onpopstate*	page or window	Triggers an event when the current window's history changes.
onprogress*	media element	Triggers an event when the browser is in the process of accessing the media content.
onratechange*	media element	Triggers an event when the rate of playback changes (such as when it switches to slow motion).
onreadystatechange*	media element	Triggers an event when the ready state (whether the media element can be played) changes.
onredo*	page or window	Triggers an event when the page is refreshed.
onscroll*	user action	Triggers an event when the scroll bar is in use.
onseeked*	media element	Triggers an event when the browser has finished seeking (moving to) a new playback position (either forward or backward).
onseeking*	media element	Triggers an event when the browser is seeking (moving to) a new playback position (either forward or backward).
onselect	form	Triggers an event when text in an element is selected.
onstalled*	media element	Triggers an event when the browser is not able to continue loading the media element's data.
onsuspend*	media element	Triggers an event when loading of the media element's data is stopped unexpectedly.
onstorage*	page or window	Triggers an event when the web storage is updated.
onsubmit	form	Triggers an event when a form is submitted.
ontimeupdate*	media element	Triggers an event when the playing position is changed (such as when the user fast-forwards).
onundo*	page or window	Triggers an event when the Undo option is selected.
onunload	page or window	Triggers an event after the page is closed.
onvolumechange*	media element	Triggers an event when the user changes the volume.
onwaiting*	media element	Triggers an event when the media element is paused temporarily (such as when it needs to load more data).

* New in HTML5

Group Type: Intl

Attribute	Uses
dir	Indicates the direction of the content flow.
lang	Indicates the language of the content.

HTML Tags

The following table provides a reference for the HTML elements discussed in this book. Although I have removed most of the deprecated (outdated) elements from this table, there are some deprecated attributes that remain. Those are marked with a (D) to help make them easily recognizable. These deprecated tags and/or attributes are not supported in HTML5. Tags and attributes new to HTML5 are marked with an asterisk.

One additional note—some attributes are only deprecated in certain cases. For example, while it is not acceptable to use the `align` attribute with the p tag, it is okay to use it within a table (such as in the `colgroup` or `tr` tags).

Element	Attributes	Uses
<!--...-->	n/a	Inserts comments into the page that aren't seen when the page is viewed in the browser.
<!doctype>	n/a	Indicates the version of HTML used. Must be placed on the first line of the document.
<a></a>	*core, events, intl*	Creates links and anchors.
	href	*Specifies the location (URL) of the link.*
	media*	*Identifies the media for which the linked document is optimized.*
	target	*Identifies the target window where the link will be displayed.*
	type*	*Identifies the MIME type of the linked document.*
<abbr></abbr>	*core, intl*	Indicates the content is an abbreviation.
<address></address>	*core, events, intl*	Formats the contact information for a page.

Element	Attributes	Uses
<area>	n/a	Defines links and anchors within an image map.
	alt	*Identifies alternate text for the area. (Required if the href attribute is used.)*
	coords	*Specifies the size of the hot spot.*
	href	*Specifies the location (URL) of the link.*
	hreflang*	*Specifies the language of the target URL.*
	media*	*Identifies the media (or device) for which the target URL is optimized.*
	rel*	*Identifies the relationship between the current page and the target URL.*
	shape	*Defines the shape of a hot spot in an image map.*
	target	*Identifies the target window where the link will be displayed.*
	type*	*Specifies the MIME type of the target URL.*
<article></article>*	*core, events, intl*	Defines a section of self-contained content.
<aside></aside>*	*core, events, intl*	Defines a section of content that is separate but related to surrounding content.
<audio></audio>*	*core, events, intl*	Defines audio to be included in the page.
	autoplay*	*Specifies the audio should start playing as soon as it's loaded.*
	controls*	*Specifies the audio controls should be displayed.*
	loop*	*Specifies the audio should play again after it's finished.*
	preload*	*Specifies what to do with the audio when the page first loads.*
	src*	*Identifies the URL of the audio file.*
<b></b>	*core, events, intl*	Makes text bold. (Should be used as a last resort. Style sheets are preferred.)
<base>	*intl*	Identifies the default path for links specified within the document.
	href	*Defines the location (URL) of the link.*
	target	*Specifies the window in which the URL should open.*

Element	Attributes	Uses
`<blockquote>` `</blockquote>`	*core, events, intl*	Identifies a section that is quoted from another source.
	cite	*Identifies the source of the quotation.*
`<body></body>`	*core, events, intl*	Encloses the contents of the document.
` `	*core, events, intl*	Causes a line break.
`<button></button>`	*core, events, intl*	Creates a button.
	autofocus*	*Specifies a button should receive focus as soon as the page loads.*
	disabled	*Specifies a button should be disabled.*
	form*	*Identifies the form to which the button belongs.*
	formaction*	*Defines where to send the form data when it is submitted.*
	formenctype*	*Defines how form data is encoded when it is submitted.*
	formmethod*	*Defines how form data is sent when it is submitted.*
	formnovalidate*	*Specifies the form shouldn't be validated upon submission.*
	formtarget*	*Identifies the window name where the form's response should be shown after it is submitted.*
	name	*Defines the name of the button.*
	type	*Defines the type of button.*
	value	*Specifies the value or type of button.*
`<caption>` `</caption>`	*core, events, intl*	Defines a table caption.
`<cite></cite>`	*core, events, intl*	Formats a short quote or reference.
`<code></code>`	*core, events, intl*	Defines text as code.
`<col>`	*core, events, intl*	Specifies subgroups of columns within a column group to allow them to share attributes.
	span	*Specifies the number of columns the subcolumn group spans.*
`<colgroup>` `</colgroup>`	*core, events, intl*	Defines a group of columns.
`<datalist>` `</datalist>`*	*core, events, intl*	Defines a group of options for an input element.

Element	Attributes	Uses
<dd></dd>	*core, events, intl*	Defines the description of a term in a definition list.
<del></del>	*core, events, intl*	Formats the text as deleted by marking a line through it.
	cite	*References another document with a URL.*
	datetime	*Identifies the date and time of the deletion.*
<details></details>*	*core, events, intl*	Defines additional content that can be viewed or hidden by the user. (Not supported by any browser as of this writing.)
	open*	*Identifies what should be shown to the user when the details are opened.*
<dfn></dfn>	*core, events, intl*	Specifies a definition.
<div></div>	*core, events, intl*	Identifies a block-level section (or division) of the page.
<dl></dl>	*core, events, intl*	Creates a definition list.
<dt></dt>	*core, events, intl*	Defines a term in a definition list.
<em></em>	*core, events, intl*	Gives emphasis to text.
<embed>*	*core, events, intl*	Defines content to be embedded via external application or plug-in.
	height*	*Defines the height of the embedded content.*
	src*	*Defines the location of the embedded content.*
	type*	*Defines the MIME type of the embedded content.*
	width*	*Defines the width of the embedded content.*
<fieldset></fieldset>	*core, events, intl*	Creates a group of form controls.
	disabled*	*Specifies that the group's fields should be disabled.*
	form*	*Defines the form to which the group belongs.*
	name*	*Defines the name of the group.*
<figcaption></figcaption>*	*core, events, intl*	Defines a caption for a figure element.
<figure></figure>*	*core, events, intl*	Contains content that is independent but related to the surrounding content, such as diagrams, photos, or illustrations.
<footer></footer>*	*core, events, intl*	Defines a footer section.

Element	Attributes	Uses
<form></form>	*core, events, intl*	Creates a form where users can enter information.
	action	*Specifies the location (URL) of the script to process the form.*
	autocomplete*	*Specifies whether a form can be autocompleted by the browser.*
	enctype	*Specifies the MIME type used to encode the content of the form.*
	method	*Defines how the form will be processed (get or post).*
	name	*Defines the name of the form.*
	novalidate*	*Specifies whether the form should be validated at submission.*
	target	*Defines the window where the results should be shown after the form is submitted.*
<h1></h1>	*core, events, intl*	Creates six levels of headline (h1 being the largest and most important; h6 being the smallest and least important).
<head></head>	*intl*	Contains the header information for the page (such as the title and information for search engines).
<header></header>*	*core, events, intl*	Defines a header section, within the body of the page.
<hgroup></hgroup>*	*core, events, intl*	Groups related heading elements.
<hr>	*core, events, intl*	Defines a thematic break.
<html></html>	*intl*	Contains and identifies the document.
	manifest*	*Defines the location of the document's cache manifest for offline browsing.*
<i></i>	*core, events, intl*	Defines text as using an alternate voice or mood.
<iframe></iframe>	*core, events, intl*	Creates an inline, floating frame.
	name	*Defines the name of the frame.*
	sandbox*	*Specifies additional guidelines or restrictions for the content.*
	seamless*	*Specifies that the frame is intended to look like it is part of the containing page.*
	src	*Defines the initial document (URL) that should be loaded into the frame.*
	srcdoc*	*Defines the HTML (code) of the initial content that should be loaded into the frame.*
	width	*Defines the width of the frame in pixels or percentages.*

Element	Attributes	Uses
\<img\>	*core, events, intl*	Embeds an image in a page by linking to its source.
	alt	*Specifies a text description of the image (required).*
	crossorigin*	*Defines the cross-origin access used in the canvas.*
	height	*Defines the height of the image in pixels.*
	ismap	*Defines the image as a server-side image map.*
	src	*Defines the location of the image file (required).*
	usemap	*Defines the image as a client-side image map and specifies the location (URL) of the map properties.*
	width	*Defines the width of the image in pixels.*
\<input\>	*core, events, intl*	Creates types of form input controls for users.
	accept	*Defines the file types allowed in a file upload control.*
	alt	*Defines an alternative text description. (Used only when type=image.)*
	autocomplete*	*Defines whether an input control can be automatically completed by the browser.*
	autofocus*	*Defines whether an input control should automatically receive focus when the page is loaded.*
	checked	*Specifies that the input control should be checked by default when the page is loaded.*
	disabled	*Specifies that the input control cannot be used.*
	form*	*Defines which form an input control belongs to.*
	formaction*	*Specifies the document (URL) that will process the input control when the form is submitted.*
	formenctype*	*Defines the type of encoding used when the form is submitted.*
	formmethod*	*Defines the HTTP method used when the form is submitted.*
	formnovalidate*	*Specifies the input control should not be validated when the form is submitted.*
	formtarget*	*Defines the name of the window where the form response should be shown after it is submitted.*
	height*	*Defines the height of the input control. (Used only when type=image.)*
	list*	*Identifies the location of a data list when an input control should have predefined options.*

Element	Attributes	Uses
<input>	max*	Defines the maximum value for an input control.
	maxlength	Defines the maximum number of characters a user can enter in a text field or password box.
	min*	Defines the minimum value for an input control.
	multiple*	Specifies the input control as capable of receiving more than one value.
	name	Defines the name of the input control used when processing the form.
	pattern*	Defines a value pattern that the input control's value should be checked against.
	placeholder*	Defines a short phrase to be used to help the user know what type of value is expected.
	readonly	Specifies that a user can read, but cannot edit, an input control.
	required*	Defines the input control as one that must be completed before the form can be submitted.
	size	Defines the size of a text field or password box.
	src	Defines the location (URL) of an image used in an input control.
	step*	Identifies the number of steps, or intervals, for the input control.
	type	Identifies the type of input control (text, check box, radio button, and so forth).
	value	Defines the initial value of an input control.
	width*	Defines the width, in pixels, for an input control. (Used only when type=image.)
<ins></ins>	core, events, intl	Formats text as inserted since the last change.
	cite	References another document with a URL.
	datetime	Identifies the date and time of the insertion.
<kbd></kbd>	core, events, intl	Formats text as something the user should type on his or her keyboard.

Element	Attributes	Uses
<keygen>*	core, events, intl	Defines a key-pair generator input control so when the form is submitted, the private part of the key is stored locally, while the public part is sent with the form. (Note: This is not fully supported by modern browsers.)
	autofocus*	Specifies the input control should automatically receive focus when the page first loads.
	challenge*	Defines whether the value of the input control should be challenged when the form is submitted.
	disabled*	Specifies the input control should be disabled.
	form*	Specifies the form(s) to which the input control belongs.
	keytype*	Defines the security algorithm of the key generator.
	name*	Defines the name of the input control.
<label></label>	core, events, intl	Specifies a label for a form input control.
	for	Identifies to which input control the label belongs.
	form*	Identifies to which form(s) the label belongs.
<legend></legend>	core, events, intl	Defines a caption for a form fieldset.
<li></li>	core, events, intl	Defines an item in an ordered or unordered list.
	value	Specifies the initial value of the first item in a numbered list.
<link>	core, events, intl	Indicates a relationship between the current document and another resource (such as a style sheet).
	href	Specifies the location of the resource.
	hreflang	Defines the language of the text in the linked file.
	media	Defines the device(s) for which the linked file is optimized.
	rel	Specifies the relationship between the current document and the linked file.
	sizes*	Defines the size of the linked file. (Used only when rel=icon.)
	type	Defines the MIME type of the linked file.
<map></map>	core	Defines the properties of a client-size image map.
	name	Names the map so that it can be referenced by other aspects of the page.
<mark></mark>*	core, events, intl	Defines text to be differentiated from other text around it.

Element	Attributes	Uses
<menu></menu>*	*core, events, intl*	Specifies a list, or menu, of commands from which the user can choose.
	label*	*Defines a caption, or label, for the menu, to be displayed in the browser.*
	type*	*Defines which type of menu is displayed. (Default is list.)*
<meta>	*intl*	Gives information about the document.
	charset*	*Defines the character encoding for the document.*
	content	*Contains specified information.*
	http-equiv	*Assigns a header field, which then can be used to transfer the user to another page or otherwise process the document.*
	name	*Defines what type of information the content attribute specifies.*
<meter></meter>	*core, events, intl*	Defines a scalable measurement, or a gauge, such as one used to show the relevance of a search result.
	form*	*Defines to which form(s) the meter belongs.*
	high*	*Defines the high value of the meter's range.*
	low*	*Defines the low value of the meter's range.*
	max*	*Defines the maximum value of the meter.*
	min*	*Defines the minimum value of the range.*
	optimum*	*Defines the optimal value of the meter's range.*
	value*	*Defines the current value of the range. (Required.)*
<nav></nav>	*core, events, intl*	Defines a section of navigational links.
<noscript></noscript>	core	Defines the content displayed in browsers that don't support scripts.
<object></object>	*core, events, intl*	Embeds an object in the page.
	data	*Defines the URL of the object's resource.*
	form*	*Defines the form(s) to which the object belongs.*
	name	*Defines the name of an object.*
	type	*Defines the MIME type of the data.*
	usemap	*Identifies the object as a client-side image map and specifies the location (URL) of the map properties.*
	width	*Defines the width, in pixels, of the object.*

Element	Attributes	Uses
<ol></ol>	*core, events, intl*	Creates an ordered list.
	reversed*	*Specifies the order of the list should be reversed.*
	start	*Defines the starting value of the ordered list.*
	type	*Defines the type of ordered list by indicating the kind of marker to be used (1, A, a, I, i).*
<optgroup></optgroup>	*core, events, intl*	Groups related options in a drop-down list.
	disabled	*Specifies the option group should be disabled.*
	label	*Defines a label (caption) for the option group.*
<option></option>	*core, events, intl*	Creates choices in a form select menu.
	disabled	*Specifies the specific option as viewable, but not selectable.*
	label	*Specifies a short label for the option.*
	selected	*Defines the option as selected by default when the page is loaded.*
	value	*Defines the initial value of the option; used when processing the form.*
<output></output>*	*core, events, intl*	Identifies content as the result of a calculation, such as one performed by a script.
	for*	*Defines the relationship between the result of the calculation and its parts.*
	form*	*Defines the form(s) to which the output belongs.*
	name*	*Defines a name for the output control.*
<p></p>	*core, events, intl*	Specifies a paragraph of text (inserts a blank line by default above the paragraph).
<param>	id	Contains parameters for an object.
	name	*Defines the parameter's unique name.*
	value	*Defines the parameter's value.*
<progress></progress>	*core, events, intl*	Displays the progress of a task.
	max*	*Identifies the total amount of work in the task.*
	value*	*Identifies the current amount of progress in completing that task.*
<q></q>	*core, events, intl*	Formats a short quotation.
	cite	*Defines the source (URL) of the quote.*
<s></s>	*core, events, intl*	Defines text content that is no longer accurate or relevant.
<samp></samp>	*core, events, intl*	Formats text as a sample computer output, usually in a monospaced font.

Element	Attributes	Uses
\<script>\</script>	None	Contains scripts, such as those written in JavaScript, executed in the page by the browser.
	async*	*Specifies that an external script should be executed asynchronously.*
	charset	*Defines the character encoding used in the script file.*
	defer	*Indicates the script is not going to generate any document content and the browser can continue drawing the page.*
	src	*References an external script by giving its location (URL).*
	type	*Specifies the MIME type of the script. (Required)*
\<section>\</section>	core, events, intl	Defines a section of content.
\<select>\</select>	core, events, intl	Creates a form menu with choices (using the option element) users can select.
	autofocus*	*Defines whether the menu should automatically receive focus when the page is first loaded.*
	disabled	*Specifies the menu as viewable, but not usable.*
	form*	*Defines the form(s) to which the field belongs.*
	multiple	*Enables users to select multiple choices.*
	name	*Identifies the name of the menu; used when processing the form.*
	size	*Defines the number of choices visible in the menu when the page loads.*
\<small>\</small>	core, events, intl	Formats the text as one size smaller than the default size.
\<source>\</source>*	core, events, intl	Defines media resources for audio and video elements.
	media*	*Defines the type of media resource.*
	src*	*Specifies the location (URL) of the media.*
	type*	*Defines the MIME type of the media resource.*
\\	core, events, intl	Defines a section of content.
\\	core, events, intl	Defines important text content.
\<style>\</style>	events, intl	Adds an internal style sheet to a page.
	media	*Specifies the destination medium for the style information (such as print, screen, all, and so forth).*
	scoped*	*Enables a set of styles to be specified for a particular section of the page, as opposed to a style element added to the head section, which then applies to the entire page.*
	type	*Defines the MIME type of the content. (Required.)*

Element	Attributes	Uses
	core, events, intl	Formats the text as subscript.
	core, events, intl	Formats the text as superscript.
<table></table>	*core, events, intl*	Creates a table.
	border	*Specifies whether the table should have its borders displayed.*
<textarea></textarea>	*core, events, intl*	Creates a form input control where users can enter multiple lines of text.
	autofocus*	*Defines whether the text area should receive focus automatically when the page first loads.*
	cols	*Defines the height of the text area in the number of character columns visible.*
	disabled	*Prevents users from entering text in the area.*
	form*	*Defines the form(s) to which the text area belongs.*
	maxlength*	*Defines the maximum number of characters allowed in the text area.*
	name	*Identifies the name of the text area; used when processing the form.*
	placeholder*	*Defines a short phrase that helps the user know what content is expected in the text area.*
	readonly	*Specifies the text area as viewable, but not editable.*
	required*	*Defines whether the text area must be completed before the form can be submitted.*
	rows	*Defines the width of the text area in the number of character rows visible.*
	wrap*	*Defines whether the content of the text area should be wrapped when the form is submitted.*
<tbody></tbody>	*core, events, intl*	Defines the table's body (must be used with tfoot and thead).
<td></td> <th></th>	*core, events, intl*	Defines an individual cell (td) or header cell (th).
	colspan	*Defines how many columns the cell spans.*
	headers	*Defines the header cell(s) to which the cell is related.*
	rowspan	*Defines how many rows the cell spans.*
<tfoot></tfoot>	*core, events, intl*	Defines the table's footer (must be used with thead and tbody).
<thead></thead>	*core, events, intl*	Defines the table's header (must be used with tbody and tfoot).

Element	Attributes	Uses
<time></time>*	*core, events, intl*	Defines a time and/or date.
	datetime*	Identifies the time/date being specified.
	pubdate*	Identifies the time/date as the publication date of the document.
<title></title>	*intl*	Gives a name to your page that will be displayed in the title bar of the browser.
<tr></tr>	*core, events, intl*	Defines a table row.
<track></track>*	*core, events, intl*	Specifies the text track for an audio or video element.
	default*	*Defines the default track.*
	kind*	*Identifies the type of text track (captions, chapters, descriptions, metadata, or subtitles).*
	label*	*Identifies the title label of the text track.*
	src*	*Defines the URL of the track file. (Required.)*
	srclang*	*Defines the language of the text track. (Required when kind=subtitles.)*
<u></u>	*core, events, intl*	Describes text as important in an effort to differentiate it from its surroundings.
<ul></ul>	*core, events, intl*	Creates an unordered list.
<var></var>	*core, events, intl*	Describes text as important in an effort to differentiate it from its surroundings.
<video></video>*	*core, events, intl*	Defines video content to be embedded.
	autoplay*	*Identifies that the video should start playing as soon as its content is ready.*
	controls*	*Specifies whether the video player's controls should be displayed.*
	height*	*Defines the height of the video player.*
	loop*	*Specifies that the video should start over again after it's finished playing.*
	muted*	*Mutes the audio playback of the video file.*
	poster*	*Defines the image to be shown until the video is played.*
	preload*	*Defines if and how the video should be loaded when the page first loads.*
	src*	*Defines the source (URL) of the video file.*
	width*	*Defines the width of the video player.*
<wbr></wbr>*	*core, events, intl*	Specifies a point where the browser can break a word or line that is long.

*New in HTML5

CSS Properties

This table acts as a reference for the style sheet properties used throughout this book. Because this is a beginner's guide, this table does not include every possible CSS property.

When listing values, those within brackets, such as <length>, indicate value concepts as opposed to actual values. For example, when a value is listed as <length>, you might use a pixel dimension, as in 10px. By contrast, a value of "left" is an actual value term, as in `float:left`. Here are a few more tips regarding value concepts:

- Length units take two-letter abbreviations, with no space between number and unit, as in `width: 100px` or `padding-top: 2cm`.

- Percentage units are calculated with regard to their default size.

- Color units can be specified by hexadecimal code: `color: #ffffff`; RGB value: `color: rgb(255, 255, 255)`; or name: `color: white`.

- Transparency can be added to color units using RGBA, where `color: rgba(0,0,0,0.5)` creates a black that is semitransparent, or HSLA, where `color: hsla(120%, 100%, 50%, .08)` creates an 80% opaque green.

- URLs are relative to the style sheet, *not the HTML document,* and are defined like this: `list-style-image: url(star.gif)`.

Those properties new in CSS3 are marked with an asterisk. Remember that these properties may or may not be supported by all the browsers in your target audience, which means testing is of significant importance when they are used.

NOTE

All these properties can also have a value of *inherit,* which tells the browser to use whichever value has already been assigned to the element's parent/container object.

Property	Use	Values	Default Value
background	*Shorthand for any of the background properties.*		
background-attachment	Defines whether a background image scrolls when the page is scrolled or remains fixed in its original location.	scroll, fixed	scroll
background-clip*	Defines where the background image/color is applied relative to the content box.	border-box, padding-box, content-box	border-box
background-color	Defines the background color of an element.	<color>, transparent	transparent
background-image	Defines an image to be used as the background pattern.	<URL>, none	none
background-position	Defines the starting position of the background color or image.	<percentage>, <length>, top, center, bottom, left, center, right	0% 0%
background-origin*	When the background position is relative, this property defines what it is relative to.	padding-box, border-box, content-box	padding-box
background-repeat	Specifies how a background image repeats.	repeat, no-repeat, repeat-x, repeat-y	repeat
background-size*	Specifies the size of a background image.	<percentage>, <length>, cover, contain	auto
border	*Shorthand for all the border properties.*		
border-collapse	Specifies whether the borders of each table cell are merged or separated from one another. Applies to table elements.	collapse, separate	collapse
border-color	Defines an element's border color. Can be specified for each side individually (as in border-top-color).	<color>, transparent	Varies
border-radius*	Enables rounded corners. Can be specified for each side individually (as in border-top-right-radius).	<length>, <percentage>	Varies

Property	Description	Values	Default
border-style	Defines an element's border style. Can be specified for each side individually (as in border-top-style).	none, hidden, dotted, dashed, solid, double, groove, ridge, inset, outset	none
border-width	Defines an element's border width. Can be specified for each side individually (as in border-top-width).	thin, medium, thick, <length>	medium
border-image*	Shorthand for all the border-image properties.		
border-image-outset*	Defines the distance beyond the border box where the border image displays.	<length>, <percentage>	0
border-image-repeat*	Defines how the border image is scaled and repeated.	stretch, repeat, round, space	stretch
border-image-slice*	Defines inward offsets from the top, right, bottom, and left edges of the image to divide it into nine available regions (four corners, four edges, and a middle).	<length>, <percentage>	100%
border-image-source*	Defines the location of an image to be used in a border.	<URL>	none
border-image-width*	Defines the width of the border image.	<length>, <percentage>	1
bottom	Specifies the location of the bottom of positioned elements.	<length>, <percentage>, auto	auto
box-shadow*	Enables drop shadows on box elements using the following syntax: horizontal_offset vertical_offset blur spread_distance color.	none, inset, <length> (for the offset, blur, and distance values), <color> (for the color value)	none
caption-side	Specifies the location of a table caption.	top, bottom, left, right	top
clear	Specifies whether an element can have floating elements around it.	none, left, right, both	none
color	Specifies the color of the element by hexadecimal code, RGB values, or keyword.	<color>	Varies

Property	Use	Values	Default Value
cursor	Changes the display of the cursor.	\<URL\>, auto, crosshair, default, pointer, move, e-resize, ne-resize, nw-resize, n-resize, se-resize, sw-resize, s-resize, w-resize, text, wait, help	auto
direction	Specifies in which direction the text flows.	ltr, rtl	ltr (left to right)
display	Specifies how the item should be displayed within the page flow.	inline, block, list-item, run-in, compact, marker, table, inline-table, table-row-group, table-header-group, table-footer-group, table-row, table-column-group, table-column, table-cell, table-caption, none	inline
empty-cells	Specifies whether to display empty table cells.	show, hide	show
float	Pushes an element to the left or right of other page elements. Can be applied to any element that is not absolutely or relatively positioned.	left, right, none	none
font	*Shorthand for all font properties.*		
font-family	Changes the font family in which text is displayed.	\<family name\>, \<generic family\>	*Varies*
font-size	Changes the font size in which the text is displayed. Absolute sizes include pixels, ems, points, and picas. Relative sizes are keywords such as small, medium, and large.	\<absolute size\>, \<relative size\>, \<length\>, \<percentage\>	medium
font-size-adjust	Adjusts the font size up or down relative to the current font size.	\<number\>, none	none
font-stretch	Changes the horizontal width of the font.	normal, wider, narrower, ultra-condensed, extra-condensed, condensed, semi-condensed, semi-expanded, expanded, extra-expanded, ultra-expanded	normal
font-style	Adjusts whether text is italicized.	normal, italic, oblique	normal
font-variant	Adjusts whether text is displayed in small-caps.	normal, small-caps	normal

Property	Description	Values	Initial
font-weight	Adjusts the heaviness of the text.	normal, bold, bolder, lighter, 100, 200, 300, 400, 500, 600, 700, 800, 900	normal
height	Specifies the height of an element. (Does not apply to table columns or column groups.)	<length>, <percentage>, auto	auto
left	Specifies the location of the left edge of positioned elements.	<length>, <percentage>, auto	auto
letter-spacing	Adjusts the amount of space between letters.	normal, <length>	normal
line-height	Adjusts the amount of space between lines of text.	<length>, <percentage>	normal
list-style	*Shorthand for all list-style properties.*		
list-style-image	Uses an image before each item in a list.	<URL>, none	none
list-style-position	Specifies whether items in a list display inside or outside of the "bullet."	inside, outside	outside
list-style-type	Specifies the type of "bullet" that precedes items in a list.	disc, circle, square, decimal, decimal-leading-zero, lower-roman, upper-roman, lower-greek, lower-alpha, upper-alpha, upper-latin, lower-latin, hebrew, armenian, georgian, cjk-ideographic, kiragana, katakana, hiragana-iroha, katakana-iroha, none	disc
margin	*Shorthand for all margin properties.*		
margin-top margin-right margin-bottom margin-left	Defines the amount of blank space around the outside of an element's box.	<margin width>	0
max-height min-height	Defines the maximum and minimum allowable height of an element. (Does not apply to table elements.)	<length>, <percentage>, none	none

Property	Use	Values	Default Value
max-width min-width	Defines the maximum and minimum allowable width of an element. (Does not apply to table elements.)	\<length>, \<percentage>, none	0
opacity*	Defines an element's level of transparency, where 0 is fully transparent and 1 is fully opaque. (Use decimal values between those two.)	\<alphavalue>	1
overflow	Defines how to handle content that does not fit within a particular block-level box. Updated in CSS3 to allow the use of two keywords to specify the horizontal and vertical overflow separately.	visible, hidden, scroll, auto, no-display, no-content	visible
padding	*Shorthand for all padding properties.*		
padding-top padding-right padding-bottom padding-left	Specifies the amount of blank space around the content within a box.	\<padding width>	0
position	Specifies how an element is positioned on the page.	static, relative, absolute, fixed	static
right	Defines the location of the right edge of a positioned element.	\<length>, \<percentage>, auto	auto
text-align	Defines the horizontal alignment of text and block-level elements.	left, right, center, justify, \<string>	Varies
text-decoration	Adds lines above, below, or through text.	none, underline, overline, line-through, blink	none
text-indent	Specifies the amount text is indented.	\<length>, \<percentage>	0
text-transform	Changes the case of text.	capitalize, uppercase, lowercase, none	none
top	Defines the location of the top edge of a positioned element.	\<length>, \<percentage>, auto	auto

vertical-align	Specifies the vertical alignment of text and inline-level elements (including table cells).	baseline, sub, super, top, text-top, middle, bottom, text-bottom, \<percentage>, \<length>	baseline
visibility	Specifies whether/how an element is displayed on the page when it first loads.	visible, hidden, collapse	inherit (the default value is inherited from the parent element)
white-space	Defines how white space is handled within block-level elements.	normal, pre, nowrap	normal
width	Defines the width of an element. (Does not apply to table rows or row groups.)	\<length>, \<percentage>, auto	auto
word-spacing	Defines the amount of space displayed between words.	normal, \<length>	normal
z-index	Specifies the stacking order of the element. (Applies only to absolutely or relatively positioned elements.)	auto, \<integer>	auto

*New in HTML5

Appendix C

Troubleshooting (FAQs)

This resource lists some of the most common problems encountered when writing HTML. If none of these answers solves the trouble you're experiencing, try running your page through an online validator, such as the one offered by the W3C at **validator.w3.org**. A service like this tests your page against the HTML specifications and displays a list of errors that makes it easy to locate problems.

Or, you could use Dave Raggett's HTML Tidy program (available for download at **http://sourceforge.net/projects/tidy/**). This handy program actually attempts to fix any problems on your page, if possible. It can also display a list of errors to alert you to things you can look for in the future.

Also, consider downloading a few very helpful free add-ons for your Firefox browser. (Don't have Firefox? Download it here: **www.firefox.com**.) The following two add-ons are those I find most helpful when coding HTML, especially for pesky details like aligning CSS boxes or tweaking CSS styles. These and plenty of others are available by searching **addons.mozilla.org**.

- **Web Developer** gives you a special toolbar filled with features that help you debug and test your pages right within the browser. For more information from the add-on's creator, visit **http://chrispederick.com/work/web-developer/**.

- **Firebug** is different from Web Developer in that it actually lets you edit HTML and CSS live while it is viewed in the browser. For more information from Firebug's creator, visit **http://getfirebug.com/**.

Finally, don't overlook the basic troubleshooting tools built into modern browsers. In most cases, you can access them simply by right-clicking (or control-clicking on the Mac) a page element and choosing Inspect Element.

My Page Is Blank in the Browser!

Yikes! You lost everything? Don't worry—it's probably all there, but an unclosed tag or quote somewhere may be causing the browser to ignore everything else on the page.

In my experience, the number-one cause for a page displaying blank or empty in a browser is an unclosed container tag, such as the `table` tag. So, if your page uses tables, go back through the code and identify each opening and closing `table` tag to make sure you didn't leave one off accidentally. Also, be sure to check you've closed your title tag.

The number-two cause of a missing section of a page is an unclosed quotation mark. For example, in the following code, the lack of closing quotes in the first a tag causes all the text after it to be considered part of the link URL. No text is displayed in the browser until another set of quotes is encountered that can be considered the closing quotes for the first link.

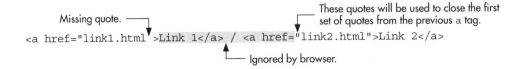

All I See Is Code in the Browser!

This occurs when the page doesn't have an HTML extension (such as .htm or .html) or when the page is saved in a format other than text-only. If you encounter this problem, return to your text editor and save the file again, making sure to choose Text Only or ASCII Text from any list of format types. When naming the file, be sure the text editor doesn't add a .txt extension, because only .htm or .html extensions are recognized as HTML by a browser. Finally, make sure your page includes opening and closing html tags.

My Images Don't Appear!

When images don't appear in a page, they are often replaced with a question mark graphic or a broken image symbol. Here's a quick checklist to run through if you encounter this problem:

- **Check filenames**   Perhaps you named a file image.jpg, but in the HTML, you referenced it as IMAGE.JPG. Any difference at all causes the image to appear "broken" in the browser. In addition, be sure your filename doesn't include spaces, because those also cause problems.

- **Check file locations**   If you tell the browser your image is in the photos folder when you write your HTML, make sure to upload the image to that folder. If the image is in a different folder, the browser won't be able to find it.

- **Check file types**   Remember, most graphical editors can view only GIF, JPEG, and PNG files. Other file types, such as BMP or TIFF, may be displayed as a broken image if the browser doesn't understand them.

- **Check img tags**   It's common for beginners to write out "image" instead of img when referencing an image. The tag is img, however, not image, and therefore, you must write it as such.

I Tried to Change the Font, But Nothing Happened!

First, make sure the font name is spelled correctly. If it is spelled correctly, make sure you actually have that font running on your system. Try launching your word processor to see if the font is available in that program. If it isn't, chances are you don't have that font loaded on your system. You might try a different font or download the font in question. And, remember, your users may not have that font, either.

When I Use a Special Character, It Doesn't Appear!

This happens for one of two reasons:

- **Missing ampersand and/or semicolon**   Don't forget, all entities—whether named or numbered—must begin with an ampersand and end with a semicolon.

- **Lack of browser support**   Certain browsers don't support some entities. If you double-checked that you're typing the entity correctly and it still doesn't appear, it might not be supported by your browser.

In something like a trademark symbol, which is not supported by all browsers, try using the superscript tag (`<sup>`) instead, as in the following example:

```
My Product<sup>TM</sup>
```

My Links Don't Work!

If your links don't work, check to make sure you typed them correctly. For example, a link to another web site should look something like this:

```
<a href="http://www.wendywillard.com">Wendy Willard</a>
```

while a link to another page in your site might look like this:

```
<a href="contactme.html">Contact Me</a>
```

Be sure to surround the link name with quotes and, if you are linking to another web site, don't forget the `http://`.

Unfortunately, if you are linking to another person's web site, it may be beyond your control to ensure the link works all the time. If a user clicks a link to another site from one of your pages and that site is unavailable, the link won't work. For this reason, it's important to check your links often, making sure they haven't become extinct. You might also contact the owner of the page you're linking to, as the owner might be able to provide a specific link address he or she can guarantee won't change.

My Page Looks Great in One Browser, But Terrible in Another!

Unfortunately, I must say this is not an uncommon problem. In most cases, though, the page's developer never takes the time to look at the site in another browser and, therefore, never knows how bad the page looks. Take heart—you're halfway to making your page look great in both browsers just because you know there's a problem! The following are a few things to consider when you have this problem:

- **Did you use Microsoft Word to create your page?** This program sometimes adds proprietary code that works great in Internet Explorer, but looks terrible in any other browser. You can use a validation service (such as **validator.w3.org**) to identify any code that isn't part of the official W3C spec. In addition, some HTML editors, like Dreamweaver, have a function to delete all the Microsoft HTML code from a Microsoft Word document. If that doesn't work, keep reading….

- **Did you use emerging technologies in HTML5 or CSS3?** Certain aspects of these emerging technologies are supported differently by some browsers. This means you may have to create multiple versions of your pages if the formatting is important to the page display, or just know your pages will look different according to the browser used. But before you set out creating multiple versions of your pages, run your page through a validator to look for hidden code errors. The most common reason for pages to display differently in multiple browsers is simply that some browsers are more forgiving than others when it comes to code errors.

Finally, remember some HTML elements are just rendered differently by some browsers. Even though you may have coded your page perfectly, there's a good chance it still might look different when viewed in certain browsers. The best advice I can offer you on this topic is to test, ask your friends to help you test, and test some more. Previewing your page in as many different browsers and computer systems as possible can help to ensure you know how it will look to the largest number of users.

When I Link My Images, They Have Little Colored Dashes Next to Them!

This happens sometimes when the browser finds a carriage return before it finds the closing a tag for a link, as in the following example:

```
<a href="home.html">
<img src="home.gif" alt="Return to the Home Page" width="25" height="25">
</a>
```

To eliminate those little dashes next to your images, run all the code on a single link, like this:

```
<a href="home.html"><img src="home.gif" alt="Return to the Home Page"
width="25" height="25"></a>
```

I Saved My Image as a JPEG, But the Browser Says It's Not a Valid File Format!

Open your image in a graphics program like Photoshop and check the color mode (in Photoshop, choose Image | Mode). JPEG files must be in the RGB color mode for the browser to be able to display them. It's not uncommon for JPEG images to mistakenly be saved in the CMYK color mode.

When this happens, the browser can't display the image, even though it's saved in the JPEG file format. To fix this, change the file format to RGB and resave the image as a JPEG.

Strange Characters Are at the Top of My Page!

If you used a word processor to write your HTML—or even if you just copied and pasted some text from Word—you may end up with some characters you didn't type at the top of your page when you view it in a browser. This occurs when the page contains hidden formatting instructions. To avoid this, return to your file in the editor and save it in Text Only or ASCII Text format, with an .html or .htm extension. Or, if you only copied text from Word, remove all Word formatting to get rid of things like curly quotes or fancy ellipses (or save the file as Text Only), and then try copying and pasting again.

I Added Internal Links to Sections of a Web Page, But When I Click Them, the Browser Launches a Brand New Window!

This occurs when the internal links within the page aren't defined properly. For instance, suppose you were trying to create a link at the bottom of your web page that took users back to the top of the page. You might use the following code:

```
<a href="#top">Back to Top</a>
```

However, unless you actually add the code to tell the browser where the top of your page is, the browser won't know what to do and will just launch a new window. In this instance, you'd need to add the following code near the top of your page:

```
<a name="top"></a>
```

If you're saying, "Wait, I already had that code at the top of my page and it still doesn't work!" then make sure both the `<a name>` reference and the `<a href>` reference match exactly. So if you used "TOP" in the `<a name>` reference, make sure to use "TOP" and not "top" in the `<a href>` reference.

I Specified One Color, But Got a Totally Different One!

This has happened to me several times, and it's caused by something that's easy to fix but hard to spot. Consider the following code:

```
<body bgcolor="#336699 text="#ffffff">
```

Did you spot the missing quotation mark after the background color value? That simple omission can cause the background color to be rendered as some odd concoction of the #336699 and #ffffff colors. So if your colors start behaving oddly, first check your quotation marks. Then make sure you haven't forgotten a hash mark (#), because missing hash marks can also cause colors to display incorrectly, or not to display at all! Finally, confirm you've included all of the necessary digits or characters for the color value.

I Need to Protect Some of My Pages from Unwanted Visitors!

Suppose you uploaded some photos of your children to a web site and now want to restrict the pages so that only your friends and family can gain access. You can add simple password protection to your site to do just that, but keep in mind most simple password protection scripts won't keep the pros out. (If someone is really determined to get in, they'll be able to unless you add more secure features to the computer your site is hosted on.)

In any case, if you're interested in adding password protection to your site, check out some of the following sites for some scripts that'll help:

- **JavaScript**   www.javascriptsource.com/passwords/
- **HTAccess**   webdesign.about.com/od/security/a/password_protec.htm

I Need to Prevent People from Stealing My Images!

Along with the question about password protection, this is another one I am asked quite frequently: "How can I protect my photography from the casual Internet thief?" Quite honestly, you can't. And most likely, you don't need to. Consider what we're talking about here—in the vast majority of cases, any photos you put on your web site are only 72 dpi (screen resolution).

This means when someone goes to print your 72 dpi photo, they will see a pretty poor representation of the image because it's so low in file resolution. To really get a nice print of an image, you need at least 300 dpi in file resolution. My guess is that no one can get that high a resolution file from you without asking for it (or breaking into your house and stealing it off your hard drive), so there's little need to worry. Hey, if the Louvre Museum (**www.louvre.fr**) is okay with putting photos of *their* artwork on a web site, you can be okay with it, too.

With that said, there are scripts available that can attempt to prevent users from right-clicking your images and saving them to your hard drives. One example can be found at **www .javascriptsource.com/page-details/no-right-click.html**. However, users who know what they are doing can disable JavaScript in their browsers or otherwise find ways around this.

If you are a photographer or artist, I suggest you use Photoshop or another graphics program to add a copyright and watermark to your images.

I Tried to Send My Web Page in an Email, But the Page Looked Terrible!

Several things could be happening here. First, you need to make sure the person you're sending the email to has an HTML-compatible email program. Not all email programs are capable of displaying HTML, and those that do sometimes support only certain aspects of HTML. For example, many email programs don't support tables or frames, even though they do support images, links, and text formatting. Furthermore, those that are capable of doing so often give the user an option to turn off the display of HTML in emails. Refer to Chapter 16 for tips on how to write pages that do look good in most email readers.

I Updated My Web Page, But I Don't See the Changes in the Browser!

First, double-check that you saved the file. If you did, indeed, save your changes, and clicking the Refresh or Reload button doesn't help, try forcing a reload by choosing File | Open Page or File | Open Location and then selecting the file in question. This ensures the browser is looking at the latest version of the file.

In some cases, you may also need to clear the browser's cache on disk. The *cache* is a place where browsers store temporary copies of web page files to avoid having to go back to the server to retrieve them multiple times. For example, you can access your browser's cache by choosing Firefox | Preferences | Privacy, and then clicking the link to clear your recent history.

My Whole Page Is _____! (Fill in the Blank)

For example, your whole page could be bold or linked or orange, and so forth. Even though this may look like a terrible error, it's relatively easy to fix. Most likely you're just missing a closing tag somewhere. For example, if your whole page is a giant link, look in your code for the place you actually wanted to create a link to be sure you included the closing a tag. Or, if all the text on your page is bold, look to make sure you included a closing b tag. Typing something like the following is actually quite common:

```
<em>Welcome to my Web site.<em>
```

At first glance it looks great, but a second look shows the closing tag is actually missing a slash. It should look like the following instead:

```
<em>Welcome to my Web site.</em>
```

My Page Has a White Background in One Browser, But Not in Others!

Some browsers set the default background color of web pages to white, while some other browsers use a default color of gray. If you only test your pages in one browser and forget to specify a background color, other users may complain that your pages look drastically different. To avoid this problem, always specify a background color in your style sheet, even if you only want that color to be white.

```
body {background-color: white;}
```

TIP

When you do specify a background color, be sure to set the text color to something readable. This is a common reason for "blank" pages: the text and background are the same color!

I Shrank My Images, But They Still Take Forever to Download!

How did you shrink your images? Did you use HTML to do so, within the height and width attributes of the img tag? If so, then you didn't really shrink your images. You just specified that they should be displayed smaller within the browser. To really shrink your images and reduce their file sizes, you need to open them in a graphics editor and cut down the physical height and width of the images.

I Embedded a Flash File That Works Fine on My Computer, But Doesn't Work Properly on Other Computers!

I suspect the other computer doesn't have the latest version of Flash Player and you haven't included code to catch that incompatibility. If this is the case, you can notify and give manual instructions for an updated Flash Player on your web page. Or, if you're up for something a bit more advanced, try implementing the deployment kit, at **www.adobe.com/products/ flashplayer/download/detection_kit/**, which can detect cases in which users do not have the appropriate version of the Flash Player and automatically reroute them. (Most plug-ins automatically detect older players, but Flash Player does not in every case.)

My Tables Look Fine in One Browser, But Terrible in Another!

First, make sure you have closed your table tags, and all tr and td tags have opening and closing versions. Consider the following example:

```
<tr>
  <td>Cell 1
  <td>Cell 2
<tr>
  <td>Cell 3
  <td>Cell 4
```

While some browsers can be forgiving when they encounter sloppy HTML that doesn't include closing tags, others refuse to display the content at all. The key to making tables that look good across multiple platforms is to use proper HTML and to test it in several browsers ahead of time.

```
<tr>
  <td>Cell 1</td>
  <td>Cell 2</td>
</tr>
<tr>
  <td>Cell 3</td>
  <td>Cell 4</td>
</tr>
```

If you continue to have table problems, try turning on the border (adding border=1 to the opening table tag will do the trick) just to help you see the outlines of your table cells. Sometimes simply making those borders visible will shed light on the problem. After you've fixed the problem, the border can be removed with border=0.

I Still Have Questions!

If the previous sections haven't answered your questions, the following are a few more things to try:

- **Take a break**   Looking at HTML code for hours on end can be quite straining, regardless of how experienced you are. If you're having trouble, take a break and don't come back to the problem page until you feel rested enough to look at the issue with fresh eyes.

- **Check for typos**   This may sound easy, but with HTML it's not. I can't tell you how many times I struggled with a certain page, only to find out three days later that it was all because I misspelled a tag or left out a quote. Printing the page and highlighting anything that seems like a potential problem area helps me. Also, reading the code on paper as opposed to on the screen can sometimes help you look at it differently. As much as 90 percent of HTML problems brought to my attention by students or coworkers involve typos!

- **Remove the styles**   If the page structure is causing headaches, try temporarily removing your style sheet. Viewing the bare-bones page elements can sometimes help structural code problems become more visible. Or, it could help identify the style sheet as the problem. If that's the case, try rebuilding your style sheet one declaration at a time until you identify the culprit.

- **Debug**   Refer back to the beginning of this chapter where I mentioned the various debugging and troubleshooting tools in the browsers. These can be invaluable for all HTML coders, especially when you feel like you're hitting your head against a brick wall with a certain bit of code.

- **Start fresh**   Begin a new HTML page and add to it from the problem page, piece by piece. For example, first add the `head` and `title` tags. Then save the page and try it in the browser. If that works, add something else. While this may take a while, it certainly can help you identify exactly where the problem lies if you didn't already know.

- **Reread the chapter**   If you're having trouble with tables, try returning to that chapter and, perhaps, even re-creating some of the examples. After all, practice makes perfect, right? Well, at least it helps….

- **Ask someone else**   If you don't have fellow students or coworkers to ask, you could try posting your problem HTML on a troubleshooting bulletin board online to see if anyone else has had the same problem.

Appendix D

Special Characters

In HTML, nonalphabetical characters that use the SHIFT key should be rendered by entities instead of being typed out. Entities can be in the form of numbers or names, but all begin with an ampersand and end with a semicolon. Some entities aren't supported by all browsers, so be sure to test your pages in several browsers to ensure they appear as you intend. For more information, visit **www.htmlhelp.com/reference/charset**.

NOTE

The following table lists the most popular entities, listed in alphabetical order by description. Most nonstandard or minimally supported entities aren't included here.

Standard HTML Entities

Character	Numbered Entity	Named Entity	Description
&	&#38;	&amp;	Ampersand
*	&#42;	n/a	Asterisk
@	&#64;	n/a	"At" symbol
´	&#180;	&acute;	Acute accent, no letter
<	&#60;	&lt;	Angle bracket (less-than symbol), left
>	&#62;	&gt;	Angle bracket (greater-than symbol), right
\	&#92;	n/a	Backslash
{	&#123;	n/a	Brace/curly bracket, opening
}	&#125;	n/a	Brace/curly bracket, closing
[	&#91;	n/a	Bracket, opening
]	&#93;	n/a	Bracket, closing
•	&#8226;	&bull;	Bullet
À	&#192;	&Agrave;	Capital A, grave accent
Á	&#193;	&Aacute;	Capital A, acute accent
Â	&#194;	&Acirc;	Capital A, circumflex accent
Ã	&#195;	&Atilde;	Capital A, tilde
Ä	&#196;	&Auml;	Capital A, dieresis, or umlaut mark
Å	&#197;	&Aring;	Capital A, ring
Æ	&#198;	&AElig;	Capital AE diphthong (ligature)
Ç	&#199;	&Ccedil;	Capital C, cedilla
È	&#200;	&Egrave;	Capital E, grave accent
É	&#201;	&Eacute;	Capital E, acute accent
Ê	&#202;	&Ecirc;	Capital E, circumflex accent

Character	Numbered Entity	Named Entity	Description
Ë	&#203;	&Euml;	Capital E, dieresis, or umlaut mark
Ì	&#204;	&Igrave;	Capital I, grave accent
Í	&#205;	&Iacute;	Capital I, acute accent
Î	&#206;	&Icirc;	Capital I, circumflex accent
Ï	&#207;	&Iuml;	Capital I, dieresis, or umlaut mark
Ñ	&#209;	&Ntilde;	Capital N, tilde
Ò	&#210;	&Ograve;	Capital O, grave accent
Ó	&#211;	&Oacute;	Capital O, acute accent
Ô	&#212;	&Ocirc;	Capital O, circumflex accent
Õ	&#213;	&Otilde;	Capital O, tilde
Ö	&#214;	&Ouml;	Capital O, dieresis, or umlaut mark
Ø	&#216;	&Oslash;	Capital O, slash
Ù	&#217;	&Ugrave;	Capital U, grave accent
Ú	&#218;	&Uacute;	Capital U, acute accent
Û	&#219;	&Ucirc;	Capital U, circumflex accent
Ü	&#220;	&Uuml;	Capital U, dieresis, or umlaut mark
Ý	&#221;	&Yacute;	Capital Y, acute accent
^	&#94;	n/a	Caret
¸	&#184;	&cedil;	Cedilla
¢	&#162;	&cent;	Cent sign
:	&#58;	n/a	Colon
,	&#44;	n/a	Comma
©	&#169;	&copy;	Copyright symbol
°	&#176;	&deg;	Degree symbol
$	&#36;	n/a	Dollar symbol
«	&#171;	&laquo;	Double-angle quote (guillemotleft), left
»	&#187;	&raquo;	Double-angle quote (guillemotright), right
"	&#34;	&quot;	Double quote
…	&#8230;		Horizontal ellipsis
—	&#8212;	&mdash;	Em dash
–	&#8211;	&ndash;	En dash
=	&#61;	n/a	Equal sign

Character	Numbered Entity	Named Entity	Description
!	&#33;	n/a	Exclamation point
ª	&#170;	&ordf;	Feminine ordinal
/	&#47;	n/a	Forward slash (virgule)
$\frac{1}{4}$	&#188;	&frac14;	Fraction one-fourth
$\frac{1}{2}$	&#189;	&frac12;	Fraction one-half
$\frac{3}{4}$	&#190;	&frac34;	Fraction three-fourths
€	&#164;	&curren;	General currency sign
`	&#96;	n/a	Grave accent, no letter
¡	&#161;	&iexcl;	Inverted exclamation
¿	&#191;	&iquest;	Inverted question mark
ß	&#223;	&szlig;	Lowercase sharp s, German (sz ligature)
à	&#224;	&agrave;	Lowercase a, grave accent
á	&#225;	&aacute;	Lowercase a, acute accent
â	&#226;	&acirc;	Lowercase a, circumflex accent
ã	&#227;	&atilde;	Lowercase a, tilde
ä	&#228;	&auml;	Lowercase a, dieresis, or umlaut mark
å	&#229;	&aring;	Lowercase a, ring
æ	&#230;	&aelig;	Lowercase ae dipthong (ligature)
ç	&#231;	&ccedil;	Lowercase c, cedilla
è	&#232;	&egrave;	Lowercase e, grave accent
é	&#233;	&eacute;	Lowercase e, acute accent
ê	&#234;	&ecirc;	Lowercase e, circumflex accent
ë	&#235;	&euml;	Lowercase e, dieresis, or umlaut mark
ì	&#236;	&igrave;	Lowercase i, grave accent
í	&#237;	&iacute;	Lowercase i, acute accent
î	&#238;	&icirc;	Lowercase i, circumflex accent
ï	&#239;	&iuml;	Lowercase i, dieresis, or umlaut mark
ñ	&#241;	&ntilde;	Lowercase n, tilde
ò	&#242;	&ograve;	Lowercase o, grave accent
ó	&#243;	&oacute;	Lowercase o, acute accent
ô	&#244;	&ocirc;	Lowercase o, circumflex accent

Character	Numbered Entity	Named Entity	Description
õ	&#245;	&otilde;	Lowercase o, tilde
ö	&#246;	&ouml;	Lowercase o, dieresis, or umlaut mark
÷	&#247;	&divide;	Division symbol
ø	&#248;	&oslash;	Lowercase o, slash
ù	&#249;	&ugrave;	Lowercase u, grave accent
ú	&#250;	&uacute;	Lowercase u, acute accent
û	&#251;	&ucirc;	Lowercase u, circumflex accent
ü	&#252;	&uuml;	Lowercase u, dieresis, or umlaut mark
ý	&#253;	&yacute;	Lowercase y, acute accent
ÿ	&#255;	&yuml;	Lowercase y, dieresis, or umlaut mark
¯	&#175;	&macr;	Macron accent
º	&#186;	&ordm;	Masculine ordinal
µ	&#181;	&micro;	Micro symbol
·	&#183;	&middot;	Middle dot
–	&#45;	n/a	Minus sign
×	&#215;	&times;	Multiplication sign
			Nonbreaking space
¬	&#172;	&not;	"Not" symbol
#	&#35;	n/a	Number symbol
¶	&#182;	&para;	Paragraph symbol
)	&#41;	n/a	Parenthesis, closing
(	&#40;	n/a	Parenthesis, opening
%	&#37;	n/a	Percent symbol
.	&#46;	n/a	Period
+	&#43;	n/a	Plus sign
±	&#177;	&plusmn;	Plus or minus symbol
£	&#163;	&pound;	Pound sterling
?	&#63;	n/a	Question mark
®	&#174;	&reg;	Registration mark
§	&#167;	&sect;	Section sign
;	&#59;	n/a	Semicolon
'	&#39;	n/a	Single quote
¹	&#185;	&sup1;	Superscript one

Character	Numbered Entity	Named Entity	Description
2	²	²	Superscript two
3	³	³	Superscript three
~	~	n/a	Tilde (equivalency symbol)
TM	™	™	Trademark symbol
··	¨	¨	Umlaut, no letter
_	_	n/a	Underscore
|	|	n/a	Vertical bar
¥	¥	¥	Yen sign

Appendix E

File Types

Multipurpose Internet Mail Extension (MIME) is an accepted system of extensions used on computer systems. Such a standardization makes it easy to specify a file type and feel confident other computers will understand it. This table includes some of the popular file types you might encounter when creating web pages.

MIME Type	File Extension(s)	Name and Description
application/excel application/msexcel	.xl .xls .xlsx	Microsoft Excel (spreadsheet)
application/mac-binhex40	.hqx	Macintosh Binhex format (file compression)
application/msword	.doc .word .docx	Microsoft Word document (word processing)
application/octet-stream	.exe	Windows/DOS programs
application/ogg	.ogg	Ogg multimedia file
application/pdf	.pdf	Adobe's Portable Document Format (PostScript/printer-friendly files)
application/postscript	.ai .eps .ps	PostScript document
application/powerpoint application/mspowerpoint	.ppt .pps .ppa .ppz	Microsoft PowerPoint document
application/rss+xml	.xml	RSS feeds
application/rtf	.rtf	Rich Text Format (word processing)
application/vnd.m-realmedia	.rm	RealMedia file (audio and video)
application/javascript	.js	JavaScript file
application/x-macbinary	.bin	Macintosh binary file (file compression)
application/x-shockwave-flash	.swf	Macromedia Flash 2.0+ file (presentation/animation/multimedia)
application/x-stuffit	.sit	Stuffit Archive (file compression)
application/zip	.zip	ZIP archive (file compression)
audio/aiff	.aif .aiff .aife	Audio Interchange File Format
audio/basic	.au .snd	AU/mlaw (basic audio)

MIME Type	File Extension(s)	Name and Description
audio/midi	.mid	Musical Instruments Digital Interface (MIDI) sound files
audio/mpeg	.mp2 .mp3 .m2a .m3u .mpg	MP2/MP3 audio file
audio/mp4	.mp4	MP4 audio file
audio/ogg	.ogg .oga	Ogg Vorbis, Speex, Flac, or other audio file
audio/vnd.rn-realaudio	.ra .ram	RealAudio file
audio/vorbis	.ogg .oga	Vorbis-encoded audio file
audio/vnd.wav	.wav	Windows Waveform audio file
audio/webm	.webm	WebM audio file
audio/xm	.xm	Extended Module audio file
audio/x-pn-realaudio	.ra .ram	RealAudio file
audio/x-pn-realaudio-plugin	.rpm	RealAudio plug-in page
image/gif	.gif	Graphics Interchange Format (GIF)
image/jpeg	.jpeg .jpg	Joint Photographic Experts Group (JPEG)
image/pict	.pic .pict	Macintosh Picture
image/png	.png	Portable Networks Graphics
image/svg+xml	.svg	Scalable Vector Graphic
image/tiff	.tif .tiff	Tag Image File Format
image/x-bitmap image/bmp image/x-windows-bmp	.xbm .bmp .bm	Windows Bitmap Format (BMP)
image/x-icon image/vnd.microsoft.icon	.ico	Icon image format (for computer icons)
text/css	.css	Cascading Style Sheet document
text/csv	.csv	Comma-separated values

MIME Type	File Extension(s)	Name and Description
text/html	.html .htm .shtm .shtml .xhtml	Hypertext Markup Language document (HTML)
text/plain	.txt	Plain-text document (no formatting)
text/vcard	.vcard	Contact information
text/xml	.xml	Extensible Markup Language document (XML)
video/mpeg	.mpg .mpeg .mpe .wmv .m1v .m2v .mp2 .mp3	MPEG video file
video/mp4	.mp4	MP4 video file
video/ogg	.ogg .ogv	Ogg Theora or other video file
video/quicktime	.qt .mov	QuickTime refers both to the file format and the helper application or plug-in used to play it
video/vnd.m-realvideo	.rv	RealVideo file
video/webm	.webm	WebM video file
video/x-flv	.flv	Flash video file
video/x-msvideo	.avi	Audio/Video Interleave Format is the standard nonstreaming Microsoft Windows Video format

Index

Special Characters

; (semicolon), 37, 325, 329
- (hyphen), 25
– (minus sign), 43
_ (underscore), 25
' (quotes), 327
" (quotation marks), 34, 37
{ } (curly brackets), 327, 329
@ (at symbol), 144–145
& (ampersand), 37
# (hash mark), 86, 87, 140
+ (plus sign), 43
< > (brackets), 28, 37

A

a tag, 34, 146, 178, 201, 327
absolute fonts, 69
absolute links, 135
absolute pathnames, 140
absolute paths, 382
absolute positioning, 115, 116
absolute sizing, 244
absolute URLs, 44
accesskey attribute, 300
ACSII mode, 364

action attribute, 292–294
ActiveX, 199
ActiveX control, 198. *See also* plug-ins
Adobe BrowserLab, 128, 362
Adobe Illustrator, 162–163
Adobe Photoshop, 162–163
aggregator, 145
AJAX (asynchronous JavaScript and XML), 328
alignment
      table cell content, 252–253
      tables, 246–247
      text, 100–103
alpha channel, 165
alt attribute, 176
Amaya, 15
ampersand (&), 37
anchors, 138, 139–142
Android browser, 205
animation, 165–166
animation frames, 165–166
answers, self-test, 405–427
APIs (application programming interfaces), 322
Apple Safari, 8, 17, 363
applets, 209
application programming interfaces (APIs), 322
area element, 180
article element, 81, 84–85
aside element, 81, 84
.asp extension, 24

asynchronous JavaScript and XML (AJAX), 328
at symbol (@), 144–145
attributes. *See also specific attributes*
    core, 430–431
    generic, 430–434
    international, 430, 434
    overview, 30–31
    placeholder, 272–273
    text fields, 272, 273
audio
    adding to web pages, 9, 203
    file formats, 204, 206
    sources, 203–207
audio element, 203, 204
autobuffer attribute, 204
autoplay attribute, 204, 208

breaks
    within code, 34
    line. *See* line breaks
    between tags, 35
Browsercam, 362
BrowserLab, 128, 362
browsers. *See* web browsers
Browsershots, 362
bullets, lists, 226–227
button element, 288–289
buttons
    forms, 275–277, 287–289, 308
    graphical, 289
    radio, 275–277
    types of, 287–288

B

background attribute, 192
background images. *See also* foreground images
    adding, 194–195
    color, 74, 75, 462
    considerations, 74, 192–193
    tables, 249
    using images as elements in, 192–195
background-image property, 192, 249
BBEdit, 15
Berners-Lee, Tim, 6
binary mode, 364
binary transparency, 165
bitmap animation, 166
bitmap applications, 162
bitmap images, 162
block-level elements, 29–30, 188–189, 300
blockquote element, 95–96
Blogger, 352
blogs, 351, 352
Blue Hornet, 380
BlueHost web hosting, 354
body element, 31, 33
bolded text, 59
border attribute, 182–184, 242–243
borders
    box model, 96–97, 99–100
    foreground images, 172–185
    images, 99–100
    tables, 242–243
box properties, 96–100
box-sizing property, 96–99, 114
br element, 28, 36, 93–94
brackets < >, 28, 37

C

calendaring, 331
Campaign Monitor, 380, 389, 395–396
canvas, 333–335
Canvas Tutorial, 345
capitalization, 33, 59
captions
    audio/video content, 209, 210
    figures, 181
    tables, 250
cascade concept, 47–48
cascading, 64
cascading order, 45
cascading style sheets. *See* CSS
case sensitivity, 25, 33, 326
cells. *See* table cells
CGI (Common Gateway Interface), 293
CGI scripts, 293–295
character entities, 36–37, 466–470
characters. *See also* text
    domain names, 351
    maximum number of, 270–271, 272, 273
    special. *See* special characters
    unusual, 459
check boxes, 277–278
checked attribute, 278
Chrome, 7, 17, 322, 324
Chrome inspection tools, 359, 360
class attribute, 87
class selectors, 87
classes, 86–87, 256
client-side validation, 315–318
closing tags, 76
CMYK mode, 168
code. *See also* HTML code
    open source, 18
    spacing in, 34

The Code Player, 346
codecs, 205. *See also* compression
CoffeeCup Free FTP, 366
CoffeeCup Pro, 15
col element, 261, 263
colgroup element, 261–264, 311
color, 48–54
    background, 74, 75, 462
    CMYK, 168
    fonts, 70
    forms, 283
    GIFs and, 167
    hexidecimal, 48–50
    JPEG and, 169
    links, 150–152
    names, 51
    PNG and, 169
    problems with, 460
    RGB, 50–51, 168
    RGBA, 52
    specifying, 52–54
    table cells, 256–257
    table rows, 256–257
    tables, 248
color pickers, 283
color values, 44
colorblender.com, 54
cols attribute, 275
colspan attribute, 258, 259
columns. *See* table columns
comments, adding to HTML files, 38
Common Gateway Interface. *See* CGI
compression
    codecs, 205
    GIF, 166
    images, 164
    JPEG, 169
    lossless, 164
    lossy, 164, 168
    LZW, 166
    video, 205
conditional statements, 329
Constant Contact, 380
Contact Us form, 289–290, 318–319
container elements, 36, 81
container format, 205
containers, 205
content
    forms, 290–292
    ID names, 128
    importance of, 106
    layering within layouts, 122–126
    linking images to, 177–181
    links to other sites, 370
    meta, 355–356

    multimedia, 202–214
    natural divisions, 80–87
    newsworthy, 370
    organizing, 12–13
    organizing sections of, 80–89
    page layout example, 109
    related, 370
    syndicated, 84–85
    tables. *See* table cells
    tips for, 58–59
context, 333
controller attribute, 208
controls attribute, 203, 204, 208
cookies, 330
CorelDraw, 163
Corel Photo-Paint, 163
CSS (cascading style sheets). *See also* style sheets
    client-side validation, 315–318
    creating structure, 44–47
    email clients, 386–389
    layouts. *See* page layouts
    properties reference, 447–453
    purpose of, 42
    reference libraries, 430
.css extension, 47
CSS selectors, 87–89, 150
CSS values, 43–44
CSS Zen Garden, 89, 90–91, 107
CSS3 properties, 72
CSS/HTML Reference Table, 429–453
curly brackets { }, 327, 329
current values, 272

D

data lists, 304
date/time inputs, 278–279
date/time script, 336
decimal units, 48–49
declaration, 43
dedicated servers, 353
default attribute, 210
definition lists, 222
descendent selectors, 87, 150
desktop FTP programs, 364–366
DHTML (Dynamic HTML), 322
disabled attribute, 286
dithering, 167
div element, 81, 85
.doc extension, 25
doctype element, 31, 32
Document Setup tags, 28
.docx extension, 25

domains
   described, 5
   names, 5, 350–351
   registering, 5, 350
   researching, 350
dongles, 8
dots per inch (dpi), 165
download times, 462
downloadable files, 146
dpi (dots per inch), 165
drag-and-drop editing, 17
Draw program, 163
Dream Host web hosting, 354
Dreamweaver, 15, 17, 362, 367
drop-down menus, 284–285
Dynamic HTML (DHTML), 322
dynamic navigation bar, 337–340

E

editing. *See also* HTML editors
   drag-and-drop, 17
   images, 331
   text-based, 14, 16–17
   WYSIWYG, 16–17, 27
editors. *See* HTML editors
elements. *See also specific elements*
   block-level, 29–30, 188–189, 300
   capitalization, 33
   container, 36, 81
   described, 27
   empty, 30
   inline, 29–30, 231, 300
   quotations, 34
   text-level, 29–30
   types of, 28–30
email, 373–400
   @ symbol, 144–145
   attachments, 376
   bulk mail, 379–380
   customizing, 143–144
   Flash in, 393
   forms in, 145, 393–395
   FTC rules, 378
   hiding address, 144, 145
   HTML. *See* HTML email
   image blocking, 382–384
   images in, 376, 382–384
   links in, 382
   links to, 143–145
   most popular clients, 380–381
   "opt out" options, 377, 378
   overview, 374
   plain-text vs. HTML, 375–377

purpose of, 375
RSS feeds, 145
sending form data via, 293
sending web pages with, 378–379
spam. *See* spam
standards, 374–375
unsubscribing, 377, 378
video in, 389
email clients, 380–381, 386–389
email programs, 375–376
email service provider (ESP), 379–380
embed element, 202, 211
embedded items
   HTML tags, 28
   multimedia content, 202–214
   style sheets, 45–46
Emma program, 380
ems, 68, 69
encryption, 308
enctype attribute, 295
ESP (email service provider), 379–380
event handlers, 327–328, 430, 431–434
Expression Studio 4 Web Professional, 15
Extensible Hypertext Markup Language (XHTML), 9
Extensible Markup Language. *See* XML
extensions, file, 172, 199–200, 471–474
external style sheets, 45, 46–47, 111, 126–127

F

Facebook ads, 371
FAQs (frequently asked questions), 455–464
Fetch, 366
fieldset element, 302–303
fieldset tags, 311–313
fieldsets, 311–315
figcaption element, 181
figure captions, 181
figure element, 181
file extensions, 172, 199–200, 471–474
file formats, 164–172
   audio, 204, 206
   GIF, 166–167, 169
   images. *See* image formats
   JPEG, 167–169, 459
   PDF, 72–73
   PNG, 169
   terminology, 164–166
   video, 204, 206
File Transfer Protocol. *See* FTP
file types, 199–200, 471–474
files
   downloadable, 146
   Flash, 208, 393, 463

HTML. *See* HTML files
multimedia, 200–202, 214–215
PDF, 72–73
PostScript, 72
resolution, 164–165
uploading, 286–287
FileZilla, 364–366
Firebug, 324
Firefox, 7, 17, 324
Firefox Web Developer tools, 356–359
FireFTP, 367
firmlist.com, 161
Flash, 9, 199–200, 393
 HTML5 and, 331
Flash files, 208, 393, 463
Flash player, 199–200
float property, 185–187
floats, 185–187
folder names, 25
folders, 25
font faces, 63–66
font formats, 66
font-family property, 63–64
fonts. *See also* text
 accessing, 66
 colors, 70
 Google Web Fonts, 65–66
 licenses, 66
 links, 152
 names, 65
 printed pages, 75
 sizes, 66–69
 style properties, 70–72
 unable to change, 457
 Web, 64–66
 web browsers and, 67, 68, 69
footer element, 81, 84
footers, 84, 119–120
foreground images. *See also* background images
 borders, 172–185
 centering, 188–189
 floats, 185–187
 margins, 187–188
 padding, 187–188
 styling, 182–191
 using images as elements in, 172–173
form element, 268
Form tags, 28
formats. *See* file formats
formatting. *See also* style sheets; styles
 forms, 308–319
 HTML basics, 27–36
 links, 149–152
 lists, 226–233
 multimedia content, 212–214

page elements, 102–103
paragraphs, 102–103
preformatting, 94–95
table cell content, 252–259, 264–265
tables, 242–252
forms, 267–295
 buttons, 275–277, 287–289, 308
 check boxes, 277–278
 color selectors, 283
 contact methods, 281–282
 creating basic, 268–290
 data lists, 304
 date/time inputs, 278–279
 disabling input elements, 286
 in email, 145, 393–395
 file uploads, 286–287
 formatting, 308–319
 grouping related controls, 302–303
 hidden fields, 286
 improving usability, 299–300, 307–308
 input controls, 268–289
 keyboard shortcuts, 300
 labels, 298, 299, 301–302, 307
 links in, 307
 menus/submenus, 284–285
 number inputs, 279–281
 overview, 268
 passwords, 274
 patterns, 291–292
 processing methods, 292–295
 progress bar, 304–307
 purpose of, 268, 269
 radio buttons, 275–277
 read-only, 286
 required fields, 307
 scroll bars, 275
 search boxes, 274
 select menus, 284–285
 spacing, 300
 style sheets, 308–319
 tab order, 300
 tables in, 298–299, 300, 311–315
 text areas, 275
 text fields, 270–274
 text input controls, 270–275
 validating content, 290–292, 315–318
frequently asked questions (FAQs), 455–464
FTP (File Transfer Protocol), 146
FTP programs
 desktop, 364–366
 uploading web sites via, 363–367
 web-based, 367
FTP servers, 146
FTP sites, 146
FTP Voyager, 366

G

gaming, 331
gamma correction, 169
geolocation, 332, 340–343
get method, 295
GIF format, 166–167, 169
GIMP (GNU Image Manipulation Program), 163
GNU Image Manipulation Program (GIMP), 163
Google, 369
Google ads, 371
Google Analytics, 370
Google Blogger, 352
Google Chrome. *See* Chrome
Google Maps, 340, 344, 345
Google search engine, 8
Google Sites, 351
Google Web Fonts, 65–66
graphics. *See also* images
    creating your own, 161
    software for, 162–163
grouping
    content, 28
    form controls, 302–303
    table columns, 261–264
    table rows, 259–261

H

"hacks," 346
hash mark (#), 86, 87, 140
head element, 31, 32–33, 84
header element, 81, 84
headers, 84, 114–117
heading tags, 88–89
headings, 87–89
headlines, 13, 59
height attribute, 204, 208
height property, 253–255
helper applications, 198–199, 200
hexidecimal color, 48–50
hexidecimal units, 48–49
hidden fields, 286
HostMonster web hosting, 354
hot spots, 178–181
href attribute, 20, 34, 135, 178, 327
.htm extension, 7, 24
HTML. *See also* code; HTML5
    considerations, 4
    current version of, 9
    FAQs, 455–464
    getting started with, 3–20
    "hacks," 346

    vs. JavaScript, 323
    learning, 4
    reference libraries, 430
    "shorthand," 98–99, 100, 389
    troubleshooting, 356–359, 455–464
    validating, 359–360
    viewing, 17–18
HTML editors. *See also* editing
    choosing best, 14–17
    previewing files in, 26–27
    WYSIWYG, 27
    WYSIWYG vs. text-based, 16–17
html element, 31, 32
HTML email. *See also* email
    absolute paths, 382
    bulk mail, 379–380
    considerations, 400
    designing, 399–400
    email clients, 380–381
    email service provider, 379–380
    end-user display, 375–376
    fixed-width vs. liquid pages, 388
    Flash and, 393
    hiding address, 145
    image blocking, 382–384
    images in, 376, 382–384
    inline CSS, 386–389
    links in, 382
    marketing with, 376–377, 378
    "opt out" options, 377, 378
    vs. plain-text email, 375–377
    pros/cons, 375–377
    RSS feeds, 145
    sending web pages, 378–379, 461
    spam. *See* spam
    tables for layout, 380, 384–386
    testing, 395–399
    unsubscribing, 377, 378
    video in, 389
HTML entities, 466–470
.html extension, 7, 24, 25
HTML files. *See also* web pages
    adding comments, 38
    creating, 24–25
    displays blank in browser, 456
    formatting basics, 27–36
    naming conventions, 24–25
    previewing in browser, 17, 25–27
    previewing in HTML editor, 26–27
    setting up, 23–40
HTML standards, 9
HTML tags. *See also specific tags*
    attributes. *See* attributes
    closing tags, 76
    considerations, 27–28

deprecated, 434
described, 24
document setup, 28
embedding, 28
event handlers, 430, 431–434
forms, 28
grouping, 28
international, 430, 434
nesting, 34
opening/closing, 30
reference, 434–446
required, 31–33
Sectioning, 28
spacing between, 35
tables, 28
text-level semantics, 28
types of, 30
HTML5. *See also* HTML
caching applications, 331
canvas, 333–335
described, 9
Flash and, 331
free scripts, 345–346
geolocation, 332, 340–343
multitasking and, 330
new features, 9, 330–335
offline capabilities, 331
references, 345–346
storage, 330
HTML5 Canvas Element Guide, 345
HTML5Rocks resources, 330
HTML5Studio, 345
HTML/CSS Reference Table, 429–453
HTTP (Hypertext Transfer Protocol), 5
HTTP servers, 146
HTTPS (Hypertext Transfer Protocol Secure), 5
hyperlinks. *See* links
Hypertext Markup Language. *See* HTML
Hypertext Transfer Protocol. *See* HTTP
Hypertext Transfer Protocol Secure (HTTPS), 5
hyphen (-), 25

I

iContact, 380
id attribute, 86, 301, 311
ID attribute, 85–86
ID names, 86, 128
ID selectors, 87
Illustrator, 162–163
image formats
choosing between, 170–171
GIF, 166–167, 169
JPEG, 167–169, 459

PNG, 169
saving images in different formats, 171–172
image maps, 178–181
images, 159–195
adding to pages, 191
alternative text/titles, 175–176, 354
animated, 165–166
in background. *See* background images
bitmap, 162
borders, 172–185
centering, 188–189
compression, 164
creating your own graphics, 161
customizing, 191
download time, 462
editing, 331
in email, 376, 382–384
figure captions, 181
file formats for. *See* image formats
floats, 185–187
in foreground. *See* foreground images
GIF, 166–167, 169
graphics software, 162–163
height/width, 173–174
hot spots, 178–181
JPEG, 167–169, 459
licensed, 161
linking to site content, 177–181
links to, 177–181, 459
locating sources for, 160–161
margins, 187–188
not appearing in pages, 175–176, 457
overview, 160
padding, 187–188
problems displaying, 459
resolution, 75, 164–175
Save for Web feature, 170–172
size, 173–174
stock, 160–161
in table cells, 241–242
transparency, 165
vector, 162
img element, 173
!important declaration, 47–48
indenting
paragraphs, 36, 92–93
quotation blocks, 95–96
index page, 7
initial values, 272
inline elements, 29–30, 231, 300
inline style sheets, 44, 45
input controls, 268–289
input element, 270, 271, 272, 287–289
interactivity. *See* multimedia
internal style sheets, 44, 45–46, 111, 126

international attributes, 430, 434
Internet. *See also web entries*
    disseminating information on, 4–8
    history of, 6
    publishing web sites on, 363–367
Internet Explorer, 7–8, 324
Internet service providers (ISPs), 8, 352, 379
IP addresses, 5
iPadPeek, 360
ISPs (Internet service providers), 8, 352, 379
italics, 59

J

Java applets, 209
Java language, 322
JavaScript. *See also* scripts
    AJAX, 328
    basic example, 322
    case sensitivity, 326
    event handlers, 327–328
    free scripts, 345–346
    functions, 326–327
    geolocation, 332, 340–343
    "hacks," 346
    hiding email address, 145
    vs. HTML, 323
    vs. Java, 322
    launching new browser window, 344–345
    logic, 329–330
    methods, 325
    multitasking and, 330
    objects, 325
    operators, 326
    overview, 322–330
    properties, 325
    references, 345–346
    reserved words, 327
    terminology, 324–328
    troubleshooting, 323–324
    variables, 326–327
    Web Workers, 330
javascripts.com, 346
joshdock.com, 28
JPEG format, 167–169, 459

K

keyboard shortcuts, 153–154, 300
keywords, 44, 67, 113, 354, 355
kind attribute, 210

L

label attribute, 210
label element, 301
labels
    forms, 298, 299, 301–302, 307
    tracks, 210
layers, in web pages, 122–126
layouts. *See* page layouts
legend tag, 303
li element, 28
line breaks
    table cells, 257
    text, 93–95
    web pages, 93–95
link element, 32
links, 133–155. *See also* URLs
    absolute, 135
    anchors, 138, 139–142
    colors, 150–152
    considerations, 74, 134
    to content, 370
    customizing, 152–155
    described, 6
    to downloadable files, 146
    effective, 146–149
    to email addresses, 143–145
    to external style sheets, 126–127
    in forms, 307
    to FTP sites, 146
    Google Maps, 345
    to images, 177–181, 459
    internal, 74, 460
    keyboard shortcuts, 153–154
    mailto, 140–145
    multimedia files, 200–202, 214–215
    navigation bar, 13
    not working, 458
    to other web pages, 134–138, 148
    problems with, 149
    relative, 135–138
    to RSS feeds, 145
    within same web page, 138–142, 148
    to site content, 177–181
    spam-proofing, 144–145
    styles, 149–152
    tab order, 153
    target windows, 154
    titles, 152–153
    video, 214–215
lists, 217–233
    bullets, 226–227
    changing layout of, 228–232
    combining, 223–225
    data, 304

definition, 222
formatting, 226–233
navigation bar, 228–232
nesting, 223–225
numbered, 218–221
ordered, 218–221
overview, 59, 218
padding, 227–228
spacing, 227–228
style sheets, 232–233
unordered, 221
using, 225
Litmus tool, 397
local storage, 330
location, displaying on map, 332, 340–343
loop attribute, 204, 208
lossless compression, 164
lossy compression, 164
Lyris program, 380
LZW compression, 166

M

MailChimp, 380
mailto links, 140–145
map, displaying user location on, 332, 340–343
map element, 180
margin property, 227
margins
    alignment, 100–103
    box model, 99
    foreground images, 187–188
    printed pages, 75
    tables, 242–243
markup text, 60–61
measurement units, 44
media. *See* multimedia
menus/submenus, 284–285
meta content, 355–356
meta element, 32
meta tags, 355–356
meter element, 305–307
method attribute, 295
Meyer, Eric, 117
Microsoft Internet Explorer. *See* Internet Explorer
Microsoft Word, 25
MIME (Multipurpose Internet Mail Extension), 472
MIME types, 471–474
minus sign (-), 43
mobile devices
    contact input controls, 281–282
    geolocation, 332, 340–343
    previewing web sites on, 360–362

Mobile Emulator, 361, 362, 363
Mobilizer, 361
monitor size, 107
Mosaic browser, 6
Mozilla, 17
Mozilla Developer Center, 345
MPEG codec, 205
MPEG-4 format, 207
MSN search engine, 8
multimedia, 197–215
    audio. *See* audio
    embedding in web pages, 202–211
    file extensions, 199–200
    file types, 199–200
    formatting content, 212–214
    links to, 200–202, 214–215
    overview, 198
    plug-ins, 198–200
    sources, 203–207
    video. *See* video
multiple selectors, 87
Multipurpose Internet Mail Extension. *See* MIME
multitasking, 330

N

name attribute, 208, 276–277
named entities, 37, 466–470
naming conventions, 24–25
National Center for Supercomputing Applications
    (NCSA), 6
nav element, 81, 84
navigation, 13–14, 114–117
navigation bar, 13, 228–232, 337–340
NCSA (National Center for Supercomputing
    Applications), 6
nesting
    lists, 223–225
    tags, 34
Netscape, 322
Network Solutions, 351
newsgroups, 6
Nielsen, Jakob, 58
nonbreaking space, 37
Notepad, 17
NoteTab, 16
number inputs, 279–281
numbered entities, 37, 466–470
numbered lists, 218–221

O

object element, 202, 207–208
object-oriented applications, 162
objects, 325
Official Google Analytics Blog, 370
Ogg format, 207
online reference libraries, 430
opacity values, 52
open source code, 18
Opera Mobile Emulator, 361, 362, 363
optgroup element, 285
ordered lists, 218–221

P

p element, 28, 36, 89–93
padding
    box model, 96–99, 114
    content, 98–99
    described, 98
    foreground images, 187–188
    lists, 227–228
    printed pages, 75
    table cells, 255–256
padding property, 98–99, 227
page layouts. *See also* style sheets
    browser support, 111, 120–121
    considerations, 121–122
    fluid, multicolumn, 111–121
    fluid, single-column, 107–111
    header example, 114
    layering content within, 122–126
    navigation example, 114–117
    references, 122
    screen size and, 107
pages. *See* HTML files; web pages
paragraphs, 89–93
    formatting, 102–103
    indenting, 36, 92–93
    overview, 89–92
param tag, 207
password protection, 460–461
passwords, 274, 460–461
pathnames, 140
pattern attribute, 291–292
patterns, 291–292
PDF (Portable Document Format), 72
PDF files, 72–73
percentage widths, 98
Periodic Table of Elements, 28, 29
Photo-Paint program, 163
Photoshop, 162–163

.php extension, 24
pixels, 44, 68, 69, 98, 237
pixels per inch (ppi), 164–165
placeholder attribute, 272–273
plug-ins, 198–200
plus sign (+), 43
PNG format, 169
point sizes, 68, 69
Portable Document Format. *See* PDF
poster attribute, 204
PostScript files, 72
ppi (pixels per inch), 164–165
pre tag, 94–95
preformatting, 94–95
preload attribute, 203, 204
previewing
    files in HTML editors, 26–27
    HTML files in browser, 17, 25–27
    web pages in browser, 17, 25–27, 362–363
    web sites on mobile devices, 360–362
printer-friendly text, 72–76
printer-specific style sheets, 73–75
progress bar, 304–307
progress element, 305–307
publishing web sites, 363–367

Q

QuickTime, 9
quotation blocks, 95–96
quotation marks ("), 34, 37
quotes ('), 327

R

radio buttons, 275–277
raster applications, 162
readonly attribute, 286
Really Simple Syndication. *See* RSS
reference libraries, 430
regular expressions, 291–292
relative links, 135–138
relative pathnames, 140
relative percentages, 44
relative positioning, 115
relative sizing, 245
relative URLs, 44
resolution
    files, 164–165
    images, 75, 164–175
    screen, 107
RGB mode, 49, 168

RGB percentages, 51
RGB values, 49, 50–51
RGBA color, 52
rows. *See* table rows
rows attribute, 275
rowspan attribute, 259
RSS feeds, 145
RSS news readers, 145
rules, 43, 99–100
ruleset, 43

S

Safari, 8, 17, 363
screen resolution, 107
screen size, 107
script element, 32
scripts. *See also* JavaScript
    adding current date/time, 336
    creating dynamic navigation bar, 337–340
    formatting new window, 336–337
    free, 345
    launching new windows, 344–345, 460
    online references, 345
    sample, 336–345
scroll bars, 275
search boxes, forms, 274
Search Engine Land, 370
search engine optimization (SEO), 369–370
search engines
    considerations, 113, 355
    page rankings, 369
    paid ads on, 369
    submitting URLs to, 368–370
section element, 81, 84–85
Sectioning tags, 28
Secure Sockets Layer (SSL), 308
security
    CGI scripts and, 293
    encryption, 308
    passwords, 274, 460–461
select element, 284–285
selected attribute, 285
selector, 42–43
selectors, 87–89, 150
self-test answers, 405–427
semicolon (;), 37, 325, 329
SEO (search engine optimization), 369–370
SEO Fast Start, 370
servers
    CGI scripts and, 293
    dedicated, 353
    described, 5

FTP, 146
home directory, 137
HTTP, 146
index page, 137
shared, 353
web, 6, 7, 25
session storage, 330
shared servers, 353
SimpleText, 17
Site5 web hosting, 354
SitePoint.com, 345
sites. *See* web sites
SmartFTP, 366
source code. *See* code; HTML
source element, 206
spacing, 34–36
    blank spaces, 272
    within code, 34
    forms, 300
    between lines of text, 35–36
    lists, 227–228
    table cells, 243, 300
    between tags, 35
spam, email, 376, 377–378, 397–399
spam-proofing email links, 144–145
special characters, 465–470
    considerations, 25
    display problems, 457–458
    displaying with character entities, 36–37
    overview, 466
    references, 466
    standard HTML entities, 466–470
spreadsheets, 236. *See also* tables
src attribute, 203, 204, 210
srclang attribute, 210
SSL (Secure Sockets Layer), 308
standby attribute, 208
start attribute, 220
static positioning, 115
stock images, 160–161
style element, 32
style sheets, 41–55. *See also* CSS; formatting; styles
    advantages of, 106
    applying to files, 128–129
    basics, 106–107
    color changes with, 54
    combining, 127
    defining, 42–43
    embedded, 45–46
    external, 45, 46–47, 111, 126–127
    fluid, multicolumn, 111–121
    fluid, single-column, 107–111
    forms, 308–319
    importing, 127
    inline, 44, 45

style sheets (*cont.*)
    internal, 44, 45–46, 111, 126
    links to, 126–127
    lists, 232–233
    page layout and. *See* page layout
    precedence, 47–48
    printer-specific, 73–75
    problems with, 129
    setting up, 42–48
styled text, 61–72, 76
styles. *See also* formatting; style sheets
    foreground images, 182–191
    headings, 88–89
    links, 149–152
    lists, 226–233
    precedence, 47–48
subheads, 59
subtitles, 209, 210
Sun Microsystems, 322
syndicated content, 84–85

T

tabindex attribute, 153, 300
table cells
    adding content, 239–242
    adding images, 241–242
    aligning content, 252–253
    color, 256–257
    customizing text in, 240–241
    empty, 239
    formatting content, 252–259, 264–265
    line breaks, 257
    padding, 255–256
    size, 253–255
    spacing, 243, 300
    wrapping content, 240
table columns. *See also* table cells
    grouping, 261–264
    spanning, 257–258
    width, 263–264
table element, 238, 239
table rows. *See also* table cells
    color, 256–257
    grouping, 259–261
    spanning, 258–259
Table tags, 28
tables, 235–265
    alignment, 246–247
    background images, 249
    borders, 242–243
    captions, 250
    cells. *See* table cells

color, 248
columns. *See* table columns
creating, 237–242, 250–252
formatting, 242–252
in forms, 298–299, 300, 311–315
HTML email and, 380, 384–386
margins, 242–243
missing, 252
overview, 236–237
problems displaying, 463
rows. *See* table rows
size, 244–246
structure, 238–239
tag selectors, 87
tags. *See* HTML tags
target attribute, 154
target windows, 154
td element, 238
test answers, 405–427
testing
    HTML email, 395–399
    web sites, 128, 354–359, 362, 368
text, 57–76. *See also* characters; fonts
    alignment, 100–103
    bolded, 59
    borders, 99–100
    capitalized, 59
    centering, 59
    code examples, 94–95
    column width, 59
    emphasis, 59
    figure captions, 181
    in forms, 270–275
    images, 175–176, 354
    indenting, 36, 92–93
    italics, 59
    line breaks, 93–95
    lists, 59
    margins, 75, 99
    markup, 60–61
    monospaced, 94–95
    onscreen readability, 58–59
    organizing on page, 89–103
    padding, 75, 98–99
    paragraphs. *See* paragraphs
    preformat function, 94–95
    printer-friendly, 72–76
    quotation blocks, 95–96
    spacing between lines, 35–36
    styled, 61–72, 76
    in table cells, 240–241
    underlined, 59
text fields, 270–274
text tracks, 209–211
text-align property, 100–103, 252

text-based editors, 14, 16–17
text-level elements, 29–30
text-level semantics, 60–61, 62
Text-Level Semantics tags, 28
TextWrangler, 15
th element, 238
time/date inputs, 278–279, 336
title attribute, 152–153
title element, 31, 32
titles
      images, 175–176
      links, 152–153
      web pages, 13, 354
tool tips, 152
tr element, 238
track element, 209–211
Transmit, 366
transparency, 52, 165
tree diagrams, 12
troubleshooting
      browser issues, 458–459
      color problems, 460
      common problems, 455–464
      in different environments, 356–359
      displaying special characters, 457–458
      HTML code, 356–359
      image display, 459
      JavaScript, 323–324
      link problems, 149
      style sheet problems, 129
      table problems, 463
      web pages, 356–359
type attribute, 206, 208, 219

U

underlining, 59
underscore (_), 25
uniform resource locators. *See* URLs
units of measurement, 44
Universal Serial Bus. *See* USB
unordered lists, 221
updating web pages, 461–462
uploading files, 286–287
URLs (uniform resource locators). *See also* links
      absolute, 44
      considerations, 7, 74, 75
      not working, 458
      overview, 4–6
      relative, 44
      submitting to search engines, 368–370
USB ports, 8
usemap attribute, 179
user location, 332, 340–343

V

validation
      client-side, 315–318
      forms, 290–292, 315–318
      HTML code, 359–360
value attribute, 221, 276–277
variable transparency, 165
vector applications, 162
vector images, 162
vertical-align property, 252
VicomsoftFTP, 366
video. *See also* multimedia
      adding to web pages, 203
      compression, 205
      considerations, 9
      in email, 389
      file formats, 204, 206
      links to, 214–215
      sources, 203–207
video element, 203, 204
View Source command, 17–18
Visual Web Developer, 16
volume attribute, 208

W

W3C (World Wide Web Consortium), 9
Web Analytics Demystified, 370
web browsers. *See also specific browsers*
      Adobe BrowserLab, 128, 362
      color input and, 283
      considerations, 8
      date/time inputs and, 278–279
      different versions, 458–459
      features supported, 9
      fonts and, 67, 68, 69
      formatting new window, 336–337
      geolocation feature, 332, 340–343
      images in. *See* images
      launching new windows, 344–345, 460
      number input and, 281
      overview, 7–8
      page displaying blank, 456
      page layouts, 111, 120–121
      plug-ins, 198–200
      previewing HTML files in, 17, 25–27
      previewing web sites in, 17, 25–27, 362–363
      table display, 463
      testing web sites in, 128, 354–359, 362, 368
      text-only, 175
      troubleshooting JavaScript in, 323–324
      updated pages and, 461–462

web browsers (*cont.*)
    validation, 315–318
    versions, 8
    viewing source code, 17–18
web designers, 161
Web fonts, 64–66
web pages. *See also* HTML files; web sites
    background color, 462
    comments, 38
    creating first page of site, 38–40
    displays blank in browser, 456
    filename, 13
    foregrounds. *See* foreground images
    headers/footers, 84
    headline, 13
    images in. *See* images
    keywords, 354, 355
    line breaks, 93–95
    links in. *See* links
    multimedia in. *See* multimedia
    organizing sections of content, 80–89
    organizing text on, 89–103
    overview, 7
    password protection, 460–461
    previewing, 17, 25–27
    printer-friendly, 72–76
    problems with different browsers, 458–459
    ranking, 369
    sending in email, 461
    setting outline, 87–89
    structure, 79–103
    text in. *See* text
    titles, 13, 354
    troubleshooting, 455–464
    updating, 461–462
    using layers in, 122–126
Web Reference JavaScript Articles, 345
web rings, 370
web servers, 6, 7, 25
web sites. *See also* Internet; web pages
    anatomy of, 4–7
    blogs, 351, 352
    competitors, 10, 369
    content management systems, 7
    cookies, 330
    creating first page, 38–40
    described, 7
    developing, 19–20
    domain names, 5, 350
    domain registration, 5
    goals, 11–12
    going live, 371
    hosting (business), 353–354
    hosting (personal), 351–352
    marketing tips, 370–371
    navigation, 13–14
    organizing content, 12–13
    planning tasks, 10–14
    preparing for public debut, 354–363
    previewing in browsers, 17, 25–27, 362–363
    previewing on mobile devices, 360–362
    publicizing, 368–371
    structure, 12
    target audience, 10–11
    testing, 128, 354–359, 362, 368
    uploading to host computer, 363–367
    URLs for. *See* URLs
    viewing source code, 17–18
Web Workers, 330
web-based FTP, 367
Webs site, 351, 354
WebVideo Text Tracks (WebVTT), 210
WebVTT (WebVideo Text Tracks), 210
Weebly, 351, 354
white-space property, 257
width attribute, 204, 208
WordPad, 25
Wordpress, 7, 352
World Wide Web (WWW), 5, 6
World Wide Web Consortium (W3C), 9
WS-FTP, 366
WWW (World Wide Web), 5, 6
www.w3schools.com, 51, 87, 107, 208
WYSIWYG editors, 16–17, 27

X

Xara tools, 163
XHTML (Extensible Hypertext Markup Language), 9
XML (Extensible Markup Language), 9
.xml extension, 24

Y

Yahoo! search engine, 8
Yahoo! web hosting, 354
Yola, 351
YummyFTP, 366

Essential Web Development Skills—Made Easy!

The Beginner's Guide series provides everything you need to get started in modern web development. Featuring a practical, hands-on approach, these fast-paced tutorials contain expert insights, sample projects, and downloadable code to help you create dynamic websites quickly and easily.

HTML: A Beginner's Guide, Fifth Edition
Willard | 0-07-180927-9

JavaScript: A Beginner's Guide, Fourth Edition
Pollock | 0-07-180937-6

Also available

HTML5 Multimedia Developer's Guide
Bluttman | 0-07-175282-X

jQuery: A Beginner's Guide
Pollock | 0-07-181791-3
(Available Winter 2014)

 Follow us on Twitter @MHcomputing